ADVANCES IN ECONOMETRICS

Volume 3 · 1984

ECONOMIC INEQUALITY: MEASUREMENT AND POLICY

GP89 01730

ADVANCES IN ECONOMETRICS

A Research Annual

ECONOMIC INEQUALITY: MEASUREMENT AND POLICY

Editors: R. L. BASMANN
             Department of Economics
             Texas A & M University

             GEORGE F. RHODES, JR.
             Department of Economics
             Colorado State University

VOLUME 3 · 1984

ᏖᎯᎥ JAI PRESS INC.
Greenwich, Connecticut   *London, England*

CONTENTS

v

LIST OF CONTRIBUTORS

R. L. Basmann

Department of Economics
Texas A & M University

Charles Blackorby

Department of Economics
University of British Columbia
Vancouver, Canada

David Donaldson

Department of Economics
University of British Columbia
Vancouver, Canada

James E. Foster

Department of Economics
Purdue University

L. Dwight Israelson

Department of Economics
Utah State University

Dale W. Jorgenson

Department of Economics
Harvard University

Nanak Kakwani

Department of Economics
University of New South Wales
Australia

James B. McDonald

Department of Economics
Brigham Young University

David J. Molina

Department of Economics
Louisiana State University

Whitney K. Newey

Department of Economics
Massachusetts Institute of
Technology

Daniel T. Slesnick

Department of Economics
University of Texas at Austin

D. J. Slottje

Department of Economics
North Texas State University

INTRODUCTION

George F. Rhodes, Jr.

Apart from the question as to whether welfare economics is a science, is the question as to whether it should be a science. But even before the normative question, "Should welfare economics be a science?" is the question, "Can welfare economics be a science?" It is not the aim of this brief essay to answer that question, as it appears premature to do so. Rather, it is the aim to suggest a foundation paradigm to use in investigating the question. Here is due an immediate disclaimer: the paradigm is not original to this essay, nor to any in this decade. But it does appear to be the appropriate one in the current context.

Why the question, "Can welfare economics be a science?" and why the use of a paradigm in seeking an answer? My own reply to these issues discloses a particular outlook in the philosophy of science and the pursuit of knowledge. I am persuaded that a field of knowledge cannot be "scientific" until it is capable of producing logical conjunctions of observational premises and pure deductive theories capable of producing logical contradictions, thereby falsifying deductive implications of pure or uninterpreted economic theories. It must be added here that "scientific" knowledge is not the only valuable kind; indeed, for many uses it may have less value than others. But the distinction between falsifiable claims and others is essential in the economical use of scarce resources devoted to learning, as also in the management of society.

The basic premise of this essay is that it is premature to decide whether welfare economics can be a science. Support for this premise comes through comparing the research reported in this volume (and many similar pieces) with the simple framework presented by J. von Neumann and H. H. Goldstine and discussed by Oskar Morgenstern in his book, *On the Accuracy of Economic Observations*.[1] The framework consists of four possible sources of error that could account for contradiction between theory and observations. Examination of proposed measures of well-being in light of the four sources of error indicates that it is too early to decide whether it is possible to test propositions regarding measured well-being of consumers and workers, either as individuals or in aggregate.

The framework is proposed as a paradigm because it contributes to *explanation* and *prediction* of contradictions between deductive implications of theories and corresponding observations designed to test them. A contradiction between theory and observation can be attributed to any combination of the four possible sources of error:

1. Errors of computation made in carrying through deductive steps in theory creation and in the processing of observational information.
2. Errors of measurement in collecting observational information either in experimental settings or in survey sampling.
3. Errors of approximation through use of transcendental functions and other approximations required in carrying out mathematical deductions and operations in creating, exploring, and completing theories.
4. Direct errors of theory creation: the theory does not match the observations. As an approximation, the proposed theory is too crude to adequately explain the phenomena under study.

The hierarchy of these sources of error is obvious. The fourth source of error, inadequate theory, is the primary focus of scientific work, but it cannot be warranted as the source of contradictions between deductive implications and observations until the first three sources have been eliminated or controlled within known bounds. The ordering of the first three is based on economy of resource use. Each is more difficult to detect than its predecessor, so that it is least expensive to begin with computational error and proceed through the others in order to end with theory error.

Measurement error and theoretical error present the greatest difficulties in economics. This is not to say that computational and function approximation errors are not important or difficult. Computational error has been a source of severe difficulty in sampling experiments, econometric model estimation and statistical inference. But the latter two sources of error are better left as the subject for another volume, since their effect on measurement of well-being is indirect and their effect on the testing of theoretical propositions can usually be controlled within required bounds. Measurement error and theoretical error are closely intertwined through their common role in the interpretation systems constructed and used in testing pure economic theories.[2] It is study of the current status of interpretation systems that makes it clear that we cannot yet discern whether welfare economics is or can be a science.

INTERPRETATION SYSTEMS AND TESTING BASIC PROPOSITIONS

Logical contradiction between a pure economic theory and observational premises is made possible by metalanguage components known as interpretation systems. For any economic theory to be empirically falsifiable it must contain names of elements that are not defined as part of the theory; "primitive elements" is the common term given to them. An interpretation system performs the function of separating those objects that come into question in the theory and those that do not. Until it is functioning it is not possible to interpret the theory and therefore it is impossible to confront the pure theory with observational statements. A pure theory remains just that until there is an interpretation system available capable of distinguishing whether objects encountered in the observational process are indeed in the classes of objects discussed in the theory.

Measurement error comes into play after the interpretation system is in place. A contradiction or agreement between a pure theory and observational evidence may be only apparent, rather than actual, due to errors in measurement. The value of any empirical test of a pure theory is compromised until the measurement error component of the problem is controlled. While this fact is not news to research economists, it may nonetheless be the most ubiquitously ignored and therefore underrated problem in modern empirical economics.

To pass judgment on the scientific stature of welfare economics, particularly as it deals with measures of well-being, is premature precisely because the requisite work on interpretation systems and measurement errors still has too far to go. Theoretical development has yet to specify primitive terms and testable propositions with sufficient clarity to warrant thorough construction of interpretation systems. Methods of measuring and controlling measurement error will develop as required for implementation of the interpretation systems as they themselves develop in the testing process.

One does not expect, of course, that the discipline will suddenly appear full-blown. As the field evolves, there is need for construction of preliminary interpretation systems and measurement procedures. It is that development process that is represented by the papers in this volume. They survey the status of measures of well-being, assess the effects of measurement errors, and purpose measures of well-being in the process of creating temporary interpretation systems. Each fills an essential function in the evolution of welfare economics and each will eventually be recognized as having contributed to solving the problem, "Can welfare economics be a science?"

NOTES

1. *Bulletin of the American Mathematical Society* 53:1021–99 (1947), Part II *Proceedings of the American Mathematical Society,* vol. 2 (1951), pp. 188–202. Cf. V. Bargmann, et al., *Solution of Linear Systems of High Order* (Princeton, 1946). Oskar Morgenstern, *On the Accuracy of Economic Observations,* (Princeton University Press: Princeton, N.J.), 1950 and 1963.

2. For an introduction to the role of interpretation systems in testing pure economic theories, as well as to the testing process discussed in this introduction, see R. L. Basmann, "Modern Logic and the Suppositious Weakness of the Empirical Foundations of Economic Science," *Schweiz. fur Volkswirtschaft und Statistik,* Heft 2/1975, 153–176.

VARIABLE CONSUMER PREFERENCES, ECONOMIC INEQUALITY, AND THE COST-OF-LIVING CONCEPT:

PART ONE

R. L. Basmann, D. J. Molina and D. J. Slottje

I. INTRODUCTION

A. Objectives and Aims

Retaining the concept of the utility-maximizing consumer, we dispense with the conventional neoclassical assumption that individual consumers' preference fields are independent of the usual budget constraint on utility maximization. We relax that conventional assumption in order to:

1. Simplify the rationalization of systems of empirical per capita de-

Advances in Econometrics, vol. 3, pages 1–65
Copyright © 1984 by JAI Press Inc.
All rights of reproduction in any form reserved.
ISBN: 0-89232-443-0

mand functions by *aggregation of direct utility functions of individual consumers.*

2. Relate the representation and analysis of comprehensive *economic inequality* in a population of consumers to the preference fields of its individual members.

3. Go beyond Samuelson and Swamy (1974) in extending the theoretical economists' concept of *cost-of-living* index (of prices) to the case in which consumers' preference fields are dependent on the budget constraint. Extension of the *cost-of-living* concept is required to yield the conventional construction of a "true cost-of-living" price index (see Klein and Rubin, 1947), in the case where consumers' preferences (in the aggregate) are independent of budget constraints. At the same time, the extended concept of *cost-of-living* index (of prices) is required to explicate the lay public's notion of price indexes based on a fixed market basket of goods as a measure of the *cost of living*.

We require, too, that relaxation of this conventional neoclassical assumption shall not alone bring the resulting theory into contradiction with any of the few empirical regularities that are already well established in economic science.

Because of the length of this study in the original manuscript, we have divided it into two parts for separate publication. Part One, containing Sections I–III, in which objectives (1) and (2) are achieved, covers the unification of the extended theory of the individual utility maximizing consumer and a theory of the multivariate personal distribution of components of wealth, components of income, and expenditures on commodities. As a consequence of the form of this unification, the *direct utility function,* which rationalizes all systems of individual consumer demand functions regardless of whether the conventional neoclassical assumption holds or not, is found to take on the character of a *cardinal measure.* That is, the numerical magnitude of the direct utility function becomes a measure of a substantive *quantitative property* of real-world consumer behavior. In Part Two (to be published in the next volume of this series) we shall call this "new" quantity *utility$_2$. Utility$_2$* is a derived quantity whose determination in economics is analogous to the determination of temperature in thermodynamics (see Hempel, 1952, esp. pp. 71–73; Basmann, 1972a, p. 39). Of course, it would be a mistake to confuse *utility$_2$* with the ordinal *satisfaction* or *utility* that is conceptually priced by a "true" *cost-of-living* index (of prices) (see Norwood, 1970, p. 158; Deaton, 1980, p. 17). Empirical magnitudes of *utility$_2$* can be meaningfully correlated with other empirical magnitudes of other economic quantities in a way that ordinal utility cannot (see Basmann, 1972a, pp. 31–31; 1972b, p. 107). In advance of knowing results of such empirical correlations, however, purely mathematical speculation is unlikely to produce any new conclusions of much practical interest. How this *utility$_2$* correlates empirically with other quantitative economic measurements such as (but not limited to) *price indexes* and various *cost-of-living* indexes (of prices) is to be examined in Part Two.

Perhaps the relevance of the restrictive neoclassical assumption that individual consumers' preference fields are independent of budget constraints is more readily apparent in the case of objective (3) and the subject matter of Part Two. The neoclassical assumption states the real-world conditions under which use of the theoretical economists' *definition* of the term "true cost of living" is valid. The hypothesis that consumers' preference fields remain undistorted by changes in the budget constraint prices is the antecedent clause, or *justificatory sentence,* for valid use of the stipulative clause of the definition itself (see Hempel, 1952, esp. pp. 18–20). If this antecedent hypothesis is confirmed, then the "true-cost of living" is the minimum expenditure required to reach a standard indifference surface of a preference field given a specified vector of budget constraint prices (see Konüs, 1924, transl. 1936; Fisher and Shell, 1968, pp. 102–103; Samuelson and Swamy, 1974, esp. p. 586). Obviously, the theoretical definition is not intended to hold when the *justificatory sentence* is false. In other words, the neoclassical assumption describes he only set of real-world circumstances in which it would be valid (say) for theoretical economists to criticize the lay public as mistaken in referring to the U.S. Consumer Price Index (CPI) produced by the Bureau of Labor Statistics (BLS) as a "cost-of-living index" of prices (see Moore, 1970; Dalton, 1970; Vartia, 1978, p. 275; Deaton and Muellbauer, 1980a, p. 169; Bureau of Labor Statistics, 1977, pp. 2–3). The neoclassical assumption, if true of real-world circumstances, would validate the assertion deduced with help of the definition that the CPI overstates the "true cost-of-living index" of prices (Norwood, 1970, p. 159). On the other hand, if the neoclassical assumption is false, then there is no such thing as a "true cost-of-living" in the sense of the theoretical economists' definition above, so the assertion that the CPI overstates the "true cost of living index" does not make sense. Consequently, the relevance of some (but not all) political arguments to the effect that recipients of Social Security, military, and other government pensions have been over compensated by COLAs (cost-of-living adjustments) because they are tied to the CPI rests ultimately on the empirical truth of the neoclassical hypothesis that consumers' preference fields are independent of budget constraints. When put forward without empirical evidence to confirm the hypothesis that consumers' preference fields are independent of budget constraints, such assertions (understandably) are likely to be regarded as capricious or merely as attempts to engage the prestige of economic science in support of a partisan economic program.

There are sound practical reasons for pursuing objectives (1)–(3), above, rather than attempting to perform empirical tests of the neoclassical assumption that consumers' preference fields are independent of their budget constraints. As we have shown elsewhere, Basmann et al. (1983a), it is not difficult to prescribe experimental conditions under which it is in principle possible for an accumulation of *confirming instances* to *establish* specific cases of the neoclassical hypothesis that a real individual consumer's preference field is independent of the operative budget constraint (cf. Braithwaite, 1955, p. 14).

In such incentive-compatible experiments the experimenter would barter in pure exchange with the experimental subjects (real consumers), who would always have the option of purchasing commodities at stated *fixed* prices.

Cost considerations, ethical considerations, and political considerations militate effectively against the actual performances of such experiments on a scale sufficient to establish (if that were to be the outcome) the neoclassical hypothesis as a widely acceptable basis for constructing *true cost-of-living* indexes for practical policy formation and implementation. Time-series market data and data produced by *revealed preference experiments*, even under controlled conditions such as described in Battalio et al. (1973), are capable in principle only of falsifying the neoclassical hypothesis that consumers' preference fields are independent of operative budget constraints. It often turns out that such data do appear to disconfirm some of the deductive consequences of that assumption (see Christensen et al., 1975; Barten and Geyskens, 1975; Theil, 1975; Berndt et al., 1977; Lau et al., 1978; Conrad and Jorgenson, 1979; Deaton and Muellbauer, 1980). The disconfirmations are very weak, however, and it is easy to "rescue" the neoclassical hypothesis by alluding to the very real inadequacies in the currently available "large sample" statistical tests of several of the deductive consequences of that hypothesis (see Laitinen, 1978; Meisner, 1979; Bera et al., 1981). Of course, it is legitimate and highly desirable that outcomes of tests of hypotheses be scrutinized in this way. Sometimes failure of an empirical test to disconform one or more of the deductive consequences of a hypothesis affords a suitable *confirming instance*, and an accumulation of such confirming instances *establishes* the hypothesis as already mentioned. The trouble is, however, that time-series market data and revealed preference data are logically incapable of providing confirming instances for the neoclassical hypothesis that consumer preference fields are independent of the operative budget constraint. For, as we shall show in Section II.E, if any sample of market data or revealed preference data provides a confirming instance for the neoclassical hypothesis, then at the same time it nullifies that confirming instance by providing an equally cogent confirming instance for the contrary hypothesis, namely, that consumers' preference fields actually do depend on the operative budget constraints (Basmann et al., 1983a).

Not empirically meaningless in an absolute sense, the neoclassical assumption that consumers' preference fields are independent of operative budget constraints is nonetheless *empirically meaningless* in terms of the time-series and revealed-preference data, the only kind of data that are now available or likely to become available for econometric analysis for many decades to come. The foregoing comment is not a criticism of the adoption of this neoclassical assumption as a stylized "fact" for internal "normal science" purposes of the economics profession (see Basmann, 1956, pp. 47–48; also Kuhn, 1962, pp. 35–37). Real economic policy problems are not respecters of the arbitrary boundaries of academic disciplines and specializations, however. A definition of "true cost-of-living" validated only by a stylized "fact" is unlikely to afford a basis for a policy consensus respecting (say) the desirability of tying COLAs to the theoretical economists' "true cost-of-living index" of prices rather than to (say) the CPI on the assertion that the latter, in consequence of the definition, overstates the "true cost-of-living."

Part One of this study lays the theoretical and empirical basis for an important new definition of the term "cost of living" and construction of a *basic cost-of-living price index$_2$* (BCLI$_2$) corresponding to that new concept. A formal definition will be presented in Part Two. A brief description of the BCLI$_2$ will be helpful in Part One.

Consumers' preference fields may change in response not only to parameters of the budget constraint but also to other variables that do not affect the budget constraint; BCLI$_2$ is designed to apply in both cases.

Let X^0 be a *fixed market basket of goods*. Let p^0 be a vector of budget constraint prices in a specified *base period*, 0. Let $I^0(X; X^0)$ be the indifference surface (containing X^0) of a direct utility function that represents the consumers' preferences in the base period, 0. Let C^0 be the *minimum expenditure* required to reach the indifference surface $I^0(X; X^0)$, given the base period price vector p^0.

Now let $I^1(X; X^0)$ be the indifference surface (containing X^0) of a direct utility function that represents the consumers' preferences in the comparison period, 1. Assume that the comparison period indifference surface $I^1(X; X^0)$ is not identical to the base period $I^0(X; X^0)$. The specific cause of this change of preference field between the base period and the comparison period is not relevant to the definition of BCLI given here. Let p^1 be the vector of budget constraint prices in comparison period, 1, and let C^1 be the minimum expenditure required to reach the indifference surface $I^1(X; X^0)$ given the comparison period price vector p^1 is not necessarily different from p^0. The *basic cost-of-living* index of prices (BCLI$_2$) is defined as the ratio of the comparison period minimum expenditure, C^1, to the base period minimum expenditure, C^0. In Part Two we shall examine several analytic properties of this *basic cost-of-living* index. For the purpose of this introduction, however, only its deductive relation to the conventional "true cost-of-living index" requires emphasis. The empirical scope of application of BCLI$_2$ includes, but is not limited to, the scope of the conventional concept of the "true cost-of-living price index." If the conventional neoclassical hypothesis that consumers' preference fields are independent of budget constraint prices holds, and if changes in other variables do not change the preference fields (Basmann, 1956, pp. 47–48), then a conventional "true cost-of-living index" of prices exists and is identical to the BCLI$_2$.

Suppose a change of the preference field is caused by some variable while total expenditure and budget constraint prices remain constant, that is, $p^1 = p^0$. Without loss of essential generality suppose, too, that standard market basket of goods X^0 is also the equilibrium system of demands in the base period, 0. In other words, in the base period, X^0 is preferred to all other commodity bundles that are attainable in the base period, 0. As a consequence of the change in the preference field from what it was in the base period to what it is in the comparison period, the indifference surface $I^1(X; X^0)$ containing X^0 now cuts through the fixed budget constraint. Some attainable bundles, all of which were preferentially inferior to X^0 in the base period, have become preferentially equivalent or preferentially superior to X^0 in the comparison period. It follows that the minimum expenditure required to reach the indifference surface containing X^0 in the comparison period is smaller than the minimum expenditure required to reach the prevailing indifference surface containing X^0 in the comparison period. In other words, BCLI$_2$ diminishes in the circumstances just described and is smaller than 1.00.

In the same circumstances, a Laspeyres index like the CPI, based on some fixed market basket X^0, remains equal to 1.00 in the comparison period. Another useful *cost-of-living* index designed by Samuelson and Swamy (1974, p. 586) to apply to concomitant (not necessarily causally connected) changes of prices and preference fields, remains equal to 1.00 in the comparison period. The Laspeyres index of prices, e.g., the CPI, is numerically different from the BCLI$_2$ in this case because the two indexes measure different aspects (properties or relations) of real-world economic behavior: The aspect of the real-world *cost of living* measured by the CPI does not change between the base period and the comparison period in the circumstances just described. Let us call that property *cost* *of living$_1$*. In like manner, let us refer to the property of real-world economic behavior measured by BCLI$_2$ as *cost of living$_2$* and that aspect of real-world economic behavior measured by the Samuelson–Swamy index as *cost of living$_3$*. The Samuelson–Swamy index is defined as the ratio of minimum expenditures required to reach the new indifference surface $I^1(\mathbf{X}; \mathbf{X}^0)$ under $\mathbf{p}^1$ and $\mathbf{p}^0$, respectively. It preserves (as the other two indexes do not) the notion that a *cost-of-living* index of prices should price a fixed level of utility or satisfaction. A similar *cost-of-living* index is defined in terms of the base period indifference surface $I^0(\mathbf{X}; \mathbf{X}^0)$. This construction of a *cost-of-living* index of prices is not an innovation relative to the Samuelson–Swamy definition, of course. These two versions of the Samuelson-Swamy *cost-of-living* index effectively ignore changes of the preference field between the base period and the comparison period: In the first case, the definition in effect calls for the construction of a "true cost-of-living index" based on the comparison period preference field *as if* that preference field had been prevailing in the base period; for the second case interchange the words "base" and "comparison" in the preceding clause. A designer of coopers' mallets is not to be faulted for ignoring carpenters' needs for a hammer with claws for pulling nails; Samuelson and Swamy, in designing a *cost-of-living* index that has some foreseeable policy uses (we discuss them in Part Two), are not to be faulted for ignoring the need for a *cost-of-living* index serving other purposes.

Attachment of the numerical subscripts (as above) should remove what little disadvantage might arise from the fact that the term "cost of living" has more than one meaning in the language of everyday economic life and economic science. Admittedly, it is not mistaken to say that it is a great merit of (say) BASIC that terms like "FOR–TO," "GOSUB" and "GOTO" are definienda of complete "if, and only if" definitions and have a strict, single, meaning to the recipient of the communications in which they occur; but saying so is merely to make a virtue out of a necessity that is due only to the nature of that recipient. There is nothing especially meritorious about "if, and only if" definitions in economic science and economic policymaking. Indeed, the use of conditional definitions, allowing for different meanings of (say) the term "cost of living" under empirically distinguishable different justificatory conditions, is often more advantageous for the development of a science.

Openness of meaning appears to be a characteristic of the more fruitful technical terms of science (see Hempel, 1952, pp. 28–29; also Pap, 1962, pp. 32–34). The classical concept of the term "cost of living" due to Konüs (1924, transl. 1936) and, in an important practical form, to Klein and Rubin (1947) possesses such openness of meaning. This is due, in turn, to the openness of meaning possessed by the terms "rational consumer" or "utility-maximizing consumer," terms with potentiality for application to real consumers whose preference fields are not fixed and may actually depend on budget constraint price and total expenditure.

Benefiting from the openness of meaning of technical terms such as "cost of living" is much more a matter of conducting empirical work with data at hand or in the process of becoming available than in purusing purely mathematical consequences of complete definitions. Empirical interdependences among the $BCLI_2$ and other price indexes (some already mentioned) as well as diverse measures of economic inequality will be the chief subject matter of Part Two of this study. The remainder of this Introduction is concerned with the contents of Part One and objectives (1) and (2) mentioned at the outset.

B. Related Literature

Otherwise not in principle testable in terms of empirical data available, or likely ever to become available, the neoclassical assumption that consumers' preference fields are independent of operative budget constraints can be rescued from meaninglessness by conjoining it with the special hypothesis that the fixed preference fields are homothetic in form. This meaningfulness in terms of data actually available is purchased (in most cases) at the cost of more or less decisive *rejection* of the conjoint null hypothesis, namely, that consumer preferences are fixed and homothetic in form. However, the usual (and logically arbitrary) interpretation of this failure of the conjoint null hypothesis to agree with available data has been to attribute that failure to the specification of the homothetic form of the preference field. The belief is widespread that "everybody knows that consumers preferences are not homothetic in form," and because of that belief there is not much reviewable literature that is directly relevant to the actual subject matter of Part One of this study. Too quickly attributing the rejection of *fixed* homothetic preferences to the specification of homotheticity rather than to the assumption of fixity obscures the following important analytic property of homothetic preference fields with parameters that are dependent on the budget constraint: Whatever form of system of demand functions might agree (even perfectly if you will) with time-series market data or revealed-preference data, a homothetic preference field with parameters dependent on the budget constraint can be found to rationalize that system of demand functions (Basmann et al, 1983a). Demonstration of this property and its consequences will be the subject of Section II. Use of the deductive consequences of this analytic property of budget-constraint–dependent preference fields in establishing an explicit unifying theoretical link between individual consumers preference fields and the multivariate personal distribution of components of wealth, components of income, and expenditures on commodities and securities is the central topic of Section III.

Such related literature as there is may be reviewed usefully under two main heads: (a) presentations of purely schematic theory of variable consumer preferences, and (b) discussions of substantive aspects of variable preference. Under heading (a) it is useful to distinguish between articles that discuss preference-changing variables *not* related to changes in budget constraints and articles that discuss schematically the notion of "price-dependent" preferences. The former are concerned with hypotheses that are meaningful in terms of available market and revealed preference data; the latter are concerned with hypotheses that are meaningful only in terms of the experimental data of the kind described in Section II.E.

Economists concerned with empirical analysis of variable preferences and causes of changes in "taste" tended to put greater emphasis on psychosocial and technological factors such as "quality changes" (Scitovsky, 1945); habit persistence (Duesenberry, 1949), advertising and other forms of selling effort, income, and parameters of the income distribution (Johnson, 1952), than on changes in market prices. Ichimura (1951) and Tintner (1952) defined changes in preferences as nonvacuous changes in the form of the ordinal utility function and indifference map and derived the corresponding shifts in demand as linear combinations of Slutsky-Hicks terms (Basmann, 1954a,b; also 1956, pp. 48–51). Tintner (1960, p. 109) was concerned with interdependence of consumers' utility functions; he considered the case of direct utility functions that incorporate as parameters the incomes of *all* individuals in society, including the consumer's own, i.e., the utility function is dependent on the empirical income distribution. In the same paper, Tintner also considered the case of direct utility functions that include the quantities of all commodities consumed by all other individual consumers (pp. 110–112).

Samuelson, in his *Foundations of Economic Analysis* (1947, p. 118), credits Léon Walras with having shown many years ago that it is possible to modify utility analysis so as to take account of the peculiar properties of money. In response to Walras's critics who feared "that there was something viciously circular in assuming the existence of prices and of a 'value for money' in the midst of the process by which that value was to be determined," Samuelson sought to clear up such misconceptions by deriving the consumer's demand function for holding of money from a utility function subject to a linear budget constraint in which the price of "gold" and the rate of interest, as well as commodity prices and total expenditure, appear as parameters (pp. 119–121). Samuelson introduced commodity prices and the price of "gold" into the consumer's ordinal direct utility function as parameters. Apart from the usual restrictions on fixed-preference utility functions, only homogeneity of degree zero in all prices was imposed. Even without an explicit form of direct utility function, that restriction is sufficient to imply the meaningful, refutable hypothesis that the demand for (holding) money has unitary own-price elasticity (p. 121). Subsequent writers on this aspect of price-dependent utility functions seldom mention Samuelson's contribution specifically. Kalman (1968), Dusansky and Kalman (1972, 1974), Clower and Riley (1976), Wichers (1976), and Dusansky and Kalman (1976) were concerned primarily with demand functions that are not homogeneous of degree zero in all prices and money income, i.e., with the presence of "money illusion." The question of whether absence of zero homogeneity of demand functions alone can exhaust the meaning of "money illusion" is still open and interesting, especially in reference to the representative consumer in statistical demand analysis (see Schultz, 1938, esp. p. 630), but it need not detain us here.

In small compass Samuelson laid out a schematic framework for a theory of price-dependent direct utility functions, which—as he mentioned—had much broader theoretical and empirical scope than rationalization of consumer demand for holding money. In that connection, Samuelson (1947, p. 119) mentioned the need to introduce prices into indifference loci in the case of commodities that are valued for their exclusiveness so that preferences are altered by changes in their relative prices. Kalman (1968, p. 497) mentions the Veblen effect, or snob appeal, and the Scitovsky hypothesis that consumers often consider commodity prices and commodity price changes as indicators of quality and quality changes.

Pollak (1977) has provided some additional important interpretations of price-dependent preferences. In Section III of his article, Pollak offers two alternative interpretations of price-dependent preferences and discusses the implications of price-dependent preferences for welfare economics. He distinguishes two paradigms of price-dependent preferences: in the first, the objects of choice are commodity bundles and the ordering is dependent on prices; in the second, the objects of choice are "quantity-price situations" (Pollak, 1977, pp. 65 and 74). The subject of the present study falls completely within the scope of the former, of course, and has no specific relevance to Pollak's innovation (the latter paradigm). It is interesting to note that Pollak (pp. 65, 69, 73) argues correctly that a system of Slutsky–Hicks demand functions derived from a price-dependent preference ordering can *sometimes* also be derived from another preference ordering that is independent of prices. Pollak substantiates his argument (p. 70) by describing a Klein-Rubin *direct* utility function in which the lower terminal parameters depend on prices in an explicit form; he argues that the implied Slutsky–Hicks demand functions can also be derived from an alternative preference ordering that does not depend on prices, namely, a preference ordering that corresponds to the "indirect utility function" derived from the system of demand functions.

Leaving behind the purely schematic theories of variable preferences, we now turn to some related literature on substantive hypotheses.

Our notion that real consumers tend to regard changes in market prices as social signals, or as cues to which they adapt their behavior, is hardly a new one. Modern research in the psychology of human conformity suggests how the human need to feel that one's values, decisions, and behavior are "correct" may lead individual consumers to be sensitive to some commodity market price increases as signaling the tendency of their relevant reference group to view the commodity in question as of different "worth" from what it had before. This may in turn lead to the attempt to validate the correctness of their own behavior by making their consumption patterns conform to the perceived behavior and valuations of the group; (see Kiesler and Kiesler, 1970, p. 44). For instance, a consumer might take an observed increase in the market price of (say) a brand of designer jeans in Neiman-Marcus Department Store as a signal that her reference group has come to view the wearing of that brand of jeans as being of greater "worth" than before, and she might then respond by making the same upward reevaluation of that brand of apparel and choose to wear it. (It cannot be concluded from this, however, that a personal opportunity to purchase the same brand of jeans at a discount price would cause her to revise the "marginal utility of brand Z jeans" downward.) Results of some recent experimental work by McConnell (1968a, 1980, p. 30), Gardner (1971), Monroe (1973), Riesz (1980), Etgar and Malhotra (1981, p. 221), and Venkataraman (1981, p. 50) provide some confirming instances for the hypothesis that individual consumers tend to interpret prices as indicators of commodity "quality," as was foreseen by Scitovsky (1945).

Moreover, there are Thorstein Veblen's remarks to be considered. In the light of modern social psychology, Veblen's famous hypotheses about primary and secondary utility can no longer be so easily dismissed as limited to a few goods the purchase of which acquires greater or less "snob appeal" accordingly as their prices increase or decrease. Veblen (1899, reprint 1931) put forward an explanatory theory of the substantive utility of commodities that attempts to account for the formation and change of consumer preferences over time.

Veblen did not propose a mathematical form for a utility function. His remarks about utility as a property of the act of purchasing, owning, controlling, and consuming commodities are open to a variety of reasonable interpretations when it comes to describing substantive utility in the transparently consistent with attribution or maximizing behavior to real consumers (cf. Veblen, 1899, reprint 1931, p. 158).

Veblen was very critical of the classical school and the marginal utility school—W. S. Jevons and the Austrians—for their uncritical acceptance of the hedonistic calculus (see Veblen, 1908, reprint 1969, pp. 181–182; also 1909, pp. 232–235; cf. also Phillips and Slottje, 1983, pp. 198–199). According to Veblen, utility is a property of the acts of purchasing, owning or controlling, and consuming commodities. Actually, the utility of commodities is viewed as a resultant of two kinds of utility that compete with each other in affecting the consumers' responses to changes in market prices and to the consumers' abilities to pay, i.e., the total expenditure of which a consumer is capable. Primary utility arises from the direct service of consumption to enhance life and well-being on the whole (Veblen 1899, reprint 1931, p. 99), the purchase, ownership, and consumption of commodities is invested with secondary utility as evidence or social confirmation of the consumer's relative ability to pay. Goods are produced and consumed as a means to the fuller unfolding of human life and their utility consists, in the first instance, in their efficiency as a means to this end. But the human proclivity to emulation has seized upon the consumption of goods as a means to an invidious comparison, thereby investing consumable goods with a secondary utility as evidence of relative ability to pay (pp. 154–155). Expenditure that is motivated chiefly by anticipated secondary utility and which does not serve human life or well-being in obvious ways Veblen called conspicuous consumption or "waste," an admittedly unfortunate piece of technical jargon (p. 97) since such expenditure is not recognized as conspicuous consumption or waste in the vulgar sense by the consumer who makes it (p. 99).

In the present connection it must be emphasized that Veblen considered this secondary utility of commodities to be pervasive rather than confined to a few unusual commodities. According to Veblen, consumption goods, and even productive goods, generally possess and exhibit a mixture of primary and secondary utility:

> It would be hazardous to assert that a useful purpose is ever absent from the utility of any article or of any service, however obviously its prime purpose and chief element is conspicuous waste; and it would be only less hazardous to assert of any primarily useful product that the element of waste is in no way concerned in its value, immediately, or remotely (p. 101).

Later, in the chapter "Pecuniary Canons of Taste," Veblen (p. 151) suggests that there are no goods supplied in any trade which do not have secondary utility in greater or less degree.

According to Veblen, conspicuous consumption, or the consumption of goods and services that is motivated predominantly by secondary utility, is not confined to the leisure class but prevails over all the social and income classes from richest to poorest. The less affluent classes emulate the consumption patterns and thereby learn and internalize the tastes of the more affluent so far as ability to pay will permit (pp. 83–85, 103). Finally, secondary utility is not weak relative to primary utility and has far-reaching consequences for economic growth and change. According to Veblen, next to the instinct for self-preservation "the propensity for emulation is probably the strongest and most alert of the economic motives proper. . . . The need of conspicuous waste, therefore, stands ready to absorb any increase in the community's industrial efficiency or output of goods, after the most elementary physical wants have been provided for" (pp. 110–111).

This brief review of Veblen's remarks about the utility of commodities may help to make clear one practical motive for assuming that prices and total expenditure have some influence on the parameters of a direct utility function that is supposed to be a mathematical description of the result- and effects of primary and secondary utility in Veblen's sense. Price changes and changes in ability to pay affect consumer demand in two distinct ways: (1) a change in the budget constraint on utility maximization; and (2) at each point of the commodity space a change in the marginal rates of substitution between commodities via effect on the relative secondary utilities of commodities. It must be borne in mind that the term "utility" as it appears in "primary utility" and "secondary utility" on these pages (and as it appears in Veblen's own remarks) does not refer to the numerical values of the utility functions introduced in the section to follow. Nor does it refer to some additive property of the act of consuming or owning goods. We shall not proffer any definition of the term "Veblen effect" in this article. Although our econometric work has yielded much empirical information about the dependence of utility function parameters on prices and total expenditures, at present it appears that much more analysis of the statistically estimated utility function parameters will be needed in order to specify a feasible empirical antecedent condition for a definition of (say) the "Veblen effect" or measurement of (say) the "Veblen secondary utility effect." In a discussion of our empirical work elsewhere (in Phillips and Slottje, 1983), it is clearly indicated to be of only a tentative character.

Veblen's emphasis on the pervasiveness of secondary utility constitutes the main relevance of his remarks to our subject. Review of the immense secondary and tertiary literature devoted to Velben's concepts of conspicuous consumption would probably mislead rather than enlighten (see Holton, 1969).

This completes the review of literature that is related to our study in a more or less general way. Many other titles, directly and specifically relevant, will be cited in due course.

II.   DIRECT UTILITY FUNCTIONS: INDIVIDUAL AND AGGREGATE

A.   Properties of Demand Functions That Depend on the Budget Constraint Only

The letters i, j, and k are pronouns for which names or descriptions of specified commodities may be substituted depending on the application in question: $i, j, k = 1, 2, \ldots, n$. Greek letters μ and ν are pronouns for which names or descriptions of real consumers may be substituted, again depending on the application in question: $\mu = 1, 2, \ldots, N$. The letter t is a pronoun for which the name or description of a specified time period, e.g., week, month, year, or fiscal year, may be substituted, depending on the application in question: $t = 1, 2, \ldots, T$. In much of the ensuing discussion we will be referring to the demand behavior of a single consumer during a single time period. For such cases it will be possible to supress superscripts ν and subscripts t without much risk of confusion.

Here M is reserved for designating total expenditure on all commodities, $i = 1, 2, \ldots, n$; $\mathbf{p}$ is reserved for designating an n-tuple $\langle p_1, \ldots, p_n \rangle$ of prices; $\boldsymbol{\alpha}$ is reserved for designating an r-tuple $\langle \alpha_1, \ldots, \alpha_r \rangle$ of real economic variables which we shall interpret later on; $\Psi_i(\boldsymbol{\alpha})$, for $i = 1, 2, \ldots, n$, is a positive-valued real function of *the argument* $\boldsymbol{\alpha}$. Whenever a definite form of $\Psi_i(\boldsymbol{\alpha})$ is specified in an application it will be necessary to introduce signs designating its adjustable parameters, of course. However, we shall sometimes be able safely to abbreviate the expression $\Psi_i(\boldsymbol{\alpha})$ by Ψ_i alone. This principle of abbreviation will apply to the expressions for other functions as well: Ψ designates the n-tuple of functions. $\langle \Psi_1, \Psi_2, \ldots, \Psi_n \rangle$; $\boldsymbol{\gamma}$ designates an n-tuple $\langle \gamma_1, \ldots, \gamma_n \rangle$ of real valued parameters not restricted in sign (the use of $\boldsymbol{\gamma}$ in specifying the domains of systems of demand functions will be made clear below); $\mathbf{X}$ designates an n-tuple $\langle x_1, \ldots, x_n \rangle$ of real variables; X_i, for $i = 1, 2, \ldots, n$, is reserved to designate quantities of the commodity denoted by i. The term $X_i(M, \mathbf{p}, \boldsymbol{\alpha})$, for $i = 1, 2, \ldots, n$, is used to designate *any* function of $M, \mathbf{p}, \boldsymbol{\alpha}$ whose value is measured in units of the commodity designated by i and without prejudice respecting its status as member of a system of demand functions derived from a utility function, direct or indirect. The sign X_i^* is reserved exclusively for designating demand functions derived from direct utility functions or for designating the magnitudes of such derived demand functions.

The following mathematical theorem, first proved rigorously by Seo in his doctoral dissertation (1973, pp. 35–36), will play a very important part in the discussion that follows: *Let* $\mathbf{X}(M, \mathbf{p}, \boldsymbol{\alpha})$ *be any system of positive valued functions* $X_i(M, \mathbf{p}, \boldsymbol{\alpha})$, *for* $i = 1, 2, \ldots, n$, *satisfying the restriction*

$$\sum_{i=1}^{n} p_i X_i(M, \mathbf{p}, \boldsymbol{\alpha}) = M \qquad (2.1a)$$

for all M, $\mathbf{p}$, $\boldsymbol{\alpha}$ *such that*

$$M - \sum_{k=1}^{n} \gamma_k p_k > 0. \qquad (2.1b)$$

Then

$$X_i(M, \mathbf{p}, \boldsymbol{\alpha}) = \frac{g_i(M, \mathbf{p}, \boldsymbol{\alpha})}{g p_i} \left[M - \sum_{k=1}^{n} \gamma_k p_k \right] + \gamma_i, \qquad (2.2a)$$

where

$$\left. \begin{array}{l} g_i(M, \mathbf{p}, \boldsymbol{\alpha}) > 0 \qquad\qquad\qquad\qquad (2.2b) \\[4pt] g = \displaystyle\sum_{i=1}^{n} g_i(M, \mathbf{p}, \boldsymbol{\alpha}) \qquad\qquad (2.2c) \end{array} \right\} i = 1, 2, \ldots, n.$$

The selection of parameters γ_k, for $k = 1, 2, \ldots, n$, is arbitrary. *Every system of demand functions that satisfy the budget constraint* (2.1a) *can be expressed in the form* (2.2a–c) *as follows:* Let the *expenditure share functions* $E_i(M, \mathbf{p}, \boldsymbol{\alpha})$, for $i = 1, 2, \ldots, n$, be determined from the specified arbitrary form of demand functions. To obtain the $g_i(M, \mathbf{p}, \boldsymbol{\alpha})$, substitute $E_i(M, \mathbf{p}, \boldsymbol{\alpha})$ into the definitional identity

$$\frac{g_i(M, \mathbf{p}, \boldsymbol{\alpha})}{g(M, \mathbf{p}, \boldsymbol{\alpha})} = \frac{M}{M - \displaystyle\sum_{k=1}^{n} \gamma_k p_k}$$

$$\times \left[E_i(M, \mathbf{p}, \boldsymbol{\alpha}) - \frac{\gamma_i p_i}{M} \right] \qquad i = 1, 2, \ldots, n, \quad (2.3a)$$

where

$$g(M, \mathbf{p}, \boldsymbol{\alpha}) = \sum_{i=1}^{n} g_i(M, \mathbf{p}, \boldsymbol{\alpha}). \qquad (2.3b)$$

We illustrate the construction of the functions $g_i(M, \mathbf{p}, \boldsymbol{\alpha})$, for $i = 1, 2, \ldots, n$, from some empirical *indirect translog demand functions* published by Christensen et al. [1975, p. 374, Eq. (52) and (53)]. Using parameter estimates presented in Table 2, col. 3, p. 379 of that paper, namely,[1]

$$E_1(M, \mathbf{p}) = \frac{-.125 - .0970 \ln p_1/M + .0816 \ln p_2/M - .0174 \ln p_3/M}{D}$$

(2.4a)

$$E_2(M, \mathbf{p}) = \frac{-.468 + .139 \ln p_1/M - .334 \ln p_2/M + .361 \ln p_3/M}{D}$$

(2.4b)

$$E_3(M, \mathbf{p}) = \frac{-.407 - .0744 \ln p_1/M - .237 \ln p_2/M - .624 \ln p_3/M}{D},$$

(2.4c)

where

$$D = -1 - .0324 \ln \frac{p_1}{M} - .489 \ln \frac{p_2}{M} - .280 \ln \frac{p_3}{M}. \quad (2.4d)$$

Substituting (2.4a-d) into (2.3a-b) we can determine the functions g_i/g, for $i = 1, 2, 3$ corresponding to (1) the estimates of Christensen et al. of parameters of the translog demand functions for services of consumers' durables, nondurable goods, and other services and (2) the arbitrarily specified parameters γ. For instance, specifying that $\gamma_i = 0$, for $i = 1$, 2, 3, we can make the $g_i(M, \mathbf{p})$, for $i = 1, 2, 3$, identical to the numerators of the expenditure shares $E_i(M, \mathbf{p})$ in (2.4a-c).

It is obvious that (2.2a-c) is not limited to the representation of translog systems of demand functions. Only limitations of space have precluded our giving illustrations of the use of (2.2a-c) in representing an *Almost Ideal Demand System* (AIDS) proposed by Deaton and Muellbauer (1980b, p. 316) and in representing a *Rotterdam System* of demand functions (Theil, 1975, p. 185).

Any system of positive functions $X_i(M, \mathbf{p}, \boldsymbol{\alpha})$ possessing first-order partial derivatives at a specified point $\langle M^0, \mathbf{p}^0, \boldsymbol{\alpha}^0 \rangle$ and satisfying the constraint (2.1a) also satisfies the condition

$$\det \begin{bmatrix} \dfrac{\partial x_1}{\partial M}, & \dfrac{\partial X_2}{\partial M}, & \cdots, & \dfrac{\partial X_n}{\partial M}, & -1 \\[2ex] \dfrac{\partial X_1}{\partial p_1}, & \dfrac{\partial X_2}{\partial p_1}, & \cdots, & \dfrac{\partial X_n}{\partial p_1}, & X_1 \\[2ex] \dfrac{\partial X_1}{\partial p_n}, & \dfrac{\partial X_2}{\partial p_n}, & \cdots, & \dfrac{\partial X_n}{\partial p_n}, & X_n \end{bmatrix} = 0 \quad (2.5)$$

at this point $\langle M^0, \mathbf{p}^0, \boldsymbol{\alpha}^0 \rangle$. It is convenient to express this relation among the partial derivatives of the system $X(M, \mathbf{p}, \alpha)$ of functions for the more compact form obtained by making the obviously called-for elementary row operations on the determinant (2.5), thus obtaining the equation

$$\det[K_{ij}] = 0, \tag{2.6a}$$

where

$$K_{ij} = \frac{\partial X_i}{\partial p_j} + X_j \frac{\partial X_i}{\partial M}, \qquad i, j = 1, 2, \ldots, n. \tag{2.6b}$$

The functions $\delta_i(M, \mathbf{p}, \alpha)$ defined by

$$\delta_i(M, \mathbf{p}, \alpha) = df \sum_{j=1}^{n} K_{ij} p_j, \qquad i = 1, 2, \ldots, n, \tag{2.7}$$

play an important part in the discussion of consumer preferences below. If any $X_i(M, \mathbf{p}, \alpha)$ is homogeneous in M and $\mathbf{p}$, then δ_i is a constant over all $\langle M, \mathbf{p}, \alpha \rangle$. If all $X_i(M, \mathbf{p}, \alpha)$, for $i = 1, 2, \ldots, n$, are homogeneous, then the average degree of homogeneity is equal to zero, since

$$\sum_{i=1}^{n} p_i \delta_i = 0. \tag{2.8}$$

Consequently, if all of the functions $X_i(M, \mathbf{p}, \alpha)$ have the same degree, δ, of homogeneity in M and $\mathbf{p}$, then they are all homogeneous of degree zero in M and $\mathbf{p}$.

Viewed retrospectively, a chief aim of early scientific theorizing about consumer demand[2] was to account deductively for those empirical regularities that have come to be called "the law of market demand."[3] A means of achieving that aim was formation of a system of definitions and economic premises characterizing behavior of a conceptual *ideal*, individual, consumer from which "laws" of market conduct can be deduced (see Hicks, 1946, esp. p. 23).[4] It was a natural first step to make those definitions and premises respecting the behavior of the *ideal* individual consumer strictly analogous in mathematical form to those of the theory of the profit-maximizing firm and thereafter, as Hicks (1956, p. 5) says, "to look about for something which he might be considered to maximize. Thus we got the Utility Theory, the consequences of which were set out by Marshall in classic form."

Thus, the *ideal* consumer of traditional demand theory is characterized by a system of demand functions displayed as solutions of a constrained maximization problem.[5] If the constraint on the maximization is (2.1a), then any system of demand functions that can be derived as solutions can be represented in the form (2.2a-c).

On the principle of *Occam's razor* we consider the most weakly restricted, or most robust, form of direct utility function that yields demand functions (2.2a-c) when maximized subject to the budget constraint (2.1a). Thus we shall go a step beyond Hicks and Allen (1934), in doing without a concept of quantitative utility (Hicks, 1946, p. 18); we shall also do without any restrictive assumptions on maximizing behavior that are not necessary in order to explain individual and market behavior and are also extremely unlikely ever to be tested empirically. We shall retain the concept of the utility-maximizing consumer, however, as will be made clear in the next subsection.

B.   The Least Restricted Direct Utility Function

Given that every system $\mathbf{X}(M, \mathbf{p}, \mathbf{\alpha})$ of demand functions whatsoever that satisfy the budget constraint (2.1a-b) can be expressed in the form (2.2a-c), the following question naturally arises: What is the most robust, or least restricted, form of *direct utility function* that can rationalize demand functions (2.2a-c)? The question is an extremely important one because its answer defines the natural scientific boundaries of a *theory of the utility-maximizing consumer*. Special, restricted forms (or algorithms) for direct utility functions imply "straightjackets on the facts," to borrow a term from Samuelson (1947, p. 88) which permit such restricted forms to be disconfirmed in principle, at least, by empirical data. Their potential empirical disconfirmation makes such restricted direct utility functions unsuitable for use in defining boundaries of a theory of the utility-maximizing consumer, especially where the theory is expected to have policy relevance, e.g., in the construction of *cost-of-living indexes*.

It turns out that the direct utility function characterized by (2.9a-b), below, rationalizes every system of demand functions that satisfy the budget constraint (2.1a). Discussion of the practical consequences of this robustness of (2.9a-b) is postponed to Section II.D.

The *generalized Fechner-Thurstone* form of direct utility function with argument $\mathbf{X}$ is defined by

$$U(\mathbf{X}; \mathbf{\Psi}) = \prod_{i=1}^{n} (X_i - \gamma_i)^{\Psi_i(\alpha)} \tag{2.9a}$$

$$X_i \geqq \max(0, \gamma_i). \tag{2.9b}$$

The n-tuple $\mathbf{\Psi}$ of positive valued functions $\Psi_i(\alpha)$, for $i = 1, 2, \ldots, n$, is (said to be) the parameter of $U(\mathbf{X}; \mathbf{\Psi})$. The notational device of separating the *argument parameter* of a function by a semicolon will be used throughout this study whenever it is essential to distinguish between them.

The *generalized Fechner–Thurstone* direct utility function (2.9a-b) looks superficially like the *Stone-Geary* and *Cobb-Douglas* direct utility function,[6] the latter being, from the formal point of view at least, highly restricted special cases of (2.9a-b). First- and second-order partial derivatives of (2.9a-b) with respect to elements of X will be designated by $U_i(X; \Psi)$ and $U_{ij}(X, \Psi)$, respectively, or, as is usually done, by U_i and U_{ij}. The *marginal rate of substitution* of commodity k *for* commodity i at a point X of the domain (2.9b) is defined by

$$R_i^{(k)}(X; \alpha) = df \frac{U_i(X, \Psi)}{U_k(X, \Psi)} \tag{2.10a}$$

$$= \frac{\Psi_i(\alpha)}{\Psi_k(\alpha)} \frac{X_k - \gamma_k}{X_i - \gamma_i}. \tag{2.10b}$$

The preference field, or system of indifference surfaces determined by (2.9a-b), remains invariant against the replacement of (2.9a-b) by any monotonically increasing function of $U(X; \Psi)$ (see Hicks, 1946, pp. 306–307).

In aggregating individual consumers' utility functions we find it very convenient to use the following replacement of $U(X, \psi)$ by another *generalized Fechner-Thurstone* direct utility function $U(X; \theta)$:

$$\Psi(\alpha) = df \sum_{i=1}^{n} \Psi_i(\alpha). \tag{2.11}$$

The new parameter θ is required to satisfy the condition

$$\sum_{i=1}^{n} \theta_i(\alpha) = \theta, \tag{2.12}$$

where the numerical value of θ is specified. This requirement is satisfied by the definition

$$U(X; \theta) = [U(X; \Psi)]^{\theta/\Psi} \tag{2.13a}$$

$$= \prod_{i=1}^{n} (X_i - \gamma_i)^{\theta_i(\alpha)}. \tag{2.13b}$$

From (2.9a-b) and (2.13a-b) it follows that

$$\theta_i(\alpha) = \frac{\Psi_i(\alpha)\theta}{\Psi}, \quad i = 1, 2, \ldots, n. \tag{2.14}$$

Consequently, for every X in the domain (2.9b), $R_i^{(k)}$, the *marginal rate of substitution of commodity k for commodity i,* remains invariant:

$$R_i^{(k)}(\mathbf{X}; \boldsymbol{\theta}) = df \frac{U_i(\mathbf{X}; \boldsymbol{\theta})}{U_k(\mathbf{X}; \boldsymbol{\theta})} \tag{2.15a}$$

$$= R_i^{(k)}(\mathbf{X}; \boldsymbol{\Psi}) \tag{2.15b}$$

at *every* point $\mathbf{X}$ of the domain (2.9a-b).

In view of this invariance of preference maps defined by *generalized Fechner-Thurstone* direct utility functions we are able validly to specify that for every pair of distinct individual consumers μ and v, the parameters $\boldsymbol{\theta}^{(v)}$ and $\boldsymbol{\theta}^{(\mu)}$ satisfy the condition

$$\sum_{i=1}^{n} \theta_i^{(v)}(\boldsymbol{\alpha}) = \sum_{i=1}^{n} \theta_i^{(\mu)}(\boldsymbol{\alpha}). \tag{2.16}$$

This respecification does not involve any interpersonal comparison of utility or levels of satisfaction.

In Section III the theory of the utility-maximizing consumer will be linked up with a theoretical representation of the *personal multivariate distribution of expenditures on commodities and components of income and wealth*. This linkage will be found to destroy the ordinal character of utility as far as the combined theory is concerned. It will remain true, of course, that *preference fields* will be invariant against replacement of (2.13a-b) by a monotonically increasing function of itself. However, such a replacement of (2.13a-b) will imply empirically testable changes in measures of inequality in the personal distributions of expenditures on commodities and components of income and wealth. The parameter $\boldsymbol{\theta}$, which is a parameter of every individual consumer's direct utility function, turns out to be an inequality parameter of the personal distribution of income. A ceteris paribus increase of $\boldsymbol{\theta}$ causes an increase in, e.g., the *Gini measure* of income inequality. Consequently the values of the parameters θ_i, for $i = 1, 2, \ldots, n$, in (2.13b) cannot be changed arbitrarily as they can with purely ordinal utility functions.

The direct utility function (2.9a-b) is a straightforward generalization of an experimentally *interpreted* direct utility function first introduced by the experimental psychologist L. L. Thurstone in his well-known article "The Indifference Function" (1931). What economists call a direct utility function is some monotonically increasing function or other of what Thurstone referred to as a *satisfaction curve*. In order to write an equation for this *satisfaction curve*, Thurstone (1931, pp. 141–142) laid down five psychological assumptions. The fifth assumption was that *motivation*, i.e., the slope of the *satisfaction curve* in the direction of increasing X_i, is inversely proportional to the amount X_i already possessed,[7] which is G. T. Fechner's proffered psychophysical law, or universalization, of well-known *empirical regularity* discovered by E. H. Weber: The increase of a stimulus to produce a given increase of sensation bears a constant ratio to the total stimulus (see James, 1890, reprint 1950, pp. 539–548). According to Thurstone, the psychological hypothesis that led him to use the Fechner "law" fit the experimental data better than other hypotheses that were tried (see Thurstone, 1931, pp. 142–143). Consequently he proffered the special case of the form (2.9a-b) with the parameters Ψ_i fixed (p. 147). Aware of the arbitrariness of the choice of the origin of the domain γ (p. 142), Thurstone used $\gamma = 0$ (p. 141).

C. Substitution Terms and Nonvacuous Preference Changers

The components of α, are called *nonvacuous preference changers*. These are classified under two main heads: (1) preference changers that are *systematic and observable*, and (2) preference changers that are *stochastic and nonobservable*. In order to define the term "nonvacuous" we consider some elementary geometry of the preference field defined by the *Fechner-Thurstone* direct utility function (2.13a-b).

Cofactors of elements of the bordered Hessian of partial derivatives of direct utility functions play an important part in the theory of consumer demand. Let $|U|$ be the bordered Hessian for (2.13a-b). We have

$$|U| = \frac{(-1)^n\{U(\mathbf{X}; \boldsymbol{\theta})\}^{n+1} \left(\prod_{k=1}^{n} \theta_k\right) \left(\sum_{k=1}^{n} \theta_k\right)}{\prod_{k=1}^{n} (X_k - \gamma_k)^2} \tag{2.17}$$

The magnitude of the cofactor of U_{ii} in $|U|$ at the point $\mathbf{X}$ is determined by (2.8) and

$$\frac{|U_{ii}|}{U} = \frac{-(\theta - \theta_i)(X_i - \gamma_i)^2}{\theta_i\theta[U(\mathbf{X}; \boldsymbol{\theta})]} ; \tag{2.18}$$

the magnitude of the cofactor of U_{ij}, for $i \neq j$, in $|U|$ at the point $\mathbf{X}$ is determined by (2.17) and

$$\frac{|U_{ij}|}{U} = \frac{(X_i - \gamma_i)(X_j - \gamma_j)}{\theta[U(\mathbf{X}; \boldsymbol{\theta})]} ; \tag{2.19}$$

finally, the magnitude of the cofactor of U_i in $|U|$ at the point $\mathbf{X}$ is determined by

$$\frac{|U_{i0}|}{|U|} = \frac{X_i - \gamma_i}{\theta[U(\mathbf{X}; \boldsymbol{\theta})]} . \tag{2.20}$$

Let $\mathbf{X}^0$ designate any given point of the domain (2.9b). Let $S(\mathbf{X}^0, \boldsymbol{\theta})$ be the set of points satisfying

$$U(\mathbf{X}; \boldsymbol{\theta}) = U(\mathbf{X}^0; \boldsymbol{\theta}). \tag{2.21}$$

Here $S(\mathbf{X}^0; \boldsymbol{\theta})$ is the indifference hypersurface passing through $\mathbf{X}^0$. Let

$$q^0 - \sum_{k=1}^{n} X_k^0 \cos \phi_k = 0, \qquad 0 \le \phi_k < \frac{\pi}{2}, \tag{2.22}$$

be the equation of the hyperplane tangent to $S(\mathbf{X}^0; \boldsymbol{\theta})$ at $\mathbf{X}^0$. Finally let the real number λ^0 be defined at the point $\mathbf{X}^0$ by

$$\lambda^0 = \theta[U(\mathbf{X}^0; \boldsymbol{\theta})] \left[q^0 - \sum_{k=1}^{n} \gamma_k \cos \phi_k \right]^{-1} \tag{2.23}$$

We define S_{ii}, S_{ij}, and S_{i0} at $\mathbf{X}^0$ in domain (2.9b) by

$$S_{ii} = \frac{\lambda^0 |U_{ii}|}{|U|} \tag{2.24a}$$

$$= \frac{-(\theta - \theta_i)(X_i^0 - \gamma_i)^2 \left[q^0 - \sum_{k=1}^{n} \gamma_k \cos \phi_k \right]^{-1}}{\theta_i} ; \tag{2.24b}$$

$$S_{ij} = \frac{\lambda^0 |U_{ij}|}{|U|} \tag{2.25a}$$

$$= (X_i^0 - \gamma_i)(X_j^0 - \gamma_j) \left[q^0 - \sum_{k=1}^{n} \gamma_k \cos \phi_k \right]^{-1}, \qquad j \ne i; \tag{2.25b}$$

and

$$S_{i0} = \frac{\lambda^0 |U_i|}{U} \tag{2.26a}$$

$$= (X_i^0 - \gamma_i) \left[q^0 - \sum_{k=1}^{n} \gamma_k \cos \phi_k \right]^{-1}. \tag{2.26b}$$

The functions S_{ij}, for $i, j = 1, 2, , , , , n$, form a symmetric negative semidefinite matrix; and

$$\sum_{j=1}^{n} S_{ij} \cos \phi_j = 0, \tag{2.27a}$$

$$\sum_{i=1}^{n} S_{ij} \cos \phi_i = 0. \tag{2.27b}$$

The functions S_{ij} look like *Slutsky-Hicks substitution terms* (see Hicks, 1946, pp. 309–310). However, Eq. (2.22) describes any tangent hyperplane, not necessarily a budget hyperplane. In the special case of a budget hyperplane the expressions S_{ij} do, indeed, reduce to the ordinary Slutsky-Hicks substitution terms *defined in terms* of *direct utility functions*; S_{i0} reduces to the ordinary income term *defined in terms of direct utility functions* (see Hicks, 1946, p. 309). We shall refer to S_{ij} as the *substitution term proper* (to the direct utility function) and to S_{i0} as the *expansion term proper* (to the direct utility function). We are now in position to define the concept of a *nonvacuous preference changer*.

A component α_h of α is (said to be) a *nonvacuous preference changer* with respect to the direct utility function $U(\mathbf{X}; \boldsymbol{\theta})$ if, and only if, for at least one point $\mathbf{X}^0$ of the domain (2.9b) a change in α_h causes a change in at least one of the *expansion terms proper*, S_{i0}, or at least one of the *substitution terms proper*, S_{ij}, for $i, j = 1, 2, \ldots, n$, at $\mathbf{X}^0$. Notice that this concept of a *nonvacuous preference changer* is always defined relative to a specified direct utility function.

Alternatively, and equivalently, a component α_h of α is (said to be) a *nonvacuous preference changer* with respect to $U(\mathbf{X}; \boldsymbol{\theta})$ if, and only if, for at least one point $\mathbf{X}^0$ of the domain (2.9b) a change in α_h causes a change in at least one *marginal rate of substitution* $R_i^{(k)}(\mathbf{X}; \boldsymbol{\theta})$ at $\mathbf{X}^0$; see (2.15a-b) (cf. Ichimura, 1951; also Tintner, 1952; Basmann, 1954b, 1956).

The concept of *nonvacuous preference changer* (as defined above) will be exemplified many times in the sections that follow.

D. Demand Functions Derived from $U(\mathbf{X}; \boldsymbol{\theta})$

In this section, let $\mathbf{p}$ be interpreted as a vector of budget constraint prices and let M be total expenditure on commodities $i = 1, 2, \ldots, n$. The consumer is assumed to select a definite equilibrium n-tuple $\langle X_1^*, \ldots, X_n^* \rangle$ such that the direct utility function (2.13a-b) is maximized subject to the budget constraint (2.1a). Equation (2.1a) is said to be a constraint because (as is usually assumed in the theory of consumer demand for one reason or other) the consumer does not treat M and $\mathbf{p}$ as choice variables in this optimization process.

The derived demand functions are expressed by

$$X_i^* = \frac{\theta_i(\alpha)p_i^{-1}}{\displaystyle\sum_{k=1}^{n} \theta_k(\alpha)} \left[M - \sum_{k=1}^{n} \gamma_k p_k \right] + \gamma_i, \qquad i = 1, 2, \ldots, n. \quad (2.28)$$

Notice that the derived demand function (2.28) has the form (2.2a-c).

Since every system of demand functions can be represented in the form (2.2a-c), it follows that every system of demand functions can be derived from the *generalized Fechner-Thurstone* direct utility function (2.9a-b). This assures us that, in accord with the principle of Occam's razor, the *generalized Fechner-Thurstone* form of direct utility function does not embody any excessively restrictive assumptions about maximizing behavior of consumers.

The consumer demand depends on, and only on, the parameters of the specified *Fechner-Thurstone* direct utility function $U(\mathbf{X}; \boldsymbol{\theta})$ and the parameters of the budget constraint (2.12).

The economic theorists' concern with the Giffen paradox of Hicks (1946, p. 35), with the possible existence of *inferior goods* and *nonlinearity* of Engel curves (Engel, 1861, p. 249), the interrelatedness of goods in consumption, i.e., their *substitutability* and *complementarity* (Hicks, 1946, Chap. III), and with *shifts in demand* (Lange, 1940; Robertson et al., 1944; Ichimura, 1951; Tintner, 1952; Basmann, 1954a,b, 1956), make those topics matters of concern to the econometrician involved in estimating (and testing hypotheses about) the parameters of systems of demand functions. Definitions of the above concepts are usually stated in terms of partial derivatives of demand functions. Since the derived demand functions (2.28) allow for the possibility of total expenditure M and budget constraint prices being systematic preference changers, definitions of "inferior good," "Giffen good," "substitutability," and "complementarity" need restatement in order to avoid an otherwise unsuspected change of their usual meanings in use.

Let y be any real variable. The partial derivative of X_i^* with respect to y is formally expressed by

$$\frac{\partial X_i^*}{\partial y} = \frac{\theta_i(\boldsymbol{\alpha})}{\sum\limits_{k=1}^{n} \theta_k(\boldsymbol{\alpha})} \frac{\partial}{\partial y} \left\{ p_i^{-1} \left[M - \sum_{k=1}^{n} \gamma_k p_k \right] \right\}$$

$$+ p_i^{-1} \left[M - \sum_{k=1}^{n} \gamma_k p_k \right] \left\{ \sum_{k=1}^{n} \left(\frac{\theta_k}{\theta} \right)^2 \frac{\partial}{\partial y} \left(\frac{\theta_i}{\theta_k} \right) \right\},$$

$$\tag{2.29}$$

$$i = 1, 2, \ldots, n.$$

In order that the expression (2.29) be nonzero it is necessary that one or more of M, the budget constraint prices $\mathbf{p}$, or one or more elements of $\boldsymbol{\alpha}$ be (specified as) dependent on y.

Stochastic variables are assumed to affect demand functions (2.29) solely by way of the parameters $\theta_i(\boldsymbol{\alpha})$. Random variables will not be "tacked on" to demand functions in this study. Partial derivatives of X_i^*, for $i = 1, 2, \ldots, n$, with respect to M and the budget constraint prices **p** necessarily satisfy (2.6a-b). Using K_{ij}^* to describe (2.6b) when the functions differentiated are (2.28), we find that the K_{ij}^* are related to substitution terms proper to $U(\mathbf{X}; \boldsymbol{\theta})$ at $\mathbf{X}^*$ by the equations

$$K_{ij}^* = S_{ij} + p_i^{-1} \left[M - \sum_{k=1}^n \gamma_k p_k \right] \sum_{k=1}^n \left(\frac{\theta_k}{\theta} \right)^2 \left(\frac{\partial}{\partial p_j} + X_j^* \frac{\partial}{\partial M} \right) \frac{\theta_i}{\theta_k},$$

(2.30)

$$i, j = 1, 2, \ldots, n.$$

We shall refer to K_{ij}^* as *apparent substitution terms*. The *apparent income term*, or partial derivative of the demand function with respect to M, is designated by K_{i0}^* and is related to S_{i0}, the *expansion term proper* to $U(X; \theta)$ at X^*, by the equations

$$K_{i0}^* = S_{i0} + p_i^{-1} \left[M - \sum_{k=1}^n \gamma_k p_k \right] \left\{ \sum_{k=1}^n \left(\frac{\theta_k}{\theta} \right)^2 \frac{\partial}{\partial M} \left(\frac{\theta_i}{\theta_k} \right) \right\},$$

(2.31)

$$i = 1, 2, \ldots, n.$$

Concepts of *inferior good, Giffen good, substitutability,* and *complementarity* as usually defined tacitly presuppose that the consumers' preferences are not dependent on total expenditure M and/or budget constraint prices, **p**. This tacit presupposition is an untested assumption about empirical "facts." It is testable in principle but not feasible to test in practice—nor is such testing probably socially desirable even were it to become feasible to do so. Accordingly, we restate all of those definitions with an explicit, much weaker antecedent condition for their use and which does not imply that consumers' preferences are independent of the budget constraint parameters: *If at a specified point $Q^0 = (M^0, \mathbf{p}^0, \alpha^0)$ of the domain of demand functions (2.28), the matrix $[K_{ij}^*]$ defined by (2.30) is symmetric and negative semidefinite, then*

(a)   *commodity i is an* **inferior good** *at Q^0 iff K_{i0} * < 0 at Q^0;*

(b)   *commodity i is a* **Giffen good** *at Q^0 iff $\dfrac{\partial X_i^*}{\partial p_i} > 0$ at Q^0;*

(c)   *commodity j is a* **substitute** *for i at Q^0, iff $j \neq i$ and $K_{ij}^* \geq 0$;*

(d)   *commodity j is a* **complement** *of commodity i at Q^0 iff $j \neq i$ and $K_{ij}^* < 0$.*

The conditional definitions (a)–(d) include as special cases the neoclassical concepts as they are defined under the tacit presupposition that consumers' preferences are independent of total expenditure M and budget constraint prices. By relaxing the tacit, highly restrictive neoclassical antecedent condition to include a nonempty subclass of demand function systems derived from direct utility functions with parameters that are dependent on total expenditure M and/or budget constraint prices $\mathbf{p}$, we have extended the scopes of concepts of an inferior good, a Giffen good, substitutability, and complementarity somewhat. The particular extension of these neoclassical concepts does seem more or less natural in the case of systems of demand functions (2.28) such as Leser-Houthakker additive logarithmic demand functions (see Houthakker, 1960, p. 263), i.e., where $\theta_i = \beta_i M^{\sigma_{i0}} p_i^{-(1+\sigma_{i0})}$, for $i = 1, 2, \ldots, n$, in (2.28), with $\beta_i > 0$, $\beta_1 + \cdots + \beta_n = 1$. Moreover, Arrow (1961, p. 177) has already extended implicitly the neoclassical concepts of "substitutability" and "complementarity" to the K_{ij}^* derived from the additive logarithmic demand functions.[8] However, to extend the scopes of those neoclassical terms beyond the class of systems of demand functions characterized by the antecedent condition we set forth would dissolve their neoclassical meaning, lead to no greater understanding of empirical consumer behavior, and (probably) stand in the way of forming more fruitful theoretical concepts out of accumulated experience with systems of empirical demand functions (2.28) derived from the less restricted forms of the *generalized Fechner-Thurstone* direct utility function (2.13a-b).

If α_h is an element of α other than current total expenditure M or a current budget constraint price, then the derivative of any demand function (2.28) is a *pure Ichimura-Tintner shift in demand*:

$$\frac{\partial X_i^*}{\partial \alpha_h} = p_i^{-1} \left[M - \sum_{k=1}^{n} \gamma_k p_k \right] \left\{ \sum_{k=1}^{n} \left(\frac{\theta_k}{\theta} \right)^2 \frac{\partial}{\partial \alpha_h} \left(\frac{\theta_i}{\theta_k} \right) \right\}$$

$$= -p_k \sum_{j=1}^{n} \sum_{m=1}^{n} \frac{\partial \theta_j}{\partial \alpha_h} \frac{\partial R_m^{(k)}}{\partial \theta_j} S_{ki} \qquad (2.32)$$

(see Basmann, 1956, p. 51). Notice that the pure shifts in demand are direct by related to the *substitution terms* S_{ij} *proper* to the direct utility function (2.13a-b). Interpretation of pure shifts in demand remains the same as in neoclassical theory.

E.   On Making Sense of the Neoclassical Notion of Fixed Consumer Preferences

We must do this before discussing aggregation of individual consumers' *generalized Fechner-Thurstone* direct utility functions. Precedent, as the preceding discussion of neoclassical substitutability and complementarity indicates, and practical concerns in the construction of cost-of-living indexes, measures of economic inequality, consumer equivalence scales, and welfare functions from systems of empirical demand functions that satisfy the ordinary budget constraint (2.1a) make it convenient to study systems of demand functions under two mutually exclusive heads—

A. Systems of demand functions (2.28) that satisfy all of the following properties: (a) homogeneity of zero degree in prices and income; (b) symmetry of the K_{ij}^*, defined in Section II.D, above; and (c) negative semidefiniteness of the matrix $[K_{ij}^*]$

B. Systems of demand functions (2.28) that fail to possess at least one of the properties (a), (b), or (c) listed above

Every system of demand functions belongs to (A) or (B) and can be rationalized by a *generalized Fechner-Thurstone* direct utility function (2.13a-b). Empirical systems of demand functions that fall under heading (A) do not logically contradict and, consequently, do not empirically disconfirm the tacit neoclassical assumption that the utility maximizing consumers' preferences are independent of total expenditure M and budget constraint price p_i, for $i = 1, 2, \ldots, n$.

A system of demand functions falling under heading (B) represents the equilibrium of a *utility-maximizing consumer* whose preferences are influenced by changes in at least one of the budget constraint prices and changes in the level of attainable total expenditure. Empirical systems of demand functions that fall under heading (B) do logically contradict and factually disconfirm the hypothesis that the underlying consumer preferences are independent of budget constraint prices **p** and total expenditure M.

Meaningfulness of the neoclassical interpretation of the term "cost of living" depends on the empirical truth of its *justificatory antecedent condition*, namely, that consumers' preferences are independent of their budget constraint prices and total expenditure. Consequently, empirical systems of demand functions that fall under heading (B) dissolve the meaningfulness of the neoclassical interpretation of "cost of living"[9] and call for a reinterpretation on the basis of a broader justificatory antecedent condition that includes the old one as an important but special case.

Need for such a reformulation is not limited to cases falling under heading (B). The need would remain even if all samples of longitudinal survey data and even the price-quantity variations of controlled revealed preference experiments were always to yield systems belonging to (A). It might be supposed that empirical systems of demand functions falling under heading (A)—at least those that are estimated from samples of price and quantity variations that favor the *strong axiom of revealed preference* in nonparametric tests—would validate the neoclassical assumption that the underlying consumer preferences are independent of total expenditure and budget constraint prices (see Koo, 1963, p. 646). True enough, if a system $\mathbf{X}(M, \mathbf{p}, \boldsymbol{\alpha})$ of demand functions falls under heading (A), not only can that system be rationalized by a *generalized Fechner-Thurstone* direct utility function $U(\mathbf{X}; \boldsymbol{\theta})$, (2.13a-b), but it may be possible to find a closed form direct utility function $V(\mathbf{X})$ with parameters that are independent of budget constraint prices and total expenditure and which also rationalize the same system of demand functions as $U(\mathbf{X}; \boldsymbol{\theta})$. We are indebted to Angus Deaton for pointing out the possibility of constructing such a fixed preference direct utility function $V(\mathbf{X})$ algorithmically that rationalizes the same system as $U(\mathbf{X}; \boldsymbol{\theta})$ even when the derivation of a closed form would be excessively intractable.[10] However, the actual finding (not to mention the mere possibility of finding) of a fixed preference direct utility function that rationalizes the same observed demand functions as $U(\mathbf{X}; \boldsymbol{\theta})$ does not suffice to prove or even establish a prima facie case for the assumption that the underlying preferences are independent of budget constraint prices and total expenditure. Here the "remarkable way of producing rabbits out of a hat—apparently *a priori* propositions which apparently refer to reality" (Hicks, 1946, p. 23) cannot make sense out of the concept of fixed preferences. Meaningfulness of the neoclassical hypothesis that consumer preferences are independent of budget constraint prices and total expenditure can be soundly established, however, without a priori sleight of hand, as we shall show now. The meaningfulness of the above neoclassical assumption rests on the possibility of detecting an observational difference between a specified fixed preference direct utility function $V(\mathbf{X})$ and a specified *generalized Fechner-Thurstone* direct utility function $U(\mathbf{X}; \boldsymbol{\theta})$ yielding the same system of demand functions falling under heading (A). In revealed preference data, even if it could be completely error-free, nothing observable in those data would be different under the alternative hypotheses even in principle. On the other hand, in an incentive-compatible experiment in which the experimenter barters with consumer subjects, the budget constraint prices and total expenditure remaining constant,[11] an observational difference can be detected. We present a simple example:

Figure 1 depicts isoquants of the price-dependent direct utility function

$$U(\mathbf{X}; \boldsymbol{\theta}) = X_1^{\sqrt{p_1}} X_2^{\sqrt{p_2}}; \qquad (2.33a)$$

$$X_i > 0, \qquad i = 1, 2; \qquad (2.33b)$$

$$\theta_i = \sqrt{p_i}. \qquad (2.33c)$$

for a given market price situation: (i) $p_1^0 = 9$ and $p_2^0 = 1$. Here p_1 and p_2 are market prices known to the individual consumer. They are not necessarily market equilibrium prices.

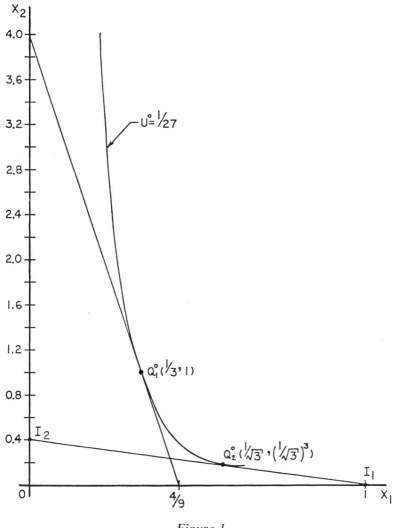

Figure 1

The budget constraint (solid line) assumes that the individual consumer's total expenditure is $M^0 = 4$.

The isoquant marked $U^0 = 1/27$ is tangent to the market price budget constraint, $\mathbf{p}^0 \cdot \mathbf{X} = M^0$, at Q_1^0, which depicts the consumer's *purchase of commodities from the market* given M^0 and market price vector $\mathbf{p}^0$. Let Q_2^0 be any other point on $U^0 = 1/27$. The isoquant shows the maximum

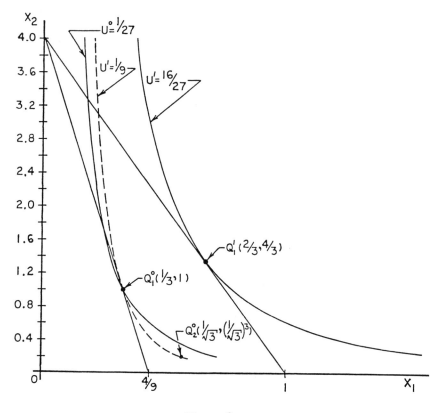

Figure 2

amount of commodity-2 that the individual consumer will exchange (barter) for the additional quantity $(X_1^2 - X_1^0)$ of commodity-1.

Figure 2 displays two distinct sets of isoquants of the price-dependent direct utility function (2.1a-b) corresponding to two distinct market price situations:(i) $p_1^0 = 9$ and $p_2^0 = 1$; (ii) $p_1^1 = 4$ and $p_2^1 = 1$. Budget constraints (solid lines) assume that the consumer's total expenditure is the same ($M^1 = M^0 = 4$) in both cases.

The isoquant under market price situation (i) is shown as a dashed line; it coincides with the isoquant shown in Figure 1. The isoquants under market price situation (ii) are exhibited by solid lines.

In particular, the isoquant $U^1 = 16/27$ shows the maximum amount of commodity-2 that the individual consumer will exchange for any specified additional amount of commodity-1 under market price situation (ii).

Figure 3 depicts isoquants of the price-independent direct utility function

$$V(\mathbf{X}) = (X_1^{-1} + X_2^{-1})^{-2} \tag{2.34a}$$

$$X_i > 0, \qquad i = 1, 2. \tag{2.34b}$$

Isoquants $V^0 = 1/16$ and $V^1 = 16/81$ of the fixed-preference direct utility function (2.34a-b) [we call (2.34a-b) a fixed-preference direct utility function because its expression contains no variable parameters] are shown in heavy lines. Market price budget constraints for market price situations (i) and (ii), above, assume total expenditure $M = 4$. Labeled points Q_1^0, Q_2^0, and Q_1^1 are the same as in Figure 1 and 2. Isoquants $V^0 = 1/16$ and $U^0 = 1/27$ of the price-dependent direct utility function $U(X; \mathbf{p}^0)$ are

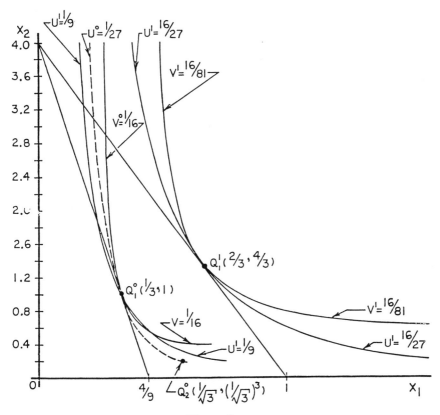

Figure 3

mutually tangent at Q_1^0. Isoquants $V^1 = 16/81$ and $U^1 = 16/27$ of $U(X; \mathbf{p}^1)$ are mutually tangent at Q_1^1.

Figure 3 illustrates the following easily demonstrated theorem:

For every market price budget $(\mathbf{p}, M)$, *maximization of either direct utility function (2.33a-b) or (2.34a-b) subject to the market price budget constraint* $\mathbf{p} \cdot \mathbf{X} = M$ *yields the same demand functions:*

$$X_i^*(p, M) = \frac{\sqrt{p_i}}{(\sqrt{p_1} + \sqrt{p_2})} \left(\frac{M}{p_i}\right), \qquad i = 1, 2. \qquad (2.35)$$

The system (2.35) belongs to heading (A). If we entertain $U(\mathbf{X}; \boldsymbol{\theta})$ as a hypothesis, it is not to rescue utility analysis from disconfirmation but because it refers to a wider range of aspects of consumer behavior than does the fixed-preference utility function $V(X)$.

In Figure 4 five distinct budgets and consumer's purchases of X_1 and X_2 are plotted. They exemplify all that we can know in principle about consumer preferences underlying the demand functions (2.35) from revealed preference techniques. Suppose a large number of such price-expenditure-quantity data were obtained for a given individual consumer by *revealed preference* experimentation techniques (Battalio et al., 1973, 1975, 1981a,b). From these revealed preference data, the econometrician can confirm consistency of the *weak axiom of revealed preference* (Samuelson, 1938; Houthakker, 1950) with the consumer's behavior and, moreover, determine that the demand functions are those shown for Figure 1, but revealed preference data like those shown in Figure 4 can never distinguish between the alternative direct utility functions $U(\mathbf{X}; \boldsymbol{\theta})$ and $V(\mathbf{X})$, whose indifference maps are depicted in Figures 1 and 3.

Finally, revealed preference data cannot in principle tell us anything about the maximum amount of commodity-2 that the individual consumer will exchange with the experimenter for the additional quantity $(X_1^2 - X_1^0)$ of commodity-1 in market price situation (i) with $M^0 = 4$ (see Figures 1–3).

What makes sense out of the assumption that the consumers' preferences are *really* given by $V(\mathbf{X})$ and not by the price dependent (2.33a-c) is the possibility of empirically disconfirming (2.34a-b) in the following incentive-compatible experiment:[12]

Let the market prices p_1 and p_2 be as in market price situation (i) and let total expenditure be $M^0 = 4$. In every period the consumer may purchase X_1^0, X_2^0 as at Q^0 in Figure 1. He is not required to barter. Offer to take the fixed amount $X_2^0 - X_2^2$ of commodity-2 from the consumer in return for an amount of $\Delta X_1 = X_1^2 - X_1^0 > 0$ to be determined in the

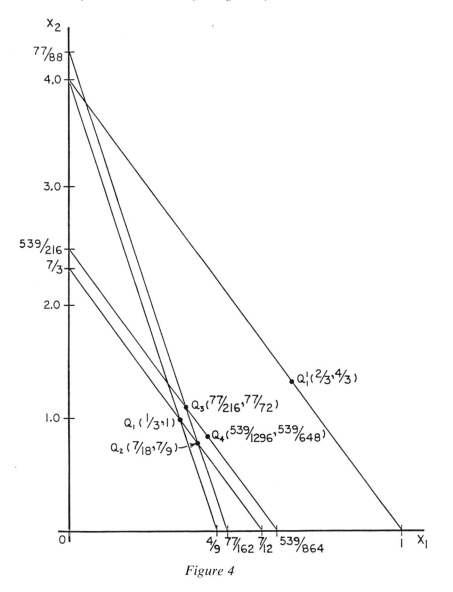

Figure 4

following way: The experimenter draws at random a positive number ΔX_1^e (say) from a suitable range of numbers written on slips of paper. The consumer is instructed to say how much, ΔX_1^c, additional commodity-1 he requires to be exactly as well-off as at Q^0. If $\Delta X_1^e \geq \Delta X_1^c$, then the consumer receives ΔX_1^e; that is, he receives more than (he says) he requires. If $\Delta X_1^c < \Delta X_1^c$, then no trade takes place. Under these conditions, the consumer has an incentive to reveal where his actual barter indifference curve through Q^0 intersects the ordinate X_2^2 in Figure 2. The experiment has to be repeated over a wide range of starting points. It may turn out, of course, that the hypothesis $U(\mathbf{X}; \boldsymbol{\theta})$ would be rejected in favor of $V(\mathbf{X})$.

Merely showing how empirical sense can be made out of the neoclassical assumption of fixed consumer preferences on a case-by-case basis does not establish the empirical truth of that assumption, of course. It does show that there can be no ground for ignoring the need to reformulate the concept of "true cost of living" to apply to direct utility functions with price-dependent parameters, especially where systems of demand functions fall under the heading (A). For it is in such systems of demand functions that the potential for price-dependent preferences to fool policymaking and pure economic science is masked from observation by variations in prices and total expenditure. The case for reformulating concepts of "true cost of living" and measures of "economic inequality" and "economic welfare" with more readily testable justificatory antecedent conditions does not stand or fall on the failure of empirical demand functions to fit under heading (A).[13]

F.   The Aggregate Direct Utility Function and Per Capita Demand Functions

As its heading indicates, this section is concerned with the representation of per capita (per consumer unit) market demands as magnitudes of consumer demand functions that are derived by constrained maximization of a direct utility function that is a definite aggregation of individual consumers' direct utility functions. Maximization of this *aggregate direct utility function* is subject to a per capita budget constraint, which itself is an arithmetic average of the individual consumer's budget constraints. In this section attention is confined to the matter of aggregation over a population of individual consumers. The matter of aggregation of commodities into commodity groups will come up in Section III, but it need not detain us here.

This article emphasizes two practical motives for aggregating individual consumers' *Fechner-Thurstone* direct utility functions into an aggregate direct utility function. The first of these has to do with formulating a specific theoretical connection between individual consumers' preferences, on the one hand, and the personal marginal multivariate distribution of components of received income and components of wealth, on the other; the theoretical connection we propose as an initial hypothesis will be described in Section III. A second practical motive for construction of an aggregate direct utility function is its use in the construction of *cost-of-living* indexes that can retain meaningfulness even when extended to a population of utility-maximizing individual consumers whose preferences are nonvacuously dependent on total expenditure or one or more budget constraint prices. In particular the aggregate direct utility function is constructed in order to extend the Klein-Rubin approach to constructing a "true cost-of-living" index based on statistical estimates of per capita demand functions (Klein and Rubin, 1947, p. 87). That is to say, the practical motive for constructing an aggregate direct utility function that is derived from individual consumers' direct utility functions is to extend the Klein-Rubin approach to systems of per capita demand functions that fall under heading (B) in Section II.E, above, and which *fail* to possess *any* of the properties listed under heading (A).

The need for an extension of the concept of *cost of living* that is based on systems of per capita demand functions falling under heading (B) has been made clear by the record of a half-century of demand analysis. Furthermore, the insufficiency of empirical systems of demand functions falling under heading (A) to establish that individual consumers' preferences are independent of budget constraint prices and total expenditure severely handicaps the use of indirect utility functions in the construction of *cost-of-living* indexes in all cases save that originally presented by Klein and Rubin (1947).

From Schultz (1938, pp. 628–633) to Muellbauer (1975), theoretical demand analysts have stressed that "there is, in general, no reason why aggregated market data should obey the same rules as the micro data of any individual, even when, as econometricians usually assume, everyone has the same tastes. Thus the symmetry restrictions do not hold in the aggregate, even if they hold at the micro level" (Muellbauer, 1975, p. 525). An important line of pure theoretical investigation has been concerned with deriving the mathematical consequences (for aggregate demand functions) of the assumption that individual consumers' direct utility functions have preference parameters that are independent of the budget constraint parameters (e.g., see Sonnenschein, 1972, 1973). Other theorists have formulated additional theoretical constraints on individual consumers' direct utility functoins that are sufficient to imply deductively that aggregate demand functions satisfy the conditions (a), (b), and (c) under heading (A) in Section II.E, above. Gorman (1953), Berndt et al. (1977), Deaton and Muellbauer (1980), and Jorgenson et al. (1982) are representative of that approach.[14] All start from the assumption that, in addition to the assumption that the individual consumers' system of demand functions fall under heading (A), the direct utility function actually underlying the demand functions has its parameters independent of total expenditure M and budget constraints prices $\mathbf{p}$. As we have seen in Section

II.E., this assumption is, in principle, at least, testable experimentally against the ever-present alternative *Fechner-Thurstone* direct utility function that also rationalizes each individual consumers' system of demand functions. The potential empirical disconfirmation of the fixed preference assumption (embodied in a specified fixed preference direct utility function) affords the fixed preference assumption and the concept of "cost of living" (as equivalent to the "cost of level of utility") their empirical meaningfulness. The alternative *Fechner-Thurstone* direct utility function and the concept of "cost of living" that emerges from it acquire their meaningfulness in precisely the same way: If the incentive-compatible experiment described in Section II.E were actually performed, the *Fechner-Thurstone* form $U(\mathbf{X}; \mathbf{\theta})$ of direct utility function might well be disconfirmed in favor of a specified fixed preference direct utility function $V(\mathbf{X})$.

The aggregation of individual consumers' *Fechner-Thurstone* direct utility functions involves no "aggregation problem" at all. That is to say, it offers no hope or challenge to prove oneself an expert "puzzle solver" (see Kuhn, 1962, pp. 36–37).

Let $\mathcal{P}$ be a specified population of individual consumers v, where $v = 1, 2, \ldots, N$. Let $X^{(v)}(M^{(v)}, \mathbf{p}; \mathbf{\alpha})$ be a system of n commodity demand functions ascribed to individual consumer v. Again, the individual consumer's demand function may fall under either heading (A) and (B) in Section II.E; it makes no difference in what follows. Here $M^{(v)}$ is the total money expenditure on commodities by v in a specified time period; $\overline{M}$ is the per capita total expenditure of $\mathcal{P}$; $\mathbf{p}$ is a vector of n market prices for that time period; and $\mathbf{\alpha}$ is a vector of personal and population characteristics. The system of demand functions can be rationalized by a direct utility function $U^{(v)}(X; \mathbf{\theta}^{(v)})$ having the *generalized Fechner-Thurstone* form (2.13a-b) with its vector $\mathbf{\theta}^{(v)}$ of preference parameters dependent on budget constraint prices $\mathbf{p}$, $M^{(v)}$, and $\mathbf{\alpha}$. That is, the system of demand functions $\mathbf{X}^{(v)}(M^{)v)}, \mathbf{p}; \mathbf{\alpha})$ can always be derived from the ordinal direct utility function:

$$U^{(v)}(\mathbf{X}; \mathbf{\theta}^{(v)}) = \prod_{i=1}^{n} (X_i - \gamma_i)^{\theta^{(v)}} \qquad (2.36a)$$

$$X_i > \max\{0, \gamma_i\} \qquad (2.36b)$$

$$\sum_{i=1}^{n} \theta_i^{(v)}(M^{(v)}, \mathbf{p}, \mathbf{\alpha}) = \theta, \qquad (2.36c)$$

for every $v = 1, 2, , , , , N$; here $\mathbf{\theta}$ is a positive but otherwise arbitrarily valued function of $\mathbf{p}$, $\mathbf{\alpha}$, and all individual consumers' expenditures. The positive-valued utility function parameters $\theta_i^{(\nu)}(M^{(\nu)}, \mathbf{p}, \boldsymbol{\alpha})$ are dependent on the characteristics $\boldsymbol{\alpha}$, on one or more of the prices $\mathbf{p}$, and on total expenditure, $M^{(\nu)}$, that appear in the consumer's budget constraint

$$\sum_{i=1}^{n} p_i X_i = M^{(\nu)}. \tag{2.37}$$

Note: Hereafter we shall use $\theta_i^{(\nu)}$ as an abbreviation of $\theta_i^{(\nu)}(M^{(\nu)}, \mathbf{p}, \boldsymbol{\alpha})$.

We define the *aggregate Fechner-Thurstone direct utility function*[15] as a weighted geometric mean of the individual consumers' direct utility functions, as follows:

$$U(\mathbf{X}, \boldsymbol{\theta}) \underset{df}{=} \sum_{\nu=1}^{n} [U^{(\nu)}]^{\kappa^{(\nu)}} \tag{2.38a}$$

where

$$\kappa^{(\nu)} > 0 \tag{2.38b}$$

and

$$\sum_{\nu=1}^{N} \kappa^{(\nu)} = 1. \tag{2.38c}$$

If the weights $\kappa^{(\nu)}$ are made proportional to the individual consumer's positive "supernumerary" expenditure, i.e., where

$$\kappa^{(\nu)} = M^{(\nu)} - \sum_{i=1}^{n} \gamma_i p_i, \tag{2.39}$$

then the *equilibrium demands* $\overline{X}_i^*$, that is, the magnitudes of demand functions derived from the *aggregate direct utility function* (2.38a-c) subject to the arithmetic mean of budget constraints (2.37), are identical with the per capita demands over the population of individual consumers. We assume that all consumers face the same budget constraint prices.

With much gain of simplicity of expression and without loss of essential generality, we present the mathematical derivations only for the case in which each of the artibrary parameters γ_i is zero. From (2.38a-c) and (2.39) we obtain

$$U(\mathbf{X}; \overline{\boldsymbol{\theta}}) = \prod_{\nu=1}^{N} \left\{ \prod_{i=1}^{n} X_i^{\theta} \right\} \tag{2.40a}$$

$$= \prod_{i=1}^{n} X_i^{\overline{\theta}_i}, \tag{2.40b}$$

where

$$\overline{\theta}_i \sum_{\nu=1}^{N} \kappa^{(\nu)} \theta_i^{(\nu)}, \qquad i = 1, 2, \ldots, n. \tag{2.40c}$$

Let $\overline{M}$ be the arithmetic mean of individual consumer's total expenditures $M^{(\nu)}$, for $\nu = 1, 2, \ldots, N$. Demand functions derived by maximizing (2.40a-c) subject to the per capita budget constraint are

$$\overline{X}_i^* = \frac{\sum_{\nu=1}^{N} \kappa^{(\nu)} \theta_i^{(\nu)}}{\sum_{j=1}^{n} \sum_{\nu=1}^{N} \kappa^{(\nu)} \theta_j^{(\nu)}} p_i^{-1} \left[\overline{M} - \sum_{k=1}^{n} p_k \gamma_k \right] + \gamma_i \tag{2.41a}$$

$$= \frac{1}{\theta} \left(\sum_{\nu=1}^{N} \kappa^{(\nu)} \theta_i^{(\nu)} \right) p_i^{-1} \left[\overline{M} - \sum_{k=1}^{n} p_k \gamma_k \right] + \gamma_i, \tag{2.41b}$$

$$i = 1, 2, \ldots, n.$$

From (2.40b-c) it is apparent that the *aggregate direct utility function* has the same form in its arguments and parameters as has each individual consumer's *Fechner-Thurstone* direct utility function (2.36a-c); from (2.41b) it is readily apparent the per capita demand functions derived from the *aggregate direct utility function* have the same form in its arguments and parameters as those derived from the individual consumer's direct utility function. Using the relation

$$\frac{\theta_i^{(\nu)}}{\theta} = \frac{p_i X_i^{(\nu)}(M^{(\nu)}, \mathbf{p}; \boldsymbol{\alpha})}{M^{(\nu)}}, \qquad i = 1, 2, \ldots, n, \tag{2.42}$$

we get

$$\overline{X}_i^* = \sum_{\nu=1}^{N} \frac{\kappa^{(\nu)} X_i^{(\nu)}(M^{(\nu)}, \mathbf{p}; \boldsymbol{\alpha})}{M^{(\nu)}} \overline{M}, \qquad i = 1, 2, \ldots, n. \tag{2.43}$$

In the special case where weights are specified by

$$\kappa^{(\nu)} = \frac{m^{(\nu)}}{\sum_{\nu=1}^{N} m^{(\nu)}}, \qquad \nu = 1, 2, \ldots, N, \tag{2.44}$$

we obtain

$$\overline{X}_i^* = \frac{1}{N} \sum_{\nu=1}^{N} X_i^{(\nu)}(M^{(\nu)}, \mathbf{p}, \boldsymbol{\alpha}), \qquad i = 1, 2, \ldots, n. \tag{2.45}$$

In other words, under specification (2.44) the magnitude of the aggregate demand function (2.41b) derived from the *aggregate direct utility function* (2.40a-c) is the arithmetic mean of magnitudes of individual consumer demand functions derived from (2.36a-c).

The parameters $\bar{\theta}_i$ of the *aggregate Fechner-Thurstone direct utility function* (2.40a-c) constitute the theoretical link between the individual consumers' preferences, on the one hand, and the *personal multivariate distribution of components of received income, wealth,* and *expenditures on the n commodities,* as we shall explain in Section III. The parameters $\bar{\theta}_i$ appear as parameters of that theoretical specification of the personal multivariate distribution. For instance, a ceteris paribus increase of $\bar{\theta}_i$ theoretically increases the Gini concentration ratio for the personal distribution of any component of income. Such is one aspect of the theoretical dependence of economic inequality on individual consumers' preferences.

III.   COMPREHENSIVE ECONOMIC INEQUALITY AND THE FECHNER-THURSTONE AGGREGATE DIRECT UTILITY FUNCTION

A.   Preliminary Remarks, Notation, and Concepts

In this section we describe an explicit theoretical link between individual consumer preferences and comprehensive economic inequality and explore some of the consequences of their interdependence. The aggregate direct utility function (2.40a-c) is conjoined with a model of comprehensive economic inequality that is designed for analysis and prediction of directions and rates of intertemporal change of inequality in the personal joint distribution of household expenditures on commodities and on securities, tax payments, and the separate components of individual consumers' income and wealth. The macroeconomic character and the modest number of dimensions of the multivariate distribution reflect an effort to keep the model usable by private participants in the policymaking process generally, and by executive policymakers and their advisers. The multivariate personal distribution of consumption of goods and services, of the payments of taxes, of the ownership and control of various forms of property, and of the receipt of various forms of income constitute the subject matter—a meeting ground of policymaking and the several distinct social sciences. Politics, according to Harold Lasswell, is the perennial question of *Who Gets What, When, and How?* [as the subtitle of his famous book (1958) puts it]. Political science is concerned at bottom with the changing joint distribution of commodities, wealth, and income, especially as it affects the distribution of consumption, deference, and safety in a society. Actualized and developing inequalities in the distribution of wealth and commodities (including safety and deference) constantly provoke attacks on the political and economic systems that are perceived to cause or to permit trends in such inequalities to develop or continue (see Lasswell, 1958, p. 26, p. 73; Sen, 1973, p. 1; Brandt, 1980, p. 49).

Multivariate personal distribution models of economic inequality have many different uses in policy-oriented positive research, normative policy formation, and policy evaluation. A complete list of uses of the multivariate personal distribution model of economic inequality in policy-oriented research would include all of the by now familiar uses of single variable personal distributions (say) of pretax income, of tax payments, of posttax income, of public transfer payments, and so on.[16] Those single variable personal distributions of economic variables are derivable as marginal distributions from the multivariate personal distribution model. However, the multivariate personal distribution model of economic inequality is able to measure some additional aspects of progressivity of direct and indirect taxation, of horizontal and vertical equity of income tax burdens, and of the redistributive effects of public transfer payments. For instance, an extended Dagum (1980) measure of "distance" between the related marginal distributions of total pretax income and of tax payments casts some additional light on the hypothesis that households whose total income is predominantly obtained from an owned business generally pay less tax than households receiving an equal total income composed predominantly of wages and salaries. Aspects of horizontal and vertical equity measured by the "distance" between the marginal distribution of pretax income and the marginal distribution of tax payments derived from the joint distribution model are supplementary to the aspects captured by other useful measures of the resdistributive effects of taxation such as those proposed by Kakwani (1982; also 1983, pp. 21–24). Use of the multivariate distribution model in policy-oriented research is not limited to those just mentioned, of course. The joint distribution approach extends in the same way to the measurement of aspects of the redistributive effects of public transfer payments, as well as the measurement of other aspects of economic welfare and the incidence of poverty.

Like any other meaningful policy-relevant ethical principle, the *normative* principles of horizontal and vertical equity presupposes some empirically established *positive* theory. That is to say, their application in practice presupposes (a) that the antecedent conditions for the valid use of certain definitions are empirically established, (b) that the definitions are empirically nonempty, and (c) that certain general assumptions are in reasonably good agreement with accepted empirical assumptions called "facts."[17] The normative principles of horizontal and vertical equity presuppose, in the sense just indicated, the basic definitions and general propositions of the theory of the utility-maximizing individual consumer—and some ad hoc assumptions, too (see Feldstein, 1976; Rosen, 1978). Other microtheoretical concepts used normatively such as *welfare functions* and *cost-of-living indexes,* presuppose the empirical truth of much of microeconomic theory.[18] The multivariate personal distribution model of economic inequality described in this section is designed to preserve a useful connection with the basic definitions and general propositions of the utility-maximizing individual consumer. However, it is important to bear in mind that the theoretical connection we establish between the aggregate direct utility function (2.40a-c) and the multivariate personal distribution of components of income and expenditures on commodities in Section III.B (below) has no *necessary* ethical or normative presuppositions.

We begin by introducing some additional notation. In terms of notation introduced in Section II.A, the symbol $m_{ti}^{(v)}$ is defined by

$$m_{ti}^{(v)} =_{df} p_{ti}(X_{ti}^{(v)} - \gamma_i) \qquad \begin{cases} i = 1, 2, \ldots, n; \\ v = 1, 2, \ldots, N. \end{cases} \qquad (3.1)$$

It is readily apparent that (3.1) is merely a translation of the expenditure on commodity i by the consumer v in the period t. In this section we shall find it convenient to reduce the notational burden by omitting the individual superscript v and the temporal subscript t, writing m_i for $m_{ti}^{(v)}$. This practice should cause no confusion since the density functions to be presented here will refer to a single population such as an occupation, age group, or family-size stratum, and to a single time period. From (2.39) and (3.1) we obtain

$$m = \sum_{i=1}^{n} m_i. \qquad (3.2)$$

A consumer (household) holds wealth and receives income in several forms, such as *wages and salaries, public transfer payments, private transfer payments, profit on owned enterprises, income from capital assets, sales of securities,* and *inheritances.* We shall use $W_{t1}^{(v)}, \ldots, W_{tq}^{(v)}$ to designate various components of consumer income.[19] We shall also translate these income components as follows:

$$w_{tj}^{(v)} =_{df} W_{tj}^{(v)} - \lambda_{tj} \qquad \begin{cases} j = 1, 2, \ldots, q; \\ v = 1, 2, \ldots, N. \end{cases} \qquad (3.3)$$

where λ_{tj} is a population parameter similar to $p_i\gamma_i$ in (3.1).[20] Again, it will be convenient to omit the individual superscript v and the time period subscript t, writing w_j for $w_{tj}^{(v)}$ ($j = 1, 2, \ldots, q$).[21]

For every consumer population $\mathscr{P}$ and every time period t the existence of an *empirical personal multivariate distribution function* of components of wealth and income and expenditures on commodities is nonproblematical. There is an important and clear sense in which this complete population empirical distribution function incorporates all of the *positive* information about economic inequality that can be extracted from unlabeled observations of individual consumers' components of income and expenditures on commodities. The empirical marginal multivariate distribution function $\bar{F}(m_1, \ldots, m_n, w_1, \ldots, w_q)$ of components of income and expenditures on commodities is obtained by "integrating out" with respect to the wealth components. This marginal distribution of components $w_1, \ldots, w_q$ of income and expenditures $m_1, \ldots, m_n$ on commodities is discrete, and it possesses N points of $(n + q)$-fold discontinuity.[22]

The empirical distribution function $\bar{F}(m_1, \ldots, m_n; w_1, \ldots, w_q)$ necessarily possesses moments of every integer order. Let $\bar{m}$ designate the mean of translated expenditures on commodities (3.1); then the population mean $\bar{M}$ in Eqs. (2.41a-b) is related to the distribution function $\bar{F}(m_1, \ldots, m_n; w_1, \ldots, w_q)$ by the equation

$$\bar{M} = \bar{m} + \sum_{k=1}^{n} p_k \gamma_k \qquad (3.4)$$

Now let $\bar{m}_i$, for $i = 1, 2, \ldots, n$, designate the population mean expenditure on commodity i. Then

$$\bar{M} = \bar{m}_i + p_i \gamma_i \qquad (3.5a)$$

$$= p_i \bar{X}_i^*, \qquad i = 1, 2, \ldots, n, \qquad (3.5b)$$

where $\bar{X}_i^*$ is per capita demand for commodity i appearing in (2.41a-b) under the specification (2.42) of the direct utility function parameters; cf. also (2.45).

In Section III.B we shall introduce a theoretical distribution function $F(m_1, \ldots, m_n; w_1, \ldots, w_q)$ as a model of the complete population empirical distribution function $\bar{F}(m_1, \ldots, m_n; w_1, \ldots, w_q)$. Let r_i and s_k ($i = 1, 2, \ldots, n; k = 1, 2, \ldots, q$) be nonnegative integers such that $r_1 + \cdots + r_n + s_1 + \cdots + s_q \leq N - 1$. Conceptually, the mathematical expectations of the product $m_1^{r_1} m_2^{r_2} \ldots m_n^{r_n} w_1^{s_1} w_2^{s_2} \ldots w_q^{s_q}$ taken with respect to the complete population empirical distribution function $\bar{F}$ and taken with respect to the theoretical distribution function F are indentical.

B. Theoretical Connection Between Consumer Preferences and Comprehensive Economic Inequality

Selection of initial forms of theoretical models of the multivaritae personal distribution of components of income and expenditures has beei guided by several criteria of research economy (see Basmann, 1968, esp. pp. 154–157, 178–186). The first of these criteria is—obviously—the maintenance of the objective of identifying the conditional expectations of commodity expenditures given mean total expenditure with the aggregate demand functions (2.41a-b) derived from the aggregate direct utility function (2.40a-c). The second criterion calls for minimization of the number of ad hoc parameters in the theoretical multivariate personal distribution and the number of different forms of marginal distributions derivable from it. We explain briefly: Consider the aggregate direct utility function (2.40a-c) and derived per capita demand functions (2.41a-b). Together there are $2n$ parameters γ_i ($i = 1, 2, \ldots, n$) and $\overline{\theta}_i$ ($i = 1, 2, \ldots, n$), all of which have a theoretical interpretation in terms of economic theory. The criterion of minimizing the number of ad hoc parameters calls for the theoretical conditional density function of commodity expenditures $m_1, \ldots, m_n$, given total expenditure m to contain just those parameters $\overline{\theta}_i$ and γ_i ($i = 1, 2, \ldots, n$) and no other parameters. Such an extraneous parameter is considered to be an ad hoc parameter relative to the economic theory being considered in Section III. The second part of the criterion calls for the selection of a multivariate form such that derived marginal distributions of sums of one or more expenditures and components of income shall have the same form as the multivariate personal distribution. For instance a selection of a multivariate *lognormal* distribution function would be ruled out on the ground that sums of lognormal variables are not lognormally distributed as well as on the ground that it introduces a great many ad hoc parameters.

The last criterion calls for conservation of empirically well-tested hypotheses where they are explicitly relevant to the hypothesis formation problem at hand. Since the multivariate personal distribution function that present hypothesis formation aims to link explicitly with the aggregate direct utility function (2.40a-c) necessarily implies a form of the marginal distribution of total income, results of previous empirical studies of alternative forms of income distribution are explicitly relevant.[23] To make a long story short, the conclusion arrived at was this: The form of multivariate distribution initially selected should imply that the marginal distribution of total income satisfy the *weak Pareto law* (see Mandelbrot, 1960, p. 81; Dagum, 1977, pp. 414, 420).[24]

All of these criteria are met by the theoretical personal multivariate distribution characterized by the following density function:

$$f(m_1, \ldots, m_n; w_1, \ldots, w_q)$$

$$= \frac{K^{b*} m_1^{a_1-1} \ldots m_n^{a_n-1} w_1^{c_1-1} \ldots w_q^{c_q-1}}{B(a_1, \ldots, a_n; c_1, \ldots, c_q; b^*)[K + m + w]^b} \tag{3.6a}$$

$$m_i > 0; \quad w_k > 0 \tag{3.6b}$$

$$= 0 \text{ otherwise,}$$

where

$$w = w_1 + \cdots + w_q, \tag{3.6c}$$

and all of the parameters a_i ($i = 1, 2, \ldots, n$), c_k ($k = 1, 2, \ldots, q$), b^*,

b, and K are positive, and

$$b^* = b - \sum_{i=1}^{n} a_i - \sum_{k=1}^{n} c_k. \qquad (3.6d)$$

Parameters a_i, c_k, b^*, K, and b are population parameters and do not properly bear individual consumer superscripts (v). However, they do properly bear time-period subscripts t, which are supressed here for convenience. In Basmann et al. (1983b) we studied the intertemporal dependence of parameters a_i on commodity prices and various measures of economic development in Mexico and the United States over the years 1947–1978. Slottje (1983) has studied the intertemporal dependence of 10 income component parameters c_k on commodity prices and several economic growth variables in the United States for the period 1952–1978. We mention this empirical work here only to emphasize that the parameters of the personal multivariate distribution of components of income and expenditures on commodities are not fixed constants.

The form in the term $(m_1, \ldots, m_n; w_1, \ldots, w_q)$ in the numerator of (3.6a) is suggested (but not deductively implied, of course) by the requirement that conditional expectations of m_i given the sum m be a linear function of m taken in conjunction with the form of the *Fechner-Thurstone* aggregate direct utility function (2.40a-c). More precisely, what is suggested is to specify that the conditional density function of expenditures m_i, given their sum m, is a product of powers of m_i ($i = 1, 2, \ldots, n$), i.e., that this conditional density have a singular Beta I form (see Basmann et al., 1976, pp. 166–171, for an application to panel data on revealed preferences). Obviously, the hypothesis (3.6a-d) is not the only one meeting the requirement that conditional expectations, given a sum, be linear functions of that sum. A multivariate normal distribution function would meet that requirement, too, but at the expense of creating $[(n + q - 1)(n + q)]/2 - 1$ ad hoc parameters. For instance, in the case of the application mentioned in connection with Table 1 in Section III.C and Table 2 in Section III.D, below, the use of a multivariate normal distribution function in lieu of (3.6a-d) would involve 560 additional parameters.

Let y designate the sum of one or more of the expenditures $m_1, \ldots,$ m_n and components of income and let α designate the sum of the corresponding exponents in (3.6a). The marginal distribution function of y derived from (3.6a-d) is

$$H(y; \alpha, b^*, K) = 0 \qquad (y < 0) \quad (3.7a)$$

$$= 1 - \left[\left(\frac{K}{K + y} \right)^{b^*} \Big/ b^* B(\alpha, b^*) \right] {}_2F_1 \left(b^*; 1 - \alpha; b^* + 1; \frac{K}{K + y} \right)$$

$$(y \geq 0), \quad (3.7b)$$

where the symbol $_2F_1(A; B; C; Z)$ stands for the ordinary hypergeometric function. Notice that for $\alpha = 1$, Eq. (3.7a-b) becomes the ordinary *Pareto* distribution function with parameter b^* and lower terminal K. As $y \to \infty$, the hypergeometric function in (3.7a-b) converges to unity; consequently for any α the marginal distribution function (3.7a-b) satisfies the *weak Pareto law*. For this reason we call b^* the *generalized Pareto parameter*. In the special case for which y is the sum of income components we have $\alpha = c$, where c is the sum of $c_1, \ldots, c_q$, so that the marginal personal distribution of total income $H(w; c, b^*, K)$ that is deductively implied by (3.6a-d) satisfies the *weak Pareto law* as required.

Conditional expectations of expenditures m_i, given the sum of expenditures m, are of the required form, namely,

$$E(m_i \mid m) = \frac{a_i}{a} m, \qquad i = 1, 2, \ldots, n. \tag{3.8}$$

Given price vector $\mathbf{p}$, (2.39) and (3.1), the conditional expectation of a consumer's demand, given total expenditure M, is

$$E(X_i^* \mid M) = \frac{a_i}{a} p_i^{-1} \left[M - \sum_{k=1}^{n} p_k \gamma_k \right] + \gamma_i,$$

$$i = 1, 2, \ldots, n. \tag{3.9}$$

Note that the $E(X_i^* \mid M)$ satisfy (2.1a-b) and (2.2a-c). When the population mean expenditure $\overline{M}$, (3.4), is substituted for M in the conditional expectation (3.9), the theoretical personal multivariate distribution of components of income and expenditures on commodities (3.6a-d) implies that the magnitude of $E(X_i^* \mid \overline{M})$ is equal to the per capita demand $\overline{X}_i^*$, (2.45), in Section II.F.

Parameters a_i $(i = 1, 2, \ldots, n)$ of the personal multivariate distribution function (3.6a-d) are expressed in terms of the aggregate *Fechner-Thurstone* direct utility function (2.40a-c) by equating (3.9) and (2.41a-b) term by term. Under this identification we have

$$a_i = \overline{\theta} \tag{3.10a}$$

$$= \sum_{v=1}^{N} \kappa^{(v)} \theta_i^{(v)}, \qquad i = 1, 2, \ldots, n, \tag{3.10b}$$

where $\kappa^{(v)}$ is defined by (2.44). In addition, the parameter b^*, defined by (3.6d), is found to be a linear function of the parameters $\overline{\theta}_i$ of the *Fechner-Thurstone* aggregate direct utility function (2.40a-c) and, in turn, a function of the parameters $\theta_i^{(v)}$ of individual consumers' *Fechner-Thurstone* direct utility functions (2.13a-b).

Such is the theoretical link between individual consumers' preferences represented, as is always possible, by the *generalized Fechner-Thurstone* direct utility function (see Section II.E).

C.   Interdependence of Variable Preferences and Overall Economic Inequality

An obvious consequence of the linking up of the aggregate *Fechner-Thurstone* direct utility function (2.40a-c) and the multivariate personal distribution (3.6a-d) of components of income and expenditures by (3.10a-b) is the interdependence of changes in consumers' preferences, reflected in $\bar{\theta}_i$ ($i = 1, 2, \ldots, n$), and changes in parameters and *functions of parameters* (e.g., variances and correlations) of the multivarate personal distribution (3.6a-d). In this subsection we shall present several of the *interdependences* of the parameters $\bar{\theta}_i$ ($i = 1, 2, \ldots, n$) of the aggregate direct utility function (2.40a-c) and the multivariate personal distribution (3.6a-d) that are deductive consequences of the identification (3.10a-b). We do this partly in order to answer some questions that are most likely to occur to the reader at this point. After all, this subject matter is unfamiliar territory even if it is not very forbidding mathematically. We shall consider a few of the definite ways in which the multivariate personal distribution (3.6a-d) adjusts to ceteris paribus changes in the parameters $\bar{\theta}_i$ ($i = 1, 2, \ldots, n$) of the aggregate direct utility function (2.40a-c). Two points need to be borne in mind as we do this: (i) Remarks of the form "a ceteris paribus increase in $\bar{\theta}_i$ produces an increase in the correlation between (say) the wages component and the interest component of total income" are not to be interpreted *here* as expressing a *causal relation* between occurrences of events in economic reality. Right now we are discussing some numerical properties of partial derivatives of some specific functions of the parameters of (3.6a-d). (ii) In respect of empirical applications of the model formed by the conjunction of (2.40a-c), (3.6a-d), and (3.10a-b), the concept of "ceteris paribus change in $\bar{\theta}_i$" is more or less artificial. In our empirical work with that model[25] we have specified the parameters $\bar{\theta}_i$ ($i = 1, 2, \ldots, n$) to be *causally* dependent on all market prices and other economic magnitudes of interest or importance in policy discussions. Consequently we expect changes in such exogenous variables to cause changes in all of the aggregate direct utility function parameters $\bar{\theta}_i$ ($i = 1, 2, \ldots, n$) simultaneously. On the other hand, the concept of a ceteris paribus change in $\bar{\theta}_i$ is not at all artificial with respect to intertemporal *random preference changers*[26] ξ_{ti} ($i = 1, 2, \ldots, n$), where $\bar{\theta}_{ti}$ is dependent only on ξ_{ti}.

Refer to (2.13a-b) in Section II.B again. Let **X** designate any point in the domain of (2.13a-b). A ceteris paribus increase (decrease) of $\theta_i^{(\nu)}$ has associated with it a proportional increase (decrease) of the individual consumer's *Fechner-Thurstone* marginal utility of commodity i. As we shall see in Section III.D, this marginal utility is not arbitrary in the same way that neoclassical marginal utility is arbitrary. A ceteris paribus change in the parameter $\bar{\theta}_i$ of the aggregate direct utility function (2.40a-c) at $\mathbf{X}$ is proportional to a weighted average of changes in all individual consumers' respective marginal utilities of commodity i at $\mathbf{X}$.

The validity of the analysis of interdependence of the parameters of the aggregate direct utility function (2.40a-c) and the multivariate personal distribution of components of income and expenditures on commodities (3.6a-d) is independent of the empirical truth or falsity of alternative "stories" that might be told in order to account for changes in the individual consumers' valuations of the want-satisfying capabilities of commodities.

A ceteris paribus increase (decrease) of the population average $\bar{\theta}_i$ of individual consumers' *Fechner-Thurstone* utility function parameters $\theta_i^{(\nu)}$ ($\nu = 1, 2, \ldots, N$) has associated with it a variety of changes in the personal multivariate distribution of components of income and expenditures on commodities characterized by (3.6a-d). In some cases directions of the associated changes are analytic consequences of the conjunction of (2.40a-c), (3.6a-d), and (3.10a-b) and are easily deduced. For instance, a ceteris paribus increase of the parameters $\bar{\theta}_i$ of the aggregate *Fechner-Thurstone* direct utility function produces an increase in the theoretical population mean of every component of income w_k and in the theoretical populations mean of every component of expenditure m_j. For example, since the theoretical population mean of a component k of income (e.g., wages) is

$$\mu_{w_k} = Kc_k(b^* - 1)^{-1}, \qquad (3.11)$$

K and c_k being independent of $\bar{\theta}_i = a_i$, and

$$\frac{\partial b^*}{\partial \bar{\theta}_i} = -1, \qquad (3.12)$$

we have

$$\frac{\partial \mu_{w_k}}{\partial \bar{\theta}_i} = Kc_k(b^* - 1)^{-2} \qquad (3.13)$$

necessarily. A ceteris paribus increase of $\bar{\theta}_i$ increases the population mean of expenditure on commodity j, where $j \neq i$, but it increases the population mean of expendure on commodity i by a greater amount.

The *generalized variance* Δ of (3.6a-d) is expressed in terms of parameters by

$$\Delta = \frac{K^{2(n+q)}(a_1 a_2 \ldots a_n)(c_1 \ldots c_q)(b - 1)}{(b^* - 2)^{n+q}(b^* - 1)^{n+q+1}}, \qquad b^* > 2. \quad (3.14\text{a-b})$$

Here Δ is the theoretical counterpart of the determinant of the variance-covariance matrix of the empirical multivariate personal distribution of components of income and expenditures that we described in Section III.A. In view of (3.10a-b), a ceteris paribus increase of the parameter $\bar{\theta}_i$ of the aggregate *Fechner-Thurstone* direct utility function produces an increase of the generalized variance (3.14a-b).[27] In other words, when the weighted average of individual consumers' parameters $\theta_i^{(v)}$ increases ceteris paribus, there is a concomitant increase in the overall dispersion of individual consumers' components of received income and expenditures. Indeed, a ceteris paribus increase of $\bar{\theta}_i$ associates with itself an increase of each variance and covariance element of the generalized variance Δ and an increase of every correlation coefficient between components of income $w_1, \ldots, w_q$ and expenditures on commodities $m_1, \ldots, m_n$.

Let y be any of $m_1, \ldots, m_n$ $w_1, \ldots, w_q$ and let α be the exponent of y in (3.6a-d). The *coefficient of variation*[28] of y is

$$c_y = \left[\frac{\alpha + b^* - 1}{\alpha(b^* - 2)} \right]^{1/2}. \tag{3.15}$$

A ceteris paribus increase in $\bar{\theta}_i$ associates with itself an increase in the coefficient of variation of each of the components of income $w_1, \ldots, w_q$ and in the coefficient of variation of each of the expenditures other than m_i.

The foregoing conclusions about ceteris paribus effects of increases in $\bar{\theta}_i$ are necessary consequences of the logical conjunction of (2.40a-c), (3.6a-d), and (3.10a-b). As such they do not depend on which population of consumers the model is applied to, or what are the commodities designated by $i = 1, 2, \ldots, n$, or what are the components of income designated by $k = 1, 2, \ldots, q$; nor do they depend on the numerical magnitudes of the parameters of (3.6a-d) in a given time period. They characterize relations we expect to find in all numerical estimates of (3.6a-d) whether, for example, they are computed from the U.S. Consumer Expenditure Survey or from the Encuesta Nacional de Ingresos y Gastos de los Hogares (Mexico).[29] The remaining two analytic results we shall present in this subsection are of a different character in that they raise questions for empirical analysis and scientific explanation of consumer behavior. The partial derivative of $C_{m_i}^2$ with respect to $\bar{\theta}_i$ ($= a_i$) is

$$\frac{\partial C_{m_i}^2}{\partial a_i} = \frac{(a_i + b^* - 1)[a_i - (b^* - 2)]}{a_i^2(b^* - 2)^2}, \qquad i = 1, 2, \ldots, n. \tag{3.16}$$

The partial derivative (3.16) has the sign of the linear factor $a_i - (b^* - 2)$. Consequently a ceteris paribus increase in the aggregate direct utility function parameter $\bar{\theta}_i$ increases (decreases) the coefficient of variation of m_i if $\bar{\theta}_i > b^* - 2$ ($\bar{\theta}_i < b^* - 2$).

The ratio of the generalized variance (3.14a-b) to the product of the squares of means of $m_1, \ldots, m_n w_1, \ldots, w_q$ affords an overall measure of the relative concentration of the multivariate personal distribution (3.6a-d). Similar to the coefficient of variation of a single expenditure or component of income, this ratio is expressed by

$$\Delta^* = \frac{(b - 1)(b^* - 1)^{n+q-1}(b^* - 2)^{-(n+q)}}{(a_1 a_2 \ldots a_n)(c_1 c_2 \ldots c_q)}, \qquad b^* > 2. \quad (3.17)$$

The partial derivative of Δ^* with respect to $\bar{\theta}_i$ $(= a_i)$ has the sign of the following quadratic in $b^* - 2$:

$$Q(b^* - 2) = a_i(b^* - 2)^2 + [a_i(n + q) - 1](b^* - 2) - 1. \quad (3.18)$$

It is apparent that, given a_i, $Q(b^* - 2)$ is negative for $b^* - 2$ sufficiently small, and positive for $b^* - 2$ sufficiently large. Consequently a ceteris paribus increase in the aggregate direct utility function parameter $\bar{\theta}_i$ can produce either an increase of the ratio Δ^* or a decrease (or no change), depending on the magnitudes of $\bar{\theta}_i$ and b^*.

Real-world commodities (such as are named in Table 1) can be classified (and rank-ordered) accordingly as a ceteris paribus increase of a_i $(= \bar{\theta}_i)$ decreases (increases or leaves unchanged) its own coefficient of variation (3.15). (The same kind of classification can be applied to components of income, of course.) For instance, if there is a ceteris paribus increase in the average of individual consumers' marginal utilities of (say) food, as reflected by an increase of $\bar{\theta}_i$, in addition to an increase of per capita expenditures and per capita receipts of components of income there will be a tendency for individual consumers to become less alike in respect of expenditures on other goods (and components of received income). Will there also be a tendency for individual consumers to become less alike in respect of their expenditures on food itself? In a like manner commodities (and components of income) may be classified (and rank-ordered) accordingly as a ceteris paribus increase of a_i $(= \bar{\theta}_i)$ decreases (increases or leaves unchanged) the overall ratio Δ^*. Cross-classification (and rank-ordering) of commodities (and components of income) according to both of the foregoing criteria is indeed possible. Such classifications require empirical data, of course, and may change from period to period as the parameters of the multivariate personal distribution (3.6a-d) of components of income and expenditures vary under intertemporal changes of market prices and other causal variables. The sample survey estimates shown in Table 1 suggest that for only a very few commodities i (in the United States, 1973) does a ceteris paribus increase in the aggregate direct utility function parameter $\bar{\theta}_i$ produce an increase in the coefficient of variation (3.15) of expenditure on that commodity, namely, food, shelter, and transportation $(i = 1, 5, 15)$. On the other hand, these survey estimates

Table 1. Estimates of the Parameters of the Joint Distribution Function from the U.S. Consumer Expenditure Survey for 1973[a]

Estimates[b] of the Expenditure Components, a_i

	Component Name	Estimate	Concentration Ratio $g(a_i, b^*)$
$i = 1$	Food	2.902	0.443
2	Alcoholic beverages	0.134	0.870
3	Tobacco products	0.205	0.820
4	Shelter	2.233	0.470
5	Residential fuel	0.678	0.637
6	Household operations	0.500	0.686
7	House furnishings	0.684	0.636
8	Dry cleaning	0.129	0.874
9	Mens' clothing	0.288	0.733
10	Boys' clothing	0.085	0.911
11	Womens' clothing	0.433	0.710
12	Girls' clothing	0.100	0.897
13	Infants' clothing	0.027	0.968
14	Clothing materials	0.046	0.949
15	Transportation	2.713	0.449
16	Health care	0.787	0.613
17	Personal care	0.163	0.848
18	Owned vacation home	0.016	0.981
19	Vacation trips	0.408	0.719
20	Recreational vehicles	0.160	0.850
21	Other recreation	0.525	0.679
22	Reading	0.083	0.912
23	Education	0.191	0.829
24	Miscellaneous	0.142	0.863
25	Insurance and pensions	1.367	0.531
26	Gifts and contributions	0.897	0.593
27	Purchase of securities	1.433	0.529

Estimates of the Income Components, c_i

	Component Name	Estimate	Concentration Ratio $g(c, b^*)$
$i = 1$	Wages and salaries	15.674	0.350
2	Private transfer payments	0.271	0.782
3	Public transfer payments	1.349	0.532
4	Own enterprise	2.735	0.449
5	Interest and dividends	0.744	0.622
6	Sale of financial assets	0.881	0.595
7	Refunds and gifts	0.822	0.606

Table 1. (*Continued*)

Sums of Components	Concentration Ratio
$a = \sum\limits_{i=1}^{27} = 17.332$	$g(a,b^*) = 0.345$
$c = \sum\limits_{i=1}^{7} = 22.475$	$g(c,b^*) = 0.337$

Note: For 1973, the Generalized Pareto Parameter b^* is 3.796; the parameter $b = b^* + a + c = 43.6$; the lower terminal K is 1882.

[a] 1972/73 Consumer Expenditure Survey (CES). U.S. Department of Labor, Bureau of Labor Statistics, Washington, D.C.

[b] These overall estimates were constructed by taking the weighted average of the mean income of all 12 populations. See Table 2.

suggest that for only a very few commodities does a ceteris paribus increase in $\bar{\theta}_i$ of (2.40a-c) produce a decrease in the overall ratio Δ^* defined by (3.17); namely, infants' clothing, clothing materials, and expenditures on owned vacation homes ($i = 13, 14, 18$). From Table 1 it appears that commodities for which a ceteris paribus increase of $\bar{\theta}_i$ has associated with it an *increase* of the corresponding coefficient of variation (3.15) are commodities which are usually offered as examples of "necessities" in textbooks and empirical demand analysis. On the other hand, it appears that those commodities for which a ceteris paribus increase $\bar{\theta}_i$ has associated with it a *decrease* of the overall ratio Δ^* (3.17) are commodities usually offered as examples of "luxuries." This correspondence between classifications is merely suggestive. For the majority of the 27 commodities an increase of $\bar{\theta}_i$ has associated with it a *decrease* in the coefficient of variation of expenditure m_i and an increase in the overall ratio Δ^*.

In empirical demand analysis the classification of real-world commodities as *necessities, normal goods,* and *luxuries* is made on the basis of logarithmic derivatives of demand functions with respect to total expenditure. In the case of the per capita demand functions (2.41a-b) derived from the aggregate direct utility function (2.40a-c), these total expenditure elasticities will depend on partial derivatives in all parameters $\bar{\theta}_i$ ($i = 1, 2, \ldots, n$) with respect to per capita total expenditure [cf. the equation for K_{i0}^*, (2.31)]. Furthermore, these derivatives may vary in sign from point to point in the domain of the system of demand functions (2.41a-b), depending on the specification of $\bar{\theta}_i$ ($i = 1, 2, \ldots, n$) as functions on that domain. Still, the conjunction of the *Fechner-Thurstone* aggregate direct utility function (2.40a-c), the multivariate personal distribution of components of income and expenditures on commodities (3.6a-d) and (3.10a-b), establishes a *theory schema* within which are explicit, empirically testable hypothetical relations between the attributes of commodities that cause them to be *necessary goods, normal goods,* and *luxury goods,* on the one hand, and the effect of changes in preference parameters of $\bar{\theta}_i$ in the aggregate direct utility function (2.40a-c) on economic inequality, on the other.

In Section II.E, we classified systems of demand functions under two mutually exclusive heads, (A) and (B), for the purpose of making sense of the neoclassical notion of fixed preferences. If the per capita demand functions (2.41a-b) derived from (2.40a-c) fall under heading (A),[30] i.e., so that the functions are homogeneous of zero degree, and the matrix in (2.6a-b) is symmetric negative semidefinite, then the neoclassical concepts of "inferior good," "Giffen good," "pair of substitutes," and "pair of complements" can validly be defined in terms of (2.41a-b); see Section II.D. Again, the conjunction of (2.40a-c), (3.6a-d), and (3.10a-b) affords a *theory schema* within which new empirically answerable questions can be asked in respect of the interdependence of various aspects of economic inequality, on the one hand, and the attributes of commodities that cause them to be *inferior goods, Giffen goods, substitute pairs,* or *complement pairs* at given points of the domain of aggregate and individual demand functions. Within this framework there are many such normal science puzzles to be worked out (see Kuhn, 1962, p. 69). However, their discussion is beyond the scope of the present study.

D.   Income Inequality and the Cardinality of the Aggregate Direct Utility Function

Inequality in the empirical mutivariable distribution of components of income and expenditures on commodities described in Section III.A and inequality in its theoretical counterpart (3.6a-d) have many diverse aspects for which there are a number of *different inequality measures.*[31] For purposes of this section we can make do with only one aspect of economic inequality and its corresponding inequality measure based on (3.6a-d) in order to relate economic inequality and the aggregate direct utility function (2.40a-c). Referring to the marginal distribution function (3.7a-b), we note that the *Gini concentration ratio* for the sum y is

$$g(\alpha, b^*) = \frac{\Gamma(\alpha + b^*)\Gamma(\alpha + \frac{1}{2})\Gamma(b^* + \frac{1}{2})}{\Gamma(\frac{1}{2})\Gamma(\alpha + 1)\Gamma(b^*)\Gamma(\alpha + b^* + \frac{1}{2})}$$

$$\times \left[1 + \frac{2\alpha}{2b^* - 1} \right], \qquad b^* > 1. \quad (3.19)$$

As either α or b^* (the other being fixed) increases, $g(\alpha, b^*)$ diminishes to a limit determined by the fixed parameter. As both increase, $g(\alpha, b^*)$ decreases to zero. As $\alpha \rightarrow 0$, $g(\alpha, b^*) \rightarrow 1$; as $b^* \rightarrow 1$, $g(\alpha, b^*) \rightarrow 1$. Formula (3.19) holds for all sums y of one or more components of income and expenditures on commodities. If, and only if, y contains one or more expenditures, m_i, for instance, where $y = m$, then the sum α involves one or more of the parameters a_i ($= \bar{\theta}_i$). Suppose α involves $\bar{\theta}_j$. Then the effect of a ceteris paribus increase in $\bar{\theta}_j$ is to increase α at the same time that it decreases b^*, and the direction of change of the concentration ratio (3.19a-b) is not analytically determined but has to be learned from empirical analysis. However, in case y is the sum of one or more components of income, then α is the sum of the corresponding parameters c_k and is not affected by the ceteris paribus change in the parameter θ_j of the aggregate *Fechner-Thurstone* direct utility function (2.40a-c). The generalized Pareto parameter b^* is, however, affected by the change in $\bar{\theta}_j$ [cf. Eq. (3.12)]. Consequently, a ceteris paribus increase in $\bar{\theta}_j$ associates with itself an increase in the concentration ratio (3.19a-b) for the sum y at the same time it produces an increase in the population mean of y. This holds whether y is itself a single component of income, w_k, or is total income.

As we have said, other measures of inequality in the distribution (3.7a-b) can be derived from the *Lorenz curve* implied by (3.7a-b). Measures such as the *relative mean deviation, Theil's entropy measure, Kakwani's measure,* and several new measures of other aspects of inequality developed by Basmann (see Basmann et al. (1983b), Tables 1.1 and 1.2) are derived directly from the *Lorenz curve,*[32] but still indirectly from (3.7a-b). Consequently, they depend on the parameters α, b^*, and, in turn, they also depend on the parameters $\bar{\theta}_i$ of the aggregate *Fechner-Thurstone* direct utility function (2.40a-c). These measures of income inequality depend on α, b^* in different ways from the concentration ratio (3.19) and, for that reason, measure different aspects of real inequality that is incorporated in (3.7a-b). Consequently, it is not surprising that there often are great differences in the magnitudes of the different inequality measures proposed. *It is important in the context of what follows here and in Section IV Part Two) to recognize that the different measures of income inequality that have been proposed are not different estimators of some single* "true" *income inequality* that merely differ in statistical efficiency as do the alternative estimates of a single aspect (Gini) of *income inequality* in Table 2. The estimates of $g(c, b^*)$ in the column under the heading GVMM (generalized variance method of moments) are computed from the joint statistical estimates of parameters of (3.6a-d) such as those in Table 1 and are functions of survey sample components of both income and commodity expenditures. The estimates of $g(c, b^*)$ in the column under the heading SVMM (single variable method of moments) are estimated (in

Table 2. Estimates of Income Inequality Utilizing
Different Amounts of Sample Information
(Beta II)[a]

	GVMM[b]			SVMM[c]		
Pop^d	c	b^*	$g(c,b^*)$	c	b^*	$g(c,b^*)$
1	19.2	2.4	0.456	29.9	3.1	0.377
2	38.6	3.5	0.352	47.8	4.1	0.319
3	28.9	2.8	0.405	37.0	3.3	0.363
4	26.9	5.0	0.293	19.0	3.8	0.344
5	17.4	3.8	0.345	19.5	4.2	0.328
6	26.9	6.9	0.251	29.6	7.5	0.240
7	22.1	4.7	0.305	25.6	5.3	0.285
8	22.9	3.7	0.348	25.7	4.0	0.331
9	12.8	4.8	0.318	11.4	4.4	0.336
10	8.5	3.2	0.406	7.3	2.9	0.433
11	8.6	2.2	0.495	8.5	2.2	0.499
12	15.8	2.6	0.432	21.5	3.2	0.378
			Weighted averages:[e]			
	23.0	3.8	0.340	27.1	4.1	0.324

[a] Data used to derive the estimates in this table are from the CES (1973); see Table 1.
[b] GVMM is defined as Generalized Variance Method of Moments.
[c] SVMM is defined as Single Variable Method of Moments.
[d] The 12 populations represent the different occupations of the consumer unit head, and they are respectively: (1) self-employed, including farm operators; (2) salaried professional, technical, and kindred workers; (3) salaried managers and administrators, and kindred workers; (4) clerical workers; (5) sales workers; (6) craftsmen; (7) operatives; (8) unskilled laborers, including household workers; (9) service workers; (10) not working, not retired; (11) retired; (12) other (armed forces living off post, working without pay, invalid codes, not reported).
[e] These overall estimates were constructed by taking the weighted average of the mean income of all 12 populations.

the most usual way) from the marginal distribution function of total income alone, ignoring the interdependence of expenditures and components of income. Numbers in both columns are merely different estimates of the concentration ratio $g(c, b^*)$, measuring a single aspect of income inequality, but computed from different estimates of c and b^*. The difference between the GVMM estimate, 0.456, and the SVMM estimate, 0.377, for the self-employed group is due to the differing amounts of sample information about Eqs. (3.6a–d) that those estimates incorporate. On the other hand, given this SVMM estimate of $g(c, b^*)$ for the self-employed group in 1973, a sound prediction of the corresponding magnitudes of Theil's *entropy measure* (normalized) and Basmann's *geometric mean measure* of income inequality are 0.095 and 0.57, respectively.[33] The corresponding prediction for *Kakwani's measure* is 0.087. It would be incorrect to attribute the numerical differences among these three numbers as being due to differences in methods of estimation of a single aspect of income inequality from the same data. The *geometric mean measure* of income inequality measures an aspect of inequality that increases very rapidly with transfer of income from the poorest decile (say) to the richer deciles; the *entropy measure* of income inequality measures a different aspect of inequality that is much less sensitive to such a transfer of income from the poorest decile. For example, if the entire share of the poorest decile were to be transferred upward, the minimum magnitude of the *geometric mean measure* would be equal to 1, whereas the minimum magnitude of the *entropy measure* would be 0.0458.

The concept of the alternative inequality measures as measuring different aspects of economic inequality can be elucidated in simple physical geometric terms by comparing the *Gini measure* and the *Kakwani measure* based on a given *Lorenz curve* represented on the Cartesian plane. As is well known, the empirical *Gini coefficient of concentration* measures a property of distributional inequality that (conceptually) varies in direct proportion to the *area* of a closed geometric figure bounded below by the (horizontal) axis, on the right by the equation $z = 1$, and from above by the *Lorenz curve* itself. The *Kakwani measure* correlates a property of distributional inequality that (conceptually) varies directly with the *perimeter* of the closed geometric figure described above. It is easy to see that the *Kakwani measure* and the *Gini coefficient* measure very different properties of this geometric figure. Given that the figure represents "income inequality," from that recognition it is but a small step to the concept that the *Kakwani measure* and the *Gini concentration ratio* measure different properties of this distributional inequality.

The chief theoretical significance of the interdependence of consumers' direct utility function parameters $\theta_i^{(\nu)}$ ($i = 1, 2, \ldots, n$) and measures of economic inequality is that it confers *cardinal measurability* on *generalized Fechner-Thurstone* "utility." True enough, the per capita demand functions (2.41a-b) remain invariant against the substitution for (2.40a-c) of an arbitrarily chosen monotonically increasing function of $U(\mathbf{X}; \bar{\boldsymbol{\theta}})$. For instance, one might replace (2.40a-c) by its square, i.e., by replacing $\bar{\theta}_i$ by $2\bar{\theta}_i$ ($i = 1, 2, \ldots, n$). Demand functions (2.41a-b) would remain invariant against this replacement. However, the various theoretical measures of inequality, such as the *Gini concentration ratio* (3.19), would not remain invariant against such a monotonically increasing transformation of $U(\mathbf{X}; \bar{\boldsymbol{\theta}})$. Agreement of theoretical measures such as (3.19) with empirical observations would be changed arbitrarily. Since $\bar{\theta}_i$ ($i = 1, 2, \ldots, n$) in (2.40a-c) are weighted averages of the parameters $\theta_i^{(\nu)}$ of individual consumers' *Fechner-Thurstone* direct utility functions (2.13a-b), the latter also cannot be replaced by an arbitrary monotonically increasing function of itself, as we remarked in Section II.B.

Like the *Gini concentration ratio* (3.19) and the other measures of inequality in marginal personal distributions of commodity expenditures and components of income, the numerical magnitude of the *generalized Fechner-Thurstone* direct utility function measures a quantitative real aspect of individual/social behavior in a way that the ordinal utility function of neoclassical demand theory cannot do. Barring effects of mere changes of scale in the measurement of commodities of X_i $(i = 1, 2, \ldots, n)$, a doubling of the numerical magnitude of the aggregate *Fechner-Thurstone* direct utility function (2.40a-c) indicates a corresponding doubling of this real quantitative aspect of consumer behavior. This is not at all to say that we know what this real quantitative aspect of economic behavior "is," any more than anyone knows what any of the derived quantities of physics "are," e.g., quantities such as temperature, time, or density (see Carnap, 1966, pp. 96–104; Hempel, 1952, pp. 69–74). See also Von Neumann and Morgenstern (1953, pp. 31–43). We shall begin to understand this derived quantitative aspect of economic reality only by seeing how numerical magnitudes of (2.40a-c) correlate with other numerical measurements of quantitative economic behavior. It is probable that the quantitative property measured by cardinal magnitudes of the *Fechner-Thurstone* direct utility function will turn out to be something quite different from the quantitative properties measured by other empirically interpreted direct utility functions, e.g., as is certainly the case with the Von Neumann-Morgenstern interpretation already mentioned. In the case of schematic forms of direct utility functions such as those that are *vacuously price dependent* [see Basmann et al., 1983a, Eq. (1)] or that possess only verbal or story interpretations at present, it is difficult to foresee the nature of the association between their future empirical interpretations and the quantitative property measured by the *Fechner-Thurstone* direct utility function. Consequently, for the time being it seems prudent to refrain from assigning a verbal interpretation or telling a "story" in order to render the existence of this new quantity more plausible.

*   *   *

Part Two of this study, which is to appear in the next volume of *Advances in Econometrics,* presents empirical applications and commences with a brief summary of how the objectives listed in Section I.A have been achieved. The empirical "law of downward slope demand" will be explained in terms of a readily testable hypothesis about relations between changes in the measurable marginal utilities of commodities brought about by ceteris paribus increases of a budget constraint price.

ACKNOWLEDGMENTS

This research was supported in part by National Science Foundation Grant SOC 77-27068.

The authors are indebted to R. C. Battalio, R. M. Harstad, D. W. Jorgenson, Thomas M. Stoker, G. Tintner, and Stephen White for helpful comments and criticisms. The authors bear sole responsibility for errors and omissions.

NOTES

1. Christensen et al. (1975) estimated (2.4a-b) using budget share equations of the form

$$E_i = \frac{a_i + B_{i1} \ln \frac{P_1}{M} + B_{i2} \ln \frac{P_2}{M} + B_{i3} \ln \frac{P_3}{M}}{-1 + B_{M1} \ln \frac{P_1}{M} + B_{M2} \ln \frac{P_2}{M} + B_{M3} \ln \frac{P_3}{M}}, \quad i = 1, 2.$$

The aforementioned authors impose the restrictions of symmetry and equality and report in Table 2, col. 3 (p. 379) results for durables and nondurables [Eqs. (2.4a-b) in our study]. We use the results they report for durables and nondurables and, given the restrictions they impose (symmetry and equality), are able to solve for the third equation in the system (other services), i.e., (2.4c). The equality restrictions forces D [Eq. (2.4d) in our study] to be the same for all three equations and the result (2.4c) follows easily.

2. For example, see Cournot (1838), esp. Chap. 4.

3. Perhaps the most widely cited empirical regularity of this sort has been the the empirical demand schedule published by Davenant in 1699 and attributed by him to Gregory King. (See Jevons, 1957 [1871]; also Wold, 1953, p. 140; Stigler, 1954, pp. 103–104. Stigler's paper includes additional examples.)

4. For the sake of economy only, reference will be made here to just one presentation of the theory of utility-maximizing (ideal) individual consumer, namely, that of Hicks (1946, pp. 305–314).

5. The methodological directive to account deductively for empirical regularities by mathematical functions which are solutions of constrained maximization problems, called the *principle of least action*, has been attributed in the first instance to Pierre Louis de Maupertuis in 1747 by Lindsay and Margenau (1936; see 1957 reprint, p. 133). See also Edgeworth (1881, pp. 89–91). Paul Samuelson has emphasized from time to time that the use of this methodological principle does not imply purposiveness of the maximizing behavior in question (e.g., Samuelson, 1948, p. 23).

6. If the ψ_i are assumed to be constant, then (2.9a-b) is essentially the form first proposed for indifference maps by L. L. Thurstone (1931, pp. 142–147). We call (2.9a-b) a *generalized Fechner-Thurstone* direct utility function. Roughly speaking, G. T. Fechner's logarithmic law makes motivation (marginal utility of a commodity) vary inversely with the amount of that commodity already possessed. Note that in the special case of fixed preferences, i.e., the ψ_i are constant for all $i = 1, \ldots, n$, the utility function $U(\mathbf{X}; \psi)$ reduces to a monotonically increasing function of the well-known *Cobb-Douglas* utility function, also called the *Stone-Geary* utility function (cf. Deaton and Muellbauer, 1980a, pp. 103, 201, 253). Notice that (2.9a-b) is closely related to transcendental logarithmic systems (cf. Christensen et al., 1975).

7. Thurstone (1931, p. 141) states that motivation is equivalent to the economists "marginal utility."

8. Arrow (1961, p. 177) noted the emptiness of the definition of complementarity: "There is no room for specialized relations of complementarity or substitution among particular pairs of commodities."

9. Klein and Rubin (1947) discuss the "cost of living" as the cost of getting back to the same level of utility after relative prices change. This definition is, of course, only meaningful under the assumption of fixed preferences.

10. A. Deaton pointed this out at the Latin American Econometric Society meetings in Mexico City in July 1982. Jean Dufour also made helpful comments at these meetings.

11. The graphic presentation in Section II.E (Figures 1–4) was first given in a working paper by Basmann et al. (1983a) that became a short paper in the *American Economic Review*.

12. Ray Battalio and Ron Harstad suggested this experiment to us.

13. An impressive amount of econometric talent and labor has been expended on the formation of statistical estimators of systems of demand functions falling under heading (A), the devising of statistical tests of the theoretical restrictions (a), (b), and (c), and the critical evaluation of the shortcomings of such tests, e.g., bias in favor of committing Type I error. Statistical tests with outcomes favorable to one or more of the properties listed under heading (A) have been reported by many econometricians, among them being Barten and Geyskens (1975), Theil (1975), and Conrad and Jorgenson (1979). Recent tests with unfavorable outcomes for hypothetical restrictions listed under (A) have been reported by Christensen et al. (1975), Berndt et al. (1977), Rosen (1978), and Conrad and Jorgenson (1979). Laitinen (1978), Meisner (1979), and Bera et al. (1981) have demonstrated the existence of bias in favor of Type I error in "large sample" tests of homogeneity and symmetry of Rotterdam systems of demand functions.

14. Stoker (1981a,b, 1982) has done the most recent work on the aggregation question. He places restrictions on the distribution of expenditures and taste differences and demonstrates the existence of Generalized Slutsky Conditions to be equivalent to (generalized) exact aggregation demand structures. Diewart (1977) also dealt with the issue of aggregation by restricting the number of consumers into particular groups.

15. The authors do not interpret (2.38a-c) as affording a *community preference field*, although it may serve some functions for which community preference fields are intended (cf. Gorman, 1953; also Muellbauer, 1976, p. 979).

16. Most of these uses are exemplified in the recent study of redistribution effects of income tax and cash benefits in Australia by Kakwani (1983).

17. For a nonmathematical but rigorous treatment of the underlying concepts, see the paper by Basmann (1975), esp. Secs. 2 and 5.

18. Literature is voluminous on the construction of *cost-of-living* indexes and *welfare functions* based on the assumption that consumer preferences are fixed. We cite only a few major works: Konüs (1924; see 1936 transl., p. 11); Klein and Rubin (1947, p. 87); Samuelson and Swamey (1974, p. 587). For recent surveys see Deaton (1980) and Diewert (1981).

19. Late, in Section III.B., we present the multivariate distribution [Eqs. (3.6a-d)] with wealth integrated out of the distribution. We do so without loss of generality in our analysis. We integrate out wealth because the estimates of parameters we will discuss in this section come from recent studies where only the parameters of marginal distributions of components of commodity expenditure (see Basmann et al., 1983b) and parameters of marginal distributions of components of income (see Slottje, 1983) were estimated.

20. A recent study by Basmann et al. (1983b) found that prices of five commodity groups, several economic growth variables, and per capita total expenditure all had varying degrees of influence on affecting inequality in the marginal distributions of expenditures on various commodity groups. One major result of the study was that the prices of the commodity groups had greater relative impact on inequality in the marginal distributions of expenditures

on the commodity groups than did the growth variables. Slottje (1983) did a similar study on components of income and found similar results. Slottje examined inequality in the marginal distributions of 10 income components using U.S. Internal Revenue Service (IRS) data. He used 11 commodity groups instead of the 5 groups used by Basmann et al. (1983b). Slottje, too, concluded that prices of commodity groups were important in affecting inequality in the size distribution of 10 components of income. He also found that in 9 out of 10 income components all 11 prices affected inequality in the respective marginal distributions but that in fully half the income components economic growth variables had no affect on inequality in the marginal distributions.

21.   It is assumed that the survey data available are *unlabeled observations* (cf. Cassel et al., 1977, p. 5). This assumption holds for the U.S. Consumer Expenditure Survey data.

22.   Note that N here is referring to the entire population size, not just a particular sample size in the population.

23.   Although normative analysis of economic inequality is important (cf. Tinbergen, 1970; Sen, 1973), it is not at all relevant to the present matter. It is certainly the case that theories of the generation of marginal distributions of total income are important [see Sahota's (1978) survey of this literature], but they are not directly relevant to the present matter. However, empirical results such as those of Champernowne (1952), Aitchison and Brown (1957), Fisk (1961), Thurow (1970), Salem and Mount (1974), Singh and Maddala (1976), and McDonald and Ransom (1979) are directly relevant.

24.   Dagum (1977, esp. pp. 414–420) has put forward a number of useful criteria to guide the selection of forms or models of the personal income distribution. Most of Dagum's criteria are readily extended to the selection of forms of multivariate distributions of components of income and expenditures on commodities. It should be noticed that his criterion 2.11 (p. 419) calling for derivation of explicit mathematical form of the Lorenz curve is not met by Eqs. (3.6a-d) that follow in Section III.B.

25.   Basmann (1954a,b, 1956) first used the model to study advertising as a preference-changing parameter in the demand for tobacco. Stecher (1978) examined expenditure functions derived from the model in his dissertation. Basmann et al. (1982a,b) used the model to estimate the parameters of a price-dependent utility function and gave one possible interpretation of the significant impact of budget constraint prices changing preferences as Veblen effects. In the paper given by these authors (1982b) at the Latin American Econometric Society Meetings, Mexico City, in June 1982, the model was used to analyze the sensitivity of changes in preferences to different specifications of the random preference-changing component of an assumed first-order autoregressive process. Basmann et al. (1983b) used the model in examining differences in preferences between Mexico and the United States and the implications this had for inequality and development differences between the two countries.

26.   See Basmann et al. (1983b, pp. 35–36) for a specification of the intertemporal random preference changer.

27.   This theorem and the others to follow are easy plums, even if proofs are tedious to read. For that reason we omit proofs, which the interested reader can supply for himself.

28.   The coefficient of variation is defined as the standard deviation of the distribution divided by the mean. It is a measure of dispersion (see Kakwani, 1980, p. 85).

29.   If the numerical estimates fail to satisfy those analytic relations, then we have failed to use a method of statistical estimation that is *consistent* with the specification of (3.6a-d) or we have made some other mistake somewhere in the computations.

30.   For example, let $\theta_i = \beta_i P_i^\gamma$; see Basmann et al. (1983a) for this specification.

31.   The recent study by Basmann et al. (1983b) discusses several of these measures and also presents three new measures of inequality invented by Basmann (see Tables 1.1 and 1.2 in that study, pp. 8–12). Of course, different measures discuss different aspects of in-

equality in the distributions, so comparisons of measures are not meaningful in the sense that one dominates another.

32. Kakwani (1980) defines his measure of inequality on p. 83. He also defines Theil's measure on inequality on p. 89.

33. These values are based on frequency distributions of income for various countries given in the World Bank's (1981) *World Development Report* and computed in Tables 1.1 and 1.2 of Basmann et al. (1983b).

REFERENCES

Aitchison, J. and J. A. Brown (1957). *The Lognormal Distribution*, Cambridge, MA: Cambridge University Press.

Arrow, K. J. (1961). Additive logarithmic demand functions and the Slutsky relations, *Review of Economic Studies* 28, 176–181.

Barten, A. P. and E. Geyskens (1975). The negativity condition in consumer demand, *European Economic Review* 6, 227–260.

Basmann, R. L. (1954a). A note on an invariant property of shifts in demand, *Metroeconomica* 6, 69–71.

Basmann, R. L. (1954b). A note on Mr. Ichimura's definition of related goods, *Review of Economic Studies* 22, 67–69.

Basmann, R. L. (1956). A theory of demand with variable consumer preferences, *Econometrica* 24, 47–59.

Basmann, R. L. (1968). Hypothesis formation in quantitative economics: A contribution to demand analysis. In Quirk, J., and A. Zarley (eds.), *Papers in Quantitative Economics*, Lawrence, KS: University of Kansas Press.

Basmann, R. L. (1972a). The Brookings quarterly econometric model: Science or number mysticism? In K. Brunner (ed.), *Problems and Issues in Current Econometric Practice*, Columbus, OH: Ohio State University.

Basmann, R. L. (1972b). Argument and evidence in the Brookings-SSRC philosophy of economics. In K. Brunner (ed.), *Problems and Issues in Current Economic Practice*, Columbus, OH: Ohio State University.

Basmann, R. L. (1974). Exact finite sample distributions for some econometric estimators and test statistics. In Intriligator, M. and D. Kendrick (eds.), *Frontiers of Quantitative Economics* 2, New York: North-Holland Publishing Co., Chapter IV.

Basmann, R. L. (1975). Modern logic and the suppositious weakness of the empirical foundations of economic science, *Schweiz. Zeitschrift für Volkswirtschaft und Statistik* 2, 153–176.

Basmann, R. L., R. C. Battalio, and J. H. Kagel (1976). An experimental test of a simple theory of aggregate per capita demand functions, *Schweiz. Zeitschrift für Volkswirtschaft und Statistik* 2, 153–173.

Basmann, R. L., D. J. Molina, and D. J. Slottje (1982a). Measuring Veblen primary and secondary effects utilizing the Fechner-Thurstone direct utility function, Working Paper No. 82-07, TX: Texas A&M University.

Basmann, R. L. (1982b). The sensitivity of tests of fixed preferences against price-dependent preferences to alternative specification of auto-correlated random preference-changers, Working Paper No. 82-08, TX: Texas A&M University.

Basmann, R. L. (1983a). Budget constraint prices as preference-changing parameters of generalized Fechner-Thurstone direct utility functions, *American Economic Review*, 73, 411–413.

Basmann, R. L., D. J. Molina, M. Rodarte, and D. J. Slottje (1983b). Some new methods of predicting changes in economic inequality associated with trends in growth and development. In Nobe, K. and R. K. Sampath (eds.), *Issues in Third World Development*. Boulder, CO: Westview Press.

Battalio, R. C., E. B. Fisher, J. H. Kagel, R. C. Winkler, L. Krasner, and R. L. Basmann (1973). A test of consumer demand theory using observations of individual purchases, *Western Economic Journal* 11, 411–428.

Battalio, R. C. and J. H. Kagel (1975). Experimental studies of consumer behavior using laboratory animals, *Economic Inquiry* 13, 22–38.

Battalio, R. C., L. Green, and H. Rachlin (1981a). Consumer demand behavior with pigeons as subjects, *Journal of Political Economy* 89, 67–91.

Battalio, R. C., L. Green, and J. H. Kagel (1981b). Income-leisure tradeoffs of animal workers, *American Economic Review* 65, 367–384.

Bera, A. K., R. P. Byron, and C. M. Jarque (1981). Further evidence on asymptotic tests for homogeneity and symmetry in large demand systems, *Economics Letters* 8, 101–105.

Berndt, E. R., M. N. Darrough, and W. E. Diewert (1977). Flexible functional forms and expenditure distributions: an application to Canadian consumer demand functions, *International Economic Review* 18, 651–676.

Braithwaite, R. B. (1955). *Scientific Explanation*, Cambridge, MA: Cambridge University Press.

Brandt, W. (1980). *North-South: A Program for Survival*. Cambridge, MA: M.I.T. Press.

Bureau of Labor Statistics (1977). *The Consumer Price Index: Concepts and Content over the Years*, Report 517, Washington, D.C.: U.S. Department of Labor.

Carnap, R. (1966). *Philosophical Foundations of Physics*, New York: Basic Books.

Cassel, C. M., C. E. Sarndal, and J. H. Wretman (1977). *Foundations of Inference in Survey Sampling*, New York: John Wiley and Sons.

Champernowne, D. G. (1952). The graduation of income distribution, *Econometrica* 20, 312–335.

Christensen, L. R., D. W. Jorgenson, and L. J. Lau (1975). Transcendental logarithmic utility functions, *American Economic Review* 65, 367–383.

Clower, R. W. and John G. Riley (1976). The foundations of money illusion in a neoclassical micro-monetary model: comments, *American Economic Review* 66, 184–185.

Conrad, K., and D. W. Jorgenson (1979). Testing the integrability of demand functions, *European Economic Review* 12, 115–147.

Cournot, A. (1838). *Recherches sur les principes mathématiques de la théorie des richesses*, Paris, L. Hachette.

Dagum, C. (1977). A new model of personal income distribution: specification and estimation, *Economic Appliquee* 30, 413–436.

Dagun, C. (1980). Inequality measures between income distributions with applications, *Econometrica* 48, 1791–1804.

Dalton, K. (1970). Compilation of the consumer price index in the United States. *Proceedings of the Central Treaty Organization (CENTO): Symposium on Price Statistics*, Ankara and Istambul, Turkey: pp. 106–112.

Davenant, C. (1699). *An Essay Upon the Probable Methods of Making a People Gainers in the Balance of Trade*, London.

Deaton, A. (1980). Measurement of welfare: theory and practical guidelines, LSMS Working Paper No. 7, Washington, D.C.: World Bank.

Deaton, A. and J. Muellbauer (1980a). *Economics and consumer behavior*, Cambridge, Cambridge University Press.

Deaton, A. and J. Muellbauer (1980b). An almost ideal demand system, American Economic Review 70, 312–326.

Diewert, W. E. (1977). Generalized Slutsky conditions for aggregate consumer demand functions, *Journal of Economic Theory* 15, 353–362.

Diewert, W. E. (1981). The economic theory of index numbers: a survey, in Deaton, A. (ed.), *Essays in the Theory of Measurement of Consumer Demand*, Cambridge, MA: Cambridge University Press.

Duesenberry, J. S. (1949). *Income, Savings, and the Theory of Consumer's Behavior*, Cambridge, MA: Harvard University Press.

Dusansky, R. and P. J. Kalman (1972). The real balance effect and the traditional theory of consumer behavior: a reconciliation, *Journal of Economic Theory* 5, 336–347.

Dusansky, R. and P. J.Kalman (1974). Foundations of money illusion in a neoclassical micro-monetary model, *American Economic Review* 64, 115–122.

Dusansky, R. and P. J. Kalman (1976). The foundations of money illusion in a neoclassical micro-money model: reply, *American Economic Review* 66, 192–195.

Etgar, M. and N. K. Malhotra (1981). Determinants of price dependency: personal and perceptual factors, *Journal of Consumer Research* 8, 217–222.

Edgeworth, F. Y. (1881). *Mathematical Psychics*, London: C. Kegan Paul and Co.

Feldstein, M. (1976). On the theory of tax reform, *Journal of Public Economics* 6, 77–104.

Fisher, F. and K. Shell (1968). Tastes and quality change in the pure theory of the true cost-of-living index, in J. N. Wolfe (ed.), *Value, Capital and Growth: Papers in Honour of Sir John Hicks*, Edinburgh, England: University of Edinburgh Press, 97–139.

Fisk, P. R. (1961). The graduation of income distributions. *Econometrica* 29, 171–185.

Gardner, D. M. (1971). Is there a generalized price-quality relationship? *Journal of Marketing Research* VIII, 241–243.

Gorman, W. M. (1953). Community preference fields, *Econometrica* 21, 63–80.

Hempel, C. (1952). *Fundamentals of Concept Formation in Empirical Science*, Chicago, IL: University of Chicago Press.

Hicks, J. R. (1946). *Value and Capital*, 2d ed. Oxford: Clarendon Press.

Hicks, J. R. (1956). *A Revision of Demand Theory*. Oxford: Clarendon Press.

Hicks, J. R. and R. G. D. Allen (1934). A reconsideration of the theory of value, *Economica* 1, 196–219.

Holton, G. (1969). Einstein, Michelson, and the "crucial" experiment, *Isis* 60, 133–197.

Houthakker, H. S. (1950). Revealed preferences and the utility function, *Economica* 17, 159–174.

Houthakker, H. S. (1960). Additive preferences, *Econometrica* 28, 244–257.

Ichimura, S. (1951). A critical note on the definition of related goods, *Review of Economic Studies* 18, 179–183.

James, W. (1890). *Principles of Psychology*, Vol. I. Reprinted (1950), New York: Dover Publications.

Jevons, W. S. (1957). *The Theory of Political Economy*, 5th ed. New York, Kelley and Millman, Inc. [First published, 1871.]

Johnson, H. G. (1952). The effects of income redistribution on aggregate consumption with interdependence of consumer preferences, *Economica* 19, 131–147.

Jorgenson, D. W., L. J. Lau, and T. M. Stoker (1982). The transcendental logarithmic model of aggregate consumer behavior. In Basmann, R. L. and G. F. Rhodes, Jr. (eds.), *Advances in Econometrics*, Vol. 1, Greenwich, CT: JAI Press, pp. 97–238.

Kakwani, N. C. (1980). *Income Inequality and Poverty*, Oxford: Oxford University Press.

Kakwani, N. C. (1982). On the measurement of tax progressivity and redistribution effect of taxes with applications to horizontal and vertical equity (mimeo), Department of Econometrics, Kensington, Australia: University of New South Wales.

Kakwani, N. C. (1983). Redistribution effects of income tax and cash benefits in Australia, Working Paper No. 18, Center for Applied Research, Kensington, Australia: University of New South Wales.

Kalman, P. J. (1968). Theory of consumer behavior when prices enter the utility function, *Econometrica* 36, 497–510.

Kiesler, C. A. and S. B. Kiesler (1970). *Conformity*, Reading, MA: Addison-Wesley Publishing Co.

Klein, L. R. and H. Rubin (1947). A constant-utility cost of living index, *Review of Economic Studies* 15, 84–87.

Konüs, A. A. (1924). The problem of the true index of the cost-of-living, *Economic Bulletin of the Institute of Economic Conjuncture*, Moscow: No. 9–10; English translation (1936), *Econometrica* 7, 110–129.

Koo, A. (1963). An empirical test of revealed preference theory, *Econometrica* 31, 646–664.

Kuhn, T. (1962). *The Structure of Scientific Revolutions*, Chicago, University of Chicago Press.

Laitinen, K. (1978). Why is demand homogeneity so often rejected? *Economics Letters* 1, 187–191.

Lange, O. (1940). Complementarity and interrelations of shifts in demand, *Review of Economic Studies* 8, 58–63.

Lasswell, H. D. (1958). *Politics: Who Gets What, When, and How?* New York: Meridian Books.

Lau, J., W. L. Lin and P. A. Yotopoulos (1978). The linear logarithmic expenditure system: an application to consumption-leisure choice, *Econometrica* 46, 843–869.

Lindsay, R. B. and H. Margenau (1936). *Foundations of Physics*. Reprinted (1957), New York: Dover Publications, Inc.

McConnell, J. Douglas (1968a). An experimental examination of the price-quality relationship, *Journal of Business* 41, 439–444.

McConnell, J. Douglas (1968b). Effect of pricing on perception of product quality. *Journal of Applied Psychology* 52, 331–334.

McConnell, J. Douglas (1968c). The price-quality relationship in an experimental setting, *Journal of Marketing Research* 5, 300–303.

McConnell, J. Douglas (1968d). Comment on "A Major Price-Perceived Quality Study Reexamined," *Journal of Marketing Research* 27, 263–264.

McDonald, J. B. and M. Ransom (1979). Functional forms, estimation techniques, and the distribution of income, *Econometrica* 47, 1513–1526.

Mandelbrot, B. (1960). The Pareto-Lévy Law and the distribution of income, *International Economic Review* 1, 79–106.

Meisner, J. F. (1979). The sad fate of the asymptotic Slutsky symmetry test for large systems, *Economics Letters* 2, 231–233.

Monroe, K. B. (1973). Buyers' subjective perceptions of price, *Journal of Marketing Research* X, 70–80.

Moore, G. (1970). Objectives for price and wage statistics at the Bureau of Labor Statistics, *The Econometrics of Price Determination: Proceeding of Symposium sponsored by the Board of Governors of the Federal Reserve System and the Social Science Research Council*, Washington, D.C.: pp. 386–395.

Muellbauer, J. (1975). Aggregation, income distribution, and consumer demand, *Review of Economic Studies* 42, 525–543.

Muellbauer, J. (1976). Community preferences and the representative consumer, *Econometrica* 44, 979–999.

Norwood, J. (1970). Plans for a comprehensive system of price statistics of the United States, *Proceedings of the Central Treaty Organization (CENTO): Symposium on Price Statistics*, Turkey: Ankara and Istambul, pp. 158–162.

Pap, A. (1962). *An Introduction to the Philosophy of Science*, Glencoe, Ill: Free Press.

Phillips, R. J. and D. J. Slottje (1983). The importance of relative prices in analyzing Veblen effects, *Journal of Public Issues* XVII, 197–206.

Pollak, R. A. (1977). Price-dependent preferences, *American Economic Review* 67, 64–75.

Pollak, R. A. (1978). Endogenous tastes in demand and welfare analysis, *American Economic Review* 68, 374–379.

Riesz, P. C. (1980). A major price-perceived quality study reexamined, *Journal of Marketing Research* 27, 259–262.

Robertson, D. H., J. R. Hicks, and O. Lange (1944). The interrelations of shifts in demand, *Review of Economic Studies* 12, 71–78.

Rosen, H. S. (1978). The measurement of excess burden with explicit utility functions, *Journal of Political Economy* 86, S121–S137.

Rosen, H. S. (1980). An approach to the study of income utility and horizontal equity, *Quarterly Journal of Economics* 42, 307–322.

Sahota, G. (1978). Theories of personal income distribution: a survey, *Journal of Economic Literature* 16, 1–55.

Salem, A. B. Z. and T. D. Mount (1974). A convenient descriptive model of income distribution: the gamma density, *Econometrica* 42, 1115–1127.

Samuelson, P. A. (1938). A note on the pure theory of consumer behavior, *Economica* 5, 61–71.

Samuelson, P. A. (1947). *Foundations of Economic Analysis*, Cambridge, MA; Harvard University Press.

Samuelson, P. A. (1948). Some implications of linearity, *Review of Economic Studies* 15, 88–90.

Samuelson, P. A. and S. Swamy (1974). Invariant economic index numbers and canonical duality: a survey and synthesis, *American Economic Review* 64, 566–593.

Schultz, H. (1938). *The Theory and Measurement of Demand*. Chicago: University of Chicago Press.

Scitovsky, T. (1945). Some consequences of judging quality by price, *Review of Economic Studies* 11, 100–105.

Sen, A. K. (1973). *On Economic Inequality*, Oxford, Clarendon Press.

Seo, T. K. (1973). On Systems of Demand Functions, Ph.D. Dissertation, TX; Texas A&M University.

Singh, S. K. and G. S. Maddala (1976). A function for the size distribution of incomes, *Econometrica* 44, 963–970.

Slottje, D. J. (1983). Inferences on Interincome Inequality Parameters of a Joint Distribution of Components of Income and Commodity Expenditure, Ph.D. Dissertation, Texas A&M University.

Sonnenschein, H. (1972). Market excess demand functions, *Econometrica* 40, 345–354.

Sonnenschein, H. (1973). The utility hypothesis and market demand theory, *Western Economic Journal* 11, 404–411.

Stecher, E. (1978). An Empirical Estimation of the Parameters of the Joint Relative Frequency Function of Consumer Demand and Planned Income for the United States, 1952–1975, Ph.D. Dissertation, Texas A&M University.

Stigler, G. (1954). The early history of empirical studies of consumer behavior, *Journal of Political Economy* 42, 198–233.

Stoker, T. (1981a). The use of average and distribution data to characterize micro functions, Cambridge, MA: M.I.T. Working Paper No. 1207-81.

Stoker, T. (1981b). Distribution restrictions and the form of aggregate functions, Cambridge, MA: M.I.T. Working Paper No. 1277-81.

Stoker, T. (1982). Exact aggregation and generalized Slutsky conditions, unpublished mimeo, Cambridge, MA: M.I.T.

Theil, H. (1975). *Theory and Measurement of Consumer Demand Vol. I,* Amsterdam: North-Holland Publishing Co.

Thurow, L. (1970). Analyzing the American income distribution, *American Economic Review* 60, 261–269.

Thurstone, L. L. (1931). The indifference function, *Journal of Social Psychology* 2, 139–166.

Tinbergen, J. (1970). A positive and normative theory of income distribution, *Review of Income and Wealth* 16, 3–17.

Tintner, G. (1952). Complementarity and shifts in demand, *Metroeconomica* 4, 1–4.

Tintner, G. (1960). External economies in consumption, in Ralph W. Pfouts, (ed.), *Essays in Economics and Econometrics,* Chapel Hill, NC, University of North Carolina Press, 107–112.

Vartia, Y. (1978). Fisher's five tines fork and other quantum theories of index numbers. In W. Eichhorn, R. Henn, O. Optiz and R. W. Shephard (eds.), *Theory and Applications of Economic Indices: Proceedings of an International Symposium held at the University of Karlsruhe,* Würzburg: Physica-Verlag, pp. 271–295.

Veblen, T. (1899). *Theory of the Leisure Class.* Reprinted (1931), New York: Modern Library.

Veblen, T. (1908). Professor Clark's economics, *Quarterly Journal of Economics* 22 Reprinted in Veblen, T. (1969). *Marx, Race, Science and Economics,* New York, Capricorn Books.

Veblen, T. (1909). The limitations of marginal utility, *Journal of Political Economy,* 17. Reprinted in Veblen, T. (1969). *Marx, Race, Science and Economics,* New York: Capricorn Books.

Venkataraman, V. K. (1981). The price-quality relationship in an experimental setting, *Journal of Advertising Research* 21, 49–52.

Von Neumann, J. and O. Morgenstern (1953). *Theory of Games and Economic Behavior.* Princeton, NJ: Princeton University Press.

Wichers, C. R. (1976). The foundations of money illusion in a neoclassical micro-monetary model: comment. *American Economic Review* 66, 186–191.

Wold, H. (1953). *Demand Analysis,* New York: John Wiley and Sons.

World Bank (1981). *World Development Report,* Oxford: Oxford University Press.

INEQUALITY IN THE DISTRIBUTION
OF INDIVIDUAL WELFARE

Dale W. Jorgenson and Daniel T. Slesnick

I. INTRODUCTION

The purpose of this paper is to present an econometric approach to the
measurement of inequality in the distribution of individual welfare. This
approach meets the objectives of inequality measurement identified by
Dalton (1920) more than 60 years ago: "For the economist is primarily
interested, not in the distribution of income as such, but in the effects of
the distribution of income upon the distribution and total amount of economic welfare, which may be derived from income." [1]

Since the pioneering work of Atkinson (1970) and Kolm (1969, 1976a,b),
inequality measurement has been based on explicit social welfare functions. However, the resulting measures of inequality have been defined
on the distribution of individual income rather than the distribution of
individual welfare, "which may be derived from income." Muellbauer

Advances in Econometrics, vol. 3, pages 67–130
Copyright © 1984 by JAI Press Inc.
All rights of reproduction in any form reserved.
ISBN: 0-89232-443-0

(1974b,c) and Roberts (1980c) have shown that measures of inequality based on income rather than welfare are subject to very stringent limitations.

Measures of social welfare defined on the distribution of individual income coincide with measures defined on the distribution of individual welfare if and only if preferences are identical and homothetic for all consumers.[2] However, homothetic preferences are inconsistent with well-established empirical regularities in the behavior of individual consumers.[3] Further, identical preferences are inconsistent with empirical findings that expenditure patterns depend on the demographic characteristics of consumers.[4]

Our approach to inequality measurement is based on an econometric model of aggregate consumer behavior. The novel feature of this model is that systems of individual demand functions can be recovered uniquely from the system of aggregate demand functions. By requiring that the individual demand functions are integrable, we can also recover indirect utility functions for all consumers. Finally, we can define measures of individual welfare in terms of these indirect utility functions.

In Section II we outline an econometric methodology for developing a model of aggregate consumer behavior. In this model, systems of individual demand functions depend on the prices faced by all households. These systems also depend on total expenditures and attributes such as demographic characteristics that vary among households. We obtain aggregate demand functions by summing over individual demand functions. The resulting system of aggregate demand functions depends on summary statistics of the joint distribution of total expenditures and attributes among all households.

In Section III we implement our econometric model of aggregate consumer behavior for the United States. For this purpose we employ cross-section data on individual expenditure patterns. We combine these data with time-series data on aggregate expenditure patterns and prices for all commodities. We also employ time-series data on the distribution of total expenditures among households.

In Section IV we present methods for evaluating the level of social welfare. For this purpose we construct an explicit social welfare function. This social welfare function incorporates measures of individual welfare based on indirect utility functions for all consumer units. In addition, this social welfare function employs normative criteria based on horizontal and vertical equity for evaluating transfers among units.

In Section V we develop indexes of inequality in the distribution of individual welfare. For this purpose we express the measures of social welfare presented in Section IV as the sum of measures of efficiency and equity. Efficiency is the maximum level of social welfare that is potentially available through redistributions of aggregate expenditure. Equity is the difference between the actual level of social welfare and the measure of efficiency.

We can define an absolute index of inequality as the negative of the measure of equity. This index reflects the differences between a perfectly egalitarian distribution of individual welfare and the actual welfare distribution. Similarly, we can define a relative measure of inequality as the ratio between the absolute index of inequality and the measure of efficiency. We implement these measures of inequality for the United States for the years 1958–1978.

In Section VI we develop indexes of inequality within subgroups of the population. For this purpose we introduce group welfare functions that are precisely analogous to the social welfare functions of Section IV. We decompose these measures of group welfare into measures of group efficiency and equity. Finally, we implement the resulting absolute and relative measures of group inequality for subgroups of the U.S. population, classified by age of head of household, for the years 1958–1978.

In Section VII we decompose indexes of inequality in the distribution of individual welfare into the sum of indexes of inequality between and within subgroups of the population. The index of inequality between groups represents the loss in social welfare due to an inequitable distribution of welfare between groups. The index of inequality within groups represents the loss in social welfare due to an inequitable distribution within each group. We implement these indexes for age groups of the U.S. population for the years 1958–1978.

In order to quantify the gains to society that can accrue from redistributional policies, we find it useful to express social welfare in terms of aggregate expenditure. For this purpose we introduce the social expenditure function, defined as the minimum level of aggregate expenditure required to attain a given level of social welfare. The social expenditure function is analogous to an individual expenditure function, which gives the minimum level of individual expenditure required to attain a stipulated level of utility.

In Section VIII we define money metric inequality as the difference between money measures of potential and actual social welfare. This measure is the amount that society as a whole would gain from a perfectly egalitarian distribution of aggregate expenditure. We also consider money measures of group inequality, corresponding to the amounts that each group would gain from an egalitarian distribution within the group. Finally, we decompose money metric inequality into the sum of money measures of between- and within-group inequality. These measures provide the amounts society would gain from redistribution between and within groups.

In Section IX we implement the money measures of inequality presented in Section VIII. We first present money metric inequality for the U.S. population as a whole for the years 1958–1978. We find that society as a whole can gain the equivalent of 30–34% of aggregate expenditure by redistributional policies. Second, we decompose money measures of inequality between and within age groups. We find that redistribution between age groups could produce gains of 6–8% of aggregate expenditure, whereas redistribution within age groups could produce gains of 23–26%.

II. AGGREGATE CONSUMER BEHAVIOR

In this section we develop an econometric model of aggregate consumer behavior based on the theory of exact aggregation, following Jorgenson et al. (1980, 1981, 1982). Our model incorporates time-series data on prices and aggregate quantities consumed. We also include cross-section data on individual quantities consumed, individual total expenditure, and attributes of individual households such as demographic characteristics.

To represent preferences for all individuals in a form suitable for measuring individual welfare, we take households as consuming units. We assume that expenditures on individual commodities are allocated so as to maximize a household welfare function. As a consequence, the household behaves in the same way as an individual maximizing a utility function, as demonstrated by Samuelson (1956) and Pollak (1981). By assuming that each household maximizes a household welfare function, we can focus on the distribution of welfare among households rather than the distribution among individuals within households.

To construct an econometric model based on exact aggregation we first represent individual preferences by means of an indirect utility function for each consuming unit, using the following notation:

p_n—price of the nth commodity, assumed to be the same for all consuming units;

$p = (p_1, p_2, \ldots, p_N)$—the vector of prices of all commodities;

x_{nk}—the quantity of the nth commodity group consumed by the kth consuming unit ($n = 1, 2, \ldots, N; k = 1, 2, \ldots, K$);

$M_k = \sum_{n=1}^{N} p_n x_{nk}$—total expenditure of the kth consuming unit ($k = 1, 2, \ldots, K$);

$w_{nk} = p_n x_{nk}/M_k$—expenditure share of the nth commodity group in the budget of the kth consuming unit ($n = 1, 2, \ldots, N; k = 1, 2, \ldots, K$);

$w_k = (w_{1k}, w_{2k}, \ldots, w_{Nk})$—vector of expenditure shares for the kth consuming unit ($k = 1, 2, \ldots, K$);

$\ln(p/M_k) = [\ln(p_1/M_k), \ln(p_2/M_k), \ldots, \ln(p_N/M_k)]$—vector of logarithms of ratios of prices to expenditure by the kth consuming unit $(k = 1, 2, \ldots, K)$;

$\ln p = (\ln p_1, \ln p_2, \ldots, \ln p_N)$—vector of logarithms of prices;

A_k—vector of attributes of the kth consuming unit $(k = 1, 2, \ldots, K)$.

We assume that the kth consuming unit allocates expenditures in accord with the transcendental logarithmic or translog indirect utility function,[5] say V_k, where

$$\ln V_k = G\left(\ln\frac{p'}{M_k}\, \alpha_p + \frac{1}{2} \ln\frac{p'}{M_k}\, B_{pp} \ln\frac{p}{M_k} + \ln\frac{p'}{M_k}\, B_{pA}A_k, A_k \right)$$

$$(k = 1, 2, \ldots, K). \quad (2.1)$$

In this representation the function G is a monotone increasing function of the variable

$$\ln\frac{p'}{M_k}\, \alpha_p + \frac{1}{2} \ln\frac{p'}{M_k}\, B_{pp} \ln\frac{p}{M_k} + \ln\frac{p'}{M_k}\, B_{pA}A_k.$$

In addition, the function G depends directly on the attribute vector A_k.[6] The vector α_p and the matrices B_{pp} and B_{pA} are constant parameters that are the same for all consuming units.

The expenditure shares of the kth consuming unit can be derived by the logarithmic form of Roy's (1943) Identity:[7]

$$w_{nk} = \frac{\partial \ln V_k}{\partial \ln(p_n/M_k)} \Bigg/ \sum_{n=1}^{N} \frac{\partial \ln V_k}{\partial \ln(p_n/M_k)}$$

$$(n = 1, 2, \ldots, N; k = 1, 2, \ldots, K). \quad (2.2)$$

Applying this Identity to the translog indirect utility function (2.1), we obtain the system of individual expenditure shares:

$$w_k = \frac{1}{D_k(p)} \left(\alpha_p + B_{pp} \ln\frac{p}{M_k} + B_{pA}A_k \right)$$

$$(k = 1, 2, \ldots, K), \quad (2.3)$$

where the denominators $\{D_k\}$ take the form:

$$D_k = i'\alpha_p + i'B_{pp} \ln\frac{p}{M_k} + i'B_{pA}A_k \quad (k = 1, 2, \ldots, K). \quad (2.4)$$

The individual expenditure shares are homogeneous of degree zero in the unknown parameters α_p, B_{pp}, and B_{pA}. By multiplying a given set of these parameters by a constant, we obtain another set of parameters that generates the same system of individual budget shares. Accordingly, we can choose a normalization for the parameters without affecting observed patterns of individual expenditure allocation. We find it convenient to employ the normalization

$$i'\alpha_p = -1.$$

Under this restriction any change in the set of unknown parameters will be reflected in changes in individual expenditure patterns.

The conditions for exact aggregation are that the individual expenditure shares are linear in functions of the attributes $\{A_k\}$ and total expenditures $\{M_k\}$ for all consuming units.[8] These conditions will be satisfied if and only if the terms involving the attributes and expenditures do not appear in the denominators of the expressions given above for the individual expenditure shares, so that

$$i'B_{pp}i = 0$$

and

$$i'B_{pA} = 0.$$

The exact aggregation restrictions imply that the denominators $\{D_k\}$ reduce to

$$D = -1 + i'B_{pp} \ln p,$$

where the subscript k is no longer required since the denominator is the same for all consuming units. Under these restrictions the individual expenditure shares can be written:

$$w_k = \frac{1}{D(p)} (\alpha_p + B_{pp} \ln p - B_{pp} i \ln M_k$$

$$+ B_{pA} A_k) \qquad (k = 1, 2, \ldots, K). \qquad (2.5)$$

The individual expenditure shares are linear in the logarithms of expenditures $\{\ln M_k\}$ and in the attributes $\{A_k\}$, as required by exact aggregation.

Under exact aggregation the indirect utility function for each consuming unit can be represented in the form:

$$\ln V_k = F(A_k) + \ln p'(\alpha_p + \tfrac{1}{2} B_{pp} \ln p + B_{pA} A_k)$$

$$- D(p) \ln M_k \qquad (k = 1, 2, \ldots, K). \qquad (2.6)$$

In this representation the indirect utility function is linear in the logarithm of total expenditure $\ln M_k$ with a coefficient that depends on the prices p $(k = 1, 2, \ldots, K)$. This property is invariant with respect to positive affine transformations but is not preserved by arbitrary monotone increasing transformations. We conclude that the indirect utility function (2.6) provides a cardinal measure of utility for each consuming unit.

If a system of individual expenditure shares (2.3) can be generated from an indirect utility function of the form (2.1), we say that the system is *integrable*. A complete set of conditions for integrability[9] is the following:

HOMOGENEITY: *The individual expenditure shares are homogeneous of degree zero in prices and total expenditure.*

We can write the individual expenditure shares in the form:

$$\beta_{pM} = B_{pp}i. \tag{2.7}$$

Given the exact aggregation restrictions, there are $N - 1$ restrictions implied by homogeneity.

SUMMABILITY: *The sum of the individual expenditure shares over all commodity groups is equal to unity:*

$$i'w_k = 1 \quad (k = 1, 2, \ldots, K).$$

We can write the denominator $D(p)$ in (2.4) in the form:

$$D = -1 + \beta_{Mp} \ln p,$$

where the vector of parameters β_{Mp} is constant and the same for all commodity groups and all consuming units. Summability implies that this vector must satisfy the restrictions:

$$\beta_{Mp} = i'B_{pp}. \tag{2.8}$$

Given the exact aggregation restrictions, there are $N - 1$ restrictions implied by summability.

SYMMETRY: *The matrix of compensated own- and cross-price substitution effects must be symmetric.*

In the system of individual expenditure shares can be generated from an indirect utility function of the form (2.1), a necessary and sufficient condition for symmetry is that the matrix B_{pp} must be symmetric. Without imposing this condition, we can write the individual expenditure shares in the form:

$$w_k = \frac{1}{D(p)}\left(\alpha_p + B_{pp} \ln \frac{p}{M_k} + B_{pA}A_k\right) \quad (k = 1, 2, \ldots, K).$$

Symmetry implies that the matrix of parameters B_{pp} must satisfy the restrictions

$$B_{pp} = B'_{pp}. \tag{2.9}$$

The total number of symmetry restrictions is $\frac{1}{2} N(N - 1)$.

NONNEGATIVITY: *The individual expenditure shares must be non-negative.*

By summability the individual expenditure shares sum to unity, so that we can write:

$$w_k \geq 0 \qquad (k = 1, 2, \ldots, K),$$

where $w_k \geq 0$ implies $w_{nk} \geq 0$ $(n = 1, 2, \ldots, N)$, and $w_k \neq 0$.

Since the translog indirect utility function is quadratic in the logarithms of prices, we can always choose the prices so that the individual expenditure shares violate the nonnegativity conditions. Accordingly, we cannot impose restrictions on the parameters of the translog indirect utility functions that would imply nonnegativity of the individual expenditure shares. Instead we consider restrictions on the parameters that imply monotonicity of the system of individual demand functions for all nonnegative expenditure shares.

MONOTONICITY: *The matrix of compensated own- and cross-price substitution effects must be nonpositive definite.*

We introduce the definition due to Martos (1969) of a *strictly merely positive subdefinite matrix*, namely, a real symmetric matrix S such that

$$xSx < 0$$

implies $Sx > 0$ or $Sx < 0$. A necessary and sufficient condition for monotonicity is either that the translog indirect utility function is homothetic or that B_{pp}^{-1} exists and is strictly merely positive subdefinite.[10]

To provide a basis for evaluating the impact of transfers among households on social welfare, we find it useful to represent household preferences by means of a utility function that is the same for all consuming units. For this purpose, we assume that the kth consuming unit maximizes its utility, say U_k, where

$$U_k = U\left[\frac{x_{1k}}{m_1(A_k)}, \frac{x_{2k}}{m_2(A_k)}, \cdots, \frac{x_{Nk}}{m_N(A_k)}\right]$$

$$(k = 1, 2, \ldots, K), \quad (2.10)$$

subject to the budget constraint

$$M_k = \sum_{n=1}^{N} p_n x_{nk} \qquad (k = 1, 2, \ldots, K).$$

In this representation of consumer preferences the quantities $\{x_{nk}/m_n(A_k)\}$ can be regarded as *effective quantities consumed*, as proposed by Barten (1964). The crucial assumption embodied in this representation is that differences in preferences among consumers enter the utility function U

only through differences in the commodity specific household equivalence scales $\{m_n(A_k)\}$.[11]

Consumer equilibrium implies the existence of an indirect utility function, say V, that is the same for all consuming units. The level of utility for the kth consuming unit, say V_k, depends on the prices of individual commodities, the household equivalence scales, and the level of total expenditure:

$$V_k = V\left[\frac{p_1 \, m_1(A_k)}{M_k}, \frac{p_2 \, m_2(A_k)}{M_k}, \ldots, \frac{p_N \, m_N(A_k)}{M_k}\right]$$

$$(k = 1, 2, \ldots, K). \quad (2.11)$$

In this representation the prices $\{p_n \, m_n(A_k)\}$ can be regarded as *effective prices*. Differences in preferences among consuming units enter this indirect utility function only through the household equivalence scales $\{m_n(A_k)\}$ $(k = 1, 2, \ldots, K)$.

To represent the translog indirect utility function (2.1) in terms of household equivalence scales, we require some additional notation:

$\ln[p \, m(A_k)/M_k]$—vector of logarithms of ratios of effective prices $\{p_n \, m_n(A_k)\}$ to total expenditure M_k of the kth consuming unit ($k = 1, 2, \ldots, K$);

$\ln m(A_k) = (\ln m_1(A_k), \ln m_2(A_k), \ldots, \ln m_N(A_k))$—vector of logarithms of the household equivalence scales of the kth consuming unit ($k = 1, 2, \ldots, K$).

We assume, as before, that the kth consuming unit allocates its expenditures in accord with the translog indirect utility function (2.1). However, we also assume that this function, expressed in terms of the effective prices $\{p_n \, m_n(A_k)\}$ and total expenditure M_k, is the same for all consuming units. The indirect utility function takes the form:

$$\ln V_k = \ln \frac{p \, m(A_k)'}{M_k} \alpha_p + \frac{1}{2} \ln \frac{p \, m(A_k)'}{M_k} B_{pp} \ln \frac{p \, m(A_k)}{M_k}$$

$$(k = 1, 2, \ldots, K). \quad (2.12)$$

Taking logarithms of the effective prices $\{p_n \, m_n(A_k)\}$, we can rewrite the indirect utility function (2.12) in the form:

$$\ln V_k = \ln m(A_k)'\alpha_p + \frac{1}{2} \ln m(A_k)' B_{pp} \ln m(A_k) + \ln \frac{p'}{M_k} \alpha_p$$

$$+ \frac{1}{2} \ln \frac{p'}{M_k} B_{pp} \ln \frac{p}{M_k} + \ln \frac{p'}{M_k} B_{pp} \ln m(A_k) \quad (2.13)$$

$$(k = 1, 2, \ldots, K).$$

Comparing the representation (2.13) with the representation (2.6), we see that the term involving only the household equivalent scales must take the form:

$$F(A_k) = \ln m(A_k)' \alpha_p + \tfrac{1}{2} \ln m(A_k)' B_{pp} \ln m(A_k)$$

$$(k = 1, 2, \ldots, K). \quad (2.14)$$

Second, the term involving ratios of prices to total expenditure and the household equivalence sales must satisfy

$$\ln \frac{p'}{M_k} B_{pA} A_k = \ln \frac{p'}{M_k} B_{pp} \ln m(A_k) \qquad (k = 1, 2, \ldots, K) \quad (2.15)$$

for all prices and total expenditure.

The household equivalence scales $\{m_n(A_k)\}$ defined by (2.15) must satisfy the equation

$$B_{pA} A_k = B_{pp} \ln m(A_k) \qquad (k = 1, 2, \ldots, K). \quad (2.16)$$

Under monotonicity of the individual expenditure shares the matrix B_{pp} has an inverse, so that we can express the household equivalence scales in terms of the parameters of the translog indirect utility function, namely, B_{pp} and B_{pA}, and the attributes $\{A_k\}$:

$$\ln m(A_k) = B_{pp}^{-1} B_{pA} A_k \qquad (k = 1, 2, \ldots, K). \quad (2.17)$$

We can refer to these scales as the *commodity specific translog household equivalence scales.*

Substituting the commodity specific equivalence scales (2.16) into the indirect utility function (2.13), we obtain a representation of the indirect utility function in terms of the attributes $\{A_k\}$:

$$\ln V_k = A_k' B_{pA}' B_{pp}^{-1} \alpha_p + \tfrac{1}{2} A_k' B_{pA}' B_{pp}^{-1} B_{pA} A_k$$

$$+ \ln p' (\alpha_p + \tfrac{1}{2} B_{pp} \ln p + B_{pA} A_k) - D(p) \ln M_k \quad (2.18)$$

$$(k = 1, 2, \ldots, K).$$

This form of the translog indirect utility function is equivalent to the form (2.1) in that both generate the same system of individual demand functions. By requiring that the attributes A_k enter only through the commodity specific household equivalence scales, we have provided a specific form for the function $F(A_k)$ in (2.6).

Given the indirect utility function (2.18) for each consuming unit, we can express total expenditure as a function of prices, consumer attributes, and the level of utility:

$$\ln M_k = \frac{1}{D(p)} \left[A'_k B'_{pA} B_{pp}^{-1} \alpha_p + \frac{1}{2} A'_k B'_{pA} B_{pp}^{-1} B_{pA} A_k \right.$$

$$\left. + \ln p' \left(\alpha_p + \frac{1}{2} B_{pp} \ln p + B_{pA} A_k \right) - \ln V_k \right] \qquad (2.19)$$

$$(k = 1, 2, \ldots, K).$$

We can refer to this function as the *translog expenditure function*. The translog expenditure function gives the minimum expenditure required for the kth consuming unit to achieve the utility level V_k, given prices p ($k = 1, 2, \ldots, K$).

We find it useful to introduce household equivalence scales that are not specific to a given commodity.[12] Following Muellbauer (1974a), we define a general household equivalence scale, say m_0, as follows:

$$m_0 = \frac{M_k[p\, m(A_k),\, V_k^0]}{M_0(p,\, V_k^0)} \qquad (k = 1, 2, \ldots, K), \qquad (2.20)$$

where M_k is the expenditure function for the kth household; M_0 is the expenditure function for a reference household with commodity specific equivalence scales equal to unity for all commodities; and $p\, m(A_k)$ is a vector of effective prices $\{p_n\, m_n(A_k)\}$.

The general household equivalence scale m_0 is the ratio between total expenditures required by the kth household and by the reference household required for the same level of utility V_k^0 ($k = 1, 2, \ldots, K$). This scale can be interpreted as the number of household equivalent members. The number of members depends on the attributes A_k of the consuming unit and on the prices p.

If each household has a translog indirect utility function, then the general household equivalence scale for the kth household takes the form:

$$\ln m_0 = \ln M_k - \ln M_0$$

$$= \frac{1}{D(p)} \left[\ln m(A_k)' \alpha_p + \frac{1}{2} \ln m(A_k)' B_{pp} \ln m(A_k) + \ln m(A_k)' B_{pp} \ln p \right]$$

$$(k = 1, 2, \ldots, K) \qquad (2.21)$$

We can refer to this scale as the *general translog household equivalence scale*. The translog equivalence scale depends on the attributes A_k of the kth household and the prices p of all commodities but is independent of the level of utility V_k^0.

Given the general translog equivalence scale, we can rewrite the indirect utility function (2.18) in the form:

$$\ln V_k = \ln p'\alpha_p + \frac{1}{2} \ln p'B_{pp} \ln p - D(p) \ln \left[\frac{M_k}{m_0(p, A_k)}\right]$$

$$(k = 1, 2, \ldots, K). \quad (2.22)$$

The level of utility for the kth consuming unit depends on prices p and total expenditure per household equivalent member $M_k/m_0(p, A_k)$ ($k = 1, 2, \ldots, K$). Similarly, we can rewrite the expenditure function (2.19) in the form:

$$\ln M_k = \frac{1}{D(p)}\left[\ln p'\left(\alpha_p + \frac{1}{2} B_{pp} \ln p\right) - \ln V_k\right]$$

$$+ \ln m_0(p, A_k) \quad (k = 1, 2, \ldots, K). \quad (2.23)$$

Total expenditure required by the kth consuming unit to attain the level of utility V_k depends on prices p and the number of household equivalent members $m_0(p, A_k)$ ($k = 1, 2, \ldots, K$).

To construct an econometric model of aggregate consumer behavior based on exact aggregation we obtain aggregate expenditure shares, say w, by multiplying individual expenditure shares (2.5) by expenditure for each consuming unit, adding over all consuming units, and dividing by aggregate expenditure, $M = \sum_{k=1}^{K} M_k$:

$$w = \frac{\sum M_k w_k}{M}. \quad (2.24)$$

The aggregate expenditure shares can be written:

$$w = \frac{1}{D(p)}\left(\alpha_p + B_{pp} \ln p - B_{pp}i \frac{\sum M_k \ln M_k}{M}\right.$$

$$\left. + B_{pA} \frac{\sum M_k A_k}{M}\right). \quad (2.25)$$

The aggregate expenditure patterns depend on the distribution of expenditure over all consuming units through summary statistics of the joint distribution of expenditures and attributes: $\sum M_k \ln M_k/M$ and $\{\sum M_k A_k/M\}$. Systems of individual expenditure shares (2.5) for consuming units with identical demographic characteristics can be recovered in one and only one way from the system of aggregate expenditure shares (2.25).

The first step in analyzing inequality in the distribution of individual welfare is to select a representation of the individual welfare function. We assume that individual welfare for the kth consuming unit, say W_k ($k = 1, 2, \ldots, K$), is equal to the logarithm of the translog indirect utility function (2.22):[13]

$$W_k = \ln V_k$$

$$= \ln p'\alpha_p + \frac{1}{2} \ln p'B_{pp} \ln p - D(p) \ln \left[\frac{M_k}{m_0(p, A_k)} \right]$$

$$(k = 1, 2, \ldots, K). \quad (2.26)$$

To Summarize

For our econometric model a system of individual expenditure shares (2.5) can be recovered in one and only one way from the system of aggregate expenditure shares (2.25). Given a system of individual expenditure shares (2.5) that is integrable, we can recover the translog indirect utility function (2.22). This indirect utility function provides a cardinal measure of utility. We obtain a cardinal measure of individual welfare for each consuming unit (2.26) by setting this measure equal to the logarithm of the indirect utility function.

III. ECONOMETRIC MODEL

In this section we present the empirical results of implementing the econometric model of consumer behavior described in Section II. We divide consumer expenditures among five commodity groups:

1. *Energy*—expenditures on electricity, natural gas, heating oil, and gasoline
2. *Food*—expenditures on all food products, including tobacco and alcohol
3. *Consumer goods*—expenditures on all other nondurable goods included in consumer expenditures
4. *Capital services*—the service flow from consumer durables and the service flow from housing
5. *Consumer services*—expenditures on consumer services, such as car repairs, medical services, entertainment, and so on

We employ the following demographic characteristics as attributes of individual households:

1. *Family size*—1, 2, 3, 4, 5, 6, and 7 or more persons
2. *Age of head*—16–24, 25–34, 35–44, 45–54, 55–64, 65 and over
3. *Region of residence*—Northeast, North Central, South, and West
4. *Race*—white, nonwhite
5. *Type of residence*—urban, rural

Our cross section observations on individual expenditures for each commodity group and on demographic characteristics of individual households are for the year 1972 from the 1972/73 Survey of Consumer Expenditures (CES).[14] Our time series observations are based on data on personal consumption expenditures from the United States National Income and Product Accounts (NIPA) for the years 1958 to 1974.[15] Prices for each commodity group are defined in terms of translog price indexes computed from detailed prices included in NIPA for each year. We employ time-series data on the distribution of expenditures over all households and among demographic groups based on *Current Population Reports*.[16]

In our application we treat the expenditure shares for five commodity groups as endogenous variables, so that we estimate four equations. As unknown parameters we have 4 elements of the vector α_p, 4 expenditure coefficients of the vector $B_{pp}i$, 16 attribute coefficients for each of the

Table 1. Pooled Estimation Results[a]

Notation:

CONST	= constant term
ln PEN	= coefficient of log of price of energy
ln PF	= coefficient of log of price of food
ln PCG	= coefficient of log of price of consumer goods
ln PK	= coefficient of log of price of capital services
ln PCS	= coefficient of log of price of consumer services
ln M	= coefficient of log of total expenditure
S2	= coefficient of dummy for family of size 2
S3	= coefficient of dummy for family of size 3
S4	= coefficient of dummy for family of size 4
S5	= coefficient of dummy for family of size 5
S6	= coefficient of dummy for family of size 6
S7+	= coefficient of dummy for family of size 7 or more
A25–34	= coefficient of dummy for age between 25 and 34
A35–44	= coefficient of dummy for age between 35 and 44
A45–54	= coefficient of dummy for age between 45 and 54
A55–64	= coefficient of dummy for age between 55 and 64
A65+	= coefficient of dummy for age of 65 and over
RNC	= coefficient of dummy for family living in the North Central region
RS	= coefficient of dummy for family living in the South
RW	= coefficient of dummy for family living in the West
NW	= coefficient of dummy for nonwhite family
RUR	= coefficient of dummy for family living in rural area

$$D(p) = -1 \ -.03491 \ \ln PEN \ -.08171 \ \ln PF \ + \ .06189 \ \ln PCG$$
$$\qquad\quad (.000998) \qquad\quad (.00238) \qquad\quad (.00214)$$

$$-.002060 \ \ln PK \ + \ .05679 \ \ln PCS$$
$$\quad (.00300) \qquad\quad (.00233)$$

Table 1. (*Continued*)

Parameter	Estimate	Standard Error
Energy:		
CONST	−.3754	.00923
ln PEN	.09151	.0134
ln PF	−.1441	.0214
ln PCG	−.06455	.0127
ln PK	.07922	.0171
ln PCS	.003061	.0138
ln M	.03491	.000997
S2	−.02402	.00139
S3	−.02971	.00163
S4	−.03144	.00178
S5	−.03255	.00206
S6	−.03606	.00249
S7+	−.02977	.00266
A25–34	.0002010	.00197
A35–44	−.006703	.00210
A45–54	−.01155	.00199
A55–64	−.01372	.00199
A65+	−.005487	.00196
RNC	−.003277	.00131
RS	.0001280	.00131
RW	.01281	.00140
NW	.01300	.00170
RUR	−.03057	.00134
Food:		
CONST	−.8917	.0215
ln PEN	−.1441	.0214
ln PF	.3118	.0428
ln PCG	.05547	.0215
ln PK	−.1982	.0334
ln PCS	−.1066	.0259
ln M	.08171	.00238
S2	−.04859	.00333
S3	−.06730	.00390
S4	−.08881	.00428
S5	−.1108	.00496
S6	−.1185	.00598
S7+	−.1471	.00639
A25–34	−.04393	.00474
A35–44	−.08221	.00504
A45–54	−.09604	.00478
A55–64	−.1034	.00477
A65+	−.08833	.00470
RNC	.01873	.00315
RS	.01213	.00314
RW	.01856	.00337
NW	.006274	.00409
RUR	−.001793	.00323

Table 1. (Continued)

Parameter	Estimate	Standard Error
Consumer goods:		
CONST	.4053	.0194
ln PEN	− .06455	.0127
ln PF	.05547	.0215
ln PCG	.2301	.0269
ln PK	− .1056	.0195
ln PCS	− .05354	.0271
ln M	− .06189	.00214
S2	− .005594	.00300
S3	− .006290	.00351
S4	− .001941	.00385
S5	.004522	.00446
S6	.01059	.00539
S7 +	.01495	.00575
A25–34	− .02311	.00426
A35–44	− .01916	.00454
A45–54	− .005279	.00431
A55–64	− .009068	.00429
A65 +	− .01722	.00423
RNC	− .02098	.00283
RS	− .03553	.00283
RW	− .009928	.00304
NW	− .02648	.00368
RUR	− .01122	.00290
Capital services:		
CONST	− .4658	.0270
ln PEN	.07922	.0171
ln PF	− .1982	.0334
ln PCG	− .1056	.0195
ln PK	.2038	.0368
ln PCS	.01869	.0165
ln M	.002060	.00300
S2	.07355	.00421
S3	.09982	.00493
S4	.1148	.00541
S5	.1253	.00626
S6	.1284	.00756
S7 +	.1369	.00807
A25–34	.04362	.00599
A35–44	.08503	.00637
A45–54	.1166	.00605
A55–64	.1395	.00603
A65 +	.1296	.00595
RNC	.02767	.00398
RS	.05528	.00397
RW	− .004132	.00427
NW	− .003539	.00517
RUR	.05588	.00408

Table 1. (*Continued*)

Parameter	Estimate	Standard Error
Consumer services:		
CONST	.3277	.0211
ln PEN	.003061	.0138
ln PF	−.1066	.0259
ln PCG	−.05354	.0271
ln PK	.01869	.0165
ln PCS	.1952	.0375
ln M	−.05679	.00233
S2	.004666	.00327
S3	.003483	.00383
S4	.007338	.00420
S5	.01357	.00486
S6	.01561	.00587
S7+	.02508	.00627
A25–34	.02321	.00465
A35–44	.02304	.00495
A45–54	−.003805	.00470
A55–64	−.01332	.00468
A65+	−.01863	.00462
RNC	−.02214	.00309
RS	−.03200	.00308
RW	−.01731	.00331
NW	.01074	.00401
RUR	−.01229	.00317

[a] Convergence after three iterations; SSR = 37387.12; convergence criterion = .00001.

four equations in the matrix B_{pA}, and 10 price coefficients in the matrix B_{pp}, which is constrained to be symmetric. The expenditure coefficients are sums of price coefficients in the corresponding equation, so that we have a total of 82 unknown parameters. We estimate the complete model, subject to inequality restrictions implied by monotonicity of the individual expenditure shares, by pooling time-series and cross-section data.[17] The results are given in Table 1.

The impacts of changes in total expenditures and in demographic characteristics of the individual household are estimated very precisely. This reflects the fact that estimates of the expenditure and demographic effects incorporate a relatively large number of cross-section observations. The impacts of prices enter through the denominator of the equations for expenditure shares; these price coefficients are estimated very precisely since they also incorporate cross section data. Finally, the price impacts also enter through the numerators of equations for the expenditure shares. These parameters are estimated somewhat less precisely, since they are based on a much smaller number of time-series observations on prices.

To Summarize

We have implemented an econometric model of aggregate consumer behavior by combining time-series and cross-section data for the United States. This model allocates personal consumption expenditures among five commodity groups—energy, food, other consumer goods, capital services, and other consumer services. Households are classified by five sets of demographic characteristics—family size, age of head, region of residence, race, and urban versus rural residence.

IV. SOCIAL WELFARE FUNCTIONS

Our next objective is to generate a class of possible social welfare functions that can provide the basis for analyzing inequality in the distribution of individual welfare. For this purpose we must choose social welfare functions capable of expressing the implications of a variety of different ethical judgments. To facilitate comparisons with alternative approaches, we employ the axiomatic framework for social choice used by Arrow (1963), Sen (1970), and Roberts (1980a) in proving the impossibility of a nondictatorial social ordering.

We consider the set of all possible social orderings over the set of social states, say X, and the set of all possible real-valued individual welfare functions, say W_k ($k = 1, 2, \ldots, K$). A social ordering, say R, is a complete, reflexive, and transitive ordering of social states. A social state is described by the quantities consumed of N commodity groups by K individuals. The individual welfare function for the kth individual W_k ($k = 1, 2, \ldots, K$) is defined on the set of social states X and gives the level of individual welfare for that individual in each state.

To describe social orderings in greater detail we find it useful to introduce the following notation:

x—a matrix with elements $\{x_{nk}\}$ describing the social state;
$u = (W_1, W_2, \ldots, W_k)$—a vector of individual welfare functions of all K individuals.

Following Sen (1970, 1977) and Hammond (1976) we define a *social welfare functional*, say f, as a mapping from the set of individual welfare functions to the set of social orderings, such that $f(u') = f(u)$ implies $R' = R$, where

$$u = [W_1(x), W_2(x), \ldots, W_K(x)]$$

and

$$u' = [W_1'(x), W_2'(x), \ldots, W_K'(x)],$$

for all $x \in X$. Similarly, we define L_k ($k = 1, 2, \ldots, K$) as the *set of admissible individual welfare functions* for the kth individual and L as the Cartesian product $\prod_{k=1}^{K} L_k$. Finally, let **L** be the partition of L such that all elements of **L** yield the same social ordering.

We can describe a social ordering in terms of the following properties of a social welfare functional:

1. UNRESTRICTED DOMAIN: *The social welfare functional f is defined for all possible vectors of individual welfare functions u.*

2. INDEPENDENCE OF IRRELEVANT ALTERNATIVES: *For any subset A contained in X, if u(x) = u'(x) for all x ∈ A, then R:A = R':A, where R = f(u) and R' = f(u') and R:A is the social ordering over the subset A.*

3. POSITIVE ASSOCIATION: *For any vectors of individual welfare functions u and u', if for all y in X − x, such that*

$$W_k'(y) = W_k(y)$$
$$k = 1, 2, \ldots, K,$$
$$W_k'(x) > W_k(x)$$

then xPy implies xP'y and yP'x implies yPx, where P is a strict ordering of social states.

4. NONIMPOSITION: *For all x, y in X there exist u, u' such that xPy and yP'x.*

5. CARDINAL FULL COMPARABILITY: *The set of admissible individual welfare functions that yield the same social ordering **L** is defined by:*

$$\mathbf{L} = \{u': \ W_k'(x) = \alpha + \beta W_k(x), \ \beta > 0, \ k = 1, 2, \ldots, K\},$$

*and f(u') = f(u) for all u' ∈ **L**.*

Cardinal full comparability implies that social orderings are invariant with respect to any positive affine transformation of the individual welfare functions $\{W_k\}$ that is the same for all individuals. By contrast Arrow requires ordinal noncomparability,[18] which implies that social orderings are invariant with respect to monotone increasing transformations of the individual welfare functions that may differ among individuals:

5'. ORDINAL NONCOMPARABILITY: *The set of individual welfare functions that yield the same social ordering **L** is defined by*

$$\mathbf{L} = \{u': \ W_k'(x) = \phi_k[W_k(x)]; \ \phi_k \ increasing; \ k = 1, 2, \ldots, K\},$$

*and f(u') = f(u) for all u' in **L**.*

The properties of a social welfare functional corresponding to unrestricted domain and independence of irrelevant alternatives are used by Arrow in proving the impossibility of a nondictatorial social ordering:

4′. NONDICTATORSHIP: *There is no individual k such that for all x, y $\in X$, $W_k(x) > W_k(y)$ implies xPy.*

Under ordinal noncomparability the assumptions of positive association and nonimposition employed by Arrow imply the weak Pareto principle:

3′. PARETO PRINCIPLE: *For any x, y $\in X$, if $W_k(x) > W_k(y)$ for all individuals (k = 1, 2, . . . , k), then xPy.*

If a social welfare functional f has the properties of unrestricted domain, independence of irrelevant alternatives, the weak Pareto principle, and ordinal noncomparability, then no nondictatorial social ordering is possible. This result is Arrow's impossibility theorem. Since it is obvious that the class of dictatorial social orderings is too narrow to provide an adequate basis for expressing the implications of alternative ethical judgments, we propose to generate a class of social welfare functions suitable for the evaluation of alternative economic policies by weakening Arrow's assumptions.

We first consider weakening the assumption of ordinal noncomparability of individual welfare functions. Sen (1970) has shown that Arrow's conclusion that no nondictatorial social ordering is possible is preserved by replacing ordinal noncomparability by cardinal noncomparability. This implies that social orderings are invariant with respect to positive affine transformations of the individual welfare functions that may differ among individuals:

5″. CARDINAL NONCOMPARABILITY: *The set of individual welfare functions that yield the same social ordering* **L** *is defined by*

L = $(u': W'_k(x) = \alpha_k + \beta_k W_k(x); \beta_k > 0; k = 1, 2, . . . , K)$,

and $f(u') = f(u)$ for all u′ in **L**.

However, d'Aspremont and Gevers (1977), Deschamps and Gevers (1978), Maskin (1978), and Roberts (1980b) have shown that we obtain an interesting class of nondictatorial social orderings by requiring cardinal unit comparability of individual welfare functions, which implies that social orderings are invariant with respect to positive affine transformations with units that are the same for all individuals:

5‴. CARDINAL UNIT COMPARABILITY: *The set of individual welfare functions that yield the same social ordering* **L** *is defined by*

$$\mathbf{L} = \{u': \quad W_k'(x) = \alpha_k + \beta W_k(x); \quad \beta > 0; \quad k = 1, 2, \ldots, K\},$$

and $f(u') = f(u)$ *for all* u' *in* **L**.

If a social welfare functional f has the properties of unrestricted domain, independence of irrelevant alternatives, the weak Pareto principle, and cardinal unit comparability, there exist social orderings and a continuous real-valued social welfare function, say W, such that if $W[u(x)] > W[u(y)]$, then xPy. Furthermore, the social welfare function can be represented in the form:

$$W[u(x)] = \sum_{k=1}^{K} a_k W_k(x). \tag{4.1}$$

If we add the assumption that the social welfare function has the property of anonymity, that is, no individual is given greater weight than any other individual in determining the level of social welfare, then the social welfare function W in (4.1) must be symmetric in the individual welfare functions $\{W_k\}$. The property of anonymity incorporates a notion of horizontal equity into the representation of social orderings.

Under anonymity the function W in (4.1) reduces to the sum of individual welfare functions and takes the form of a utilitarian social welfare function. Utilitarian social welfare functions have been employed extensively in applications of welfare economics, especially in the measurement of inequality by methods originated by Atkinson (1970) and Kolm (1969, 1976a,b), in the design of optimal income tax schedules along the lines pioneered by Mirrlees (1971), and in the evaluation of alternative economic policies by Arrow and Kalt (1979).

The approach to the measurement of social welfare based on a utilitarian social welfare function provides a worthwhile starting point for applications. Harsanyi (1976) and Ng (1975) have pointed out that distributional considerations can be incorporated into a utilitarian social welfare function through the representation of individual welfare functions. However, Sen (1973, p. 18) has argued that a utilitarian social welfare function does not take appropriate account of the distribution of welfare among individuals:

> The distribution of welfare between persons is a relevant aspect of any problem of income distribution, and our evaluation of inequality will obviously depend on whether we are concerned only with the loss of the sum of individual utilities through a bad distribution of income, or also with the inequality of welfare levels of different individuals.

To broaden the range of possible social orderings we can require cardinal full comparability of individual welfare functions, as defined above. Roberts (1980b) has shown that a social welfare functional f with the properties of unrestricted domain, independence of irrelevant alternatives, the weak Pareto principle, and cardinal full comparability implies the existence of a social welfare function that takes the form:

$$W[u(x)] = \overline{W}(x) + g[u(x) - \overline{W}(x) i], \qquad (4.2)$$

where i is a vector of ones; the function $\overline{W}(x)$ corresponds to average individual welfare:

$$\overline{W}(x) = \sum_{k=1}^{K} a_k W_k(x);$$

and $g(x)$ is a linear homogeneous function of deviations of levels of individual welfare from the average.[19]

If the function $g(x)$ in the representation (4.2) of the social welfare function is identically equal to zero, then the social welfare function reduces to the form (4.1). If the function $g(x)$ is not identically zero, then the social welfare function incorporates both a measure of average individual welfare and a measure of inequality in the distribution of individual welfare. We conclude that the class of possible social welfare functions (4.2) includes utilitarian welfare functions but also includes functions that are not subject to the objections that can be made to utilitarianism.

Although Roberts (1980b) has succeeded in broadening the class of possible social welfare functions beyond those consistent with utilitarianism, the social welfare functions (4.2) are subject to an objection raised by Sen (1973).[20] Information about alternative social states enters only through the individual welfare functions $\{W_k\}$. Sen refers to this property of a social welfare functional f as *welfarism*. Welfarism rules out characteristics of a social state that are conceivably relevant for social orderings but that cannot be incorporated into the social welfare function through the individual welfare functions.

Roberts (1980b) has suggested the possibility of further weakening Arrow's assumptions in order to incorporate nonwelfare characteristics of social states.[21] For this purpose we can replace the weak Pareto principle by positive association and nonimposition, as defined above. We retain the assumptions of unrestricted domain, independence of irrelevant alternatives, and cardinal full comparability of measures of individual welfare. We can partition the set of social states X into subsets such that all states within each subset have the same nonwelfare characteristics. For each subset there exists a social ordering that can be represented by a social welfare function of the form (4.2).

Under the assumptions we have outlined there exists a social ordering for the set of all social states that can be represented by a social welfare function of the form:

$$W(u, x) = F\{\overline{W}(x) + g[x, u(x) - \overline{W}(x) i], x\}, \qquad (4.3)$$

where the function $\overline{W}(x)$ corresponds to average individual welfare:

$$\overline{W}(x) = \sum_{k=1}^{K} a_k(x) W_k(x).$$

As before, the function g is a linear homogeneous function of deviations of levels of individual welfare from average welfare.

The class of social welfare functions (4.3) incorporates nonwelfare characteristics of social states through the weights $\{a_k(x)\}$ in average individual welfare $\overline{W}(x)$, through the function $g(x)$, which depends directly on the social state x as well as on deviations of levels of individual welfare from the average welfare, and through the function F, which depends directly on the social state x and on the sum of the functions $\overline{W}(x)$ and $g(x)$. This class includes social welfare functions that are not subject to the objections that can be made to welfarism.

At this point we have generated a class of possible social welfare functions capable of expressing the implications of a variety of different ethical judgments. In order to choose a specific social welfare function, we must narrow the range of possible ethical judgments by imposing further requirements on the class of possible social welfare functions. First, we must limit the dependence of the function $F(x)$ in (4.3) on the characteristics of alternative social states. Second, we must select a form for the function $g(x)$ in (4.3), which depends on deviations of levels of individual welfare from average welfare $\overline{W}(x)$. Finally, we must choose representations of the individual welfare functions $\{W_k(x)\}$ that provide cardinal full comparability.

We first rule out the dependence of the function $F(x)$ in (4.3) on characteristics of social states that do not enter through the functions $\overline{W}(x)$ and $g(x)$. This restriction reduces F to a function of a single variable $\overline{W} + g$. We obtain an ordinal measure of social welfare by permitting the function F to be any monotone increasing transformation. To obtain a cardinal measure of social welfare we observe that the function $\overline{W}(x) + g$ is homogeneous of degree one in the individual welfare functions $\{W_k(x)\}$. All representations of the social welfare function that preserve this property can be written in the form:

$$W(u, x) = \beta[\overline{W}(x) + g(x)] \qquad (\beta > 0). \qquad (4.4)$$

We conclude that only positive, homogeneous, affine transformations are permitted.

The restrictions embodied in the class of social welfare functions (4.4) do not reduce social welfare to a function of the individual welfare functions $\{W_k(x)\}$ alone, since the weights $\{a_k(x)\}$ in average individual welfare $\overline{W}(x)$ and the function $g(x)$ depend on nonwelfare characteristics of the social state x. However, these social welfare functions are homogeneous of degree 1 in levels of individual welfare. This implies that doubling the welfare of each individual will double social welfare, holding nonwelfare characteristics of the social state constant. Blackorby and Donaldson (1982) refer to this class of social welfare functions as *distributionally homothetic*.[22]

We impose a second set of requirements on the class of social welfare functions (4.3) by selecting an appropriate form for the function $g(x)$. In particular, we require that this function is additive in deviations of individual welfare functions $\{W_k(x)\}$ from average welfare $\overline{W}(x)$. Since the function $g(x)$ is homogeneous of degree 1, it must be a mean value function of order $\rho(x)$:[23]

$$g[x, u(x) - \overline{W}(x) \, i] = -\gamma(x) \left[\sum_{k=1}^{K} b_k(x) \, | \, W_k - \overline{W} \, |^{-\rho(x)} \right]^{-1/\rho(x)}, \quad (4.5)$$

where

$$\gamma(x) > 0; \qquad \rho(x) \leqq -1; \qquad \sum_{k=1}^{K} b_k(x) = 1;$$

$$0 < b_k(x) < 1 \qquad (k = 1, 2, \ldots, K).$$

Under these restrictions the function $g(x)$ is negative, except at the point of perfect equality $W_k = \overline{W}(x)$ $(k = 1, 2, \ldots, K)$, where it is zero. The function $\rho(x)$ in the representation (4.5) determines the curvature of the social welfare function in the individual welfare functions $\{W_k(x)\}$. We can refer to this function as the *degree of aversion to inequality*. We assume that the degree of aversion to inequality is constant. To complete the selection of an appropriate form for the social welfare function we must choose appropriate weights $\{a_k(x)\}$ for average individual welfare $\overline{W}(x)$ and $\{b_k(x)\}$ for the measure of equality $g(x)$. We find it natural to require that the two sets of weights are the same.

To incorporate a notion of horizontal equity into the social welfare functions (4.5) we can impose a weak form of the property of anonymity. In particular, we require that no individual is given greater weight in the social welfare function than any other individual with an identical individual welfare function. This implies that the social welfare function is symmetric in the levels of individual welfare for identical individuals. The weights $\{a_k(x)\}$ in average welfare $\overline{W}(x)$ and the measure of $g(x)$ must be the same for identical individuals.

Under the restrictions presented up to this point the social welfare function W takes the form:

$$W(u, x) = \overline{W} - \gamma(x) \left[\sum_{k=1}^{K} a_k(x) \mid W_k - \overline{W} \mid^{-\rho} \right]^{-1/\rho}, \qquad (4.6)$$

where

$$\overline{W}(x) = \sum_{k=1}^{K} a_k(x) \, W_k(x).$$

The condition of positive association requires that an increase in all levels of individual welfare must increase social welfare. This condition implies that the average level of individual welfare $\overline{W}$ must increase by more than the function $g(x)$ whatever the initial distribution of individual welfare. We assume that the function $\gamma(x)$ in (4.6) must take the maximum value consistent with positive association, so that

$$\gamma(x) = \left\{ 1 + \left[\frac{\sum_{k=1}^{K} a_k(x)}{a_j(x)} \right]^{-(\rho+1)} \right\}^{1/\rho}, \qquad (4.7)$$

where

$$a_j(x) = \min_k a_k(x) \qquad (k = 1, 2, \ldots, K),$$

for the social state x.

To complete the selection of a social welfare function $W(u, x)$ we require that the individual welfare functions $\{W_k\}$ in (4.3) must be invariant with respect to any positive affine transformation that is the same for all households.[24] Under this assumption the logarithm of the translog indirect utility function is a cardinal measure of individual welfare with full comparability among households. The social welfare function takes the form:

$$W(u, x) = \ln \overline{V} - \gamma(x) \left[\sum_{k=1}^{K} a_k(x) \mid \ln V_k - \ln \overline{V} \mid^{-\rho} \right]^{-1/\rho}, \qquad (4.8)$$

where

$$\ln \overline{V} = \sum_{k=1}^{K} a_k(x) \ln V_k \left[\frac{p \, m(A_k)}{M_k} \right].$$

We can complete the specification of a social welfare function $W(u, x)$ by choosing a set of weights $\{a_k(x)\}$ for the levels of individual welfare $\{\ln V_k[p \, m(A_k)/M_k]\}$ in (4.8). For this purpose we must appeal to a notion of vertical equity. Following Hammond (1977), we define a distribution of total expenditure $\{M_k\}$ as more *equitable* than another distribution $\{M'_k\}$ if

(i) $M_i + M_j = M'_i + M'_j$;

(ii) $M_k = M'_k$ (for $k \neq i, j$);

(iii) $\ln V_i \left[\dfrac{p \, m(A_i)}{M'_i} \right] > \ln V_i \left[\dfrac{p \, m(A_i)}{M_i} \right] > \ln V_j \left[\dfrac{p \, m(A_j)}{M_j} \right]$

$> \ln V_j \left[\dfrac{p \, m(A_j)}{M'_j} \right]$.

We say that a social welfare function $W(u, x)$ is an *equity-regarding* function if it is larger for a more equitable distribution of total expenditure.

We require that the social welfare functions (4.8) must be equity-regarding functions. This amounts to imposing a version of Dalton's (1920) principle of transfers. This principle requires that a transfer of total expenditures from a rich household to a poor household that does not reverse their relative positions in the distribution of total expenditure must increase the level of social welfare.

If the social welfare functions (4.8) are required to be equity-regarding functions, then the weights $\{a_k(x)\}$ associated with the individual welfare functions $\{\ln V_k[p \, m(A_k)/M_k]\}$ must take the form:

$$a_k(x) = \frac{m_0(p, A_k)}{\sum_{k=1}^{K} m_0(p, A_k)} \qquad (k = 1, 2, \ldots, K). \tag{4.9}$$

We conclude that an equity-regarding social welfare function of the class (4.8) must take the form:

$$W(u, x) = \ln \overline{V} - \gamma(x) \left[\frac{\sum_{k=1}^{K} m_0(p, A_k) \, | \ln V_k - \ln \overline{V} |^{-\rho}}{\sum_{k=1}^{K} m_0(p, A_k)} \right]^{-1/\rho},$$

$$\tag{4.10}$$

where

$$\ln \overline{V} = \frac{\sum_{k=1}^{K} m_0(p, A_k) \ln V_k[p \, m(A_k)/M_k]}{\sum_{k=1}^{K} m_0(p, A_k)}$$

$$= \ln p' \left(\alpha_p + \frac{1}{2} B_{pp} \ln p \right)$$

$$- D(p) \frac{\sum_{k=1}^{K} m_0(p, A_k) \ln [M_k/m_0(p, A_k)]}{\sum_{k=1}^{K} m_0(p, A_k)}.$$

Furthermore, the condition of positive association implies that the function $\gamma(x)$ in (4.8) must take the form:

$$\gamma(x) = \left\{ 1 + \left[\frac{\sum_{k=1}^{K} m_0(p, A_k)}{m_0(p, A_j)} \right]^{-(\rho+1)} \right\}^{-1/\rho}, \tag{4.11}$$

where

$$m_0(p, A_j) = \min_k m_0(p, A_k) \quad (k = 1, 2, \ldots, K).$$

To Summarize

We have generated a class of social welfare functions (4.3) that has the properties of unrestricted domain, independence of irrelevant alternatives, positive association, nonimposition, and cardinal full comparability. By imposing the additional assumption that the degree of aversion to inequality is constant and requiring the social welfare function to satisfy requirements of horizonal and vertical equity, we obtain the social welfare functions (4.10).

V.   INDEXES OF INEQUALITY

In this section we develop indexes of inequality in the distribution of individual welfare. For this purpose we decompose the measures of social welfare presented in Section IV into measures of efficiency and measures of equity. Efficiency can be defined as the maximum level of welfare that is potentially available through redistributions of aggregate expenditure. We define an absolute index of inequality as the difference between the measure of efficiency and the actual level of social welfare.[25] Finally, we define a relative measure of inequality as the ratio between the absolute index of inequality and the measure of efficiency.[26]

In order to decompose social welfare into measures of efficiency and equity, we first maximize social welfare for a fixed level of aggregate expenditure. We can maximize the average level of individual welfare for a given level of aggregate expenditure by means of the Lagrangian:

$$
\begin{aligned}
Z &= \ln \overline{V} + \lambda \left[\sum_{k=1}^{K} M_k - M \right] \\
&= \ln p' \left(\alpha_p + \frac{1}{2} B_{pp} \ln p \right) \\
&\quad - D(p) \frac{\sum_{k=1}^{K} m_0(p, A_k) \ln [M_k/m_0(p, A_k)]}{\sum_{k=1}^{K} m_0(p, A_k)} \\
&\quad + \lambda \left[\sum_{k=1}^{K} M_k - M \right].
\end{aligned}
\tag{5.1}
$$

The first-order conditions for a constrained maximum of average individual welfare are

$$
\left.
\begin{aligned}
\frac{D(p)}{\sum_{k=1}^{K} m_0(p, A_k)} \cdot \frac{m_0(p, A_k)}{M_k} &= \lambda \\
\sum_{k=1}^{K} M_k &= M
\end{aligned}
\right] \quad (k = 1, 2, \ldots, K),
$$

so that total expenditure per household equivalent member $\{M_k/m_0(p, A_k)\}$ is the same for all consuming units.

Next we consider the class of social welfare functions (4.6). Since the function $g(x, u - \overline{W} i)$ is nonpositive, we obtain a maximum of the social welfare function if the function $g(x, u - \overline{W} i)$ can be made equal to zero while the average level of individual welfare $\overline{W}$ is a maximum. If total expenditure per household equivalent member $\{M_k/m_0(p, A_k)\}$ is the same for all consuming units, the function $g(x, u - \overline{W} i)$ is equal to zero, so that the social welfare function $W(u, x)$ in (4.6) is a maximum.

If aggregate expenditure is distributed so as to equalize total expenditure per household equivalent member, the level of individual welfare is the same for all consuming units. For this distribution of total expenditure the social welfare functions (4.6) reduce to the average level of individual welfare $\ln \overline{V}$. For the translog indirect utility function the social welfare function takes the form:

$$E(x, u) = \ln \overline{V} \tag{5.2}$$
$$= \ln p' \left(\alpha_p + \frac{1}{2} B_{pp} \ln p \right) - D(p) \ln \left[\frac{M}{\sum_{k=1}^{K} m_0(p, A_k)} \right].$$

This is the maximum level of welfare that is potentially available and can be taken as a measure of efficiency. We can refer to this measure as the *translog index of efficiency*. The translog index is equal to the translog indirect utility function (2.22), evaluated at aggregate expenditure per household equivalent member for society as a whole.

Given the translog index of efficiency (5.2), defined in terms of the social welfare function, we can define a measure of inequality as the difference between the translog index of efficiency and the actual value of the social welfare function:

$$I(x, u) = E(x, u) - W(x, u). \tag{5.3}$$

We can refer to this measure as the *translog index of inequality*. Since the index of efficiency is always greater than or equal to the social welfare function $W(u, x)$, the index of inequality $I(x, u)$ is nonnegative. This index is equal to zero only at the point of perfect equality, where total expenditure per household equivalent member is the same for all consuming units. Finally, the social welfare function can be decomposed into the sum of measures of efficiency and equity:

$$W(u, x) = E(u, x) - I(u, x). \tag{5.4}$$

Similarly, we can define a relative measure of inequality, say $J(x)$, as

$$J(x) = 1 - \frac{W(u, x)}{E(u, x)}$$

$$= \frac{I(u, x)}{E(u, x)}.$$

We can refer to this measure as the *translog index of relative inequality*. The index of relative inequality lies between 0 and 1 and is 0 only at the point of perfect equality. It is important to note that measures of inequality are usually defined in terms of the distribution of income or total expenditure, rather than the distribution of individual welfare.[27] The indexes of inequality I and J are defined in terms of the distribution of individual welfare.[28]

To illustrate the measurement of inequality in the distribution of individual welfare we can represent the indexes of inequality I and J in diagrammatic form. For simplicity we consider the case of a society consisting of two identical individuals ($K = 2$). In Figure 1 we have depicted

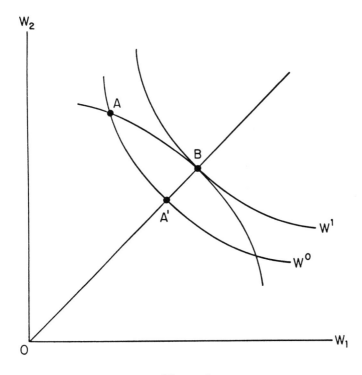

Figure 1

the contours of a concave social welfare function. The 45° line through the origin represents distributions of individual welfare characterized by perfect equality ($W_1 = W_2$). Under anonymity the contours of the social welfare function are symmetric around the line of perfect equality. Under distributional homotheticity distances between contours are in the same proportion along any ray from the origin.

We can represent the actual distribution of individual welfare by the point A with level of social welfare W^0. To measure the potential level of social welfare we consider levels of individual welfare corresponding to all possible lump sum redistributions of aggregate expenditure $M = M_1 + M_2$. The maximum level of social welfare is attained at the point B corresponding to perfect equality in the distribution of individual welfare. The potential level of social welfare is W^1.

In Figure 1, the point A' represents perfect equality in the distribution of individual welfare at the same level of social welfare W^0 as at point A. The actual level of social welfare W^0 can be represented by the distance OA'. The level of efficiency W^1 can be represented by the distance OB. The absolute index of inequality I is represented by the distance $OB - OA' = A'B$. The relative index of inequality J is represented by the ratio $A'B/OB$. Under distributional homotheticity, this ratio is the same for distances between the contours corresponding to social welfare levels W^0 and W^1 along any ray from the origin.

We can also illustrate the measurement of inequality in the distribution of individual welfare by considering actual and potential levels of social welfare over the period 1958–1978. The first step in measuring inequality is to evaluate the actual level of social welfare. Levels of social welfare for alternative values of the degree of aversion to inequality ρ are presented in Table 2. The first term in the social welfare functions (4.10) represents an average of individual welfare levels over all consuming units, while the second term in these functions is a measure of dispersion in individual welfare levels. The unit for measurement of individual welfare is the level of welfare of a white household with one family member, aged 16–24, living in the Northeast region of the United States in an urban residence, facing prices equal to unity, and having the log of total expenditure equal to unity. Social welfare is measured in the same units as individual welfare.

To decompose each measure of social welfare into measures of efficiency and equity we maximize social welfare for a fixed level of aggregate expenditure to obtain a measure of efficiency or potential social welfare. The maximum value results from equalizing total expenditure per household equivalent member over all households. This provides a translog index of efficiency that is independent of the value of the degree of aversion to inequality ρ. An index of efficiency for the years 1958–1978 is presented in Table 2.

We can define the translog index of inequality as the difference between the translog index of efficiency and the actual value of the social welfare function. This index of inequality is nonnegative and equal to zero under perfect equality with total expenditure per household equivalent member the same for all households. Since the value of the social welfare function depends on the degree of aversion to inequality ρ, we have presented measures of inequality for alternative values of this parameter for the years 1958–1978 in Table 3.

We find it useful to present our measures of inequality in relative form by means of the translog index of relative inequality. We have defined this index as the ratio of the translog index of inequality to the translog index of efficiency. This ratio varies between 0 and 1 and is equal to 0 under perfect equality. Translog indexes of relative inequality are presented for alternative values of the degree of aversion to inequality ρ for the years 1958–1978 in Table 3.

Table 2. Levels of Social Welfare

Year	Actual Levels of Social Welfare		Translog Index of Efficiency
	$\rho = -1$	$\rho = -2$	
1958	7.08032	7.32138	7.49464
1959	7.12603	7.35945	7.52364
1960	7.15476	7.38594	7.54755
1961	7.16900	7.39788	7.55669
1962	7.18551	7.41395	7.57203
1963	7.21120	7.43712	7.59225
1964	7.24447	7.47186	7.62946
1965	7.29288	7.51858	7.67355
1966	7.33922	7.56292	7.71515
1967	7.35314	7.57707	7.73013
1968	7.39051	7.61350	7.76569
1969	7.41633	7.63909	7.79087
1970	7.44096	7.66264	7.81313
1971	7.45043	7.67184	7.82248
1972	7.49446	7.71466	7.86315
1973	7.53176	7.75304	7.90208
1974	7.52867	7.75005	7.89760
1975	7.53466	7.75673	7.90548
1976	7.56748	7.78750	7.93436
1977	7.60081	7.81870	7.96333
1978	7.63985	7.85778	8.00183

Table 3. Indexes of Inequality

Year	Translog Index of Inequality		Translog Index of Relative Inequality	
	$\rho = -1$	$\rho = -2$	$\rho = -1$	$\rho = -2$
1958	0.41432	0.17326	0.05528	0.02312
1959	0.39761	0.16419	0.05285	0.02182
1960	0.39280	0.16161	0.05204	0.02141
1961	0.38769	0.15881	0.05130	0.02102
1962	0.38652	0.15808	0.05105	0.02088
1963	0.38105	0.15513	0.05019	0.02043
1964	0.38499	0.15760	0.05046	0.02066
1965	0.38067	0.15496	0.04961	0.02019
1966	0.37593	0.15224	0.04873	0.01973
1967	0.37699	0.15306	0.04877	0.01980
1968	0.37518	0.15219	0.04831	0.01960
1969	0.37454	0.15178	0.04807	0.01948
1970	0.37216	0.15049	0.04763	0.01926
1971	0.37205	0.15064	0.04756	0.01926
1972	0.36869	0.14849	0.04689	0.01888
1973	0.37032	0.14904	0.04686	0.01886
1974	0.36893	0.14755	0.04671	0.01868
1975	0.37082	0.14875	0.04691	0.01882
1976	0.36688	0.14686	0.04624	0.01851
1977	0.36253	0.14463	0.04552	0.01816
1978	0.36198	0.14405	0.04524	0.01800

To Summarize

In order to analyze inequality in the distribution of individual welfare we can decompose the measures of social welfare (4.10) into measures of efficiency and equity. Our measure of efficiency is the translog indirect utility function (5.2), evaluated at aggregate expenditure per household equivalent member for society as a whole. The translog index of inequality is the difference between the translog index of efficiency and the actual value of the social welfare function. The translog index of relative inequality is the ratio between the translog index of inequality and the translog index of efficiency.

VI. INEQUALITY WITHIN GROUPS

In Section V we have presented indexes of inequality in the distribution of individual welfare for the U.S. economy as a whole. In this section our objective is to develop indexes of inequality in the distribution of individual welfare within subgroups of the U.S. population. For this purpose we introduce group welfare functions that are precisely analogous to the social welfare functions of Section IV. We consider a group of G individuals, where $1 \leq G \leq K$; without loss of generality we can take the group to be composed of the first G individuals in the society.

To describe group orderings we find it useful to introduce the following notation:

x_{ng}—the quantity of the nth commodity group consumed by the gth consuming unit ($n = 1, 2, \ldots, N; g = 1, 2, \ldots, G$);
x_G—a matrix with elements $\{x_{ng}\}$ describing the group state;
$u_G = (W_1, W_2, \ldots, W_G)$—a vector of individual welfare functions for all G individuals.

We can define a group welfare functional as a mapping from the set of individual welfare functions to the set of group orderings. We can describe a group ordering in terms of properties of a group welfare functional that are precisely analogous to the properties of a social welfare functional considered in Section IV: unrestricted domain, independence of irrelevant alternatives, positive association, nonimposition, and cardinal full comparability. Under these assumptions there exists a group ordering for the set of all group states that can be represented by a group welfare function analogous to the social welfare function (4.3):

$$W_G(u_G, x_G) = F\{\overline{W}_G(x_G) + g[x_G, u_G(x_G) - \overline{W}_G(x_G) i], x_G\}, \quad (6.1)$$

where the function $\overline{W}_G(x_G)$ corresponds to average individual welfare:

$$\overline{W}_G(x_G) = \sum_{g=1}^{G} a_g(x_G) W_g(x_G).$$

As before, the function g is a linear homogeneous function of deviations of levels of individual welfare from average welfare for the group.

We can rule out the direct dependence of the function $F(x_G)$ in (6.1) on characteristics of group states x_G. As in Section IV, this results in a cardinal representation of group welfare. To complete the selection of a group welfare function $W_G(u_G, x_G)$ we require, as before, that the individual welfare functions $\{W_g(x_G)\}$ must be invariant with respect to any positive affine transformation that is the same for all households. Second, we require that the group welfare function be an equity-regarding function. Under these assumptions the group welfare function must take forms analogous to (4.10).

Our next objective is to decompose group welfare into measures of efficiency and equity. For this purpose we can maximize group welfare for a fixed level of group expenditure $M_G = \sum_{g=1}^{G} M_g$ by equalizing total expenditure per household equivalent member for all households in the group. The maximum value of the group welfare function, say E_G, takes the form:

$$E_G(u_G, x_G) = \ln \overline{V}_G$$

$$= \ln p'\left(\alpha_p + \frac{1}{2} B_{pp} \ln p\right) - D(p)\left[\ln \frac{M_G}{\sum_{g=1}^{G} m_0(p, A_g)}\right],$$

(6.2)

where $\ln \overline{V}_G$ is the average level of individual welfare for the group. We can refer to the maximum value of group welfare that is potentially available, E_G, as the *translog index of group efficiency*. The translog index is equal to the translog indirect utility function (2.22), evaluated at group expenditure per household equivalent member.

Given the translog index of group efficiency (6.2), defined in terms of the group welfare function (6.1), we can define a measure of group inequality as the difference between the index of efficiency and the actual level of social welfare:

$$I_G(u_G, x_G) = E_G(u_G, x_G) - W_G(u_G, x_G).$$

(6.3)

The translog index of group inequality I_G is nonnegative and equal to zero only at the point of perfect equality, where total expenditure per household equivalent member is the same for all households in the group. The group welfare function can be decomposed into the sum of measures of group efficiency and group equity:

$$W_G(u_G, x_G) = E_G(u_G, x_G) - I_G(u_G, x_G).$$

(6.4)

We can define a translog index of group relative inequality, say $J_G(u_G, x_G)$, as

$$J_G(u_G, x_G) = 1 - \frac{W_G(u_G, x_G)}{E_G(u_G, x_G)}$$

$$= \frac{I_G(u_G, x_G)}{E_G(u_G, x_G)}.$$

(6.5)

The group index of relative inequality lies between 0 and 1 and is 0 only at the point of perfect equality within the group. We can represent the indexes of group inequality I_G and J_G in the same way as in Figure 1. If we consider contours of the group welfare function, say W_G^0 and W_G^1, rather than contours of the social welfare function, W^0 and W^1, we obtain diagrammatic interpretation of the indexes I_G and J_G that is precisely analogous to the interpretation of the indexes I and J given in Section V.

We can also illustrate the measurement of group inequality by considering actual and potential levels of group welfare for subgroups of the U.S. population classified by age of head of the household. The first step in measuring group inequality is to evaluate the actual level of group welfare. Levels of group welfare for six age groups are presented for the years 1958–1978 in the Appendix (Table A-1). We take the degree of aversion to inequality ρ to be minus unity in order to simplify the presentation. It would be possible to evaluate the level of group welfare for alternative values of this parameter.

To decompose each measure of group welfare into sums of measures of group efficiency and equity we maximize group welfare for a fixed level of group expenditure. The maximum value results from equalizing total expenditure per household equivalent member over all households in the group. This provides a translog index of group efficiency that is independent of the degree of aversion to inequality ρ. Indexes of group efficiency for six age groups of the U.S. population are presented in the Appendix (Table A-2) for the years 1958–1978.

We can define the translog index of group inequality as the difference between the translog index of group efficiency and the actual value of the group welfare function. This index of group inequality is equal to zero under perfect equality. Indexes of group inequality for six age groups of the U.S. population are presented in Table 4 for the years 1958–1978. As before, we take the degree of aversion to inequality ρ equal to minus unity.

We have defined the translog index of group relative inequality as the ratio of the translog index of group inequality to the translog index of group efficiency. This ratio varies between 0 and 1 and is equal to 0 under perfect equality. Translog indexes of group relative inequality for six age groups of the U.S. population are presented in Table 5 for the years 1958–1978. Again, we take the degree of aversion to inequality ρ equal to minus unity.

To Summarize

In this section we have developed measures of inequality within subgroups of the U.S. population. For this purpose we have introduced translog indexes of group inequality and relative inequality that are analogous to the indexes for the U.S. population as a whole presented in Section V. To illustrate the population of measures of inequality within subgroups we have presented translog indexes for six age groups for the years 1958–1978. Our methodology could also be used to provide measures of inequality within subgroups classified by the other demographic characteristics employed in the econometric model of Section III. These characteristics include family size, region of residence, race, and urban versus rural residence.

Table 4. Indexes of Group Inequality

	Age Groups					
Year	16–24	25–34	35–44	45–54	55–64	65+
1958	0.32704	0.39062	0.38851	0.41726	0.39114	0.39456
1959	0.32212	0.37565	0.36677	0.40085	0.38088	0.38831
1960	0.31762	0.36945	0.36389	0.39578	0.37478	0.38181
1961	0.31584	0.36889	0.36084	0.39368	0.37202	0.37807
1962	0.31769	0.37194	0.35975	0.39129	0.37147	0.37510
1963	0.31319	0.36615	0.35213	0.38694	0.36633	0.37152
1964	0.31347	0.37040	0.35762	0.39017	0.36462	0.36858
1965	0.31009	0.36402	0.35127	0.38439	0.36200	0.36701
1966	0.30624	0.35897	0.34543	0.37989	0.35618	0.36232
1967	0.30606	0.35916	0.34372	0.37810	0.35350	0.35930
1968	0.30847	0.36035	0.34245	0.37653	0.35130	0.35639
1969	0.30855	0.35728	0.33800	0.37295	0.34990	0.35607
1970	0.30832	0.35709	0.33745	0.37053	0.34604	0.35264
1971	0.30868	0.35670	0.33874	0.37107	0.34570	0.35196
1972	0.30306	0.35147	0.33627	0.36666	0.34301	0.35075
1973	0.30649	0.35353	0.33720	0.36759	0.34458	0.35270
1974	0.31004	0.35267	0.33694	0.36598	0.34580	0.35486
1975	0.31299	0.35414	0.34175	0.36789	0.34555	0.35497
1976	0.31094	0.35045	0.33620	0.36364	0.34326	0.35336
1977	0.30782	0.34617	0.33244	0.35975	0.34006	0.35083
1978	0.31048	0.34570	0.33167	0.35857	0.34118	0.35307

Table 5. Indexes of Group Relative Inequality

	Age Groups					
Year	16–24	25–34	35–44	45–54	55–64	65+
1958	0.04198	0.05113	0.05095	0.05666	0.05302	0.05381
1959	0.04160	0.04907	0.04788	0.05433	0.05128	0.05250
1960	0.04088	0.04816	0.04731	0.05339	0.05048	0.05138
1961	0.04071	0.04804	0.04693	0.05295	0.04995	0.05073
1962	0.04086	0.04844	0.04665	0.05246	0.04970	0.05039
1963	0.04011	0.04744	0.04561	0.05175	0.04884	0.04980
1964	0.03986	0.04775	0.04602	0.05198	0.04852	0.04905
1965	0.03929	0.04665	0.04492	0.05083	0.04790	0.04874
1966	0.03860	0.04572	0.04394	0.04990	0.04691	0.04792
1967	0.03856	0.04563	0.04353	0.04960	0.04649	0.04758
1968	0.03867	0.04571	0.04313	0.04921	0.04590	0.04698
1969	0.03872	0.04521	0.04233	0.04856	0.04561	0.04689
1970	0.03849	0.04506	0.04216	0.04812	0.04495	0.04629
1971	0.03876	0.04506	0.04218	0.04812	0.04488	0.04607
1972	0.03799	0.04429	0.04161	0.04726	0.04433	0.04566
1973	0.03832	0.04436	0.04148	0.04717	0.04431	0.04567
1974	0.03877	0.04437	0.04148	0.04701	0.04442	0.04587
1975	0.03911	0.04449	0.04202	0.04720	0.04448	0.04573
1976	0.03879	0.04395	0.04118	0.04645	0.04401	0.04534
1977	0.03838	0.04339	0.04056	0.04570	0.04340	0.04488
1978	0.03848	0.04323	0.04028	0.04529	0.04330	0.04492

VII.   INEQUALITY BETWEEN GROUPS

We have presented indexes of inequality in the distribution of individual welfare within subgroups of the U.S. population in Section VI. In this section our objective is to develop indexes of inequality between subgroups. For this purpose we introduce between-group welfare functions that are precisely analogous to the social welfare functions of Section IV. We first partition the population into B mutually exclusive and exhaustive groups. We suppose that the bth group has G_b individuals ($b = 1, 2, \ldots, B$). The sum of the number of individuals over all groups, say $\sum G_b$, is equal to the total population K.

We can express the potential level of welfare for each group as a function of the price system p and the level of group expenditure, say M_{G_b} ($b = 1, 2, \ldots, B$). This level of welfare can be attained by equalizing total expenditure per household equivalent member within the group. The potential level of group welfare corresponds to the value of the translog indirect utility function (6.2) at group expenditure per household equivalent member for the group as a whole. When actual group welfare is equal to potential group welfare, the group behaves like an individual household with a number of household equivalent members equal to the total for all households in the group.

To describe between-group orderings we find it useful to introduce the following notation:

x_{nb}—the quantity of the nth commodity group consumed by the bth group with actual group welfare equal to potential group welfare ($n = 1, 2, \ldots, N; b = 1, 2, \ldots, B$);

x_B—a matrix with elements $\{x_{nb}\}$ describing the between group states;

$u_B = (E_{G_1}, E_{G_2}, \ldots, E_{G_B})$—a vector of potential group welfare functions for all B groups.

We can define a between-group welfare functional as a mapping from the set of group welfare functions to the set of between-group orderings. We can describe a between-group ordering in terms of properties of a between-group welfare functional that are precisely analogous to the properties of a social welfare functional considered in Section IV. There exists a between-group ordering for the set of all between-group states that can be represented by a between-group welfare function analogous to the social welfare function (4.3):

$$W_B(u_B, x_B) = F\{\overline{W}_B(x_b) + g[x_B, u_B(x_B) - \overline{W}_B(x_B) i], x_B\}, \quad (7.1)$$

where the function $\overline{W}_B(x_B)$ corresponds to the average level of potential group welfare,

$$\overline{W}_B(x_B) = \sum_{b=1}^{B} a_b(x_B)E_{G_b},$$

and the function g is a linear homogenous function of deviations of levels of potential group welfare from average potential group welfare.

Ruling out direct dependence of the function $F(x_B)$ in (7.1) on characteristics of between-groups states x_B results in a cardinal representation of between-group welfare. We can require that potential group welfare functions $\{E_{G_b}\}$ must be invariant with respect to any positive affine transformation that is the same for all households and that the between-group welfare function is an equity-regarding function. Under these assumptions the between-group welfare function must take forms analogous to (4.10).

The translog index of efficiency (5.2) is expressed in terms of the social state x and the vector u of individual welfare functions for all K individuals. We can also define such an index, say E_B, in terms of the between group state x_B and the vector u_B of potential group welfare functions for all B groups. Both indexes correspond to the potential level of social welfare and both are equal to the translog indirect utility function (3.13), evaluated at aggregate expenditure per household equivalent member for society as a whole.

Given the translog index of efficiency E_B, we can define a measure of between-group inequality as the difference between the translog index of efficiency and the value of the between-group welfare function:

$$I_B(u_B, x_B) = E_B(u_B, x_B) - W_B(u_B, x_B). \tag{7.2}$$

The *translog index of between-group inequality* I_B is nonnegative and equal to zero only where group expenditure per household equivalent member is the same for all groups. The between-group social welfare function can be decomposed into the sum of measures of efficiency and between group equity:

$$W_B(u_B, x_B) = E_B(u_B, x_B) - I_B(u_B, x_B). \tag{7.3}$$

Given the between-group welfare function (7.1), we can define a measure of within-group inequality, say I_W, as the difference between the actual values of the between-group welfare function and the social welfare function:

$$I_W(u, x; u_B, x_B) = W_B(u_B, x_B) - W(u, x). \tag{7.4}$$

The *translog index of within-group inequality* I_W is nonnegative and equal to zero only where group expenditure per household equivalent member is the same for all households within each group. The translog index of inequality I can be decomposed into the sum of measures of inequality between and within groups:

$$I(u, x) = I_B(u_B, x_B) + I_W(u, x; u_B, x_B)$$

$$= [E_B(u_B, x_B) - W_B(u_B, x_B)] \tag{7.5}$$

$$+ [W_B(u_B, x_B) - W(u, x)].$$

Similarly, we can define a *translog index of between-group relative inequality*, say J_B, as

$$J_B(u_B, x_B) = 1 - \frac{W_B(u_B, x_B)}{E_B(u_B, x_B)}$$

$$= \frac{I_B(u_B, x_B)}{E_B(u_B, x_B)}. \tag{7.6}$$

The between-group index of relative inequality lies between 0 and 1 and is 0 only at the point of perfect equality among groups. We can also define a *translog index of within-group relative inequality*, say J_W, as

$$J_W(u, x; u_B, x_B) = \frac{W_B(u_B, x_B) - W(u, x)}{E(u, x)}$$

$$= \frac{I_W(u, x; u_B, x_B)}{E(u, x)}. \tag{7.7}$$

The within-group index lies between 0 and 1 and is 0 only at the point of perfect equality within each group. The translog index of relative inequality J can be decomposed into the sum of measures of relative inequality between and within groups:

$$J(u, x) = J_B(u_B, x_B) + J_W(u, x; u_B, x_B)$$

$$= \frac{I_B(u_B, x_B)}{E_B(u_B, x_B)} + \frac{I_W(u, x; u_B, x_B)}{E(u, x)}. \tag{7.8}$$

The translog indexes of inequality presented in Table 3 can be decomposed into the sum of translog indexes of inequality between and within groups.[29] The index of between-group inequality is equal to zero where group expenditure per household equivalent member is the same for all groups. The index of within group inequality is equal to zero only where group expenditure per household equivalent member is the same for all households within each group. Indexes of between- and within-group inequality for the U.S. population divided among six subgroups classified by age of head of household are presented in Table 6 for the years 1958–1978. To simplify the presentation we take the degree of aversion to inequality ρ equal to minus unity.

Similarly, the translog indexes of relative inequality presented in Table

Table 6.   Decomposition of Indexes of Inequality

	Translog Indexes of Inequality		
Year	Total	Between Groups	Within Groups
1958	0.41432	0.07881	0.33551
1959	0.39761	0.07474	0.32287
1960	0.39280	0.07523	0.31757
1961	0.38769	0.06806	0.31962
1962	0.38652	0.06743	0.31909
1963	0.38105	0.06738	0.31366
1964	0.38499	0.07261	0.31239
1965	0.38067	0.07360	0.30707
1966	0.37593	0.07482	0.30111
1967	0.37699	0.08152	0.29546
1968	0.37518	0.08038	0.29479
1969	0.37454	0.08437	0.29018
1970	0.37216	0.08371	0.28846
1971	0.37205	0.08246	0.28959
1972	0.36869	0.08113	0.28756
1973	0.37032	0.08161	0.28871
1974	0.36893	0.07683	0.29210
1975	0.37082	0.07791	0.29291
1976	0.36688	0.07536	0.29151
1977	0.36253	0.07118	0.29134
1978	0.36198	0.06768	0.29430

3 can be decomposed into the sum of translog indexes of relative inequality between and within groups. Both indexes lie between 0 and 1. The translog index of relative between group inequality is equal to zero only at the point of perfect equality among groups. The translog index of relative within group inequality is equal to zero only at the point of perfect equality within each group. Relative indexes of between- and within-group inequality for the U.S. population are presented in Table 7 for the years 1958–1978. As before, we take the degree of aversion to inequality ρ equal to minus unity.

To Summarize

In this section we have developed measures of inequality between and within subgroups of the U.S. population. For this purpose we have introduced a between-group welfare function that is analogous to the social welfare function presented in Section IV, above. The translog index of between-group inequality is the difference between the translog index of efficiency for the society as a whole and the actual value of the between-

Table 7.   Decomposition of Indexes of Relative
Inequality

| Year | | Translog Indexes of Relative Inequality | |
	Total	Between Groups	Within Groups
1958	0.05528	0.01052	0.04477
1959	0.05285	0.00993	0.04291
1960	0.05204	0.00997	0.04208
1961	0.05130	0.00901	0.04230
1962	0.05105	0.00891	0.04214
1963	0.05019	0.00888	0.04131
1964	0.05046	0.00952	0.04094
1965	0.04961	0.00959	0.04002
1966	0.04873	0.00970	0.03903
1967	0.04877	0.01055	0.03822
1968	0.04831	0.01035	0.03796
1969	0.04807	0.01083	0.03725
1970	0.04763	0.01071	0.03692
1971	0.04756	0.01054	0.03702
1972	0.04689	0.01032	0.03657
1973	0.04686	0.01033	0.03654
1974	0.04671	0.00973	0.03699
1975	0.04691	0.00985	0.03705
1976	0.04624	0.00950	0.03674
1977	0.04552	0.00894	0.03659
1978	0.04524	0.00846	0.03678

group welfare function. The translog index of within-group inequality is the difference between the actual values of the between-group welfare function and the social welfare function.

To illustrate the decomposition of the translog indexes of inequality and relative inequality for society as a whole we have presented indexes of between-group and within-group inequality for the U.S. population classified by age of head of household for the years 1958–1978. Our methodology could also be used to decompose the measures of inequality by the other demographic characteristics employed in the econometric model of Section III.

VIII.   MONEY METRIC INEQUALITY

In order to quantify gains to society from redistributional policies we find it useful to express measures of inequality in terms of equivalent levels of aggregate expenditure. For this purpose we introduce the social expenditure function, defined as the minimum level of aggregate expenditure $M = \sum_{k=1}^{K} M_k$ required to attain a given level of social welfare, say W, at a specified price system p.[30] More formally, the social expenditure function $M(p, W)$ is defined by:

$$M(p, W) = \min\left\{M: \quad W(u, x) \geq W; \quad M = \sum_{k=1}^{K} M_k\right\}. \quad (8.1)$$

The social expenditure function (8.1) is precisely analogous to the individual expenditure function (2.23): the individual expenditure function gives the minimum level of individual expenditure required to attain a level of individual welfare; the social expenditure function gives the minimum level of aggregate expenditure required to attain a level of social welfare.

To construct a social expenditure function we maximize social welfare for a fixed level of aggregate expenditure by equalizing total expenditure per household equivalent member for all consuming units. The maximum level of welfare (5.2) is equal to the translog indirect utility function (2.22), evaluated at total expenditure per household equivalent member $M/\sum_{k=1}^{K} m_0(p, A_k)$ for the economy as a whole. We can solve for aggregate expenditure as a function of the level of social welfare and prices:

$$\ln M(p, W) = \frac{1}{D(p)}\left[\ln p'\left(\alpha_p + \frac{1}{2} B_{pp} \ln p\right) - W\right] \quad (8.2)$$

$$+ \ln\left[\sum_{k=1}^{K} m_0(p, A_k)\right]. \quad (8.2)$$

We can refer to this function as the *translog social expenditure function*. The value of aggregate expenditure is obtained by evaluating the translog individual expenditure function (2.23) at the level of social welfare W and the number of household equivalent members $\sum_{k=1}^{K} m_0(p, A_k)$ for the economy as a whole.

To obtain a money measure of the actual level of social welfare, say W^0, we first evaluate the social welfare function at prices actually prevailing, say p^0, and at the actual distribution of total expenditure $\{M_k^0\}$:

$$W^0 = \ln \overline{V}^0 - \left\{1 + \left[\frac{\sum_{k=1}^{K} m_0(p^0, A_k)}{m_0(p^0, A_j)}\right]^{-(\rho+1)}\right\}^{-1/\rho}$$

$$\times \left[\frac{\sum_{k=1}^{K} m_0(p^0, A_k) \mid \ln V_k^0 - \ln \overline{V}^0 \mid^{-\rho}}{\sum_{k=1}^{K} m_0(p^0, A_k)}\right]^{-1/\rho}, \quad (8.3)$$

where

$$\ln \overline{V}^0 = \frac{\sum_{k=1}^{K} m_0(p^0, A_k) \ln V_k [p^0 m(A_k)/M_k^0]}{\sum_{k=1}^{K} m_0(p^0, A_k)}$$

and

$$\ln V_k^0 = \ln p^{0\,\prime}\left(\alpha_p + \frac{1}{2}B_{pp}\ln p^0\right)$$

$$- D(p^0)\ln\left[\frac{M_k^0}{m_0(p^0, A_k)}\right] \qquad (k = 1, 2, \ldots, K).$$

We can express the actual level of social welfare W^0 in terms of aggregate expenditure by means of the social expenditure function:

$$\ln M(p^0, W^0) = \frac{1}{D(p^0)}\left[\ln p^{0\,\prime}\left(\alpha_p + \frac{1}{2}B_{pp}\ln p^0\right) - W^0\right]$$

$$+ \ln\left[\sum_{k=1}^{K} m_0(p^0, A_k)\right]. \qquad (8.4)$$

Second, we can decompose our measure of social welfare into measures of efficiency and equity. For this purpose we evaluate the social welfare function at the maximum level, say W^2, that can be attained through lump sum redistributions of aggregate expenditure $M^0 = \sum_{k=1}^{K} M_k^0$. Total expenditure per household equivalent member must be equalized for all consuming units so that the social welfare function reduces to average individual welfare:

$$W^2 = \ln \overline{V}^2 \qquad\qquad\qquad\qquad (8.5)$$

$$= \ln p^{0\,\prime}\left(\alpha_p + \frac{1}{2}B_{pp}\ln p^0\right) - D(p^0)\ln\left[\frac{M^0}{\sum_{k=1}^{K} m_0(p^0, A_k)}\right].$$

This is the maximum level of social welfare that is potentially available and can be taken as a measure of efficiency. Evaluating the social expenditure function at the potential level of welfare W^2, we obtain

$$M(p^0, W^2) = M^0, \qquad\qquad (8.6)$$

so that aggregate total expenditure M^0 is the resulting money measure of efficiency.

Given a money measure of efficiency (8.6), defined in terms of the social expenditure function, we can define a money measure of inequality, say $M^I(p^0, W^0)$, as the difference between the money measure of potential social welfare M^0 and the money measure of actual social welfare $M(p^0, W^0)$:

$$M^I(p^0, W^0) = M^0 - M(p^0, W^0). \qquad (8.7)$$

This measure of inequality is nonnegative and equal to zero only for perfect equality in the distribution of individual welfare. The money measure of inequality M^I is the amount that society as a whole would gain from a perfectly egalitarian distribution of aggregate expenditure M^0.

Using the social expenditure function, our money measure of social welfare $M(p^0, W^0)$ can be decomposed into money measures of efficiency M^0 and equity $-M^I$:

$$M(p^0, W^0) = M^0 - M^I(p^0, W^0). \qquad (8.8)$$

The level of aggregate expenditure M^0 is the amount society would be willing to pay for the level of social welfare that is potentially available. The money measure of equity $-M^I$ is the loss to society that results from an inequitable distribution of aggregate expenditure among individual households. The critical feature of this decomposition is that all three money measures are expressed in terms of the same set of prices p^0.

Similarly, we can define a money measure of relative inequality, say $M^J(p^0, W^0)$, as

$$\begin{aligned} M^J(p^0, W^0) &= 1 - \frac{M(p^0, W^0)}{M^0} \\ &= \frac{M^I(p^0, W^0)}{M^0}. \end{aligned} \qquad (8.9)$$

This money measure of relative inequality lies between 0 and 1 and is 0 only at the point of perfect equality. The money measure of relative inequality M^I is the proportion of aggregate expenditure M^0 lost owing to an inequitable distribution of aggregate expenditure.

In order to quantify gains to subgroups of the U.S. population from redistributional policies we find it useful to express measures of group inequality in terms of equivalent levels of group expenditure. For this purpose we introduce group expenditure functions that are precisely analogous to the social expenditure function (8.1). The group expenditure function is defined as the minimum level of group expenditure $M_G = \sum_{g=1}^{G} M_g$ required to attain a given level of group welfare W_G at a specified price system p. The group expenditure function gives the minimum level of group expenditure required to attain a stipulated level of group welfare.

To construct a group expenditure function we can maximize group welfare for a fixed level of group expenditure by equalizing total expenditure per household equivalent member for all households in the group. The maximum level of group welfare (6.2) is equal to the translog indirect utility function (2.22) evaluated at group expenditure per household equivalent member $M_G / \sum_{g=1}^{G} m_0(p, A_g)$ for the group as a whole. We can solve the group expenditure as a function of the level of social welfare and prices:

$$\ln M_G(p, W_G) = \frac{1}{D(p)} \left[\ln p' \left(\alpha_p + \frac{1}{2} B_{pp} \ln p \right) - W_G \right]$$

$$+ \ln \left[\sum_{g=1}^{G} m_0(p, A_g) \right]. \quad (8.10)$$

The *translog group expenditure function* is obtained by evaluating the translog individual expenditure function (2.23) at the level of group welfare W_G and the number of household equivalent members $\sum_{g=1}^{G} m_0(p, A_g)$ for the group as a whole.

To obtain a money measure of the actual level of group welfare, say W_G^0, we first evaluate the group welfare function at prices p^0 and the actual distribution of total expenditure within the group. We then express this level of welfare in terms of group expenditure by means of the group expenditure function (8.10). We can decompose this money measure of group welfare, say $M_G(p^0, W_G^0)$, into money measures of group efficiency and equity. The level of group expenditure, say M_G^0, is a money measure of efficiency, so that we can define a money measure of group inequality, say $M_G^I(p^0, W_G^0)$, as follows:

$$M_G^I(p^0, W_G^0) = M_G^0 - M_G(p^0, W_G^0). \quad (8.11)$$

This measure is nonnegative and equal to zero only for perfect equality in the distribution of individual welfare within the group. The money measure of group inequality M_G^I is the amount that the group would gain from a perfectly egalitarian distribution of group expenditure.

Using the group expenditure function, our money measure of group welfare $M_G(p^0, W_G^0)$ can be decomposed into money measures of group efficiency M_G^0 and equity $-M_G^0$:

$$M_G(p^0, W_G^0) = M_G^0 - M_G^I(p^0, W^0). \quad (8.12)$$

The level of group expenditure M_G^0 is the amount the group would be willing to pay for the level of group welfare that is potentially available. The money measure of group equity $-M_G^I$ is the loss to the group that results from an inequitable distribution of expenditure among households within the group. We can define a money measure of relative group inequality, say $M_G^I(p^0, W_G^0)$, as follows:

$$M_G^I(p^0, W_G^0) = \frac{M_G^I(p^0, W^0)}{M_G^0}. \quad (8.13)$$

This measure represents the proportion of aggregate expenditure M_G^0 lost owing to an inequitable distribution within the group.

Finally, we can decompose money measures of inequality into the sum of money measures of inequality between and within groups. For this purpose we first express differences in between-group welfare in terms of differences in aggregate expenditure. The between-group expenditure function gives the minimum level of aggregate expenditure required to attain a stipulated level of between-group welfare. We can construct this function by equalizing group expenditure per household equivalent member among all groups or total expenditure per household equivalent member among all households. We obtain the translog index of efficiency (5.2), which is equal to the translog utility function (2.13), evaluated at aggregate expenditure per household equivalent member for society as a whole. We can solve for aggregate expenditure as a function of the level of social welfare and prices, obtaining the translog social expenditure function (8.2).

To obtain a money measure of the actual level of between group welfare, say W_B^0, we first evaluate the between-group welfare function at prices p^0 and the actual distribution of aggregate expenditure among groups. We then express this level of welfare in terms of aggregate expenditure by means of the social expenditure function (8.2). We can decompose this money measure of between-group welfare, say $M(p^0, W_B^0)$, into money measures of efficiency and between-group equity. The level of aggregate expenditure M^0 is a money measure of efficiency, so that we can define a money measure of between-group inequality, say $M_B^I(p^0, W_B^0)$, as follows:

$$M_B^I(p^0, W_B^0) = M^0 - M(p^0, W_B^0). \qquad (8.14)$$

This measure of between-group inequality is nonnegative and equal to zero only for perfect equality in the distribution of aggregate expenditure among groups.

Given the money measure of between-group welfare $M(p^0, W_B^0)$, we can define a money measure of within-group inequality, say $M_W^I(p^0, W_B^0, W^0)$, as the difference between money measures of between-group welfare and the actual level of social welfare:

$$M_W^I(p^0, W_B^0, W^0) = M(p^0, W_B^0) - M(p^0, W^0). \qquad (8.15)$$

This measure of within-group inequality is nonnegative and equal to zero only for perfect equality in the distribution of group expenditure within each group. The money measure of inequality $M^I(p^0, W^0)$ can be decomposed into the sum of money measures of inequality between and within groups:

$$M^I(p^0, W^0) = M_B^I(p^0, W_B^0) + M_W^I(p^0, W_B^0, W^0),$$
$$= [M^0 - M(p^0, W_B^0)] \qquad (8.16)$$
$$+ [M(p^0, W_B^0) - M(p^0, W^0)].$$

The money measure of between-group inequality M_B^I is the amount that society as a whole would gain from a perfectly egalitarian distribution of aggregate expenditure among groups. The money measure of within-group inequality M_W^I is the amount society would gain from a perfectly egalitarian distribution of group expenditure within each group.

We can define a money measure of relative between-group inequality, say $M_B^I(p^0, W_B^0)$, as follows:

$$M_B^I (p^0, W_B^0) = \frac{M_B^I(p^0, W_B^0)}{M^0}. \tag{8.17}$$

This measure represents the proportion of aggregate expenditure M^0 lost owing to an inequitable distribution of aggregate expenditure among groups. We can also define a money measure of relative within group inequality, say $M_W^I(p^0, W_B^0, W^0)$, as follows:

$$M_W^I (p^0, W_B^0, W^0) = \frac{M_W^I(p^0, W_B^0, W^0)}{M^0}. \tag{8.18}$$

The measure represents the proportion of aggregate expenditure lost owing to an inequitable distribution of group expenditure among households within each group. The money measure of relative inequality $M^J(p^0, W^0)$ can be decomposed as the sum of money measures of relative inequality between and within groups:

$$M^J(p^0, W^0) = M_B^J(p^0, W_B^0) + M_W^J(p^0, W_B^0, W^0). \tag{8.19}$$

To Summarize

In this section we have developed methods for expressing differences in levels of social welfare in terms of differences in aggregate expenditure. These methods are useful in quantifying gains to society from redistributional policies. Money metric inequality can be defined as the difference between money measures of potential and actual social welfare. This measure of inequality is the amount that society as a whole would gain from a perfectly egalitarian distribution of aggregate expenditure. We also consider money measures of group inequality, corresponding to the amounts groups would gain from an egalitarian distribution. Finally, we decompose money metric inequality into the sum of money measures of between- and within-group inequality. These measures correspond to gains to society from redistribution between and within groups.

IX. APPLICATIONS OF MONEY METRIC INEQUALITY

To illustrate the application of the money measures of inequality presented in Section VIII we observe that the translog social expenditure function (8.2) has the same form as the translog individual expenditure function (2.23). We can express the level of social welfare as a function of the price system and aggregate expenditure M. We take this level of social welfare to be the level obtained by equalizing total expenditure per household equivalent member among all households. Under this assumption society behaves in the same way as an individual maximizing a utility function, so that we can represent social welfare in terms of the indifference map for a single representative consumer.[31]

In Figure 2 we have depicted the indifference map of the representative consumer with indirect utility function given by the average level of utility $\ln \overline{V}$ in (5.2). For simplicity we consider the case of two commodities ($N = 2$). Consumer equilibrium at the actual level of social welfare W^0 is represented by the point A. The corresponding level of aggregate expenditure $M(p^0, W^0)$, divided by the price of the second commodity

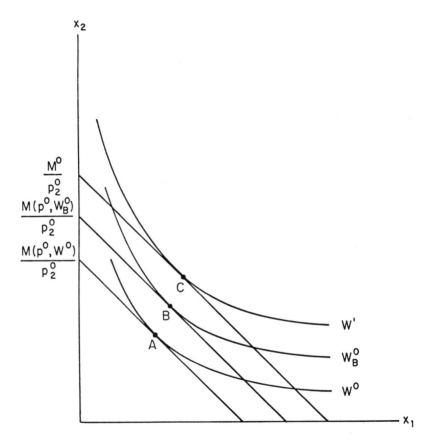

Figure 2

p_2^0, is given the vertical axis. This axis provides a representation of aggregate expenditure in terms of units of the second commodity.

Aggregate expenditure M^0 is the value of the social expenditure function at the potential level of welfare W^1. This is the maximum level of welfare that can be obtained by lump sum redistributions of aggregate expenditure. The corresponding consumer equilibrium is represented by the point C. A money measure of the loss in social welfare due to inequality, expressed in terms of units of the second commodity, is provided by the distance along the x_2 axis between aggregate expenditure M^0/p_2^0 and the value of the social expenditure function $M(p^0, W^0)/p_2^0$. This distance represents the money measure of inequality $M^I(p^0, W^0)$, divided by the price of the second commodity. The ratio between this distance and the distance corresponding to aggregate expenditure M^0/p_2^0 is the money measure of relative inequality $M^J(p^0, W^0)$.

Since the translog group expenditure function (8.11) is precisely analogous to the translog social and individual expenditure functions, we can also express group welfare in terms of the indifference map for a representative consumer. By interpreting the consumer equilibria A and C in Figure 2 as those corresponding to actual and potential group welfare, we obtain a representation of money measures of group inequality and relative inequality. These measures are analogous to the money measures of inequality for society as a whole that we have already described.

Finally, we can decompose money measures of inequality into the sum of measures of inequality between and within groups. The level of between group welfare W_B^0 can be attained by equalizing group expenditure per household equivalent member within each group. The corresponding consumer equilibrium is represented by the point B. A money measure of the loss in social welfare owing to inequality in the distribution of aggregate expenditure among groups is provided by the distance along the x_2 axis between the level of aggregate expenditure and the value of the social expenditure function $M(p^0, W_B^0)/p_2^0$. This distance represents the money measure of between group inequality $M_B^I(p^0, W_B^0)$, divided by the price of the second commodity. Similarly, the loss in social welfare owing to inequality within groups $M_W^I(p^0, W_B^0, W^0)$, divided by the price of the second commodity, is the distance between the value of the social expenditure function $M(p^0, W_B^0)/p_2^0$ and the value at the actual level of social welfare $M(p^0, W^0)/p_2^0$. Ratios between these distances and the distance corresponding to aggregate expenditure M^0/p_2^0 represents money measures of relative between-group and within-group inequality, $M_B^J(p^0, W_B^0)$ and $M_W^J(p^0, W_B^0, W^0)$, respectively.

We can also illustrate money measures of inequality in the distribution of individual welfare by considering money measures of actual and potential levels of social welfare over the period 1958–1978. We first present money measures of social welfare for alternative values of the degree of aversion to inequality ρ in Table 8. The money measure of potential social welfare is independent of the degree of aversion to inequality ρ. Money metric efficiency for the years 1958–1978 is presented in Table 8. Money metric social welfare and efficiency are measured in prices of 1972.

Money metric inequality is defined as the difference between money metric efficiency and money metric social welfare. This measure of inequality is the amount that society as a whole would gain from a perfectly egalitarian distribution of aggregate expenditure. Since money metric social welfare depends on the degree of aversion to inequality ρ, we have presented money metric inequality for different values of this parameter for the years 1958–1978 in Table 9. We also present the corresponding values of money metric relative inequality in Table 9. This measure is the proportion of aggregate expenditure lost owing to an inequitable distribution among households.

Similarly, we can illustrate money measures of group inequality in the distribution of individual welfare. For this purpose we consider money measures of actual and potential group welfare for subgroups of the U.S.

Table 8.   Money Metric Social Welfare

	Money Metric Social Welfare		Money Metric Efficiency
Year	ρ = −1	ρ = −2	
1958	247351.78	314780.43	374327.96
1959	261652.47	330441.39	389406.41
1960	269947.79	340158.88	399823.92
1961	278505.80	350136.05	410397.88
1962	288739.03	362839.33	424980.25
1963	299392.61	375280.84	438255.18
1964	313877.64	394017.70	461275.74
1965	331406.26	415320.71	484934.29
1966	350819.84	438765.73	510915.29
1967	362386.95	453337.89	528319.68
1968	378768.96	473387.80	551204.43
1969	393892.71	492177.76	572848.77
1970	408149.04	509437.21	592170.79
1971	417450.60	520910.67	605599.08
1972	439859.27	548209.69	635967.11
1973	461234.37	575467.36	667958.55
1974	463423.37	578257.88	670199.13
1975	470846.24	587924.63	682218.56
1976	491298.65	612206.60	709051.25
1977	513075.66	637987.81	737266.40
1978	538670.09	669837.30	773622.09

Table 9. Money Metric Inequality

Year	Money Metric Inequality		Money Metric Relative Inequality	
	$\rho = -1$	$\rho = -2$	$\rho = -1$	$\rho = -2$
1958	126976.18	59547.53	0.33921	0.15908
1959	127753.94	58965.02	0.32807	0.15142
1960	129876.13	59665.04	0.32483	0.14923
1961	131892.08	60261.83	0.32138	0.14684
1962	136241.21	62140.92	0.32058	0.14622
1963	138862.56	62974.34	0.31685	0.14369
1964	147398.10	67258.04	0.31954	0.14581
1965	153528.02	69613.58	0.31660	0.14355
1966	160095.44	72149.56	0.31335	0.14122
1967	165932.73	74981.79	0.31408	0.14193
1968	172435.46	77816.63	0.31283	0.14118
1969	178956.06	80671.01	0.31240	0.14082
1970	184021.75	82733.58	0.31076	0.13971
1971	188148.48	84688.42	0.31068	0.13984
1972	196107.84	87757.42	0.30836	0.13799
1973	206724.18	92491.19	0.30949	0.13847
1974	206775.76	91941.25	0.30853	0.13718
1975	211372.32	94293.93	0.30983	0.13822
1976	217752.60	96844.65	0.30710	0.13658
1977	224190.74	99278.59	0.30408	0.13466
1978	234952.00	103784.79	0.30370	0.13415

population classified by age of head of household. The first step in constructing money measures of group inequality is to present money measures of group welfare for six age groups for the years 1958–1978 (see the Appendix, Table A-3). We take the degree of aversion to inequality ρ equal to minus unity in order to simplify the presentation. The money measure of potential group welfare is independent of the degree of aversion to inequality. Money metric group efficiency for the six age groups for the years 1958–1978 is presented in the Appendix (Table A-4). Money metric group welfare and efficiency are given in prices of 1972.

Money metric group inequality is defined as the difference between money metric group efficiency and money metric group welfare. These money measures of inequality are the amounts that each group would gain from a perfectly egalitarian distribution of group expenditure. Money metric inequality for six age groups of the U.S. population is presented in Table 10 for the years 1958–1978. We present the corresponding values of money metric group relative inequality in Table 11. These measures are the proportions of group expenditure lost owing to an inequitable distribution among households within the group.

Table 10. Money Metric Group Inequality

	Age Groups					
Year	16–24	25–34	35–44	45–54	55–64	65+
1958	3447.98	20882.64	37115.51	28561.99	18468.05	13463.39
1959	3450.47	20096.69	37058.78	28308.07	19304.58	14597.27
1960	3618.72	20228.31	37473.17	29546.45	19381.75	14520.44
1961	3510.88	19797.20	37499.23	29736.95	20649.46	16245.49
1962	3619.39	19589.07	39636.20	30584.01	21632.02	16658.31
1963	3905.83	20166.12	39518.31	31338.80	22221.36	16981.93
1964	4404.91	21401.11	41552.57	33702.20	22913.60	17950.81
1965	4592.21	22587.32	42612.89	35324.76	23919.78	18520.36
1966	4880.51	23642.38	43825.51	37145.06	24759.44	19381.34
1967	4945.80	24806.21	45198.83	37891.49	25858.45	19554.78
1968	5849.16	26551.55	45830.74	38786.11	27249.57	20327.16
1969	6093.08	27708.48	47038.63	39930.96	28207.82	20909.23
1970	6915.97	28721.44	47790.69	41001.96	28905.09	21552.45
1971	7206.44	30283.43	47933.48	41622.81	29193.02	22759.84
1972	7532.08	31963.75	50143.83	42634.63	30045.18	24063.55
1973	8314.51	34780.78	52362.30	44160.97	31100.97	25692.54
1974	8265.53	35286.63	52007.73	43177.97	31754.93	26697.57
1975	8539.16	36755.43	53651.22	43093.50	31709.12	28003.10
1976	8842.40	38198.84	55219.22	43788.36	32818.55	28894.73
1977	8978.27	39241.68	57744.27	43869.41	34408.20	29820.61
1978	9923.73	40399.85	60924.00	45116.37	36005.96	32220.40

Table 11. Money Metric Group Relative Inequality

	Age Groups					
Year	16–24	25–34	35–44	45–54	55–64	65+
1958	0.27894	0.32336	0.32193	0.34115	0.32372	0.32603
1959	0.27539	0.31316	0.30703	0.33025	0.31674	0.32180
1960	0.27212	0.30889	0.30503	0.32684	0.31256	0.31737
1961	0.27082	0.30850	0.30291	0.32543	0.31066	0.31482
1962	0.27217	0.31061	0.30215	0.32382	0.31028	0.31278
1963	0.26889	0.30660	0.29681	0.32087	0.30673	0.31031
1964	0.26909	0.30954	0.30066	0.32306	0.30554	0.30828
1965	0.26662	0.30512	0.29621	0.31913	0.30372	0.30720
1966	0.26379	0.30160	0.29209	0.31606	0.29966	0.30394
1967	0.26366	0.30174	0.29087	0.31484	0.29777	0.30184
1968	0.26543	0.30257	0.28997	0.31376	0.29623	0.29980
1969	0.26549	0.30042	0.28681	0.31130	0.29524	0.29957
1970	0.26532	0.30029	0.28642	0.30963	0.29252	0.29717
1971	0.26558	0.30002	0.28734	0.31000	0.29228	0.29669
1972	0.26145	0.29634	0.28557	0.30696	0.29037	0.29584
1973	0.26397	0.29780	0.28624	0.30760	0.29148	0.29721
1974	0.26658	0.29719	0.28605	0.30648	0.29235	0.29873
1975	0.26874	0.29822	0.28947	0.30781	0.29217	0.29880
1976	0.26724	0.29563	0.28552	0.30486	0.29055	0.29767
1977	0.26495	0.29261	0.28283	0.30215	0.28827	0.29590
1978	0.26690	0.29228	0.28228	0.30133	0.28907	0.29747

Finally, we can illustrate the decomposition of the money measures of inequality presented in Table 9 into money measures of inequality between and within subgroups of the U.S. population. Money metric between-group inequality is defined as the differences between money metric efficiency and money metric between-group welfare. This measure is the amount that society as a whole would gain from a perfectly egalitarian distribution of aggregate expenditure among groups. Money metric within-group inequality is defined as the difference between money metric between-group welfare and money metric social welfare. This measure is the amount that society as a whole would gain from a perfectly egalitarian distribution of group expenditure within each group.

Money measures of between- and within-group inequality for the U.S. population divided among six groups classified by age of head of household are presented in Table 12 for the years 1958–1978. To simplify the presentation we take the degree of aversion to inequality ρ equal to minus unity. Money metric between- and within-group inequality are measured in prices of 1972. We present the corresponding money measures of between- and within-group relative inequality in Table 13. These measures

Table 12. Decomposition of Money Metric Inequality

		Money Metric Inequality	
Year	Total	Between Groups	Within Groups
1958	126976.18	28369.72	98606.47
1959	127753.94	28043.54	99710.40
1960	129876.13	28973.54	100902.60
1961	131892.08	27004.28	104887.80
1962	136241.21	27711.82	108529.39
1963	138862.56	28558.46	110304.11
1964	147398.10	32305.03	115093.07
1965	153528.02	34409.54	119118.49
1966	160095.44	36832.11	123263.33
1967	165932.73	41362.07	124570.67
1968	172435.46	42574.35	129861.11
1969	178956.06	46346.13	132609.92
1970	184021.75	47550.88	136470.87
1971	188148.48	47934.36	140214.12
1972	196107.84	49559.65	146548.18
1973	206775.76	52347.22	154376.95
1974	206775.76	49565.48	157210.29
1975	211372.32	51131.44	160240.88
1976	217752.60	51472.64	166279.96
1977	224190.74	50656.93	173533.81
1978	234952.00	50628.34	184323.66

Table 13. Decomposition of Money Metric Relative
Inequality

| | Money Metric Relative Inequality | | |
Year	Total	Between Groups	Within Groups
1958	0.33921	0.07579	0.26342
1959	0.32807	0.07202	0.25606
1960	0.32483	0.07247	0.25237
1961	0.32138	0.06580	0.25558
1962	0.32058	0.06521	0.25538
1963	0.31685	0.06516	0.25169
1964	0.31954	0.07003	0.24951
1965	0.31660	0.07096	0.24564
1966	0.31335	0.07209	0.24126
1967	0.31408	0.07829	0.23579
1968	0.31283	0.07724	0.23560
1969	0.31240	0.08090	0.23149
1970	0.31076	0.08030	0.23046
1971	0.31068	0.07915	0.23153
1972	0.30836	0.07793	0.23043
1973	0.30949	0.07837	0.23112
1974	0.30853	0.07396	0.23457
1975	0.30983	0.07495	0.23488
1976	0.30710	0.07259	0.23451
1977	0.30408	0.06871	0.23537
1978	0.30370	0.06544	0.23826

are the proportions of aggregate expenditure lost owing to inequitable
distributions between and within groups.

To Summarize

In this section we have illustrated the application of the money measures of inequality presented in Section VIII. We have first presented
money metric inequality for the U.S. population as a whole for the years
1958–1978. This money measure of inequality is the difference between
money metric efficiency and money metric social welfare. Second, to
illustrate the application of money measures of inequality within
subgroups we have presented money metric group inequality for six
groups, classified by age of head of household. Finally, we have decomposed money measures of inequality for the U.S. population as a whole
into money measures of inequality between and within age groups. Our
methodology could also be used to decompose money measures of inequality by the other demographic characteristics employed in the econometric model of Section III.

X. SUMMARY AND CONCLUSION

In this paper we have presented an econometric approach to the measurement of inequality in the distribution of individual welfare. The first step in analyzing inequality is to select a representation for individual welfare. We assume that individual welfare is equal to the logarithm of the translog indirect utility function (2.22). The indirect utility function enables us to express individual welfare in terms of the price system and the level of total expenditure.

In Section II we show how the translog indirect utility function can be determined from a system of individual expenditure shares (2.5) that is integrable. We also demonstrate how the individual expenditure shares (2.5) can be recovered uniquely from the system of aggregate expenditure shares (2.25). In Section III we fit an econometric model of aggregate consumer behavior that incorporates the restrictions implied by integrability of the individual expenditure shares.

In Section IV we generate a class of possible social welfare functions that provides the basis for analyzing inequality in the distribution of individual welfare. Each of these social welfare functions can be represented as the sum of two terms. The first term represents an average of individual welfare levels over all consuming units. The second term is a measure of dispersion in individual welfare levels. Using indirect utility functions for all households, we can express social welfare in terms of the price system and the distribution of aggregate expenditure among individuals.[32]

In Section V we develop indexes of inequality in the distribution of individual welfare. For this purpose we decompose the measures of social welfare presented in Section IV into measures of efficiency and equity. Our measure of efficiency is the translog indirect utility function (5.2), evaluated at aggregate expenditure per household equivalent member for society as a whole. Our measure of equity is the difference between the actual level of social welfare and the measure of efficiency.

In Section V we define the translog index of inequality as the difference between the measure of efficiency given by the translog indirect utility function (5.2) and the actual level of social welfare. Similarly, we define the translog index of relative inequality as the ratio between the translog index of inequality and the measure of efficiency. We implement our measures of inequality for the U.S. population as a whole for the years 1958–1978.

In Section VI we extend our measures of inequality to the distribution of individual welfare within subgroups of the U.S. population. We first introduce group welfare functions that are precisely analogous to the social welfare functions of Section IV. We define measures of group inequality and group relative inequality that are analogous to those for the U.S. population as a whole. We implement these measures of inequality for six groups, classified by age of head of household, for the years 1958–1978.

In Section VII we develop measures of inequality between subgroups of the U.S. population. We introduce between-group welfare functions that are analogous to the social welfare functions of Section IV. We define the translog index of inequality between groups as the difference between our measure of efficiency for the population as a whole and the value of the between-group welfare function. Similarly, we define the translog index of equality within groups as the difference between the values of the between-group welfare function and the social welfare functions. We implement these measures of between-group and within-group inequality for six age groups for the years 1958–1978.

For applications to the evaluation of redistributional policies we find it useful to express our measures of inequality in terms of aggregate expenditure. For this purpose we introduce the social expenditure function in Section VIII, giving the minimum level of aggregate expenditure required to attain a stipulated level of social welfare. This value of aggregate expenditure is obtained by evaluating the translog individual expenditure function (2.23) at the actual level of social welfare per household equivalent member for the U.S. population as a whole.

We define money metric inequality as the difference between money measures of potential and actual social welfare. This measure is the amount that society as a whole would gain from a perfectly egalitarian distribution of income. We also consider money measures of group inequality, and we decompose money metric inequality into the sum of money measures of between- and within-group inequality. In Section IX we implement these money measures of inequality for the U.S. population as a whole and for six age groups for the years 1958–1978.

NOTES

1. Dalton (1920, p. 348), as quoted by Atkinson (1983b, p. 3). These objectives have also been emphasized by Bentzel (1970) and Tinbergen (1970).

2. See, for example, Muellbauer (1974b, p. 498).

3. Evidence on the nonhomotheticity of preferences is presented by Houthakker (1957), Leser (1963), Muellbauer (1976), Pollak and Wales (1978), and Prais and Houthakker (1971).

4. Evidence on the impact of demographic characteristics on expenditure allocation is given by Lau et al. (1978), Muellbauer (1977), Parks and Barten (1973), Pollak and Wales (1980, 1981), and Ray (1982).

5. The translog indirect utility function was introduced by Christensen et al. (1975) and extended to encompass determinants of expenditure allocation other than prices and total expenditure by Jorgenson and Lau (1975). Alternative approaches to the representation of

the effects of prices and total expenditure on expenditure allocation are summarized by Barten (1977), Deaton and Muellbauer (1980, pp. 60–85), and Lau (1977a).

6. Alternative approaches to the representation of household characteristics in expenditure allocation are presented by Barten (1964), Gorman (1976), and Prais and Houthakker (1971). A review of the literature is presented by Deaton and Muellbauer (1980, pp. 191–213).

7. The specification of a system of individual demand functions by means of Roy's Identity was first employed in econometric modeling of consumer behavior by Houthakker (1960). A detailed review of econometric models based on Roy's Identity is given by Lau (1977a).

8. For further discussion, see Lau (1977b, 1982) and Jorgenson et al. (1980, 1981, 1982).

9. Conditions for integrability are discussed by Jorgenson and Lau (1979) and Jorgenson et al. (1982).

10. For further discussion see Jorgenson et al. (1982, esp. pp. 175–186).

11. Household equivalence scales are discussed by Barten (1964), Lazear and Michael (1980), Muellbauer (1974a, 1977, 1980), and Prais and Houthakker (1971), among others. Alternative approaches are summarized by Deaton and Muellbauer (1980).

12. The use of household equivalence scales in evaluating transfers among individuals has been advocated by Deaton and Muellbauer (1980, esp. pp. 205–212) and by Muellbauer (1974a). Pollak and Wales (1979) have presented arguments against the use of household equivalence scales for this purpose.

13. Deaton and Muellbauer (1980, pp. 227–239), King (1983a,b), and Muellbauer (1974b,c) present approaches to inequality measurement based on the distribution of "real expenditure." Measures of "real expenditure" could be derived from the individual expenditure function (2.23) by varying the level of utility V_k for a fixed set of prices p ($k = 1, 2, \ldots, K$). Restrictions on preferences under which measures of inequality defined on the distribution of real expenditure coincide with measures defined on the distribution of individual welfare are given by Roberts (1980c).

14. The 1972/73 Survey of Consumer Expenditures (CES) is discussed by Carlson (1974).

15. We employ data on the flow of services from durable goods rather than purchases of durable goods. Personal consumption expenditures in the U.S. National Income and Product Accounts (NIPA) are based on purchases of durable goods.

16. This series is published annually by the U.S. Bureau of the Census.

17. A detailed discussion of the stochastic specification of our model and of econometric methods for pooling time-series and cross-section data is presented by Jorgenson et al. (1982, Sec. 6). This stochastic specification implies that time-series data must be adjusted for heteroscedasticity by multiplying each observation by the statistic

$$\rho = \frac{(\sum M_k)^2}{\sum M_k^2}.$$

18. Arrow (1977, p. 225) has defended noncomparability in the following terms: "the autonomy of individuals, an element of mutual incommensurability among people[,] seems denied by the possibility of interpersonal comparisons."

19. It is important to note that the social welfare function in (5.2) represents a social ordering over all possible individual orderings and exemplifies the multiple profile approach to social choice of Arrow (1963) rather than the single profile approach employed by Bergson (1938) and Samuelson (1947). The literature on the existence of single-profile social welfare functions is discussed by Roberts (1980d), Samuelson (1982), and Sen (1979b).

20. See Sen (1977, 1979b) for further discussion.

21. See Roberts (1980b, esp. pp. 434–436).

22. The implications of distributional homotheticity are discussed by Kolm (1976b) and Blackorby and Donaldson (1978).

23.   Mean value functions were introduced into economics by Bergson (1936) and have been employed, for example, by Arrow et al. (1961) and Atkinson (1970). Properties of mean value functions are discussed by Hardy et al. (1959).

24.   This assumption implies that individual welfare increases with total expenditure at a rate that is inversely proportional to total expenditure. This is also implied by the utilitarian social welfare function employed by Arrow and Kalt (1979).

25.   An absolute index of inequality is invariant with respect to equal additions to the levels of individual welfare. See Blackorby and Donaldson (1980) and Kolm (1976a,b) for further discussion.

26.   A relative index of inequality is homogeneous of degree zero in the levels of individual welfare. See Blackorby and Donaldson (1978) and Kolm (1976a,b) for further discussion.

27.   A bibliography of applications of the approach to inequality measurement originated by Atkinson (1970) and Kolm (1969, 1976a,b) is given by Atkinson (1983a, pp. 32–36).

28.   The relationship between measures of inequality and social welfare functions is discussed by Atkinson (1970), Blackorby and Donaldson (1978, 1980), Dasgupta et al. (1973), Kolm (1969, 1976a,b), Roberts (1980b,d), and Sen (1973). Alternative approaches to measuring efficiency and equity are discussed by Arrow and Kalt (1979) and Sen (1979a).

29.   References on the decomposition of inequality measures by subgroups of the population are listed by Atkinson (1983a, pp. 34–35).

30.   The social expenditure function was introduced by Pollak (1981). Alternative money measures of social welfare are discussed by Arrow and Kalt (1979), Bergson (1980), Deaton and Muellbauer (1980, pp. 214–239), Roberts (1980c), and Sen (1976). A survey of the literature is presented by Sen (1979a).

31.   The indifference map for society as a whole corresponds to that for a consumer with an indirect utility function given by the translog index of efficiency (5.2). In Section III, above, we have assumed that each household has a translog indirect utility function (2.22). We can derive this representation of household preferences by first assuming that each individual has a translog indirect utility function of this form. We then assume, in addition, that the household maximizes a household welfare function of the form (4.10). Under these assumptions the distribution of individual welfare within each household is perfectly egalitarian. The household indirect utility function has the same form as the individual indirect utility functions (2.22) with the number of household equivalent members equal to the sum over all individuals. The translog indexes of inequality I and J in Section V can be interpreted as measures of inequality in the distribution of individual welfare between households by analogy with the translog indexes of between-group inequality I_B and J_B in Section VII. For further discussion, see Pollak (1981) and Samuelson (1956).

32.   Atkinson and Bourguignon (1982, p. 184) have pointed out that this approach has the effect of reducing multidimensional inequality measures, defined on the multivariate distribution of all commodities among individual households, to a single-dimensional inequality measure, defined on the univariate distribution of individual welfare. References on multidimensional inequality measures are listed by Atkinson (1983a, p. 36).

REFERENCES

Arrow, K. J. (1963). *Social Choice and Individual Values*, New Haven, Yale University Press, 2nd ed.

Arrow, K. J. (1977). "Extended Sympathy and the Possibility of Social Choice," *American Economic Review* 67, (1) February, 219–225.

Arrow, K. J., H. B. Chenery, B. S. Minhas, and R. M. Solow (1961). "Capital-Labor

Substitution and Economic Efficiency, *Review of Economics and Statistics* 43, (3) August, 225–250.

Arrow, K. J. and J. P. Kalt (1979). *Petroleum Price Regulation: Should We Decontrol*, Washington, D.C., American Enterprise Institute.

Atkinson, A. B. (1970). "On Measurement of Inequality," *Journal of Economic Theory* 2, (3) September, 244–263.

Atkinson, A. B. (1983a). "Bibliography 1970–82." In A. B. Atkinson (ed.), *Social Justice and Public Policy*, Cambridge, MA, M.I.T. Press, 31–36.

Atkinson, A. B. (1983b). "Introduction to Part I." In A. B. Atkinson (ed.), *Social Justice and Public Policy*, Cambridge, MA, M.I.T. Press, 3–13.

Atkinson, A. B. and F. Bourguignon (1982). "The Comparison of Multi-Dimensioned Distributions of Economic Status," *Review of Economic Studies* 49, (156) April, 183–201.

Barten, A. P. (1964). "Family Composition, Prices, and Expenditure Patterns." In P. Hart, G. Mills, and J. K. Whitaker (eds.), *Econometric Analysis for National Economic Planning: 16th Symposium of the Colston Society*, London, Butterworth, 277–292.

Barten, A. P. (1977). "The Systems of Consumer Demand Functions Approach: A Review." In M. D. Intriligator (ed.), *Frontiers of Quantitative Economics*, Vol. IIIA, Amsterdam, North-Holland, 23–58.

Bentzel, R. (1970). "The Social Significance of Income Distribution Statistics," *Review of Income and Wealth* 16, (3) September, 253–264.

Bergson, A. (1936). "Real Income, Expenditure Proportionality, and Frisch's 'New Methods of Measuring Marginal Utility'," *Review of Economic Studies* 4, (10) October, 33–52.

Bergson, A. (1938). "A Reformulation of Certain Aspects of Welfare Economics," *Quarterly Journal of Economics* 52, February, 310–334.

Bergson, A. (1980). "Consumer's Surplus and Income Redistribution," *Journal of Public Economics* 14, (1) August, 31–47.

Blackorby, C. and D. Donaldson (1978). "Measures of Relative Equality and their Meaning in Terms of Social Welfare," *Journal of Economic Theory* 18, (1) June, 651–75.

Blackorby, C. and D. Donaldson (1980). "A Theoretical Treatment of Indices of Absolute Inequality," *International Economics Review* 21, (1) February, 107–136.

Blackorby, C. and D. Donaldson (1982). "Ratio-Scale and Translation-Scale Full Interpersonal Comparability without Domain Restrictions: Admissible Social-Evaluation Functions," *International Economic Review* 23, (2) June, 249–268.

Bureau of the Census (various annual issues). *Current Population Reports, Consumer Income, Series P-60*, Washington, D.C., U.S. Department of Commerce.

Carlson, M. D. (1974). "The 1972–73 Consumer Expenditure Survey," *Monthly Labor Review* 97, (12) December, 16–23.

Christensen, L. R., D. W. Jorgenson, and L. J. Lau (1975). "Transcendental Logarithmic Utility Functions," *American Economic Review* 65, (3) June, 367–383.

Dalton, H. (1920). "The Measurement of Inequality of Income," *Economic Journal* 30, (119) September, 361–84.

Dasgupta, P., A. K. Sen, and D. Starrett (1973). "Notes on the Measurement of Inequality," *Journal of Economic Theory* 6, (2) April, 180–187.

d'Aspremont, C. and L. Gevers (1977). "Equity and the Informational Basis of Collective Choice," *Review of Economic Studies* 44, (137) June, pp. 199–209.

Deaton, A. and J. Muellbauer (1980). *Economics and Consumer Behavior*, Cambridge, England, Cambridge University Press.

Deschamps, R. and L. Gevers (1978). "Leximin and Utilitarian Rules: A Joint Characterization," *Journal of Economic Theory* 17, (2) April, 143–63.

Gorman, W. M. (1976). "Tricks with Utility Functions." In M. J. Artis and A. R. Nobay (eds.), *Essays in Economic Analysis: Proceedings of the 1975 AUTE Conference*, Cambridge, England, Cambridge University Press, pp. 211–243.

Hammond, P. J. (1976). "Equity, Arrow's Conditions and Rawl's Difference Principle," *Econometrica* 44, (4) July, 793–804.

Hammond, P. J. (1977). "Dual Interpersonal Comparisons of Utility and the Welfare Economics of Income Distribution," *Journal of Public Economics* 7, (1) February, 51–71.

Hardy, G. H., J. E. Littlewood, and G. Polya (1959). *Inequalities*, Cambridge, England, Cambridge University Press, 2nd ed.

Harsanyi, J. C. (1976). *Essay on Ethics, Social Behavior and Scientific Explanation*, Dordrecht, Netherlands, D. Reidel.

Houthakker, H. S. (1957). "An International Comparison of Household Expenditure Patterns Commemorating the Centenary of Engel's Law," *Econometrica* 25, (4) October, 532–551.

Houthakker, H. S. (1960). "Additive Preferences," *Econometrica* 28, (2) April, 244–257.

Jorgenson, D. W. and L. J. Lau (1975). "The Structure of Consumer Preferences," *Annals of Economic and Social Measurement* 4, (1) January, 49–101.

Jorgenson, D. W. and L. J. Lau (1979). "The Integrability of Consumer Demand Functions," *European Economic Review* 12, (2) April, 115–147.

Jorgenson, D. W., L. J. Lau, and T. M. Stoker (1980). "Welfare Comparison Under Exact Aggregation," *American Economic Review* 70, (2) May, 268–272.

Jorgenson, D. W., L. J. Lau, and T. M. Stoker (1981). "Aggregate Consumer Behavior and Individual Welfare," In D. Currie, R. Nobay, and D. Peel (eds.), *Macroeconomic Analysis*, London, Croom-Helm, pp. 35–61.

Jorgenson, D. W., L. J. Lau, and T. M. Stoker (1982). "The Transcendental Logarithmic Model of Aggregate Consumer Behavior." In R. L. Basmann and G. F. Rhodes, Jr. (eds.), *Advances in Econometrics*, Vol. 1, Greenwich, CT, JAI Press, pp. 97–238.

King, M. A. (1983a). "An Index of Inequality: With Applications to Horizontal Equity and Social Mobility," *Econometrica* 51, (1) January, 99–115.

King, M. A. (1983b). "Welfare Analysis of Tax Reforms Using Household Data," *Journal of Public Economics*, (forthcoming).

Kolm, S. C. (1969). "The Optimal Production of Social Justice." In J. Margolis and H. Guitton (eds.), *Public Economics*, London, Macmillan, pp. 145–200.

Kolm, S. C. (1976a and 1976b). "Unequal Inequalities I and II," *Journal of Economic Theory* 12, (3) June, 416–42, and 13, (1) August, 82–111.

Lau, L. J. (1977a). "Complete Systems of Consumer Demand Functions through Duality." In M. D. Intriligator (ed.), *Frontiers of Quantitative Economics*, Vol. IIIA, Amsterdam, North-Holland, 59–86.

Lau, L. J. (1977b). "Existence Conditions for Aggregate Demand Functions," Technical Report No. 248, Institute for Mathematical Studies in the Social Sciences, Stanford University, Stanford (revised 1980 and 1982).

Lau, L. J. (1982). "A Note on the Fundamental Theorem of Exact Aggregation," *Economic Letters* 9, (2) 119–126.

Lau, L. J., W. L. Lin, and P. A. Yotopoulos (1978). "The Linear Logarithmic Expenditure System: An Application to Consumption-Leisure Choice," *Econometrica* 46, (4) July, 843–868.

Lazear, E. P. and R. T. Michael (1980). "Family Size and The Distribution of Real Per Capita Income," *American Economic Review* 70, (1) March, 91–107.

Leser, C. E. V. (1963). "Forms of Engel Functions," *Econometrica* 31, (4) October, 694–703.

Martos, B. (1969). "Subdefinite Matrices and Quadratic Forms," *SIAM Journal of Applied Mathematics* 17, 1215–1223.

Maskin, E. (1978). "A Theorem on Utilitarianism," *Review of Economic Studies* 42, (139) February, 93–96.

Mirrlees, J. A. (1971). "An Exploration in the Theory of Optimal Income Taxation," *Review of Economic Studies* 38, (114) April, 175–208.

Muellbauer, J. (1974a). "Household Composition, Engel Curves and Welfare Comparisons between Households: A Duality Approach," *European Economic Review* 5, (2) August, 103–22.

Muellbauer, J. (1974b). "Inequality Measures, Prices and Household Composition," *Review of Economic Studies* 41, (128) October, 493–504.

Muellbauer, J. (1974c). "Prices and Inequality: The United Kingdom Experience," *Economic Journal* 84, (333) March, 32–55.

Muellbauer, J. (1976). "Economics and the Representative Consumer," In L. Solari and J. N. Du Pasqueir (eds.), *Private and Enlarged Consumption*, Amsterdam, North-Holland, 29–54.

Muellbauer, J. (1977). "Testing the Barten Model of Household Composition Effects and the Cost of Children," *Economic Journal* 87, (347) September, 460–487.

Muellbauer, J. (1980). "The Estimation of the Prais-Houthakker Model of Equivalence Scales," *Econometrica* 48, (1) January, 153–176.

Ng, Y. K. (1975). "Bentham or Bergson? Finite Sensibility, Utility Functions and Social Welfare Functions," *Review of Economic Studies* 42, (132) October, 545–569.

Parks, R. W. and A. P. Barten (1973). "A Cross Country Comparison of the Effects of Prices, Income, and Population Composition on Consumption Patterns," *Economic Journal* 83, (331) September, 834–852.

Pollak, R. A. (1981). "The Social Cost of Living Index," *Journal of Public Economics* 15, (3) June, 311–336.

Pollak, R. A. and T. J. Wales (1978). "Estimation of Complete Demand Systems from Household Budget Data: The Linear and Quadratic Expenditure Systems," *American Economic Review* 68, (3) June, 348–359.

Pollak, R. A. and T. J. Wales (1979). "Welfare Comparisons and Equivalent Scales," *American Economic Review* 69, (2) May, 216–21.

Pollak, R. A. and T. J. Wales (1980). "Comparisons of the Quadratic Expenditure System and Translog Demand Systems with Alternative Specifications of Demographic Effects," *Econometrica* 48, (3) April, 595–612.

Pollak, R. A. and T. J. Wales (1981). "Demographic Variables in Demand Analysis," *Econometrica* 49, (6) November, 1533–1552.

Prais, S. J. and H. S. Houthakker (1971). *The Analysis of Family Budgets*, Cambridge, England, Cambridge University Press, 2nd ed.

Ray, R. (1982). "The Testing and Estimation of Complete Demand Systems on Household Budget Surveys: An Application of AIDS," *European Economic Review* 17, (3) March, 349–370.

Roberts, K. W. S. (1980a). "Possibility Theorems with Interpersonally Comparable Welfare Levels," *Review of Economic Studies* 47, (147) January, 409–20.

Roberts, K. W. S. (1980b). "Interpersonal Comparability and Social Choice Theory," *Review of Economic Studies* 47, (147) January, 421–439.

Roberts, K. W. S. (1980c). "Price-Independent Welfare Prescriptions," *Journal of Public Economics* 13, (3) June, 277–298.

Roberts, K. W. S. (1980d). "Social Choice Theory: The Single-profile and Multi-profile Approaches," *Review of Economic Studies* 47, (147) January, 441–450.

Roy, R. (1943), *De l'utilité: contributions à la théorie des choix*, Paris, Hermann.

Samuelson, P. A. (1947). *Foundations of Economic Analysis*, Cambridge, MA: Harvard University Press.

Samuelson, P. A. (1956). "Social Indifference Curves," *Quarterly Journal of Economics* 70, (1) February, 1–22.

Samuelson, P. A. (1982). "Bergsonian Welfare Economics." In S. Rosefielde (ed.), *Economic Welfare and the Economics of Soviet Socialism: Essays in Honor of Abram Bergson*, Cambridge, England, Cambridge University Press, 223–266.

Sen, A. K. (1970). *Collective Choice and Social Welfare*, Edinburgh, Oliver and Boyd.

Sen, A. K. (1973). *On Economic Inequality*, Oxford, Clarendon Press.

Sen, A. K. (1976). "Real National Income," *Review of Economic Studies* 43, (133) February, 19–40.

Sen, A. K. (1977). "On Weights and Measures: Informational Constraints in Social Welfare Analysis," *Econometrica* 45, (7) October, 1539–72.

Sen, A. K. (1979a). "The Welfare Basis of Real Income Comparisons: A Survey," *Journal of Economic Literature* 17, (1) March, 1–45.

Sen, A. K. (1979b). "Personal Utilities and Public Judgements: Or What's Wrong with Welfare Economics," *Economic Journal* 89, (355) September, 537–558.

Tinbergen, J. (1970). "A Positive and Normative Theory of Income Distribution," *Review of Income and Wealth* 16, (3) September, 221–234.

APPENDIX

Table A-1. Levels of Group Welfare

Year	Age Groups					
	16–24	*25–34*	*35–44*	*45–54*	*55–64*	*65 +*
1958	7.46383	7.24867	7.23708	6.94668	6.98630	6.93805
1959	7.42142	7.27994	7.29390	6.97660	7.04650	7.00746
1960	7.45163	7.30163	7.32777	7.01759	7.04965	7.04909
1961	7.44188	7.31046	7.32835	7.04101	7.07588	7.07469
1962	7.45703	7.30572	7.35136	7.06735	7.10265	7.06861
1963	7.49431	7.35187	7.36828	7.09042	7.13424	7.08863
1964	7.55130	7.38741	7.41328	7.11530	7.15032	7.14529
1965	7.58140	7.43842	7.46820	7.17822	7.19604	7.16284
1966	7.62703	7.49181	7.51662	7.23272	7.23630	7.19830
1967	7.63029	7.51182	7.55249	7.24482	7.24975	7.19195
1968	7.66930	7.52383	7.59684	7.27459	7.30294	7.23013
1969	7.65965	7.54540	7.64671	7.30685	7.32121	7.23765
1970	7.70156	7.56736	7.66603	7.32931	7.35256	7.26543
1971	7.65429	7.55899	7.69283	7.34005	7.35739	7.28777
1972	7.67454	7.58487	7.74624	7.39180	7.39525	7.33059
1973	7.69195	7.61637	7.79261	7.42522	7.43223	7.36972
1974	7.68761	7.59547	7.78677	7.41857	7.43980	7.38154
1975	7.68898	7.60510	7.79119	7.42690	7.42387	7.40681
1976	7.70511	7.62282	7.82817	7.46432	7.45696	7.44067
1977	7.71316	7.63288	7.86335	7.51239	7.49471	7.46625
1978	7.75827	7.65057	7.90188	7.55815	7.53805	7.50680

Table A-2. Indexes of Group Efficiency

			Age Groups			
Year	16–24	25–34	35–44	45–54	55–64	65 +
1958	7.79087	7.63928	7.62559	7.36394	7.37744	7.33262
1959	7.74355	7.65559	7.66067	7.37745	7.42739	7.39577
1960	7.76925	7.67108	7.69166	7.41337	7.42443	7.43090
1961	7.75772	7.67935	7.68919	7.43469	7.44790	7.45276
1962	7.77472	7.67767	7.71111	7.45865	7.47412	7.44371
1963	7.80750	7.71802	7.72040	7.47736	7.50057	7.46015
1964	7.86476	7.75781	7.77090	7.50548	7.51494	7.51387
1965	7.89149	7.80244	7.81947	7.56261	7.55804	7.52985
1966	7.93327	7.85078	7.86205	7.61261	7.59249	7.56062
1967	7.93636	7.87098	7.89621	7.62292	7.60325	7.55125
1968	7.97777	7.88418	7.93929	7.65112	7.65423	7.58652
1969	7.96821	7.90267	7.98472	7.67980	7.67111	7.59371
1970	8.00988	7.92445	8.00349	7.69984	7.69860	7.61807
1971	7.96297	7.91569	8.03157	7.71112	7.70310	7.63973
1972	7.97761	7.93633	8.08251	7.75846	7.73827	7.68134
1973	7.99844	7.96990	8.12982	7.79281	7.77680	7.72243
1974	7.99765	7.94814	8.12371	7.78455	7.78560	7.73640
1975	8.00197	7.95924	8.13294	7.79479	7.76941	7.76178
1976	8.01605	7.97326	8.16437	7.82797	7.80022	7.79403
1977	8.02099	7.97906	8.19579	7.87214	7.83477	7.81708
1978	8.06875	7.99627	8.23355	7.91673	7.87923	7.85986

Table A-3. Money Metric Group Welfare

			Age Groups			
Year	16–24	25–34	35–44	45–54	55–64	65 +
1958	8912.91	43697.32	78173.49	55160.54	38581.93	27832.00
1959	9078.85	44078.05	83640.86	57409.79	41642.57	30763.98
1960	9679.34	45259.73	85376.60	60852.64	42628.57	31231.56
1961	9452.87	44375.69	86296.51	61640.31	45820.08	35357.00
1962	9678.72	43478.15	91545.49	63864.28	48084.99	36600.34
1963	10620.00	45607.15	93625.97	66329.05	50224.78	37742.90
1964	11964.68	47737.11	96652.48	70619.79	52081.00	40277.61
1965	12631.71	51439.72	101249.40	75364.58	54836.40	41767.87
1966	13620.83	54746.84	106217.51	80378.70	57866.63	44385.93
1967	13812.41	57404.54	110192.36	82460.31	60981.14	45231.33
1968	16187.51	61202.96	112220.80	84830.94	64739.29	47474.80
1969	16857.30	64523.80	116968.74	88341.78	67333.43	48887.09
1970	19150.49	66923.74	119067.10	91419.11	69909.84	50973.22
1971	19928.00	70654.50	118887.06	92642.51	70688.50	53951.55

Table A-3. Money Metric Group Welfare

Year	Age Groups					
	16–24	*25–34*	*35–44*	*45–54*	*55–64*	*65 +*
1972	21277.23	75896.27	125446.69	96260.59	73426.66	57276.64
1973	23183.24	82012.37	130571.12	99405.94	75599.71	60751.80
1974	22740.29	83446.93	129805.90	97703.93	76865.29	62672.90
1975	23235.10	86492.54	131689.92	96908.15	76821.80	65714.11
1976	24244.86	91014.62	138177.96	99845.53	80135.68	68174.14
1977	24907.82	94867.34	146423.37	101320.31	84951.80	70960.20
1978	27257.49	97825.11	154904.95	104608.89	88552.72	76094.14

Table A-4. Money Metric Group Efficiency

Year	Age Groups					
	16–24	*25–34*	*35–44*	*45–54*	*44–65*	*65 +*
1958	12360.89	64579.96	115289.00	83722.53	57049.98	41295.38
1959	12529.32	64174.73	120699.64	85717.86	60947.15	45361.25
1960	13298.06	65488.04	122849.77	90399.09	62010.32	45752.00
1961	12963.75	64172.88	123795.74	91377.26	66469.54	51602.49
1962	13298.11	63067.22	131181.69	94448.29	69717.01	53258.65
1963	14525.83	65773.27	133144.28	97667.85	72446.14	54724.82
1964	16369.60	69138.22	138205.05	104321.99	74994.60	58228.42
1965	17223.92	74027.04	143862.29	110689.34	78756.18	60288.23
1966	18501.33	78389.22	150043.02	117523.76	82626.08	63767.27
1967	18758.21	82210.75	155391.19	120351.80	86839.60	64786.11
1968	22036.66	87754.51	158051.53	123617.05	91988.86	67801.96
1969	22950.38	92232.28	164007.37	128272.74	95541.25	69796.32
1970	26066.45	95645.18	166857.79	132421.07	98814.93	72525.67
1971	27134.44	100937.92	166820.54	134265.32	99881.52	76711.39
1972	28809.31	107860.02	175590.52	138895.22	103471.85	81340.19
1973	31497.75	116793.15	182933.42	143566.90	106700.68	86444.34
1974	31005.82	118733.56	181813.64	140881.90	108620.22	89370.47
1975	31774.26	123247.97	185341.13	140001.65	108530.92	93717.21
1976	33087.26	129213.46	193397.17	143633.89	112954.22	97068.87
1977	33886.09	134109.02	204167.64	145189.72	119360.00	100780.81
1978	37181.22	138224.97	215828.95	149725.26	124558.68	108314.54

ETHICALLY SIGNIFICANT ORDINAL INDEXES OF RELATIVE INEQUALITY

Charles Blackorby and David Donaldson

I. INTRODUCTION

There are two general approaches to the construction of indexes of inequality. In the descriptive, or "mechanistic," approach, indexes are found which satisfy certain more or less plausible axioms (see, for example, Cowell and Kuga, 1981; Dasgupta et al., 1973; Eichhorn and Gehrig, 1982; Fei and Fields, 1978; Kolm, 1976; Sen, 1973, 1978 [reprint 1982]; Shorrocks, 1980). In the alternative "ethical" approach, indexes are constructed from specific social-evaluation functions (see, for example, Aigner and Heins, 1967; Atkinson, 1970, 1976; Blackorby and Donaldson, 1978, 1980; Dalton, 1920; Donaldson and Weymark, 1980; Kolm, 1969, 1976; Sen, 1973, 1978).

Advances in Econometrics, vol. 3, pages 131–147
Copyright © 1984 by JAI Press Inc.
All rights of reproduction in any form reserved.
ISBN: 0-89232-443-0

Ethical indexes have obvious normative significance, but it is not clear just how descriptive indexes can be used for ethical judgments. However, if these indexes are thought to describe inequality objectively, it seems natural to suppose that ethical judgments might be based on them. Thus, we imagine that a social-evaluation function might be written as an increasing function of per-capita (real) income and a decreasing function of an index (or several indexes) of inequality. If one index only is used, then it is normatively significant—a reduction in inequality with per-capita income constant is a social improvement. If this property is satisfied with a single *relative* index, we say that the social-evaluation function satisfies the *Relative Inequality Aggregation Property* (RIAP). When more than one relative index is used, we refer to the *Generalized Relative Inequality Aggregation Property* (GRIAP). The RIAP has been investigated by Amiel (1981), Kats (1972), and Sheshinski (1972) in the special case of the Gini index of inequality, and Kondor (1975) has discussed its ethical attractiveness.

In this paper, we investigate the relationship of the RIAP (and the GRIAP) to ethical indexes of inequality. In Section II, we discuss the best-known ethical index, the Atkinson (1970)–Kolm (1969)–Sen (1973) (AKS) index. It is the percentage of per-capita (or total) income that can be saved by moving, with social indifference, from the actual income vector to full equality. The AKS index is normatively significant, but it is not a relative index unless the social-evaluation function is homothetic. In that case, we show that the social-evaluation function satisfies the RIAP with index I if and only if the AKS index is ordinally equivalent to I.

We have suggested a method (Blackorby and Donaldson, 1978) for deriving a family of ethical indexes of relative inequality from a (possibly) nonhomothetic social-evaluation function. These indexes are numerically significant (an index value of .5 has a particular meaning) but are not always normatively significant. We show (Section III.A) that if the social-evaluation function satisfies the RIAP with index I then all the members of our family are ordinally equivalent to each other and to I. That is, all the indexes in the family rank distributions of income in exactly the same way and thus represent the same "more unequal than" relation.

In this paper, too, we provide a new method for deriving a family of indexes of relative inequality from a social-evaluation function (Section III.B). This method uses the equivalent-income function and a "reference level" of per-capita income. Again, we find that the RIAP makes the members of this family ordinally equivalent to each other and the index I.

Section IV contains a discussion of the GRIAP and its relationship to ethical indexes.

II. ATKINSON–KOLM–SEN INDEXES

We begin with a general relative index of inequality[1] $I:[\mathbf{R}^n_+ \backslash 0_n] \to \mathbf{R}$ where I is homogeneous of degree zero (a relative index) and S-convex (it agrees weakly with the Lorenz quasi-ordering), and $I(x1_n) = 0$ for any $x > 0$. For a vector $y = (y_1, \ldots, y_n)$ of individual real incomes (we abstract from the pooling problem raised by the existence of households containing several individuals), measured inequality is $I(y)$, and the index of equality corresponding to I is defined by

$$E(y): = 1 - I(y). \tag{1}$$

Here E is homogeneous of degree zero and S-concave, and $E(x1_n) = 1$ for any $x > 0$. Since S-convex and S-concave functions are symmetric, I and E are symmetric functions.

In addition to indexes of inequality and equality, we consider a social-evaluation function $W:[\mathbf{R}^n_+ \backslash 0_n] \to \mathbf{R}$. It is assumed to be S-concave (and therefore symmetric) and increasing along rays. We want to know the conditions under which it can be written as

$$W(y) = \mathring{W}(\mu(y), I(y)) = \hat{W}(\mu(y), E(y)), \tag{2}$$

where $\hat{W}$ is increasing in its arguments. This is the RIAP. The regularity conditions (above) on W are necessary conditions for it to satisfy (2).

Given a social-evaluation function, it is possible to define an index of inequality using a procedure of Atkinson (1970), Kolm (1969), and Sen (1973). This AKS index of inequality is defined as the percentage of total income or per-capita income that can be saved by moving with social indifference from the actual distribution of income to income equality. A formal definition requires the notion of the *equally-distributed-equivalent income*, i.e., that income which, if given to each person in society, results in an income vector which is ethically indifferent to the actual distribution. It is defined by

$$W(\xi 1_n) = W(y). \tag{3}$$

We assume that a solution to (3) always exists,[2] and solve (3) as

$$\xi = \Xi(y). \tag{4}$$

The mean of the income distribution is given by

$$\mu(y) = \sum_i y_i/n. \tag{5}$$

Equations (4) and (5) can be used to define the AKS index of inequality:

$$I^a(y): = \frac{\mu(y) - \Xi(y)}{\mu(y)} = 1 - \frac{\Xi(y)}{\mu(y)}. \tag{6}$$

The AKS index of equality E^a is defined by

$$E^a(y): = 1 - I^a(y) = \frac{\Xi(y)}{\mu(y)}.$$ (7)

It is easy to see [from (3) and (4)] that the *equally-distributed-equivalent-income function* Ξ is just an increasing transform of the social-evaluation function and is, therefore, ordinally equivalent to it. It follows from (7) that

$$\Xi(y) = \mu(y)E^a(y),$$ (8)

and therefore that

$$W(y) = \overset{*}{W}(\mu(y) E^a(y)),$$ (9)

where $\overset{*}{W}$ is increasing. It follows that $\Xi(y)$ is an inequality-adjusted per-capital income. Further, the product of the mean income and the AKS index of equality is ordinally equivalent to the original social-evaluation function.

Given (9), it is tempting to say that any function W satisfying our regularity conditions satisfies the RIAP. In general, however, that is not true; the AKS index E^a is not always a relative index. However, E^a and I^a are relative indexes if and only if W is homothetic (see, for example Sen, 1973). In that case, W trivially satisfies the RIAP. In addition, if any homothetic W satisfies the RIAP with some index E, then E^a and E are ordinally equivalent. That is,

$$E^a(y) = \phi(E(y))$$ (10)

for all y with ϕ increasing and $\phi(1) = 1$. These results are summarized in the following theorem.

THEOREM 1: *Given our regularity conditions,*

(i) *if W is homothetic, then it satisfies the RIAP; and*

(ii) *if W satisfies the RIAP with the index E, then E and E^a are ordinally equivalent if and only if W is homothetic.*

PROOF: See the Appendix.

III. MORE GENERAL INDEXES OF RELATIVE INEQUALITY

The result of Theorem 1 is a consequence of the fact that AKS indexes are relative indexes if and only if the corresponding social-evaluation functions are homothetic. It is possible for the RIAP to be satisfied by nonhomothetic social-evaluation functions, and this suggests that interpreting all indexes of inequality as AKS indexes is inappropriate. We have developed (Blackorby and Donaldson, 1978) a method for generating relative indexes from arbitrary social-evaluation functions. Our procedure results in a family of inequality indexes for each social-evaluation function, one index for each level surface. This is not the only procedure available for the generation of relative indexes, however. In this paper, we offer a new procedure for finding families of relative indexes, one index for each level of the per capita income. Both of these families have the same property. If the social-evaluation function satisfies the RIAP, then all the members of either family are ordinally equivalent to each other and to the index *I*.

This ordinality property is interesting in itself. The AKS index and the members of the families presented here are all numerically significant. That is, an index value of .5 or .7 has a numerical interpretation (percentage of per capital income "wasted" by inequality in the AKS case). If we interpret indexes of inequality as representations of a "more unequal than" relation, it is appropriate to abandon numerical significance in favour of ordinality. Both procedures presented here may be thought of as providing a rationale for ordinal indexes. In addition, we show that the ordinality property provides a complete characterization of the RIAP.

A.   Relative Indexes Based on the Transformation Function

The transformation function is an implicit representation of the social-evaluation function. It is defined by

$$F(w, y): = \max\{\lambda > 0 \mid W(y/\lambda) \geq w\},\tag{11}$$

and we assume that it is defined for all w and y; F is decreasing in its first argument, and it is positively linearly homogeneous and S-concave in the income vector y. The social-evaluation function can be recovered from the transformation function, since

$$F(w, y) = 1 \leftrightarrow W(y) = w.\tag{12}$$

Since F is positively linearly homogeneous in y, it represents, for each w, a set of homothetic preferences (the indifference surfaces are radial blowups of the indifference surface of W referenced by w). This allows us to construct, given w, an AKS index using F. It is a relative index and is given by

$$E^f(w, y) = \frac{F(w, y)}{\mu(y)F(w, 1_n)}.\tag{13}$$

In the case that W is homothetic, it is easily checked that the AKS index for W is E^f.[3] Homotheticity of W requires, for all y,

$$W(y) = \Lambda(\bar{W}(y)) \tag{14}$$

where $\bar{W}$ is positively linearly homogeneous and Λ is increasing. It follows that

$$E^a(y) = \frac{\bar{W}(y)}{\mu(y)\bar{W}(1_n)} . \tag{15}$$

The transformation function, in this case, is

$$F(w, y) = \frac{\bar{W}(y)}{\Lambda^{-1}(w)} , \tag{16}$$

ensuring that $E^a = E^f$.

The AKS index E^a is not always a relative index, but it is always normatively significant. That is, for all $\bar{y}$, $\hat{y}$ such that $\mu(\bar{y}) = \mu(\hat{y})$,

$$[E^a(\bar{y}) \geq E^a(\hat{y})] \leftrightarrow W(\bar{y}) \geq W(\hat{y}). \tag{17}$$

On the other hand, E^f is always a relative index but it is not necessarily normatively significant.[4] But (17) implies that an index E is normatively significant if and only if

$$W(y) = \hat{W}(\mu(y), E(y)) \tag{18}$$

where W is increasing in its second argument. Thus, the RIAP is equivalent to normative significance of E.

THEOREM 2: *Given our regularity conditions, the social-evaluation function satisfies the* RIAP *with the index* E *if and only if each member of the family of indexes* E^f *is ordinally equivalent to* E. *That is,*

$$E^f(w, y) = \phi^f(w, E(y)), \tag{19}$$

where ϕ^f *is increasing in its second argument, and*

$$\phi^f(w, 1) = 1 \tag{20}$$

for all w.

PROOF: See the Appendix.

It follows that the family of numerically significant indexes E^f is a single ordinal index only in the case that RIAP is satisfied. In this case, the indexes E^f are normatively significant. Too, ordinal equivalence of the indexes in the family E^f is a complete characterization of the RIAP.

B. Relative Indexes Based on the Equivalent-Income Function

The family of relative indexes E^f is not the only one that corresponds to the social-evaluation function W. It is possible to find another one based on the equivalent-income function Ξ. We define

$$G(m, y): = \left\{ \lambda \; \Xi\left(\frac{y}{\lambda}\right) \; \middle| \; \mu\left(\frac{y}{\lambda}\right) = m \right\}$$

$$= \frac{\mu(y)}{m} \; \Xi\left(\frac{my}{\mu(y)}\right) . \tag{21}$$

This construction is illustrated in Figure 1: AB is the set of points for which $\mu(y) = m$, a reference level of per-capita income. For an arbitrary $\bar{y}$, λ is found so that $\mu(\bar{y}/\lambda) = m$. The value of $G(m, \bar{y})$ is just λ times the equally distributed income of $\bar{y}/\lambda$. Since $\lambda = \mu(\bar{y})/m$, Eq. (21) results. Here G is positively linearly homogeneous and S-concave in its second

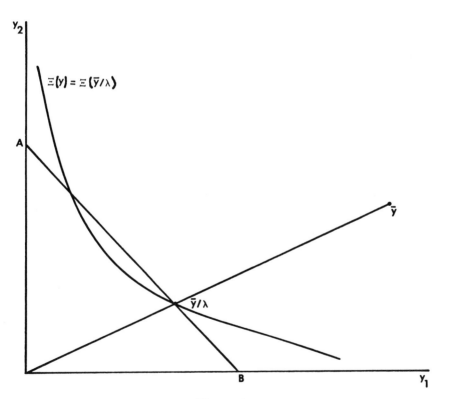

Figure 1

argument, y. The social-evaluation function W can be recovered from G by noting that

$$\Xi(y) = G(\mu(y), y). \tag{22}$$

We define the family of indexes E^g by finding the AKS index corresponding to G for each level of m. It is

$$E^g(m, y) = \frac{G(m, y)}{\mu(y)G(m, 1_n)} \tag{23}$$

$$= \frac{1}{m} \Xi\left(\frac{my}{\mu(y)}\right),$$

where the second line of (23) follows from (21) and the fact that

$$\Xi(m1_n) = m. \tag{24a}$$

It is easily checked that E^g is the AKS index for W if W is homothetic, since, in that case,

$$G(m, y) = \Xi(y). \tag{24b}$$

It is also true that E^g is independent of m if and only if W is homothetic. Of course, whenever $\mu(y) = m$ the values of the AKS index E^a and E^g coincide.

THEOREM 3: *Given our regularity assumptions, W satisfies the* RIAP *with the index E if and only if each member of the family E^g is ordinally equivalent to E. That is,*

$$E^g(m, y) = \phi^g(m, E(y)) \tag{25}$$

where ϕ^g is increasing in its second argument, and

$$\phi^g(m, 1) = 1 \tag{26}$$

for all m.

PROOF: See the Appendix.

Thus, the RIAP is completely characterized by the ordinal equivalence of the members of the family E^g. Further, the members of the family E^g are normatively significant if and only if they represent a single ordinal index.

To illustrate these results, consider an index of relative equality Q and the ordinally equivalent index Q^2, where

$$Q^2(y): = (Q(y))^2. \tag{27}$$

Interpreting these as AKS indexes, they are dual to the social-evaluation functions

$$W^Q(y) = \overset{*}{W}{}^Q(\mu(y)Q(y)) \tag{28}$$

and

$$W^{Q^2}(y) = \overset{*}{W}{}^{Q^2}(\mu(y)(Q(y))^2). \tag{29}$$

These are both homothetic functions, and they are not ordinally equivalent. They are, however, members of the larger class of functions that can be written as

$$W(y) = \hat{W}(\mu(y), Q(y)). \tag{30}$$

A nonhomothetic member of the class of functions given by (30) is

$$\overset{\circ}{W}(y) = \frac{\log(1 + \mu(y))}{1 - \log Q(y)}. \tag{31}$$

The equally-distributed-equivalent-income function corresponding to $\overset{\circ}{W}$ is

$$\overset{\circ}{\Xi}(y) = \exp\left\{\frac{\log(1 + \mu(y))}{1 - \log Q(y)}\right\} - 1, \tag{32}$$

and its AKS index is

$$\overset{\circ}{E}{}^a(y) = \frac{1}{\mu(y)}\left[\exp\left\{\frac{\log(1 + \mu(y))}{1 - \log Q(y)}\right\} - 1\right]. \tag{33}$$

Here $\overset{\circ}{E}{}^a$ is not a relative index. The transformation function corresponding to $\overset{\circ}{W}$ is

$$\overset{\circ}{F}(w, y) = \frac{\mu(y)}{(e/Q(y))^w - 1}, \tag{34}$$

and therefore the family E^f is given by

$$\overset{\circ}{E}{}^f(w, y) = \frac{\overset{\circ}{F}(w, y)}{\mu(y)\,\overset{\circ}{F}(w, 1_n)} = \frac{e^w - 1}{(e/Q(y))^w - 1}. \tag{35}$$

This index is ordinally equivalent to Q for each w [note that w must be greater than zero in (31)]. Each value of w makes E^f into a different *numerical* index, but each value of w results in a simple renumbering of the isoinequality sets. Here $\overset{\circ}{E}{}^f$ contains the unobservable w, but this may be changed to m, a reference level of per-capita income, by substituting $w = W(m1_n)$ into (35). This produces the family of indexes

$$\overset{*}{E}{}^f(m, y) := \overset{\circ}{E}{}^f(W(m1_n), y) = \frac{m}{(e/Q(y))^{\log(m+1)} - 1}. \tag{36}$$

The family E^g is found directly from $\overset{\circ}{\Xi}$ in (32), and

$$
\begin{aligned}
E^g(m, y) &= \frac{1}{m} \overset{\circ}{\Xi}\left(\frac{my}{\mu(y)}\right) \\
&= \frac{1}{m}\left[\exp\left\{\frac{\log(1 + m)}{1 - \log Q(y)}\right\} - 1\right].
\end{aligned}
\tag{37}
$$

Each member of this family is a relative index and is ordinally equivalent to Q.

IV.   THE GENERALIZED RIAP

If mechanistic indexes are incorporated into social-evaluation functions, there is no obvious reason why only a single index should be employed. Thus, we say that W satisfies the *Generalized RIAP* (GRIAP) if it can be written as

$$
W(y) = \hat{W}(\mu(y), E^1(y), E^2(y), \ldots, E^r(y)),
\tag{38}
$$

where W is increasing in its first argument, nondecreasing in the rest, and $E^1, \ldots, E^r$ are indexes of relative equality. For example, we may have

$$
W(y) = \Xi(y) = \begin{cases} \mu(y)E^G(y), & \mu(y) < 10{,}000 \\ \mu(y)E^A(y), & \mu(y) \geq 10{,}000, \end{cases}
\tag{39}
$$

where E^G and E^A are the Gini and (one of the) Atkinson indexes of equality.

Theorem 4 generalizes our previous results to the GRIAP.

THEOREM 4:   *Given our regularity conditions,*

(i) *W is homothetic and satisfies the* GRIAP *if and only if E^a is a relative index, and*

$$
E^a(y) = \psi(E^1(y), \ldots, E^r(y)),
$$

where ψ is nondecreasing and

$$
\psi(1, \ldots, 1) = 1;
\tag{41}
$$

(ii) *W satisfies the* GRIAP *if and only if*

$$
E^f(w, y) = \psi^f(w, E^1(y), \ldots, E^r(y)),
\tag{42}
$$

where ψ^f is nondecreasing in $E^j(y)$, for $j = 1, \ldots, r$, and

$$
\psi^f(w, 1, \ldots, 1) = 1
\tag{43}
$$

for all w; and

(iii) *W satisfies the* GRIAP *if and only if*

$$E^g(m, y) = \psi^g(m, E^1(y), \ldots, E^r(y)) \tag{44}$$

where ψ^g is nondecreasing in $E^j(y), j = 1, \ldots, r, and

$$\psi^g(m, 1, \ldots, 1) = 1. \tag{45}$$

for all m.

PROOF: See the Appendix.

In our example (30), E^f is not easily computable, but

$$E^g(m, y) = \begin{cases} E^G(y), & m < 10,000 \\ E^A(y), & m \geq 10,000, \end{cases} \tag{46}$$

allowing a different index for different reference levels of per-capita real income. In the general case, the GRIAP is satisfied if and only if the families E^f and E^g are functions of $E^1(y), \ldots, E^r(y)$. The function that is used to aggregate the indexes will depend on the reference level of w or m, and, of course, the members of the families are not ordinally equivalent to each other. If we want a single ordinal index

$$\overset{*}{E}(y) = \overset{*}{\psi}(E^1(y), \ldots, E^r(y)), \tag{47}$$

constructed from the indexes $E^1, \ldots, E^r$, then the results of Section III apply and

$$W(y) = \hat{W}(\mu(y), \overset{*}{\psi}(E^1(y), \ldots, E^r(y))). \tag{48}$$

V. CONCLUSION

Descriptive indexes are, at least in principle, very different from ethical indexes. They may, however, be given simple ethical interpretations. Any descriptive index that is numerically significant may be interpreted as an AKS index, and the corresponding homothetic social-evaluation function can be found. If, however, a descriptive index is an ordinal index, it is normatively consistent with all the social-evaluation functions that satisfy an appropriate RIAP or GRIAP. These ordinal indexes can be interpreted as ethical indexes as well, and our results show that they are dual to social-evaluation functions that satisfy the RIAP using the index. Thus, we have provided a rationale for ordinal ethical indexes of relative inequality and discovered all the social-evaluation functions that are consistent with these indexes. The RIAP is the ethical property of social-evaluation functions that makes this ethical interpretation of ordinal indexes possible.

Relative indexes are not the only commonly used indexes of inequality. Absolute indexes (Blackorby and Donaldson, 1980; Kolm, 1976) are invariant to equal additions to or subtractions from each person's real income. All the results of this paper may be extended to absolute indexes. We could speak of the *Absolute Inequality Aggregation Property* (AIAP) and the *Generalized* AIAP. And, given Theorems 2 and 3 in this paper, it is easy to show that a social-evaluation function satisfies the AIAP with absolute index A if and only if the members of the family described in Blackorby and Donaldson (1980) are ordinally equivalent to each other and to A. And, of course, the construction of Section III.B could be extended to absolute indexes with a similar result.

APPENDIX

THEOREM 1: *Given our regularity conditions,*

(i) *if W is homothetic, it satisfies the RIAP; and*

(ii) *if W satisfies the RIAP with the index E, then E^a and E are ordinally equivalent if and only if W is homothetic.*

PROOF: (i) Suppose that W is homothetic. Then it can be written as

$$W(y) = \psi(\bar{W}(y)), \tag{A-1}$$

where $\bar{W}$ is positively linearly homogeneous and ψ is increasing. From (3) and (7),

$$E^a(y) = \frac{\bar{W}(y)}{\mu(y)\bar{W}(1_n)}, \tag{A-2}$$

and since $\bar{W}$ is positively linearly homogeneous, E^a is a relative index. Hence, (9) guarantees that W satisfies the RIAP.

(ii) Suppose that W satisfies the RIAP and that it is homothetic. Then, using Eqs. (A-1) and (2),

$$\bar{W}(y) = \overset{*}{W}(\mu(y), E(y)). \tag{A-3}$$

From (A-2), it follows that

$$E^a(y) = \frac{\overset{*}{W}(\mu(y), E(y))}{\mu(y)\overset{*}{W}(1, 1)}. \tag{A-4}$$

Since $\bar{W}$ is positively linearly homogeneous, for any $\lambda > 0$,

$$E^a(y) = \frac{\overset{*}{W}(\mu(\lambda y), E(\lambda y))/\lambda}{\mu(\lambda y)\overset{*}{W}(1, 1)/\lambda}$$

$$= \frac{\overset{*}{W}(\lambda\mu(y), E(y))}{\lambda\mu(y)\overset{*}{W}(1, 1)} \ . \tag{A-5}$$

Setting $\lambda = 1/\mu(y)$, Eq. (A-5) becomes

$$E^a(y) = \frac{\overset{*}{W}(1, E(y))}{\overset{*}{W}(1, 1)}$$

$$= \phi(E(y)), \tag{A-6}$$

with $\phi(1) = 1$.

Now suppose that (10) is satisfied. It is immediate that E^a is a relative index; and from (9), W is homothetic.   QED

THEOREM 2: *Given our regularity conditions, the social-evaluation function satisfies the* RIAP *with the index E if and only if each member of the family E^f is ordinally equivalent to the index E. That is,*

$$E^f(w, y) = \phi^f(w, E(y)), \tag{19}$$

where the function ϕ^f is increasing in its second argument, and

$$\phi^f(w, 1) = 1 \tag{20}$$

for all w.

PROOF: (i) Let W satisfy the RIAP. Then

$$F(w, y) = \max\left\{\lambda \mid W\left(\frac{y}{\lambda}\right) \geq w\right\}$$

$$= \left\{\lambda \mid \hat{W}\left(\mu\left(\frac{y}{\lambda}\right), E\left(\frac{y}{\lambda}\right)\right) = w\right\}$$

$$= \left\{\lambda \mid \hat{W}\left(\frac{\mu(y)}{\lambda}, E(y)\right) = w\right\} \tag{A-7}$$

$$= \mu(y)\, f(w, E(y)),$$

where f is increasing in its second argument.

From (13),

$$E^f(w, y) = \frac{f(w, E(y))}{f(w, 1)} ,$$ (A-8)

satisfying (19) and (20).

(ii) Now suppose that (19) is satisfied for some index E. From (13),

$$\begin{aligned} F(w, y) &= F(w, 1_n)\mu(y)E^f(w, y) \\ &= F(w, 1_n)\mu(y) \, \phi^f(w, E(y)). \end{aligned}$$ (A-9)

Since W is found by setting $F(w, y) = 1$ and solving for w, W must satisfy the RIAP.   QED

THEOREM 3:   *Given our regularity assumptions, W satisfies the RIAP with the index E if and only if each member of the family E^g is ordinally equivalent to E. That is,*

$$E^g(w, y) = \phi^g(m, E(y))$$ (25)

where ϕ^g is increasing in its second argument, and

$$\phi^g(m, 1) = 1$$ (26)

for all m.

PROOF: (i) Let W satisfy the RIAP. Then Ξ can be written as

$$\Xi(y) = \hat{\Xi}(\mu(y), E(y)),$$ (A-10)

where $\hat{\Xi}$ is increasing in its arguments, and from (23),

$$\begin{aligned} E^g(m, y) &= \frac{1}{m} \, \Xi\left(\frac{my}{\mu(y)}\right) \\ &= \frac{1}{m} \, \hat{\Xi}\left(\mu\left(\frac{my}{\mu(y)}\right), E\left(\frac{my}{\mu(y)}\right)\right) \\ &= \frac{1}{m} \, \hat{\Xi}(m, E(y)), \end{aligned}$$ (A-11)

satisfying (25) and (26).

(ii) Now suppose that (25) is satisfied. Then, from (23)

$$\begin{aligned} \Xi\left(\frac{my}{\mu(y)}\right) &= m \, E^g(m, y) \\ &= m \, \phi^g(m, E(y)). \end{aligned}$$ (A-12)

Setting $m = \mu(y)$ in (A-12),

$$\Xi(y) = \mu(y) \, \phi^g(\mu(y), E(y)), \tag{A-13}$$

and Ξ and W satisfy the RIAP. QED

THEOREM 4: *Given our regularity conditions,*
(i) *W is homothetic and satisfies the* GRIAP *if and only if E^a is a relative index and*

$$E^a(y) = \psi(E^1(y), \ldots, E^r(y)), \tag{40}$$

where ψ is nondecreasing and

$$\psi(1, \ldots, 1) = 1; \tag{41}$$

(ii) *W satisfies the* GRIAP *if and only if*

$$E^f(w, y) = \psi^f(w, E^1(y), \ldots, E^r(y)), \tag{42}$$

where ψ^f is nondecreasing in $E^j(y)$, for $j = 1, \ldots, r$, and

$$\psi^f(w, 1, \ldots, 1) = 1 \tag{43}$$

for all w; and
(iii) *W satisfies the* GRIAP *if and only if*

$$E^g(m, y) = \psi^g(m, E^1(y), \ldots, E^r(y)), \tag{44}$$

where ψ^g is nondecreasing in $E^j(y)$, for $j = 1, \ldots, r$, and

$$\psi^g(m, 1, \ldots, 1) = 1 \tag{45}$$

for all m.

PROOF: Theorem 4 (i) is a trivial extension of Theorem 1(i).

(ii) Suppose W satisfies the GRIAP. Then

$$\begin{aligned} F(w, y) &= \max\left\{\lambda \mid \hat{W}\left(\frac{\mu(y)}{\lambda}, E^1(y), \ldots, E^r(y)\right) \geq w\right\} \\ &= \mu(y) \, f(w, E^1(y), \ldots, E^r(y)) \end{aligned} \tag{A-14}$$

where f is nondecreasing in $E^j(y)$, for $j = 1, \ldots, r$.
From (13),

$$E^f(w, y) = \frac{f(w, E^1(y), \ldots, E^r(y))}{f(w, 1, \ldots, 1)}, \tag{A-15}$$

satisfying (42) and (43).
Now suppose that E^f satisfies (42). From (13),

$$F(w, y) = F(w, 1_n)\mu(y) \, \psi^f(w, E^1(y), \ldots, E^r(y)). \tag{A-16}$$

Since W is found by setting $F(w, y) = 1$ and solving for w, W must satisfy the GRIAP.

(iii) Suppose W satisfies the GRIAP. Then Ξ may be written as

$$\Xi(y) = \hat{\Xi}(\mu(y), E^1(y), \ldots, E^r(y)), \tag{A-17}$$

and, from (23),

$$
\begin{aligned}
E^g(m, y) &= \frac{1}{m} \Xi\left(\frac{my}{\mu(y)}\right) \\
&= \frac{1}{m} \hat{\Xi}(m, E^1(y), \ldots, E^r(y)),
\end{aligned}
\tag{A-18}
$$

satisfying (44). Equation (45) follows from the fact that

$$E^g(m, x1_n) = 1 \tag{A-19}$$

for any m and $x > 0$.

Now suppose that E^g satisfies (44). Then, from (23),

$$
\begin{aligned}
\Xi\left(\frac{my}{\mu(y)}\right) &= m\, E^g(m, y) \\
&= m\, \psi^g(m, E^1(y), \ldots, E^r(y))
\end{aligned}
\tag{A-20}
$$

and, setting $m = \mu(y)$,

$$\Xi(y) = \mu(y)\, \psi^g(\mu(y), E^1(y), \ldots, E^r(y)), \tag{A-21}$$

so Ξ and W satisfy the GRIAP.   QED

NOTES

1. $[\mathbf{R}^n_+ \backslash 0_n]$ is the nonnegative Euclidean n-orthant with the origin deleted. This is done because mean income is zero at that point, causing a difficulty in Eq. (6). Some inequality indexes such as the Gini are defined on larger domains, and our analysis can be easily extended to those domains.

2. Several sets of assumptions will guarantee this. One is to assume, in addition to the regularity conditions above, that W is continuous and increasing in its arguments. Such "increasingness" of W is not, however guaranteed by (2). [Amiel (1981) contains a discussion.] We adopt the domain restrictions we do for convenience. It is possible to prove analogous theorems if Ξ is defined on a subset of $[\mathbf{R}^n_+ \backslash 0_n]$.

3. It may be objected that E^f contains the unobservable variable w. This is easily remedied by defining

$$\bar{E}^f(m, y): = E^f(W(m1_n), y).$$

Here m can be thought of as a reference level of per-capita income, and the family $\bar{E}^f$ contains a different index for each value of m.

4. See the discussion in Blackorby and Donaldson (1978, p. 64).

REFERENCES

Aigner, D. and A. Heins (1967), A social welfare view of the measurement of income inequality, *Review of Income and Wealth* 13, 13–25.

Amiel, Y. (1981) Some remarks on income inequality, the Gini index and Paretian social welfare functions, Working Paper No. 17-81, Foerder Institute for Economic Research, May.

Atkinson, A. (1970) On the measurement of inequality, *Journal of Economic Theory* 2, 244–263.

Atkinson, A. (1976) *The Economics of Inequality*, Clarendon, Oxford.

Blackorby, C. and D. Donaldson (1978) Measures of relative equality and their meaning in terms of social welfare, *Journal of Economic Theory* 18, 59–80.

Blackorby, C., and D. Donaldson (1980) A theoretical treatment of indices of absolute inequality, *International Economic Review* 21, 107–136.

Cowell, F. and K. Kuga (1981) Additivity and the entropy concept: an axiomatic approach to inequality measurement, *Journal of Economic Theory* 25, 131–143.

Dalton, H. (1920) The measurement of inequality of incomes, *Economic Journal* 20, 348–361.

Dasgupta, P., A. Sen, and D. Starrett (1973) Notes on the measurement of inequality, *Journal of Economic Theory* 6, 183–187.

Donaldson, D. and J. Weymark (1980) A single-parameter generalization of the Gini indices and inequality, *Journal of Economic Theory* 22, 67–86.

Eichhorn, W. and W. Gehrig (1982) Measurement of inequality in Economics. In B. Korte (ed.), *Modern Applied Mathematics: Optimization and Operations Research*, New York/Amsterdam, North-Holland.

Fei, G. and G. Fields (1978) On inequality comparisons, *Econometrica* 46, 303–316.

Kats, A. (1972) On the social welfare function and the parameters of income distribution, *Journal of Economic Theory* 15, 377–382.

Kolm, S. Ch. (1969) The optimal production of social justice. In J. Margolis and H. Guitton, (eds.), Public Economics, London and New York: Macmillan.

Kolm, S. Ch. (1976) Unequal inequalities I, *Journal of Economic Theory* 12, 416–412.

Kolm, S. Ch. (1976) Unequal inequalities II, *Journal of Economic Theory* 13, 82–111.

Kondor, Y. (1975) Value judgements implied by the use of various measures of income inequality, *Review of Income and Wealth* 21, 309–321.

Sen, A. (1973) *On Economic Inequality*, London: Oxford University Press (Clarendon).

Sen, A. (1982) Ethical measurement of inequality: some difficulties. In W. Krelle and A. Shorrocks (eds.), *Personal Income Distribution* North-Holland, New York/Amsterdam: 1978, reprinted in *Choice, Welfare and Measurement*, Blackwell, Oxford.

Sheshinski, E. (1972) Relation between a social welfare function and the Gini index of income inequality, *Journal of Economic Theory* 4, 98–100.

Shorrocks, A. (1980) The class of additively decomposable inequality measures, *Econometrica* 48, 613–626.

ON THE MEASUREMENT OF TAX PROGRESSIVITY AND REDISTRIBUTIVE EFFECT OF TAXES WITH APPLICATIONS TO HORIZONTAL AND VERTICAL EQUITY

Nanak Kakwani

I.   INTRODUCTION

The progressivity of a tax system is generally defined in terms of the average tax rate along the income range. A tax system is said to be (i) progressive when the average rate of tax rises with income, (ii) proportional when the average tax rate remains constant, and (iii) regressive when it decreases with rising income. A local measure of progression indicates the extent to which a given tax system deviates from propor-

Advances in Econometrics, vol. 3, pages 149–168
Copyright © 1984 by JAI Press Inc.
All rights of reproduction in any form reserved.
ISBN: 0-89232-443-0

tionality at a given level of income.[1] On the other hand, an overall measure of progressivity indicates the extent of the overall deviation of a tax system from proportionality.

Since a number of different measures of tax progression (or progressivity) have been proposed, some criteria are needed to evaluate their relative merits. This paper develops and applies such criteria.

Two basic axioms of progressivity have been proposed which provide the basis for comparing alternative measures of tax progressivity. The two recent measures of tax progressivity, one proposed by Kakwani (1977) and the other by Suits (1977), have been shown to satisfy both the axioms. Further, the sensitivity of alternative measures of progressivity to a transfer of share of tax liability has been investigated. It has been demonstrated that the sensitivity of both Kakwani's and Suit's measures increases first and then decreases. The only difference between the two measures is that Kakwani's measure gives maximum weight to transfer at the mode of the pretax income distribution whereas Suit's measure gives maximum weight at an income level beyond the mode.

If the social preference is in favor of avoiding an increase in the tax share of the poor relative to that of the rich, then it will be desirable to have a measure of progressivity which is more sensitive at the lower levels of income. A new measure of progressivity possessing this property has been derived in the present paper.

The major contribution of the paper, however, is the establishment of the conceptual distinction between measures of progressivity and those of income redistribution. It has been demonstrated that the concept of progressivity defined in terms of the deviation of a tax system from proportionality is not compatible with the redistributive effects of taxation. Clearly, then, the distinction must be made between the two concepts; much of the empirical literature seems to have ignored such a distinction.

The principles of horizontal and vertical equity play a fundamental role in any debate on taxation. The principle of horizontal equity means that people in equal positions should be treated equally.[2] The principle of vertical equity, on the other hand, requires that people with different incomes should pay different taxes. It is widely believed that a tax system should conform with both these principles.[3]

In order to see the extent to which a given tax system conforms with these principles, it is essential to develop tools for quantitative measurements.[4] In this paper, an attempt is made to develop the measures of horizontal and vertical equity and to derive their relationship with the measures of progressivity and income redistribution. It has been demonstrated that the index of overall redistributive effect of taxation (or expenditures) defined in terms of the Gini index may be decomposed into its two component parts—the index of horizontal equity and the index of vertical equity.[5] This decomposition is important because it provides the quantitative framework to analyze the contribution of horizontal and vertical equity to the total redistributive effect of taxes (or expenditures). The methods are then applied on data obtained from *The Australian Survey of Consumer Expenditure and Finances*, 1966/67 (see Drane et al., 1966–1968).

II. AXIOMS OF TAX PROGRESSIVITY AND REDISTRIBUTIVE EFFECT OF TAXES

The following two basic axioms are proposed which conform to the intuitive notion of tax progressivity.

AXIOM 2.1: *The degree of progressivity is unaffected if the share of tax liability of every individual remains the same irrespective of total tax yield.*

Any observed tax schedule incorporates two distinct factors: the average tax rate and the distribution of tax liability over the income ranges. The concept of progressivity is concerned with the second factor, i.e., the distribution of tax liability. If the tax liability is distributed among individuals in proportion to their income, the tax is said to be proportional. The tax system is said to be progressive (regressive) if the richer (poorer) individual pays higher proportion of their income as taxes. Therefore a measure of progressivity (regressivity) shows the extent of the deviation of a tax system from proportionality in favor of the poorer (richer). This interpretation of progressivity implies that a measure of progressivity should not be affected by increasing or decreasing tax by the same rates at all income levels.

AXIOM 2.2: *If the proportional share of the total tax liability of a person with income x is increased (decreased) and that of a person with lower income (x − h) is decreased (increased), then the progressivity must increase (decrease).*

This axiom conforms to the intuitive idea that if the poor person is penalized more heavily than the rich person, the progressivity must decrease.

AXIOM 2.3: *The degree of progressivity is unaffected if the aftertax income of every individual is increased or decreased by the same proportion.*

This axiom asserts that the degree of progressivity remains constant when aftertax income is changed equiproportionately, rather than when tax burden is changed equiproportionately.

Although all three axioms appear to be equally appealing, it will be shown that they are inconsistent with each other and, therefore, there is no measure of progressivity that can satisfy them all.

Musgrave and Thin (1948) proposed a measure of progressivity which is obtained by comparing the inequality indexes of the pretax and posttax income distributions. Their measure indicates the extent to which a given tax system results in a shift in the distribution of income toward equality: A progressive tax system is associated with a decrease in income inequality, whereas the regressive tax structure leads to an increase in income inequality.[6]

It can be demonstrated that Musgrave and Thin's measure of progressivity violates Axioms 2.1 and 2.2 but satisfies Axiom 2.3.

It will be argued below that progressivity and redistributive effect of taxation are two distinct, though related, concepts.

Musgrave and Thin are in fact measuring the redistributive effect of taxation rather than progressivity. It will now be demonstrated with the help of the accompanying example of two taxpayers that Axioms 2.1 and 2.2 are appropriate for measuring tax progressivity whereas Axiom 2.3 is desirable for measuring the redistributive effect of taxation.

Income Before Tax	Tax System I			Tax System II			Tax System III	
	Tax Liability	Average Tax Rate Percent	Tax Liability Percent	Tax Liability	Average Tax Rate Percent	Tax Liability Percent	Tax Liability	Average Tax Rate Percent
$100	$ 20	20	10	$ 28	28	11.67	−$400	−400
$500	$180	36	90	$212	42.4	88.33	$400	80
Total	$200	33.3	100	$240	40	100	$ 0.0	—

Tax system II is obtained by reducing the aftertax income of both individuals by 10%. According to Axiom 2.3, both these tax schedules are equally progressive despite the fact that the shares of tax liability of two individuals differ under the two tax systems. Further, note that under tax system I the poorer person pays only 10% of the total tax whereas under tax system II the poorer person pays 11.6% of the total tax. Therefore, Schedule II should be less progressive than Schedule I, but a measure based on Axiom 2.3 would indicate that both the tax systems are equally progressive. Thus, Musgrave and Thin's measure based on Axiom 2.3 violates Axioms 2.1 and 2.2.

Comparing tax systems III and I, we find that the average tax rate of the poorer person reduced from 20% to −400% whereas that of the richer person increases from 36% to 80%. Obviously, system III should be considerably more progressive than system I, but according to the Musgrave and Thin measure tax system III is in fact proportional (i.e., has zero progressivity) whereas tax system I is progressive. This suggests that the concept of progressivity (or regressivity) defined in terms of deviation of a tax system from proportionality is not compatible with the redistributive effect of taxes. Clearly then the distinction must be made between ''progressivity'' and redistributive effects; however, the empirical literature seems to have ignored such a distinction.

This distinction is important because it shows how the distributional effect of taxation is influenced by changes in the average tax rate while progressivity is constant, and vice versa. For instance, moving from tax system I to tax system II, we note that the progressivity has decreased because the proportion of total tax liability of the poor has increased and that of the rich decreased, which should have increased the aftertax income inequality except that its effect was offset by the increase in the average tax rate.

Further, note that tax system III is highly progressive owing to the fact that the average tax of the poorer person is −400% and that of the richer person is 80%, which should have increased the redistribution effect of the tax except that this effect was offset by the change in the ranking of individuals in the posttax distribution of income. Thus, the pre- and posttax income distributions are exactly identical despite the highly progressive tax structure.

One might argue that from the equity point of view we only should care about the redistributive effects of taxation and public expenditure. Since the change in ranking of individuals, tax progressivity, and the average tax rate are all important policy instruments which influence the redistribute power of a tax system, it is important to distinguish these concepts in order to measure their effects on the redistribution of economic welfare. In the subsequent sections of this paper we develop the tools that can be used to measure their effects.

III. RANKING OF TAX SYSTEMS

Among the four local measures of progression proposed by Musgrave and Thin (1948),[7] *the liability progression* is the only one that satisfies the two basic Axioms 2.1 and 2.2. This measure is equal to the tax elasticity, which is defined as the elasticity of the tax function $T(x)$ with respect to pretax income x. Since the tax elasticity is unity for a proportional tax system, the magnitude of the difference of tax elasticity from unity provides the measure of tax progressivity (or regressivity).

Let $L(p)$ be the Lorenz curve of income, which is interpreted as the fraction of total income received by the lowest pth fraction of income units. Kakwani (1977a) generalized the concept of the Lorenz curve that was later used to develop the measure of progressivity of a tax system. He introduced the idea of the concentration curve of taxes $C(p)$, which is interpreted as the proportion of tax paid by the lowest pth fraction of income units when income units are arranged in ascending order of their income.

The vertical distance between the Lorenz curve of income and the concentration curve of tax depends only on the tax elasticity. If this elasticity is unity at all income levels, the two curves coincide. It follows from Theorem 8.1 of Kakwani (1980) that the larger the deviation of tax elasticity from unity, the greater is the distance between the two curves. This suggests that for a given pretax income distribution the concentration curve can be used as a criterion for ranking alternative tax systems. If the concentration curve of one tax system is strictly inside that of an other, one can conclude from the liability progression measure that the second tax system is more progressive than the first. If, however, the two concentration curves intersect, neither tax systems can be said to be more progressive than the other. Therefore, the ranking of the tax systems provided by the concentration curve is only partial, and one has to consider a single measure of progressivity to arrive at complete ranking. Since a number of single measures of progressivity have been proposed, some criteria are needed to evaluate them. These criteria are developed in the next section.

IV.   A CRITERION FOR EVALUATING ALTERNATIVE MEASURES OF TAX PROGRESSIVITY

The basic axioms of progressivity proposed in Section II will be used to evaluate the relative merits of alternative measures of tax progressivity.

Suppose the pretax income x is a random variable with probability density function $f(x)$. If $T(x)$ is the tax paid by a unit with income x and Q and is the total tax revenue collected, then $t(x) = T(x)/Q$ will be the proportion of tax liability borne by the unit with income x.

All the progressivity measures proposed so far are of the general form

$$\theta = \int_0^\infty V[t(x), x] \, f(x) \, dx, \tag{4.1}$$

where $V[t(x), x]$ is some function of $t(x)$ and x. It is obvious that a measure of this form will always satisfy Axiom 2.1. The following lemma, which is proved in the Appendix, gives the condition under which Axiom 2.2 will also be satified.

LEMMA 4.1: *Any progressivity index which is written in the form (4.1) will satisfy Axiom 2.2 if and only if K(x) defined as*

$$K(x) = V'[t(x), x] - V'[t(x - h), x - h] \qquad (4.2)$$

is positive for all x and h > 0, where V'[t(x), x] is the first derivative of V[t(x), x] will respect to t(x).

LEMMA 4.2: *If the share of tax liability of a unit with income x is increased (decreased) and that of a person with lower income (x − h) is decreased (increased), then the magnitude of change in the tax progressivity depends on the magnitude of K(x).*

Proof follows immediately from Lemma 4.1.

Lemma 4.2 enables us to examine the relative sensitivity of the progressivity to a change in the share of tax liability at different levels of income. For instance, if the function $K(x)$ is constant, it implies that the effect of changes in the share of tax liabilities would be independent of the income levels at which the changes take place. Further, if $K(x)$ is a monotonically decreasing function of x, then the progressivity index gives higher weight to changes in the tax share at the lower end of the distribution and the weight decreases monotonically as income increases. Similarly, if $K(x)$ is a monotonically increasing function of x, then the weight increases with income. There can be a situation when $K(x)$ increases initially and then decreases. This situation implies that the progressivity index attaches more weight to changes in the share of tax liability at the middle of the distribution than at the tails.

V. EVALUATION OF MEASURES OF TAX PROGRESSIVITY

We are now in a position to examine the relative merits of alternative measures of tax progressivity.

A. The Concentration Measure of Tax Progressivity

In a recent article Kakwani (1977) has derived a measure of tax progressivity by comparing the Lorenz curve of income and the concentration curve of taxes. This measure, which will be referred to as the concentration measure, is equal to twice the area between the Lorenz curve of income and the concentration curve of taxes:

$$P = 2 \int_0^1 [L(p) - C(p)] \, dp,$$

which on integration by parts becomes

$$P = 2 \int_0^\infty \left[t(x) - \frac{x}{m} \right] F(x) \, f(x) \, dx,$$

where $f(x)$ is the probability density function of x; $F(x)$ is the probability distribution function, which is interpreted as the proportion of units having income less than or equal to x; and m is the total income of the society. This equation gives

$$K(x) = 2[F(x) - F(x - h)],$$

which is always greater than zero for $h > 0$. Thus, Axiom 2.2 is always satisfied by the concentration measure of tax progressivity.

Since $dF(x)/dx = f(x)$, the first derivative of $K(x)$ is given by

$$K'(x) = 2[f(x) - f(x - h)].$$

For a typical unimodal income distribution, $f(x)$ increases up to the mode and then decreases, which means that $K(x)$ is an increasing function of x up to the modal income and then becomes a monotonically decreasing function of x. Thus, the following conclusion immediately follows from Lemma 4.2: *The concentration measure of tax progressivity attaches maximum weight to a transfer of the share of tax liability at the mode of the income distributon.*

B.   The Measure Proposed by Suits

Suits (1977) proposed a measure of progressivity which is equal to 1 minus twice the area under the relative concentration curve of $T(x)$ with respect to x:[8]

$$S = 1 - 2 \int_0^1 C(p) \, dL(p),$$

which after integrating by parts can be written as

$$S = 2 \int_0^\infty [F_1(x) - \tfrac{1}{2}] t(x) \, f(x) \, dx,$$

where $F_1(x)$ is the cumulative proportion of income of units having income less than or equal to x. This equation gives

$$K(x) = 2[F_1(x) - F_1(x - h)],$$

which is always greater than zero for $h > 0$. Thus, Suit's measure satisfies Axiom 2.2.

The first derivative of $K(x)$ with respect to x is

$$K'(x) = \frac{2}{\mu} [x \, f(x) - (x - h) \, f(x - h)],$$

where μ is the mean income of the society. There exists an income level x^* such that

$$f(x^*) + x^* f'(x^*) = 0; \tag{5.1}$$

then it can be seen that $x \, f(x)$ is an increasing function of x up to the income level x^* and then it decreases monotonically. Obviously, then, $K(x)$ increases monotonically with x up to the income level x^* and then decreases.

Equation (5.1) shows that for a typical unimodal income distribution x^* exceeds the modal income. This leads to the following conclusion: *Suit's measure of tax progressivity attaches maximum weight to a transfer of the share of tax liability at an income level higher than the mode.*

VI.　DERIVATION OF A NEW MEASURE OF TAX PROGRESSIVITY

Let us consider a family of tax progressivity measures

$$\theta = \int_0^\infty \left(\frac{x}{m} - t(x) \right) w(x) \, f(x) \, dx, \tag{6.1}$$

where $w(x)$ is the weight attached to a unit with income x with the density function $f(x)$. Note that θ is equal to the weighted sum of the differences between income shares and tax shares of the units at different income levels.

It can be seen that Axioms 2.1 is always satisfied by θ for all $w(x)$.

It is obvious that θ will be zero if the tax system is proportional at all income levels. If the tax system is progressive (regressive) in the entire income range, θ must be positive (negative). This condition requires that the weight $w(x)$ must be positive for all x.

The function $K(x)$, defined in (4.2), is given by

$$K(x) = -[w(x) - w(x - h)], \tag{6.2}$$

which on using Lemma 4.1 shows that Axiom 2.2 will be satisfied if $w(x)$ is a monotonically decreasing function of x.

If we substitute

$$w(x) = 2[1 - F(x)]$$

into (6.1), we obtain Kakwani's concentration measure of tax progressivity. Similarly, Suit's measure is obtained if

$$w(x) = 2[1 - F_1(x)].$$

Thus, we have demonstrated that the two recent measures of tax progressivity belong to the same class of progressivity measures (6.1). The two measures differ, however, in one respect: in the case of Kakwani's measure the weight $w(x)$ depends on the number of persons or units who have income greater than x, whereas in the case of Suit's measure this weight is proportional to the total income of units with income greater than x. Because of this differing weighting scheme, the two measures may lead to quite different conclusions about the degree of progressivity, particularly when the pretax income distribution is not fixed, over time.

The problem of choosing between the two measures is a difficult one and cannot be resolved here. Nonetheless, it should be mentioned that Kakwani's measure has an advantage over that of Suits in one respect: it provides the relationship between measures of progressivity and that of the redistributive effect of taxation. This problem is the subject matter of the next section.

As regards the relative sensitivity of progressivity to a transfer of tax share, both Kakwani's and Suit's measures are almost similar in the sense that the sensitivity first increases and then decreases—or, in other words, the measures are most sensitive at the middle of the income distribution. If society is more concerned with the increase in tax share of the poor than of the rich, the progressivity measure must be most sensitive at the bottom end of the distribution and the sensitivity must decrease monotonically with income. In order that a progressivity index should possess such a property, $K(x)$ must be a monotonically decreasing function of x, which in turn implies that the first derivative of $K(x)$, given by

$$K'(x) = -[w'(x) - w'(x - h)],$$

has to be negative for all values of x. Thus, a measure of progressivity which is most sensitive at the bottom end of the distribution must satisfy the following restrictions:

$$w(x) > 0$$
$$w'(x) < 0$$
$$w''(x) > 0,$$

where $w''(x)$ is the second derivative of $w(x)$. A simplest function which satisfies all these restrictions is[9]

$$w(x) = \frac{m}{x},$$

which on substituting (6.1) leads to a new measure of progressivity:

$$\theta = 1 - \frac{1}{e} \int_0^\infty \frac{T(x)}{x} f(x) \, dx,$$

where $e = Q/m$ is the average tax rate of the society. In the discrete case, this measure can be written as

$$\theta = 1 - \frac{1}{ne} \sum_{i=1}^n e_i,$$

where e_i is the average tax rate of the ith income unit.

VII. MEASURES OF HORIZONTAL AND VERTICAL EQUITY

The principle of horizontal equity means that people in equal position should be treated equally. In other words two persons with identical incomes and needs must pay the same tax or receive the same government benefits. This principle can be violated under various circumstances. For instance, it is alleged that people earning income from business pay less tax than those earning wages. These inequities in taxation may alter the ranking of individuals in the pre- and posttax distributions of income. This led Feldstein (1976) to propose an alternative definition of horizontal equity which requires that taxes should not alter the utility ordering of individuals.

Feldstein (1976) and Rosen (1978), therefore, have proposed measures of horizonal equity in terms of the rank correlation coefficient between the pre- and posttax orderings of utilities. Their approach requires the specification of the individual or the family utility function, which has a number of well-known limitations. Moreover, the relationship between their measures of horizontal equity and the measures of income redistribution is not that obvious, although the two concepts are closely related.[10]

The change in the ranking between the pre- and posttax distributions will affect the aftertax income inequality. This effect has been examined by Atkinson (1980), who proved that the Gini index of aftertax income is reduced as a result of the reranking of individuals according to aftertax income. This result will form the basis of our measure of horizontal equity.

The principle of vertical equity requires that people with different income (adjusted for their needs) should pay different tax. The concept of progressivity, defined in terms of the distribution of tax liability among persons with different income, in fact measures the extent to which different people pay different rates of taxation. Thus, the two concepts are closely related.

It seems that principles of horizontal and vertical equity both were proposed in order to advance the general objective of income redistribution. Therefore, the measures of horizontal and vertical equities should be related to the redistributive effects of taxes. In fact we would decompose the total redistributive effects of taxation into two components such that the first component may be interpreted as a measure of horizontal equity and the second as a measure of vertical equity.

Suppose that income units are arranged in ascending order of their pretax income; then if $T(x)$ is the tax paid by a unit with income x, the aftertax income of the individual is given by

$$d(x) = x - T(x),$$

which on applying Theorem 8.2 of Kakwani (1980) yields

$$(m - Q)C_d(p) = mL(p) - QC(p),$$

where $C_d(p)$ is the concentration curve of aftertax income; $L(p)$ is the Lorenz curve of pretax income; $C(p)$ is the concentration curve of taxes; and m and Q are total pretax income and total tax revenue, respectively. This equation can also be rearranged as

$$L(p) = C_d(p) - \frac{e}{1 - e} [L(p) - C(p)], \qquad (7.1)$$

where $e = m/Q$ is the average tax rate of the entire society.

If we denote $L^*(p)$ to be the Lorenz curve of the posttax income distribution, then the index of the redistributive effect of taxes will be obtained by comparing the differences between the curves $L^*(p)$ and $L(p)$ for all values of p in the interval $0 \leq p \leq 1$. Subtracting quantities in both sides of (7.1) from $L^*(p)$, we obtain

$$[L^*(p) - L(p)] = [L^*(p) - C_d(p)] + \frac{e}{1 - e} [L(p) - C(p)], \quad (7.2)$$

which shows that the redistributive effect of taxes is equal to the sum of two components, each of which has the following interpretations.

Note that $C_d(p)$ is the proportion of the posttax income of the lowest pth fraction of units arranged in ascending order of their pretax income, while $L^*(p)$ is the proportion of the posttax income of units arranged in ascending order of their posttax income. Obviously, if the ranking of all units is unaltered between the pre- and posttax distributions of income, $L^*(p) = C_d(p)$ for all p, which suggests that an appropriate summary measure of differences between $L^*(p)$ and $C_d(p)$ will lead to an index which measures the effect of horizontal inequity on income redistribution.

In Section III it was argued that an appropriate index of tax progressivity is obtained by comparing the differences between the Lorenz curve of the pretax income and the concentration curve of taxes. It follows that the second component in (7.2) depends on the average tax rate and the progressivity [which is measured by the differences between the curves $L(p)$ and $C(p)$] and is equal to the redistributive effect of taxes when the horizontal inequity is zero. Thus, the second component represents the redistributive impact of taxation induced purely by taxing different individuals differently and, therefore, should provide an index measuring the effect of vertical equity on income redistribution.

Integrating both sides of Eq. (7.2) in the range $0 \leq p \leq 1$, we obtain

$$(G - G^*) = (C_d - G^*) + \frac{ep}{(1 - e)} ,$$

where G and G^* are the Gini indexes of the pre- and posttax income distributions, respectively; C_d is the concentration index of the posttax income distribution; and P is the concentration measure of tax progressivity.[11] Therefore, the index of redistributive effect of taxes R, measured by the percentage change in the Gini index of the pre- and posttax distribution of income, is given by

$$R = H + V, \tag{7.3}$$

where

$$H = \frac{C_d - G^*}{G}$$

and

$$V = \frac{ep}{(1 - e)G}$$

are the proposed indices measuring the effects of horizontal and vertical equity (or inequity) on income redistribution, respectively.[12]

Kakwani's (1980) Corollary 8.7 shows that $C_d \leq G^*$, which implies that $H \leq 0$. Note that $H = 0$ when the ranking remains the same between the pre- and posttax distribution of income; otherwise it will be negative. Thus, the violation of horizontal equity in the Feldstein sense will have the effect of reducing the redistributive effect of taxation.

It can be seen that V is greater (less) than zero if the tax system is progressive (regressive) and equals zero when the tax system is proportional.

Let us consider the examples shown here for four tax systems to illustrate the above methods.

Income Before Tax	Tax System I		Tax System II		Tax System III		Tax System IV	
	Tax Liability	After-tax Income	Tax Liability	After-tax Income	Tax Liability	After-tax Income	Tax Liability	After-tax Income
$100	$ 20	$ 80	$ 20	$80	$ 10	$90	$ 11	$89
$500	$180	$320	$430	$70	$440	$60	$484	$16

The results are summarized in the accompanying tabulation.

Tax System	Average Tax Rate e	Progressivity P	Horizontal Equity H(percent)	Vertical Equity V(percent)	Redistributive Effect of the Tax System R(percent)
I	.333	.134	0.0	10.00	10.00
II	.750	.245	− 20.25	110.24	89.99
III	.750	.289	− 60.04	130.04	70.00
IV	.825	.289	− 208.62	204.35	− 4.27

Tax system I is progressive and results in 10% decrease in income inequality. It does not violate the principle of horizontal equity, and as a result the index of vertical equity is equal to the index of redistributive effect of tax.

Tax system II is made more progressive than tax system I and also has a higher average tax rate. As a result, the index of vertical equity increases substantially from 10% to 110.24%; but at the same time horizontal inequity is introduced, which has the effect of increasing income inequality by 20.25%. This example shows that there can be the possible clash between horizontal and vertical equity. Increasing vertical equity may lead to horizontal inequity.

Tax system III is made even more progressive than tax system II while keeping the same average tax rate. The index of vertical equity is further increased from 110.24% to 130.04%, which should have increased the index of tax redistribution, but its effect was offset by a substantial increase in horizontal inequity. As a result, the index of redistribution decreased from 89.99% to 70%. An interesting thing to note is that, although the two tax systems give exactly the same posttax ranking of individuals, the magnitude of the index of horizontal inequity happens to be substantially different in the two systems. This observation demonstrates that the index of horizontal inequity is sensitive to changes not only in rankings but also to the magnitude of income differences produced by taxation.

Tax systems III and IV have exactly the same progressivity but differ with respect to the average tax rate. It can be seen that increasing the average tax rate while keeping the same progressivity increases substantially the index of vertical equity from 130.04% to 204.35%. This increase in vertical equity is accompanied by even greater increase in horizontal inequity. As a result, the index of tax redistribution decreases from 70% to -4.27%. Thus, a change in average tax rate can substantially alter the vertical and horizontal equity even if the progressivity of taxation has been kept constant.

VIII.   A NUMERICAL ILLUSTRATION BASED ON ACTUAL DATA

In this section, the empirical results of using the methodology developed in the previous section on the actual data are presented. The data used for this purpose are from *The Australian Survey of Consumer Expenditures and Finances*, 1966–1968, Stage Two, by Drane et al. The first stage was an inquiry into the expenditures on different commodities made by the households; the second stage, a gathering of detailed information about income, taxes, government cash benefits, assets and liabilities of the 2,757 sample households.

The definitions of the variables used in the present illustration are given below:

1.   *Original income* is defined as income received from all sources by all members of the household.
2.   *Gross family income* is defined as the sum of original income and government cash benefits received by all members of the household.
3.   *Disposable income* is equal to gross household income minus income tax paid.

The Gini index for each of the above income definitions was computed from individual household observations by means of the following formula:

$$G = \frac{2}{n-1} \sum_{i=1}^{n} i y_i - \frac{n+1}{n-1},$$

where y_i is the proportion share in income of the ith household when households are arranged in ascending order of their income, and n is the sample size. The concentration indices of various incomes and tax paid were computed by the same formula after the households were arranged

Table 1. Horizontal and Vertical Equity of Cash Benefits and
Taxation in Australia, 1967/68[a]

	Average Benefit or Tax Rate (Percent)	Progressivity	Horizontal Equity (Percent)	Vertical Equity (Percent)	Redistribution Effect (Percent)
Cash benefits	7.37	.629	− .81	13.58	12.77
Tax	11.75	.191	N.A.[b]	6.93	N.A.[b]
Combined effect of cash benefits and tax	4.39	1.568	− 2.44	19.56	17.12

[a] If the taxes are subtracted from the gross income, the additional increase in the share of the first quintile is only .46%. The vertical equity and horizontal equities account for .59% and − ,13% of this increase, respectively. The government cash benefits tend to increase the share of the first quintile only, whereas the taxes increase the shares of the first two quintiles.

From the above observations we can conclude that of the two instruments redistributing income, namely, government cash benefits and income tax, the former is considerably more redistributive than the latter. Both these instruments introduce the horizontal inequities, but the magnitude of such inequity is higher for income tax than for government cash benefits.

[b] N.A. = not applicable.

in ascending order of their original income. The numerical results are presented in Table 1.

It can be seen that the combined effect of all government cash benefits paid in the form of various types of pensions, sickness and unemployment benefits, child endowment, and scholarships and other educational grants is progressive. These benefits together reduce the income inequality by

Table 2. Changes in Quintile Shares Due to Government Cash
benefits in Terms of Horizontal and Vertical Equity

Quintiles	Quintile Share of Original Income (Percent)	Quintile Share of Gross Income (Percent)	Change of Quintile Shares (Percent)	Change in Quintile Shares due to Horizontal Equity (Percent)	Change in Quintile Shares due to Vertical Equity (Percent)
1	2.92	6.31	3.39	− .14	3.53
2	13.74	13.59	− .15	− .07	− .08
3	18.34	17.87	− .47	− .01	− .46
4	24.01	23.27	− .74	.20	− .94
5	40.98	38.94	− 2.04	0.0	− 2.04

Table 3. Changes in Quintile Shares Due to Combined Effect of
Government Cash Benefits and Tax in Terms of Horizontal and
Vertical Equity

Quintiles	Quintile Share of Original Income (Percent)	Quintile Share of Gross Income (Percent)	Change of Quintile Shares (Percent)	Change in Quintile Shares due to Horizontal Equity (percent)	Change in Quintile Shares due to Vertical Equity (percent)
1	2.92	6.77	3.85	− .27	4.12
2	13.74	14.07	.33	− .16	.49
3	18.34	18.18	− .16	− .12	− .04
4	24.01	23.29	− .72	.15	− .87
5	40.98	37.68	− 3.30	.39	− 3.69

12.77%. The vertical equity contributing to this reduction in inequality is
as high as 13.58%. There exists some horizontal inequity but its effect
amounts to increase in inequality by only .81%.

The degree of progressivity of taxes is much lower than that of government cash benefits, but the combined effect of the two is highly progressive. The vertical equity introduced by the high degree of progressivity of cash benefits and taxes would have reduced the income inequality
by 19.56%, but this effect was offset by accompanying horizontal inequity,
which had the effect of increasing inequality by 2.44%. Thus, the resulting
decrease in inequality was only 17.12%.

It is interesting to note that the magnitude horizontal inequity introduced by taxes is much higher than that by government cash benefits.

Tables 2 and 3 present the changes in the quintile shares introduced by
the government's redistributive policies in terms of the horizontal and
vertical equity. The government cash benefits increase substantially the
share of the first quintile from 2.92% to 6.31%. The increase in the share
due to vertical equity is 3.53%, but it is then reduced by .14% due to the
introduction of horizontal inequity.

APPENDIX:
PROOF OF LEMMA 4.1

PROOF: Equation (4.1) in the discrete case is equivalent to

$$\theta = \sum_{i=1}^{n} V(t_i, x_i), \qquad (A\text{-}1)$$

where n is the total number of income units and t_i is the share of tax liability of the ith person.

Suppose the share of the tax liability of the ith person is increased and that of the jth person decreased by the same amount δ. If δ is sufficiently small, we have

$$d\theta = \frac{\partial\theta}{\partial t_i}\,\delta + \frac{\partial\theta}{\partial t_j}\,(-\delta),$$

which according to Axiom 2.2 should be positive for $x_i > x_j$. Therefore, Axiom 2.3 will be satisfied if

$$\frac{\partial\theta}{\partial t_i} - \frac{\partial\theta}{\partial t_j} > 0,$$

which on using (A-1) gives

$$\frac{\partial V(t_i, x_i)}{\partial t_i} - \frac{\partial V(t_j, x_j)}{\partial t_j} > 0$$

for all $x_i > x_j$. Substituting $x_i = x$ and $x_j = x - h$ proves the necessary condition of the lemma. The sufficient condition follows immediately from the above proof.   QED

ACKNOWLEDGMENT

The author would like to thank Dr. Nripesh Podder for his valuable suggestions on the first draft of this paper.

NOTES

1. The four local measures of progression suggested by Musgrave and Thin (1948) are (1) average rate progression, (2) marginal rate progression, (3) liability progression, and (4) residual income progression.

2. For an illuminating discussion of the principle of horizontal equity and its relationship with utilitarianism, see Stiglitz (1982).

3. See Musgrave (1959, p. 160).

4. For a discussion of difficulties associated with the measurement of horizontal equity, see King (1983).

5. The Gini index is the most widely used inequality measure. The measure has recently been criticized by several authors. Their criticism is mainly based on the fact that the welfare function implied by the Gini index does not have desirable properties such as addivity and strict concavity (see Atkinson, 1970; Newbery, 1970; Dasgupta et al., 1973; Rothschild and Stiglitz, 1973). The desirability of these properties has been questioned by Sen (1973), who later in his 1974 article, has provided a complete axiomization of the Gini index as a measure of inequality.

6. Jakobsson (1976) also prefers this measure of progressivity but gives no further justification.

7. See note 1, above.

8. The graph of $C(p)$ and $L(p)$ is called the relative concentration curve of $T(x)$ with respect to x. For further details see Kakwani (1977a, 1980).

9. It seems reasonable to choose the simplest functional form in the absence of a convincing case for any alternative forms.

10. Recently King (1983) has developed a normative index of horizontal inequity by defining a social welfare function which is sensitive to changes in ranking of individuals in society. But his index cannot be empirically estimated unless some strong assumptions are made about the form of the social welfare function.

11. The concentration index is defined as 1 minus twice the area under the concentration curve.

12. It is interesting to note that Plotnick (1981) has also suggested an index of horizontal equity which is similar to H, but he does not discuss its relationship with the measures of progressivity and income redistribution. This relationship [Eq. (7.3)] is important because it provides the quantitative framework enabling us to analyze the contribution of horizontal and vertical equity to the total redistributive effect of taxes.

REFERENCES

Atkinson, A. B. (1970) On the Measurement of Inequality, *Journal of Economic Theory* 2.

Atkinson, A. B. (1980) Horizontal Equity and the Distribution of Tax Burden. In Aaron, H. and Boskin, M. J. (ed.), *The Economics of Taxation*, Brookings Institute.

Dasgupta, P., Sen, A. K. and Starrett, D. (1973) Notes on the Measurement of Inequality, *Journal of Economic Theory* 6.

Drane, N. T., H. R. Edwards, and R. C. Gates (1966–1968) *The Australian Survey of Consumer Expenditure and Finances*, Macquarie University Data Archive Ltd.

Feldstein, M. S. (1976) On the Theory of Tax Reform, *Journal of Public Economics* 6, 77–104.

Jakobsson, U. (1976) On the Measurement of Degree of Progression, *Journal of Public Economics* 12.

Kakwani, N. (1977) Measurement of Tax Progressivity: An International Comparison, *The Economic Journal* 87, (March).

Kakwani, N. (1977a) Applications of Lorenz Curves in Economic Analysis, *Econometrica*, (April).

Kakwani, N. (1980), *Income Inequality and Poverty Methods of Estimation and Policy Applications*, New York: Oxford University Press.

King, M. A. (1983) An Index of Inequality: With Applications to Horizontal Equity and Social Mobility, *Econometrica* 51, (1) 99–116.

Musgrave, R. A. (1959), *The Theory of Public Finance*, McGraw-Hill.

Musgrave, R. A. and Thin, T. (1948) Income Tax Progression 1929–48, *Journal of Political Economy* 56, (December) 498–514.

Newbery, D. M. G. (1970) A Theorem on the Measurement of Inequality, *Journal of Economic Theory* 2.

Plotnick, Robert (1981) A Measure of Horizontal Equity, *Review of Economics and Statistics* 63, 283–288.

Rosen, Harvey S. (1978) An Approach to the Study of Income, Utility and Horizontal Equity, *Quarterly Journal of Economics* XCII.

Rothschild, M. and Stiglitz, J. E. (1973) "Some Further Results on the Measurement of Inequality", *Journal of Economic Theory*, vol 6, pp 188–204.

Sen, A. K. (1973), *On Economic Inequality*, Oxford: Clarendon Press.

Sen, A. K. (1974) Informational Bases of Welfare Approaches, *Journal of Public Economics* 3.

Stiglitz, J. E. (1982) Utilitarianism and Horizontal Equity, *Journal of Public Economics* 18, 1–33.

Suits, D. (1977) Measurement of Tax Progressivity, *American Economic Review* 67, 747–52.

THE IMPACT OF MEASUREMENT
ERROR ON THE DISTRIBUTION
OF INCOME

L. Dwight Israelsen, James B. McDonald and
Whitney K. Newey

I.   INTRODUCTION

Issues surrounding the distribution of personal income have attracted the
interest of a wide range of economists since World War II. That these
issues are of practical as well as theoretical interest is evidenced by the
increasing importance of distributional considerations in the evaluation
of existing and potential government economic policies and programs.
Such evaluations, however, can be accurate only to the degree that
(changes in) measured income distributions mirror (changes in) true income distributions. This qualification is seen to be vital when it is rec-

Advances in Econometrics, vol. 3, pages 169–189
ISBN: 0-89232-443-0

ognized that much income data is subject to measurement error in general
and (in contrast to the usual errors-in-variables models) to underreporting
in particular. The present study is concerned with the impact of measurement error on measures of income inequality.

Section II contains the development of a model in which measurement
errors are assumed to be multiplicative and distributed independently of
the level of income. It is shown that the coefficient of variation of measured income will always be *larger* than the true coefficient of variation
unless the variance of measurement error is zero. The result is general,
i.e., does not depend on any particular functional form(s) for the underlying distributions of true income, measured income, or measurement
error, and holds for overreported as well as underreported data. Arnold
(1980) has recently demonstrated that the Lorenz curve associated with
true income is nested within that associated with measured income;
hence, the Gini coefficient and Pietra index of measured income increase
as a result of this type of measurement error.[1]

Alternative forms of density functions for true income, measured income, and measurement error are considered, and the density function
for true (measured) income is derived from a specification of density functions for measurement error and for measured (true) income. Gamma and
Singh-Maddala density functions for income and a beta density function
for measurement error are used in the derivations because of their flex-
ibility and fit to the distribution of income compared to other commonly
used two- and three-parameter functions. The section concludes with a
discussion of alternative approaches to the problem of estimating characteristics associated with the true distribution of income from observed
individual or grouped income data when measurement error is present.

Section III contains a discussion of extensions to the model, including
the consideration of alternative measures of inequality. The effect of
misreporting on measures of inequality when the fraction of income reported is a function of the income level is also considered.

A discussion of the implications of the study for the interpretation of
income distribution data and the evaluation of incomes policies is contained in the final section, along with the authors' conclusions. It is suggested that changes in the characteristics of the distribution of measurement errors over time may obscure the magnitude and even the direction
of change in characteristics associated with the true distribution of income. For example, if the average fraction of income reported decreased
over time and/or the variance of measurement error increased, the distribution of true income could become *more equal* while the distribution
of observed income became *less equal*. Mean income and other characteristics of income distributions could be similarly affected. Because income distribution characteristics are important inputs into the formulation

and evaluation of incomes policies, an understanding of the relationships among the distributions of true income, observed income, and measurement error is crucial.

II. DEVELOPMENT

A. General Discussion

In order to investigate the impact of measurement error upon the distribution of observed income, we assume that measured income (y) is related to true income (y^*) by

$$y = uy^*, \tag{2.1}$$

where u is the ratio of reported income to true income and is assumed to be distributed independently of y^*. The density functions of y^*, u, and y, respectively, are denoted by $f(y^*; \theta_1)$, $g(u; \theta_2)$, and $h(y; \theta)$, where θ_1, θ_2, and θ represent vectors of parameters.

We note that the density of measured income can be deduced from a knowledge of the density function of measurement errors (u) and true income using

$$h(y; \theta) = \int f\left(\frac{y}{u}\right) g(u) \left(\frac{du}{u}\right). \tag{2.2}$$

Similarly, if y and u are distributed independently, the density of y^* can be obtained from the density functions of y and u using

$$f(y^*; \theta_1) = \int h(uy^*) g(u) u \, du; \tag{2.3}$$

and if y and y^* are assumed to be distributed independently, the density of u can be obtained from the density functions of y and y^* using

$$g(u; \theta_2) = \int h(y) f\left(\frac{y}{u}\right)\left(\frac{y}{u^2}\right) dy. \tag{2.4}$$

Hence, any one of $f(y^*; \theta_1)$, $g(u; \theta_2)$, or $h(y; \theta)$ can be deduced from a knowledge of the other two, given appropriate independence assumptions.

In empirical applications we have observations on y with perhaps some information about u, and we would like to make statements about $f(y^*; \theta_1)$. The estimation of $f(y^*; \theta_1)$, however, is associated with an *identification problem*. In other words, if we assume compatible functional forms of $f(\ )$, $g(\ )$, and $h(\ )$, we need to be able to deduce θ_1 and θ_2 from a knowledge of θ.

A necessary condition for identification is that number of parameters in $h(y; \theta)$ be at least as large as the total number of parameters in $f(y^*; \theta_1)$ and $g(y; \theta_2)$. The identification problem will be considered in more detail in connection with the selection of particular functional forms for $f(\ )$, $g(\ )$, and $h(\ )$. Without specifying forms for two of the functions, there is little empirical work that can be done.

We now consider the relationship among means, Gini coefficients, and coefficients of variation associated with the measured and true distributions. Based upon the notation already introduced and (2.1), we can write

$$E(y) = E(u \cdot y^*) = E(u)E(y^*); \tag{2.5}$$

$$CV = \sqrt{\mathrm{Var}(y)}/E(y)$$

and $\tag{2.6}$

$$CV^* = \sqrt{\mathrm{Var}(y^*)}/E(y^*);$$

$$G = \int_0^\infty \int_0^\infty |x - y|\, h(x)h(y)dx\, \frac{dy}{2E(y)}$$

and $\tag{2.7}$

$$G^* = \int_0^\infty \int_0^\infty |x - y|\, f(x)f(y)dx\, \frac{dy}{2E(y^*)}.$$

An interesting relationship between the coefficients of variation for measured income (CV) and true income (CV^*) is given by

$$CV = \sqrt{(CV^*)^2\left(\frac{\sigma_u^2}{E^2(u)} + 1\right) + \frac{\sigma_u^2}{E^2(u)}} \tag{2.8a}$$

or

$$CV = \sqrt{(CV)_u^2[(CV^*)^2 + 1] + (CV^*)^2}, \tag{2.8b}$$

where σ_u^2 and $E(u)$ denote the variance and mean of the fraction of income reported;[2] $\sigma_u/E(u)$ in (2.8a) is the coefficient of variation of the fraction of income reported, $(CV)_u$. This result is independent of the functional form for true income and is valid for measurement errors which allow overreporting as well as underreporting. Several implications of (2.8a-b) are important for research using data with multiplicative measurement errors. First, variance in the fraction of income reported implies that the measured coefficient of variation (CV) will be larger than the true coefficient of variation (CV^*), but measurement errors which are constant ($\sigma_u^2 = 0$) will not affect the value of the coefficient of variation regardless of the level of $E(u)$, that is, $CV = CV^*$ for $\sigma_u^2 = 0$. Increases in the variance of the measurement error or decreases in the average fraction of income reported or, more generally, increases in the coefficient of variation of measurement errors will increase CV for a given CV^*. Finally, the larger the value of CV^*, the smaller will be the effect of a change in $(CV)_u$ on CV/CV^*. The sensitivity of CV to changes in CV^*, σ_u, and $E(u)$ is shown in Table 1 for representative values of these parameters. Table 2 shows the effect of changes in CV^* and $(CV)_u$ on CV.

B.   Functional Forms

In order to estimate the mean of true income or inequality measures for true income, it is necessary to make assumptions about the form of the underlying density functions.

Table 1.   Coefficient of Variation of Measured Income (CV) for Representative Values of CV^*, $E(U)$, and σ_u

		CV^*				
$E(u)$	σ_u	*.4000*	*.5000*	*.6000*	*.7000*	*.8000*
.50	.00	.4000	.5000	.6000	.7000	.8000
	.05	.4142	.5123	.6112	.7106	.8102
	.10	.4543	.5477	.6437	.7414	.8400
	.15	.5142	.6021	.6946	.7900	.8875
	.20	.5879	.6708	.7600	.8535	.9499
	.25	.6708	.7500	.8367	.9287	1.0247
	.30	.7600	.8367	.9217	1.0131	1.1092
	.35	.8535	.9287	1.0131	1.1045	1.2015
.60	.00	.4000	.5000	.6000	.7000	.8000
	.05	.4099	.5086	.6078	.7074	.8071
	.10	.4384	.5336	.6307	.7290	.8280
	.15	.4822	.5728	.6671	.7636	.8617
	.20	.5375	.6235	.7149	.8097	.9068
	.25	.6012	.6834	.7721	.8663	.9616
	.30	.6708	.7500	.8367	.9287	1.0247
	.35	.7448	.8218	.9071	.9985	1.0946
.70	.00	.4000	.5000	.6000	.7000	.8000
	.05	.4073	.5063	.6058	.7054	.8052
	.10	.4286	.5249	.6227	.7214	.8207
	.15	.4618	.5544	.6500	.7473	.8458
	.20	.5047	.5933	.6863	.7821	.8797
	.25	.5549	.6399	.7304	.8247	.9215
	.30	.6108	.6925	.7809	.8739	.9702
	.35	.6708	.7500	.8367	.9287	1.0247

Table 1. (Continued)

E(u)	σ_u	.4000	.5000	.6000	.7000	.8000
				CV*		

E(u)	σ_u	.4000	.5000	.6000	.7000	.8000
.80	.00	.4000	.5000	.6000	.7000	.8000
	.05	.4056	.5049	.6044	.7041	.8040
	.10	.4220	.5192	.6175	.7164	.8159
	.15	.4481	.5422	.6386	.7366	.8353
	.20	.4822	.5728	.6671	.7636	.8617
	.25	.5228	.6100	.7020	.7972	.8945
	.30	.5684	.6526	.7425	.8364	.9331
	.35	.6181	.6995	.7876	.8805	.9767
.90	.00	.4000	.5000	.6000	.7000	.8000
	.05	.4045	.5038	.6035	.7033	.8032
	.10	.4175	.5152	.6138	.7130	.8126
	.15	.4384	.5336	.6307	.7290	.8280
	.20	.4661	.5583	.6536	.7507	.8491
	.25	.4995	.5886	.6819	.7778	.8755
	.30	.5375	.6236	.7149	.8097	.9068
	.35	.5792	.6626	.7521	.8458	.9424

Hartley and Revankar (1974) base their analysis of the impact of underreporting upon the assumptions that the density function of true income is a Pareto, $f(y^*; \theta, m) = (\theta/m)(m/y^*)^{\theta+1}$ for $y^* \geq m$, and that the density of the proportion of y^* which is reported is given by $g(u; p) = pu^{p-1}$ for $0 \leq u \leq 1$. They propose estimation techniques for the associated parameters and investigate the corresponding statistical properties. The Pareto provides a good fit for income in the upper tail, but the fit is not uniform across income levels. For this reason we consider alternative specifications.

Numerous functions have been considered as models for the distribution of income. Two-parameter models include lognormal, gamma, Weibull, and Fisk, among others. Some three-parameter models include the beta of the first and second kinds, generalized gamma, and Singh-Maddala (or Burr) distributions. McDonald (1982) has considered two four-parameter generalized beta distributions which include all of the previously mentioned distributions as special or limiting cases. The Singh-Maddala function and gamma distributions provide the best fits to U.S. family income data for the three- and two-parameter models considered (see McDonald and Ransom, 1979; McDonald, 1982). For these reasons we consider these two functions as possible models for y or y^*.[3] Some results associated with the generalized beta of the second kind will also be presented.

Table 2. Coefficient of Variation of Measured Income (*CV*) for
Representative Values of *CV** and *CV$_u$*

	CV^*				
CV_u	*.4000*	*.5000*	*.6000*	*.7000*	*.8000*
.00	.4000	.5000	.6000	.7000	.8000
.05	.4036	.5031	.6028	.7027	.8026
.10	.4142	.5123	.6112	.7106	.8102
.15	.4314	.5274	.6250	.7236	.8227
.20	.4543	.5477	.6437	.7414	.8400
.25	.4822	.5728	.6671	.7636	.8617
.30	.5142	.6021	.6946	.7900	.8875
.35	.5496	.6349	.7257	.8201	.9170
.40	.5879	.6708	.7600	.8535	.9499
.45	.6284	.7093	.7971	.8898	.9860
.50	.6708	.7500	.8367	.9287	1.0247
.55	.7148	.7925	.8783	.9699	1.0659
.60	.7600	.8367	.9217	1.0131	1.1092
.65	.8063	.8821	.9667	1.0581	1.1545
.70	.8535	.9287	1.0131	1.1046	1.2015
.75	.9014	.9763	1.0607	1.1524	1.2500
.80	.9499	1.0247	1.1092	1.2015	1.2998
.85	.9990	1.0738	1.1587	1.2516	1.3509
.90	1.0486	1.1236	1.2092	1.3027	1.4030
.95	1.0986	1.1739	1.2599	1.3545	1.4561
1.00	1.1489	1.2247	1.3115	1.4701	1.5100

The gamma density is defined by

$$\ell(z) = \frac{z^{p-1}e^{-z/\lambda}}{\lambda^p \Gamma(p)} \tag{2.9}$$

and has an associated Gini coefficient of

$$G = \frac{\Gamma(p + 1/2)}{\Gamma(p + 1)\sqrt{\pi}}, \tag{2.10}$$

with mean

$$E(z) = \lambda p \tag{2.11}$$

and coefficient of variation

$$CV = 1/\sqrt{p}. \tag{2.12}$$

The Singh–Maddala function is defined by

$$k(z) = \frac{aqz^{a-1}}{b^a(1 + (z/b)^a)^{q+1}}, \tag{2.13}$$

with

$$G = 1 - \frac{\Gamma(q)\Gamma(2q - 1/a)}{\Gamma(q - 1/a)\Gamma(2q)}, \tag{2.14}$$

$$E(z) = \frac{b\Gamma(1 + 1/a)\Gamma(q - 1/a)}{\Gamma(q)}, \tag{2.15}$$

$$CV = \sqrt{\frac{\Gamma(q)\Gamma(1 + 2/a)\Gamma(q - 2/a)}{\Gamma^2(1 + 1/a)\Gamma^2(q - 1/a)} - 1}. \tag{2.16}$$

Hence, given estimates for p, q, a, b, and λ, one can obtain corresponding estimates of G, $E(z)$, and CV for the gamma or Singh–Maddala functions.[4]

Measurement errors are assumed to be of the form

$$g(u; \alpha, \beta, \gamma) = \frac{u^{\alpha - 1}(\gamma - u)^{\beta - 1}}{\gamma^{\alpha + \beta - 1}B(\alpha, \beta)} \quad (0 \le u \le \gamma)$$
$$= 0, \quad \text{otherwise}, \tag{2.17}$$

where u is the ratio of reported income to true income. This formulation includes that of Hartley and Revankar (1974) as a special case ($\beta = \gamma = 1$) and is extremely flexible, ranging from ∪- or ∩-shaped to a J-shaped density function, depending upon the values selected for α and β. If γ is greater than 1, overreporting as well as underreporting is admitted. A value of $\gamma \le 1$ does not permit overreporting.

Table 3 illustrates some alternative scenarios that might be considered. A natural procedure would be to select a function for $h(y)$ which accurately models observed income and then to determine the corresponding $g(u)$ and $f(y^*)$. There are several problems with this approach. First, either $g(u)$ or $f(y^*)$ must be specified, and even then an identification problem may exist unless values for some of the parameters are specified prior to estimation. For example, in the second case in Table 3, $h(y; \theta)$ is characterized by two parameters, and $g(u; \theta_2)$ and $f(y^*; \theta_1)$ are characterized by five parameters. Given estimates of $\theta = (p, \lambda)$, we cannot obtain estimates of the five parameters defining $f(y^*)$ and $g(u)$ without some a priori restrictions, i.e., restrictions on θ_1 and θ_2. It should be mentioned that the parameter γ in $g(u)$ is not identifiable for any of the cases shown and must be specified.

An alternative approach is to specify $f(y^*)$ as a function characterized by a few parameters which are easily interpreted and then to deduce the corresponding density for measured income. This is the methodology employed by Hartley and Revankar (1974) and would correspond to the first, third, and fifth cases in Table 3. This approach circumvents the identification problem for the cases considered, hence, given estimates of the parameters in $h(y)$, corresponding estimates of $f(y^*)$, $E(y^*)$, G^*, and CV^*

Table 3. The Relationships Among the Density Functions of True Income, Measurement Error, and Measured Income[a]

Case No.	True Income	Measurement Error	Measured Income
(1)	$\dfrac{y^{*p-1}e^{-y^*/\lambda}}{\lambda^p\Gamma(p)}$	$\dfrac{u^{\alpha-1}(\gamma-u)^{\beta-1}}{B(\alpha,\beta)\gamma^{\alpha+\beta-1}}$	$\dfrac{\Gamma(\beta)y^{(\alpha+p-3)/2}e^{-y/2\gamma\lambda}}{\Gamma(p)\beta(\alpha,\beta)(\gamma\lambda)^{(\alpha+p-1)/2}}\,W_{(p-\alpha-2\beta+1)/2,(\alpha-p)/2}\left(\dfrac{y}{\lambda\gamma}\right)$
(2)	$\dfrac{B(\beta,\alpha+p)\gamma^p y^{*p-1}}{B(\alpha,\beta)\lambda^p\Gamma(p)}\,{}_1F_1\left[\begin{array}{c}\alpha+p;\ \dfrac{-y^*\gamma}{\lambda}\\ \alpha+p+\beta;\ \lambda\end{array}\right]$	$\dfrac{u^{\alpha-1}(\gamma-u)^{\beta-1}}{B(\alpha,\beta)\gamma^{\alpha+\beta-1}}$	$\dfrac{y^{p-1}e^{-y/\lambda}}{\lambda^p\Gamma(p)}$
(3)	$\dfrac{aqy^{*a-1}}{b^a(1+(y^*/b)^a)^{q+1}}$	$\dfrac{u^{\alpha-1}(\gamma-u)^{\beta-1}}{B(\alpha,\beta)\gamma^{\alpha+\beta-1}}$	$\dfrac{aqy^{a-1}}{B(\alpha,\beta)(b\gamma)^a}\displaystyle\int_0^1\dfrac{s^{\alpha+aq-1}(1-s)^{\beta-1}}{(s^a+(y/b\gamma)^a)^{q+1}}\,ds$
(4)	$\dfrac{aqy^{*a-1}\gamma^a}{b^aB(\alpha,\beta)}\displaystyle\int_0^1\dfrac{s^{\alpha+a-1}(1-s)^{\beta-1}}{(1+(\gamma y^*/b)^a s^a)^{q+1}}\,ds$	$\dfrac{u^{\alpha-1}(\gamma-u)^{\beta-1}}{B(\alpha,\beta)\gamma^{\alpha+\beta-1}}$	$\dfrac{aqy^{a-1}}{b^a(1+(y/b)^a)^{q+1}}$
(5)[b]	$\dfrac{ay^{*ap-1}}{b^{ap}B(p,q)(1+(y^*/b)^a)^{p+q}}$	$\dfrac{u^{\alpha-1}(\gamma-u)^{\beta-1}}{B(\alpha,\beta)\gamma^{\alpha+\beta-1}}$	$\dfrac{ay^{ap-1}}{B(\alpha,\beta)B(p,q)(b\gamma)^{ap}}\,I_1$
(6)[b]	$\dfrac{ay^{*ap-1}\gamma^{ap}}{b^{ap}B(p,q)B(\alpha,\beta)}\,I_2$	$\dfrac{u^{\alpha-1}(\gamma-u)^{\beta-1}}{B(\alpha,\beta)\gamma^{\alpha+\beta-1}}$	$\dfrac{ay^{ap-1}}{b^{ap}B(p,q)(1+(y/b)^a)^{p+q}}$

[a] Here, ${}_1F_1[\ \ ]$ denotes the confluent hypergeometric series, $W_{\lambda1,\lambda2}(\ )$ denotes the Whittaker function:

$$I_1=\int_0^1\frac{s^{\alpha+aq-1}(1-s)^{\beta-1}}{(s^a+(y/b\gamma)^a)^{p+q}}\,ds;\qquad I_2=\int_0^1\frac{s^{\alpha+ap-1}(1-s)^{\beta-1}}{(1+(\gamma y^*/b)^a s^a)^{p+q}}\,ds;$$

[b] Cases (5) and (6) correspond to the generalized beta of the second kind, which includes the results for the Singh–Maddala function as a special case where $p=1$. The generalized gamma, lognormal, gamma, and Weibull are also special or limiting cases of these results (see McDonald, 1982). An outline of the derivations of these results is contained in the Appendix (Section A.3).

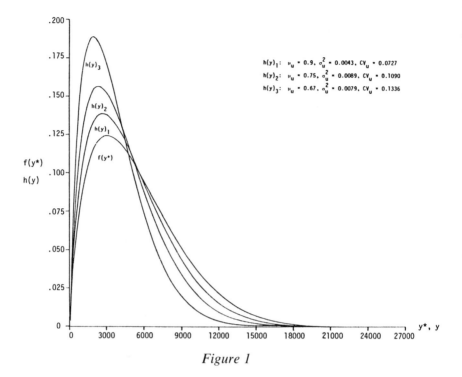

Figure 1

can be recovered using (2.9)–(2.16). In the absence of information on $g(u)$, we have elected to adopt the second approach.

Figure 1 is useful in analyzing the impact of measurement error on measured income. In this figure an assumed density for true income is compared with density functions for measured income corresponding to different combinations of expected levels of u and variance of u.[5] From the figure, it appears that the relative "dispersion" between true and measured income distributions corresponds to the ranking based on $(CV)_u$; and that the difference between central tendency of true and measured distributions corresponds to different values for $E(u)$, as would be expected.

C. Estimation

In order to estimate characteristics associated with the distribution of true income from observed income, one must obtain estimates of θ_1—a procedure which may involve the identification problem. We will assume that the model selected is identified and concentrate on estimating θ.

Maximum likelihood estimators of θ can be obtained by solving

$$\max_{\theta} \prod_{t=1}^{n} f(y_t; \theta) \qquad (2.18)$$

where $y_1, \ldots, y_n$ denote the n observed values for income. For the cases considered, this problem requires the solution of a nonlinear optimization problem.

An alternative approach which might be more tractable in some instances is the *method of moments*. The method of moments estimators of θ are obtaining by solving

$$\sum_{t=1}^{n} \frac{y_t^r}{n} = E(u^r)E(y^{*r}) \qquad (r = 1, 2, \ldots, k) \qquad (2.19)$$

for θ_1 and θ_2, where k denotes the number of unknown parameters in θ_1 and θ_2. Since

$$E(u^r) = \frac{\gamma^r(\alpha)(\alpha + 1) \cdots (\alpha + r - 1)}{(\alpha + \beta)(\alpha + \beta + 1) \cdots (\alpha + \beta + r - 1)},$$

the method of moments may prove to be tractable if $f(y^*)$ is characterized by relatively simple expressions for $E(y^{*r})$.[6]

The previously described techniques of maximum likelihood estimation and method of moments are not directly appropriate for the case in which grouped data is used. Let n_i denote the number of observations in the ith group of g groups and p_i denote the probability of income in the ith income interval I_i:

$$p_i(\theta) = \int_{I_i} f(y; \theta) \, dy. \qquad (2.20)$$

It should be noted that p_i is a function of the population parameter θ. The likelihood function associated with the $n_1, n_2, \ldots, n_g$ $(\sum_i n_i = n)$ is given by

$$L(n_1, n_2, \ldots, n_g; \theta) = n! \prod_{L=1}^{g} \frac{(p_i(\theta))^{n_i}}{n_i!}. \qquad (2.21)$$

Since $n_1, n_2, \ldots, n_g$ can be viewed as being generated by a multinomial distribution, estimators of θ which maximize the likelihood function (2.21) will be maximum likelihood estimators and will be asymptotically efficient, relative to other estimators based on grouped data (cf. Cox and Hinckley, 1974).

III. ANALYSIS: EXTENSIONS OF THE MODEL

A. Functional Forms and Alternative Measures of Inequality

Equation (2.8) and Tables 1 and 2 show the relationship between the coefficients of variation for measured and true income in the presence of measurement error. Measurement error increases inequality as measured by the coefficient of variation. Arnold has demonstrated the same result for the Gini coefficient and Pietra index. For certain density functions it is possible to infer directly changes in Gini coefficients from changes in coefficients of variation. For example, for gamma functions we note from (2.10) and (2.12) that both the Gini coefficient (G) and the coefficient of variation (CV) are functions of p only. We also note that dG/dp and dCV/dp are both negative. Thus, changes in p will move G and CV in the same direction. If the underlying density function for true (measured) income is a gamma, when CV^* (CV) changes, G^* (G) changes in the same direction.[7]

An argument similar to the above cannot be made for the Singh–Maddala function. From (2.14) and (2.16) we note that G and CV are both functions of a and q. It can be shown that $\partial G/\partial a$, $\partial G/\partial q$, $\partial CV/\partial a$ and $\partial CV/\partial q$ are all negative. Hence a change in a or in q will move G and CV in the same direction. If a and q change simultaneously, G and CV will move in the same direction as long as the changes in a and q have the same sign. However, if a increases while q decreases, or vice versa, G and CV may not change in the same direction.

The differences in the preceding examples result from the number of parameters which characterize the density functions. This suggests a general rule: For density functions with no more than two parameters (CV and G characterized by one parameter)—gamma, Pareto, lognormal, etc.—coefficients of variation and Gini coefficients will move in the same direction. For density functions with three or more parameters (CV and G characterized by two or more parameters)—Singh-Maddala, beta, etc.—coefficients of variation and Gini coefficients may not move in the same direction.[8]

This rule can be demonstrated as well for alternative measures of income inequality, such as the Pietra index, defined by

$$P = \frac{E(\mid Y - \mu \mid)}{2\mu},$$
(3.1)

and Theil's entropy (expected information) measure, defined by

$$T = \int_0^\infty \left(\frac{y}{\mu}\right) \ln\left(\frac{y}{\mu}\right) f(y)dy.$$
(3.2)

One can infer changes in *P* or *T* from changes in *CV* for specific functional forms, as was done above for the Gini coefficient. For example, the Pareto density function, defined as

$$p(y; \omega, k) = \frac{\omega k^{\omega}}{y^{\omega+1}} \qquad (y \geq k), \tag{3.3}$$

has associated with it *CV*, *G*, *P*, and *T* as follows:

$$CV = \frac{1}{\sqrt{\omega(\omega - 2)}} \; ; \tag{3.4}$$

$$G = \frac{1}{2\omega - 1} \; ; \tag{3.5}$$

$$P = \frac{(\omega - 1)^{\omega-1}}{\omega^{\omega}} \; ; \tag{3.6}$$

$$T = \frac{1}{\omega - 1} - \ln\left(\frac{\omega}{\omega - 1}\right) . \tag{3.7}$$

It is clear from Eqs. (3.4)–(3.7) that all four measures of inequality are decreasing functions of ω. By the reasoning discussed for the gamma function and the Gini coefficient, it is clear that *CV* (*CV**) increasing implies *G* (*G**), *P* (*P**), and *T* (*T**) increasing if the underlying density function for measured (true) income is a Pareto. For other density functions, the rule mentioned above for the Gini coefficient should apply as well to the Pietra and Theil measures.

B. Interdependence Between *u* and *y**

The analysis of Section II is based on the assumption that *u* is distributed independently of *y* and *y**. The nature of misreporting makes testing the assumption difficult or impossible in most cases. In preliminary testing of individual income data covering the majority of income earners in Utah for years between 1855 and 1900, where it is possible to identify "true" and "reported" income, the authors could not reject the assumption of independence between the level of true income (*y**) and the fraction of income reported (*u*).[9] Of course, that is but one example, and it seems likely that the independence assumption could be rejected in other cases. A natural extension of the model, then, might drop the assumption of independence and undertake an analysis of misreporting where the density function of *u* would be denoted by $g(u; \theta_2, y^*)$. Consider the special case where the fraction of income reported (*u*) is a deterministic (nonstochastic) function of true income (y^*). Then

$$u = g(y^*) \tag{3.8}$$

and observed income is

$$y = g(y^*)y^*, \tag{3.9}$$

where $g(y^*)$ is assumed to preserve the rank order of y^*. With these assumptions, it can be shown that the Gini coefficients and Pietra indices for measured income are greater (less) than the corresponding coefficients for true income if u is an increasing (decreasing) function of y^*:

$$G \gtreqqless G^* \quad \text{as} \quad g'(y^*) \gtreqqless 0;$$
$$P \gtreqqless P^* \quad \text{as} \quad g'(y^*) \gtreqqless 0.^{10} \tag{3.10}$$

The more general case of stochastic interdependence between measurement error and true income should include the above result as a polar case as the variance of u approaches zero.

IV.   CONCLUSIONS

A.   Data Interpretation and Policy Evaluation

The results of the foregoing analysis suggest that caution needs to be used in drawing inferences about the effectiveness of incomes policies from measured income distributions. If the underlying income data are subject to measurement error, measures of income inequality and other characteristics of reported distributions ordinarily will not reflect accurately corresponding characteristics of true income distributions. That problem may not be very serious if changes in the relative magnitudes of true and measured income distribution characteristics correspond over time. However, changes over time in the distribution of measurement errors can lead to serious misinterpretation if the effectiveness of incomes policies is judged on the evidence of changes in characteristics of observed income distributions. Two hypothetical examples will illustrate the point.

First, assume multiplicative errors and independence between the distributions of measurement errors and true income. Suppose that the variance of measurement error increased and/or the mean fraction of income reported decreased over time. It is clear that the measured coefficient of variation or Gini coefficient could increase while the true coefficient of variation or Gini coefficient decreased. It should be obvious that other characteristics of the two distributions also could move in opposite directions.

As a second example, assume that the fraction of income reported is a deterministic function of true income, that is, $u = g(y^*)$. Suppose that $g'(y^*)$ decreased over time, that is, $dg'(y^*)/dt < 0$. It follows from (3.10) that the Gini coefficient for reported income could decrease while the Gini coefficient for true income increased. In either of the above cases, an evaluation of the effectiveness of incomes policies based on observed changes in inequality measures would be wrong. Less radical divergences of the relative changes in true and observed measures of inequality also could lead to incorrect conclusions.

At this point it is natural to speculate about factors which might affect the distribution of measurement errors over time. Methods of measurement, sampling procedures, and estimation rules are obvious candidates. Changes in data collection procedures over time could affect means, variances, and other characteristics of the distribution of measurement errors.

Incentives facing suppliers of income data constitute another category of influences which may affect the distribution of measurement errors. If individuals perceive some gain from underreporting, such as tax advantages, that perception will presumably have an impact on the fraction of income reported. Differences in perceptions and motivations among individuals in the population would be expected to affect the variance of measurement errors. If taxes can be avoided by underreporting, then the structure of taxation will have an effect on the accuracy of reported income data. Other things equal, progressive income taxation would likely result in a smaller proportion of income reported at higher income levels. Changes in the structure of taxation would lead to changes in the distribution of measurement errors.

Diminishing marginal utility of income may counteract to a greater or lesser extent the impact of progressive taxation on the distribution of measurement errors by reducing the expected real gain from underreporting at higher income levels. With diminishing marginal utility of income, increases in real income over time would be associated with increases in the average fraction of income reported, other things equal.

Inflation also may have an independent effect on the distribution of measurement errors. In a progressive income tax system like that of the United States, where tax brackets are linked to nominal income, inflation would increase the incentive to underreport by facing individuals with higher real tax rates, other things equal. Thus, we would expect inflation to be accompanied by decreases in the average fraction of income reported. If tax brackets were indexed by the rate of inflation, this effect would be obviated.

Since calculations of expected net advantage from underreporting should incorporate an evaluation of potential loss as well as possible gain, penalties associated with underreporting become important determinants of the distribution of measurement errors. Changes in the structure and severity of penalties and in the effectiveness of enforcement would be expected to induce changes in characteristics of the measurement error distribution.

The importance of many of these factors in influencing income reporting in the United States has been recognized by the Internal Revenue Service. A recent statement by the IRS Commissioner identifies reporting requirements, verification techniques, risk of discovery, severity of penalties, level of enforcement, and the impact of inflation as major determinants of individual income underreporting.[11]

B.   Empirical Questions

In addition to the theoretical extensions to the model suggested in Section III, several important areas of empirical testing are indicated. First, alternative assumptions relative to the form of measurement error need to be tested. Do multiplicative, additive, or other forms best fit the relevant data? Second, are measurement errors independent of the level of income? The answer to this question most likely is interrelated with the first. Third, estimates of the value of parameters associated with the distribution of measurement errors are needed in order to assess the relative magnitude of the distortion in characteristics of observed income distributions resulting from the existence of underreporting. For example, if $E(u)$ is high and/or σ_u is low, distortions in the coefficient of variation may be minimal, as shown in Table 1. Large values of σ_u and/or low values of $E(u)$, however, may cause extreme distortions in the coefficient of variation. Fourth, has there been a trend over time in characteristics of the distribution of measurement errors? If not, relative changes in true income distribution characteristics may be accurately reflected by relative changes in corresponding characteristics of measured distributions. If there has been a trend, inferences drawn from observed income distributions about the effectiveness of incomes policies can be seriously misleading.

There is evidence for such a trend of U.S. income distribution data. According to IRS estimates, the fraction of income unreported on individual tax returns increased by 21–24% between 1965 and 1973, and by 16–17% between 1973 and 1981—an increase of some 40–45% for the entire 1965–1981 period.[12] It seems reasonable to assume that a similar increase in underreporting occurred in income data collected by the U.S. Bureau of the Census. If income misreporting in the United States is correctly characterized by the model developed here, then the time trend in underreporting implies that, other things being equal, there has been an increase in the upward bias of measured income inequality relative to actual inequality over the period mentioned, with the accompanying possibility of serious misinterpretations regarding policy impacts and effectiveness.

The nature of misreporting makes the empirical testing of assumptions and the estimation of parameters necessary to answer the questions raised in this section difficult—and perhaps impossible in some cases. Nevertheless, the potential social costs of misinterpretation and inaccurate evaluation of policies inherent in misreported data suggest that more accurate estimates of levels and trends in income inequality would be highly beneficial. The analysis and techniques developed in this study provide a framework within which such estimates might be obtained. Much remains to be done. It is the hope and anticipation of the authors that applications and extensions of this study will, indeed, prove beneficial to economic researchers and to society.

APPENDIX

A.1. Derivation of Eq. (2.8)

By definition,

$$CV = \sqrt{\mathrm{Var}(y)}/E(y),$$

where

$$E(y) = E(u)E(y^*);$$

$$\begin{aligned}
\mathrm{Var}(y) &= E(y^2)E^2(y) \\
&= E(u^2)E(y^{*2}) - E^2(u)E^2(y^*) \\
&= E(u^2)E(y^{*2}) \pm E(u^2)E^2(y^*) - E^2(u)E^2(y^*) \\
&= E(u^2)\mathrm{Var}(y^*) + E^2(y^*)\mathrm{Var}(u) \\
&= [\mathrm{Var}(u) + E^2(u)]\mathrm{Var}(y^*) + E^2(y^*)\mathrm{Var}(u).
\end{aligned}$$

Therefore,

$$\begin{aligned}
CV &= \sqrt{\frac{[\mathrm{Var}(u) + E^2(u)]\mathrm{Var}(y^*) + E^2(y^*)\mathrm{Var}(u)}{E^2(u)E^2(y^*)}} \\
&= \sqrt{(CV_u^2 + 1)CV^{*2} + CV_u^2},
\end{aligned}$$

where

$$CV_u = \sqrt{\mathrm{Var}(u)}/E(u).$$

A.2. Derivation of Eq. (2.16)

$$E(Z^r) = \frac{b^r\Gamma(1 + r/a)\Gamma(q - r/a)}{\Gamma(q)}$$

(cf. McDonald, 1982). Combining this result with

$$CV_z = \sqrt{\frac{E(z^2)}{E^2(z)} - 1}$$

yields the desired result.

A.3. Derivation of Table 3

The entries in Table 3 are obtained from an application of (2.2) and (2.3). The basic integrals involved in Cases (1) and (2) are obtained from (2.2) and (2.3) and are evaluated using results from Gradshteyn and Ryzhik [1965: 3.383(4) and 3.383(3), respectively]. The results reported for Cases (3), (4), (5), and (6) follow directly from an application of (2.2) and (2.3), respectively.

A.4. A Special Case of Interdependence Between Measurement Error and the Level of Income

Let $u = g(y^*)$ represent the fraction of income reported; then observed income is

$$y = g(y^*)y^*,$$

where $g(y^*)$ is assumed to preserve the rank order of y^*, that is, $dy/dy^* > 0$ (or $g'/g \geq -1/y^*$). Let $y_1, \ldots, y_n$ denote an ordered sample of observed income and $y_1^*, \ldots, y_n^*$ the corresponding true values. If it is assumed that $g'(y^*) > 0$, then

$$\frac{y_j^*}{y_i^*} \leq \frac{y_j}{y_i} \tag{A.4.1}$$

and

$$\frac{\sum_{j=i+1}^{n} y_j^*}{y_i^*} \leq \frac{\sum_{j=i+1}^{n} y_j}{y_i} \tag{A.4.2}$$

for $j > i$. Similarly,

$$\frac{\sum_{j=1}^{i} y_j^*}{y_i^*} \geq \frac{\sum_{j=1}^{i} y_j}{y_i}. \tag{A.4.3}$$

Cross-multiplying in (A.4.2) and (A.4.3) yields

$$\frac{\sum_{j=i+1}^{n} y_j}{\sum_{j=i+1}^{n} y_j^*} \geq \frac{y_i}{y_i^*} \geq \frac{\sum_{j=1}^{i} y_j}{\sum_{j=1}^{i} y_j^*} \tag{A.4.4}$$

or

$$\frac{\sum_{j=i+1}^{n} y_j}{\sum_{j=i+1}^{n} y_j^*} \geq \frac{\sum_{j=1}^{i} y_j}{\sum_{j=1}^{i} y_j^*} \; . \tag{A.4.5}$$

From (A.4.5) we can write

$$\frac{\sum_{j=i+1}^{n} y_j}{\sum_{j=1}^{i} y_j} \geq \frac{\sum_{j=i+1}^{n} y_j^*}{\sum_{j=1}^{i} y_j^*} \; , \tag{A.4.6}$$

or

$$\frac{\sum_{j=i+1}^{n} y_j}{\sum_{j=1}^{i} y_j} + 1 \geq \frac{\sum_{j=i+1}^{n} y_j^*}{\sum_{j=1}^{i} y_j^*} + 1$$

and

$$\frac{\sum_{j=1}^{n} y_j}{\sum_{j=1}^{i} y_j} \geq \frac{\sum_{j=1}^{n} y_j^*}{\sum_{j=1}^{i} y_j^*} \; .$$

The last inequality is equivalent to

$$\frac{\sum_{j=1}^{i} y_j}{\sum_{j=1}^{n} y_j} \leq \frac{\sum_{j=1}^{i} y_j^*}{\sum_{j=1}^{n} y_j^*} \; . \tag{A.4.7}$$

The strict inequality holds unless $y_i^* = y_j^*$, for all i and j. Thus, (A.4.7) implies that the Lorenz curve for measured income lies to the right of the Lorenz curve for true income if $g'(y^*) > 0$, lies to the left of the Lorenz curve for true income if $g'(y^*) < 0$, and the two Lorenz curves coincide if $g'(y^*) = 0$. This clearly implies that the Gini coefficients and Pietra indices for measured income are greater (less) than the corresponding coefficients for true income if $g'(y^*) > 0$ $(g'(y^*) < 0)$. The previous analysis corresponds to the case where measurement error depends upon true income, but in a deterministic manner. The case of stochastic inter-dependence between measurement error and true income should include the above result as a polar case as the variance of u approaches zero.

NOTES

1. This result follows because the Gini coefficient is twice the area between the Lorenz curve and the 45° line of equality (the area of concentration) and the Pietra index, or relative mean deviation, defined by $P = E(\mid Y - \mu \mid)/2\mu$, is twice the area of the largest triangle

that can be inscribed within the region of concentration (see Gastwirth, 1972; Kendall and Stuart, 1961).

2. See the Appendix Section A.1, for details.

3. Cramer (1980) notes that a strict application of a chi square goodness-of-fit test in the work of Kloek and van Dijk (1978) and McDonald and Ransom (1979) results in the rejection of virtually all of the models considered. He investigates whether this might be due to the presence of an error in the observed income series. He adopts methods of moments estimation and concludes that "neither the Pareto nor gamma are redeemed by the introduction of an error term" but that "the verdict on the lognormal must be postponed; as a byproduct of the analysis we find that it does better than was suggested some years ago by Salem and Mount."

4. The derivation of (2.16) is contained in the Appendix, Section A.2. Other results are contained in McDonald and Ransom (1979).

5. Figure 1 corresponds to an assumed beta density for true income, denoted by

$$f(y^*) = \frac{y^{*p-1}(b - y^*)^{q-1}}{b^{p+q-1}B(p, q)} \, ,$$

and measurement error given by (2.17); hence, the density function of measured income is given by

$$h(y) = \frac{y^{\alpha-1}(1 - y/b)^{\beta+q-1}B(\beta, q)}{(b\gamma)^{\alpha}B(p, q)B(\alpha, \beta)} \, {}_2F_1 \left[\begin{array}{c} \alpha + \beta - p, q; \quad 1 - y/b \\ \beta + q; \end{array} \right]$$

for $0 \le y \le b$. Parameter values for $g(u)$ used in Figure 1 are as follows: Case (1), $\alpha = 2$, $\beta = 18$; Case (2), $\alpha = 4$, $\beta = 16$; Case (3), $\alpha = 9$, $\beta = 18$. The scale parameter, γ, is unity in all three cases.

6. The rth moments about the origin are given by

$$E(y^r) = \lambda^r p(p + 1) \cdots (p + r - 1)$$

for the gamma and

$$E(y^r) = \frac{b^r \Gamma(1 + r/a)\Gamma(q - r/a)}{\Gamma(q)}$$

for the Singh–Maddala density function. In order to illustrate this procedure, we consider a special example of the first case (Table 3) where $\gamma = \beta = 1$. The method of moments estimators of λ, p, and α are obtained by solving

$$\sum_{t=1}^{n} \frac{y_t}{n} = \frac{\hat{\lambda} p \hat{\alpha}}{\hat{\alpha} + 1}$$

$$\sum_{t=1}^{n} \frac{y_t^2}{n} = \frac{\hat{\lambda}^2 p(p + 1)\hat{\alpha}}{\hat{\alpha} + 2}$$

$$\sum_{t=1}^{n} \frac{y_t^3}{n} = \frac{\hat{\lambda}^3 p(p + 1)(p + 2)\hat{\alpha}}{\hat{\alpha} + 3}$$

for $\hat{\alpha}$, p, and $\hat{\lambda}$. This example corresponds to the measurement error assumed by Hartley and Revankar. If the expressions for $E(y^r)$ are easy to work with, then (2.19) might be replaced with

$$\sum_{t=1}^{n} \frac{y_t^r}{n} = E(y^r), \tag{2.19'}$$

which could be solved for θ and then θ_1.

7. It is possible to construct cases in which a ranking based upon a Gini coefficient can be inferred from a ranking based upon the coefficient of variation. For example, if y^* and y are each distributed as gamma variates, the associated measurement error has an F distribution. In this case, $CV^* > CV$ implies $G^* > G$; however, this case has associated with it an identification problem.

8. In the two-parameter density functions mentioned, one parameter is a scale parameter and does not appear in the scale-free inequality measures CV and G. For a summary table of the density functions mentioned, with their associated characteristics, see McDonald (1980, 1982).

9. Utah Income and Wealth Project, Brigham Young University and Utah State University.

10. See the Appendix, Section A.4, for proof. The case of $u = g(y^*)$ is analogous to $t = g(y^*)$, where t is the tax rate on income and $dt/dy^* = g'(y^*)$ is the measure of tax progressivity. This latter case has been studied extensively in the public finance literature.

11. *Statement of Roscoe L. Egger, Jr., Commissioner of Internal Revenue, Before the Ways and Means Committee, May 18, 1982.*

12. Ibid., Attachment II; Department of the Treasury (1979), p. 152.

REFERENCES

Arnold, Barry C. (1980) Misreporting Increases Apparent Inequality, Mimeographed manuscript: University of California at Riverside. Department of Statistics.

Cox, D. R. and D. V. Hinckley (1974) *Theoretical Statistics*. London: Chapman and Hall.

Cramer, J. S. (1980) Errors and Disturbances and the Performance of Some Common Income Distribution Functions, University of Amsterdam. Mimeographed manuscript.

Department of the Treasury (1979) Internal Revenue Service. *Estimates of Income Unreported on Individual Income Tax Returns*. Washington, D.C.

Gastwirth, Joseph (1972) The Estimation of the Lorenz Curve and Gini Index, *Review of Economics and Statistics* 54, 306–316.

Gradshteyn, I. S. and I. M. Ryzhik (1965) *Tables of Integrals, Series, and Products*. New York: Academic Press.

Hartley, Michael J. and Nagesh S. Revankar (1974) On the Estimation of the Pareto Law from Under-Reported Data, *Journal of Econometrics* 2, 327–341.

Kendall, M. G. and A. Stuart (1961) "Relative Mean Deviation." *The Advanced Theory of Statistics* 1, (2nd Ed.) New York: Hafner.

Kloek, T. and H. K. van Dijk (1978) Efficient Estimation of Income Distribution Parameters, *Journal of Econometrics* 8, 61–74.

McDonald, J. B. (1981) Some Issues Associated with the Measurement of Income Inequality. In C. Taillie, et al., (eds.) *Statistical Distributions in Scientific Work* 6, 161–179.

McDonald, J. B. (1982) Some Generalized Functions for the Size Distribution of Income, *Brigham Young University*, mimeographed manuscript.

McDonald, James B. and Michael R. Ransom (1979) Functional Forms, Estimation Techniques and The Distribution of Income, *Econometrica* 47, 1513–1525.

Salem, A. B. Z. and T. D. Mount (1974) A Convenient Descriptive Model of Income Distribution: The Gamma Density, *Econometrica* 42, 1115–1127.

Statement of Roscoe L. Egger, Jr. (1982) Commissioner of Internal Revenue Before the Ways and Means Committee, May 18, (Mimeograph).

WELFARE RANKING OF INCOME DISTRIBUTIONS

Nanak Kakwani

I. INTRODUCTION

The Lorenz curve is widely used to represent and analyze the size distribution of income and wealth. It is defined as the relationship between the cumulative proportion of income units and the cumulative proportion of income received when units are arranged in ascending order of their income.

The Lorenz curve is represented by a function $L(p)$, which is interpreted as the fraction of total income received by the lowest pth fraction of income units. If every individual in the society gets exactly the same income, the Lorenz curve coincides with the egalitarian line $L(p) = p$; otherwise it falls below this line.

Because the Lorenz curve displays the deviation of each individual income from perfect equality, it captures, in a sense, the essence of in-

Advances in Econometrics, vol. 3, pages 191–213
Copyright © 1984 by JAI Press Inc.
All rights of reproduction in any form reserved.
ISBN: 0-89232-443-0

equality. The nearer is the Lorenz curve to the egalitarian line, the more equal will be the distribution of income. Consequently, the Lorenz curve could be used as a criterion for ranking income distributions. However, the ranking provided by the curve is only partial. When the Lorenz curve of one distribution is higher than that of another, it can be concluded that the first distribution is more equal than the second. But when two Lorenz curves intersect, neither distribution can be said to be more equal than the other. This partial ranking need not, however, be considered a weakness of the Lorenz curve. In fact, Sen (1973) critized complete ranking on the grounds that "the concept of inequality has different facets which may point in different directions, and sometimes a total ranking cannot be expected to emerge." The concept of inequality is, therefore, essentially a question of partial ranking, and the Lorenz curve is consistent with such a notion of inequality.

Atkinson (1970) provided a justification of the Lorenz curve in terms of social welfare by showing that, if social welfare is the sum of the individual utilities and every individual has an identical utility function which is concave, the ranking of distributions according to the Lorenz curve criterion is identical to the ranking implied by the social welfare function, provided the distributions have the same mean income and their Lorenz curves do not intersect. This is indeed a remarkable result in the sense that one can rank the distributions without knowing the form of the utility function, except that it is increasing and concave. If the Lorenz curves do intersect, however, two utility functions that will rank the distributions differently can always be found.

Atkinson's result relies on the assumptions that the social welfare function is equal to the sum of individual utilities and that every individual has the same utility function. These assumptions have been criticized by Dasgupta et al. (1973) as well as by Rothschild and Stiglitz (1973), who have demonstrated that the result is, in fact, more general and would hold for any symmetric welfare function that is quasi-concave.

Despite the fact that the Lorenz curve provides only a partial ranking of the distributions, it is a powerful device to judge the distributions from the welfare point of view provided the distributions have the same mean income. If the distributions have different means, however, the Lorenz curve criterion may fail to provide a welfare ranking of the distributions. Consider an example of two distributions X and Y which have means μ_x and μ_y, respectively. If we let X have a higher Lorenz curve than Y, then it can be unambiguously inferred that if $\mu_x \geq \mu_y$, X is a better distribution than Y. On the other hand, if $\mu_x < \mu_y$, the Lorenz curve alone does not allow us to make any normative statement about the two distributions.

The Lorenz curve makes the distributional judgments independently of the size of income, which, as Sen (1973) points out, "will make sense only if the relative ordering of welfare levels of distributions were strictly neutral to the operation of multiplying everybody's income by a given number." This is rather an extreme requirement because social welfare depends on both size and distribution of income. Sen, recognizing this limitation, concluded that "the problem of extending the Lorenz ordering to cases of variable mean income is quite a serious one, and this—naturally enough—restricts severely the usefulness of this approach."

This paper deals with the welfare ranking of income distributions which differ in mean income. Sen (1973) argued that in order to make Lorenz-curve comparisons of income distributions with different mean income one would have to bring in some symmetry axiom for income which may not be particularly justifiable. In this paper the Lorenz partial ordering has been extended to cases of variable mean income without requiring a symmetry axiom for income. The new ranking criterion developed here is justified from the welfare point of view in terms of several alternative classes of social welfare functions. This new ranking criterion is then used for international comparison of welfare using data from 72 countries.

II. RANKING OF INCOME DISTRIBUTION ON THE BASIS OF UTILITARIAN SOCIAL WELFARE FUNCTION

Assume that distributions X and Y are characterized by random variables x and y, which have the density functions $f(x)$ and $g(y)$, respectively. The utilitarian social welfare for X and Y will then be written as

$$E[u(X)] = \int_0^\infty u(x) \, f(x) \, dx \qquad (2.1)$$

and

$$E[u(Y)] = \int_0^\infty u(y) \, g(y) \, dy, \qquad (2.2)$$

respectively, where the utility function $u(x)$, which is assumed to be the same for each individual, is concave. The following theorem can now be stated.

THEOREM 1: *If X and Y are two distributions having the mean income* μ_x *and* μ_y, *respectively, the following statements are equivalent—*

(a) $\mu_x L_x(p) \geq \mu_y L_y(p)$ *(for all p in the interval $0 \leq p \leq 1$)*
(b) $E[u(X)] \geq E[u(Y)]$

where $L_x(p)$ and $L_y(p)$ are the Lorenz curves of distributions X and Y, *respectively, and the individual utility function u(x) is continuous and concave.*

PROOF: The following lemma, which is due to Hardy et al. (1929), will be useful in proving the theorem.

LEMMA: *Suppose m and n are two increasing functions. Then the necessary and sufficient conditions for*

$$\int_a^b u(m(x)) \, dx \ge \int_a^b u(n(x)) \, dx$$

to be true for every concave and continuous u is

$$\int_a^\ell m(x) \, dx \ge \int_a^\ell n(x) \, dx$$

for $a \le \ell \le b$, with equality for the extreme value of ℓ.

The Lorenz curves always satisfy the following conditions:[1]

$$x = \mu_x L_x'(p) \quad \text{and} \quad y = \mu_y L_y'(p), \tag{2.3}$$

where $L_x'(p)$ and $L_y'(p)$ are the first derivatives of $L_x(p)$ and $L_y(p)$, respectively, and p varies from zero to unity when incomes x and y vary from zero to infinity. Because $dp = f(x) \, dx$, substituting (2.3) into (2.1) and (2.2) yields

$$E[u(X)] = \int_0^1 u[\mu_x L_x'(p)] \, dp$$

and

$$E[u(Y)] = \int_0^1 u[\mu_y L_y'(p)] \, dp,$$

respectively.

Since $\mu_x L_x'(p)$ and $\mu_y L_y'(p)$ are increasing functions of p because of the fact that $L_x''(p)$ and $L_y''(p)$ are positive,[2] the lemma provides the necessary and sufficient condition for

$$E[u(X)] \ge E[u(Y)]$$

to be true for every concave and continuous u as

$$\int_0^\ell \mu_x L_x'(P) \, dp \ge \int_0^\ell \mu_y L_y'(p) \, dp \tag{2.4}$$

for $0 \le \ell \le 1$, with equality for extreme values of ℓ. When the integrals have been evaluated, Eq. (2.4) becomes

$$\mu_x L_x(\ell) \geq \mu_y L_y(\ell)$$

for all ℓ in the interval $0 \leq \ell \leq 1$, which is clearly equivalent to condition (a) in Theorem 1. This completes the proof of that theorem.   QED

The above theorem suggests an alternative criterion of ranking the distributions with variable mean income. This criterion is given by

$$L(\mu, p) = \mu L(p),$$

whereas the Lorenz ranking is based on $L(p)$. Ranking the distributions according to $L(\mu, p)$ will be identical to the Lorenz ranking if the distributions have the same mean income.

The theorem implies that, if social welfare is the sum of the individual utilities and every individual has an identical utility function, the ranking of distributions with different means according to the $L(\mu, p)$ criterion is identical to the ranking implied by the social welfare function, provided the curves $L(\mu, p)$ for the different distributions do not intersect; indeed, condition (a) requires that the $L(\mu, p)$ curves do not intersect. One can, therefore, judge between the distributions with different means without knowing the form of the utility function $u(x)$, except that it is concave. If the distributions have the same mean income, the above theorem leads to Atkinson's (1970) theorem.

The following implications emerge from Theorem 1:

1. If the two distributions have the same Lorenz curve, the distribution with larger mean income will be welfare superior.
2. Even if the Lorenz curves of two distributions intersect, it may still be possible to infer that one distribution is welfare superior to another. For example, consider the two distributions

    $$X: \quad (2, 3, 5, 6)$$

    $$Y: \quad (1, 4, 4, 5),$$

    the Lorenz curve of which intersect; but Theorem 1 implies that distribution X is welfare superior to distributions Y.
3. Even if one distribution has a higher Lorenz curve than another at all points, it may still be welfare inferior. Consider the two distributions

    $$X: \quad (3, 3, 5, 13)$$

    $$Y: \quad (2, 4, 4, 4),$$

    where X has a lower Lorenz curve than Y but still is welfare superior.

These implications suggest that the Lorenz ranking when applied to cases of variable mean income may not be very useful in making distributional judgments from the welfare point of view. Theorem 1 provides a useful alternative to the Lorenz ranking, although it is based on the restrictive assumption of the utilitarian welfare function, with every individual having the same utility function. These restrictions are relaxed in the subsequent sections.

III. ABBA LERNER'S PROBABILISTIC SOCIAL WELFARE FUNCTION

Since people's tastes do differ, the assumption of identical utility function for each person cannot be defended. It is, therefore, assumed that each individual has a different utility function. Suppose there are n individuals in the society who have n different utility functions $u_1(x)$, $u_2(x)$, . . . , $u_n(x)$. Each $u_i(x)$ is continuous and concave.

Since insufficient knowledge is available as to which person has which utility function, Lerner (1944) made the Bayesian assumption that each possibility is equally likely. Given this assumption, the expected utility of an individual with income x is

$$\bar{u}(x) = \frac{1}{n} \sum_{i=1}^{n} u_i(x).$$

If social welfare is considered to be the sum of the individual utilities, the expected social welfare for income distributions X and Y will be

$$E[\bar{u}(X)] = \int_0^\infty \bar{u}(x)f(x) \, dx$$

and

$$E[\bar{u}(Y)] = \int_0^\infty \bar{u}(y) \, g(y) \, dy,$$

respectively.

It can be easily demonstrated that $\bar{u}(x)$ is continuous and concave. Then the following theorem follows immediately from Theorem 1.

THEOREM 2: *The following statements are equivalent—*

(a) $\mu_x L_x(p) \geq \mu_y L_y(p)$ (*for all p in the interval* $0 \leq p \leq 1$)

(b) $E[\bar{u}(X)] \geq E[\bar{u}(Y)]$

where $\bar{u}(x) = \dfrac{1}{n} \sum_{i=1}^{n} u_i(x)$ *and each* $u_i(x)$ *is continuous and concave in x.*

Let $\mu_x = \mu_y = \mu$ and in distribution X let each individual receive exactly the same income, which is μ; then the Lorenz curve for X will coincide with the egalitarian line, that is, $L(p) = p$. Then condition (a) in Theorem 2 becomes $\mu p \geq \mu L_y(p)$, which is always true because p is always greater than $L_y(p)$ for all values of p. Therefore, Theorem 2 implies that condition (b) will always be true if in distribution X each individual receives exactly the same income. This leads to the following famous theorem, which is due to Lerner (1944).

THEOREM 3: *The maximization of probable total satisfaction in a society is attained by an equal division of income.*

Note that Lerner (1944) proved this theorem for a two-person model but asserted that it holds for any number of persons. Breit and Culbertson (1970) indicated that the generalization to the n-person case is not self-evident as Samuelson (1964) and Lerner (1944) have suggested. Later McManus et al. (1972) and Sen (1969) extended the proof of it to the n-person case. Our proof of this theorem is entirely different from the ones given earlier.

IV. A FURTHER GENERALIZATION OF THEOREM 1

To arrive at a stronger version of Theorem 1, a class of social welfare functions, which are not necessarily utilitarian, must be considered. For an n-person society, a general social welfare function introduced by Bergson in 1938 and subsequently developed by Samuelson in 1947 is defined as

$$W(X) = W(x_1, x_2, \ldots, x_n),$$

where $X = (x_1, x_2, \ldots, x_n)$ is a vector of incomes received by n persons in the society. The following theorem can now be stated.

THEOREM 4: *The following statements are equivalent—*

(a) $\mu_x L_x(p) \geq \mu_y L_y(p)$

(b) $W(X) \geq W(Y)$,

where $W(X)$ is a nondecreasing, symmetric, and quasi-concave in individual incomes.[3]

PROOF: If two distributions X and Y are ordered,

$$x_1 \leq x_2 \leq \cdots \leq x_n; \qquad y_1 \leq y_2 \leq \cdots \leq y_n,$$

then condition (a) is equivalent to

$$s_k \geq 0 \qquad \text{(for all } k = 1, 2, \ldots, n\text{)}, \qquad (4.1)$$

where

$$s_k = \sum_{i=1}^{k} x_i - \sum_{i=1}^{k} y_i.$$

The following lemma, which is due to Rothschild and Stiglitz (1973), will be useful in proving the theorem.

LEMMA: $W(x_1, x_2, \ldots, x_n) \geq W(x_1, x_2, \ldots, x_i - t, \ldots, x_j + t, \ldots, x_n)$, where $t \geq 0$, $x_j \geq x_i$, and $W(X)$ is symmetric and quasi-concave.

The proof of Theorem 4 consists in demonstrating (a) → (b) → (a). First, we must show that

$$\text{(a)} \rightarrow \text{(b)}.$$

This proposition will be proved by an induction method. Let us first consider a two-person society. If (a) is true, then the above lemma implies that

$$W(x_1, x_2) \geq W(x_1 - s_1, x_2 + s_1)$$

$$= W(y_1, y_2 + s_2).$$

Since $W(X)$ is a nondecreasing function of individual incomes,

$$W(y_1, y_2 + s_2) \geq W(y_1, y_2)$$

must be true. This obviously proves that

$$W(x_1, x_2) \geq W(y_1, y_2).$$

Next let us consider a three-person society. Applying the above lemma twice gives

$$W(x_1, x_2, x_3) \geq W(x_1 - t_1 - t_2, x_2 + t_1, x_3 + t_2), \qquad (4.2)$$

where $t_1 + t_2 = s_1$; $t_1 \geq 0$; $t_2 \geq 0$. If $x_2 + s_1 \leq x_3$, we can put $t_1 = s_1$ and $t_2 = 0$, which gives

$$W(x_1, x_2, x_3) \geq W(x_1 - s_1, x_2 + s_1, x_3).$$

Since $x_2 + s_1 \leq x_3$ and $s_2 \geq 0$, the above lemma is applicable again as

$$W(x_1 - s_1, x_2 + s_1, x_3) \geq W(x_1 - s_1, x_2 + s_1 - s_2, x_3 + s_2)$$

$$= W(y_1, y_2, y_3 + s_3),$$

and therefore

$$W(x_1, x_2, x_3) \geq W(y_1, y_2, y_3 + s_3),$$

which obviously proves that

$$W(x_1, x_2, x_3) \geq W(y_1, y_2, y_3).$$

But if $x_2 + s_1 \geq x_3$, determine t_1 and t_2 such that[4]

$$t_1 + t_2 = s_1$$

and

$$x_2 + t_1 = x_3 + t_2,$$

which on solving simultaneously give

$$t_1 = \tfrac{1}{2}[s_1 + x_3 - x_2] \geq 0$$

and

$$t_2 = \tfrac{1}{2}[s_1 - (x_3 - x_2)] \geq 0.$$

Equation (4.2), on substituting t_1 and t_2, can be written as

$$W(x_1, x_2, x_3) \geq W[y_1, \tfrac{1}{2}(s_3 + y_2 + y_3), \tfrac{1}{2}(s_3 + y_2 + y_3)],$$

which on using the above lemma yields

$$W(x_1, x_2, x_3) \geq W[y_1, \tfrac{1}{2}(s_3 + y_2 + y_3) - t, \tfrac{1}{2}(s_3 + y_2 + y_3) + t],$$

where $t \geq 0$. This equation, on substituting

$$t = \tfrac{1}{2}(s_3 + y_3 - y_2) \geq 0,$$

becomes

$$W(x_1, x_2, x_3) \geq W(y_1, y_2, y_3 + s_3)$$

$$\geq W(y_1, y_2, y_3).$$

The extension of the proof to the *n*-person case goes through the same steps as above and needs no further elaboration. This proves (a) → (b). The proof of (b) → (a) is given by Rothschild and Stiglitz (1973), which completes the proof of Theorem 4.[5]   QED

V.   PROBABILISTIC SOCIAL WELFARE FUNCTION WHICH IS NOT ADDITIVE SEPARABLE

Again consider a society with *n* persons who have *n* different utility functions $u_1(x)$, $u_2(x)$, . . . , $u_n(x)$. The social welfare we suppose is individualistic and can be written as

$$F[X] = F(x_1, x_2, \ldots, x_n) = W[u_1(x_1), u_2(x_2), \ldots, u_n(x_n)], (5.1)$$

where social welfare W is a nondecreasing, symmetric, and concave function of individual utility levels $u_1(x_1), u_2(x_2), \ldots, u_n(x_n)$, each of which itself is a concave function of income.

It is not known which person has which utility function. There are $n!$ different ways of assigning n individual utility functions to n persons, thus yielding $n!$ values for W, that is, $W_1, W_2, \ldots, W_{n!}$. Under the Bayesian assumption, each possibility is counted as equally probable and the mathematical expectation is

$$E(W) = \frac{1}{n!} \sum_{k=1}^{n!} W_k. \tag{5.2}$$

The following theorem can now be stated.

THEOREM 5: *The following statements are equivalent—*

(a) $\mu_x L_x(p) \geq \mu_y L_y(p)$

(b) $E_x(W) \geq E_y(W)$,

where $E_x(W)$ and $E_y(W)$ are the mathematical expectations of social welfare for distributions X and Y, respectively.

Substituting $\mu_x = \mu_y$ and $L_x(p) = p$, condition (a) will always be true and, therefore, Theorem 5 implies that condition (b) will always be true, if in distribution X each individual receives exactly the same income. This leads to the following theorem, which was proved earlier by Sen (1973a).

THEOREM 6: *The mathematical expectation of social welfare [defined in Eq. (5.2)] is maximized by an equal division of income.*

Note that this theorem is a substantial generalization of Lerner's theorem regarding the optimum distribution of income. It does not require the social welfare function to be utilitarian or even additive separable.[6]

Theorem 5 still remains to be proved. In order to do so, we denote X_k to be a permuted vector of income distribution X. Since there are n individuals, we can form $n!$ such permuted income vectors. Owing to the symmetry property of W, all possible values for W will be given by $F(X_k)$, where k varies from 1 to $n!$. Therefore, the mathematical expectation of social welfare defined in (5.2) for income distribution X can be written as

$$E_x(W) = \frac{1}{n!} \sum_{i=1}^{n!} F(X_k). \qquad (5.3)$$

As we have assumed that W is a concave function of individual utilities and each $u_i(x)$ is concave in income, $F(X_k)$ is a concave function. Therefore, $E_x(W)$, which is the average of $F(X_1), F(X_2), \ldots, F(X_{n!})$ will also be concave. Since a concave function is necessarily quasi-concave, we have proved that $E_x(W)$ is a quasi-concave function.

It can be seen that $E_x(W)$ is a nondecreasing and symmetric function of individual incomes. Therefore, Theorem 5 follows immediately from Theorem 4. QED

VI. MAXIMIN STRATEGY FOR SOCIAL WELFARE

In the previous section, the mathematical expectation of social welfare was defined on the assumption that each possible value for W is equally probable. This equiprobability assumption has been subjected to the criticism that not to be sure who has which utility function is not the same as assuming that every possible assignment is equally likely.[7]

Alternatively, the society may adopt a "maximin" policy of maximizing the minimum level of social welfare. McManus et al. (1972) call it a "play safe" policy under which the society chooses that income distribution which make the worst of the possible values for W larger than the worst W associated with other income distributions.[8]

Under this strategy the social welfare function is defined as

$$S(X) = \min_k W_k = \min_k F(X_k), \qquad (6.1)$$

where X_k is a permuted vector of income distribution vector X, and k varies from 1 to $n!$. Note that the second equality in the above equation follows from the symmetry of the social welfare function W.

In the previous section we assumed that W is a concave function of individual utilities. We can now weaken this assumption and say that it is only quasi-concave. The quasi-concave of W is a sufficient condition to prove that $F(X)$ is a quasi-concave function of individual incomes. Then we must have

$$F[\lambda X_k + (1 - \lambda)Y_k] \geq \min_k [F(X_k), F(Y_k)], \qquad (6.2)$$

where X_k and Y_k are any two permuted vectors of income distributions X and Y, respectively, and $0 < \lambda < 1$. In order to prove that $S(X)$ is a quasi-concave function, we write

$$S[\lambda X + (1 - \lambda)Y] = \min_k[F(\lambda X_k + (1 - \lambda)Y_k)],$$

which by means of Eq. (6.2) must be greater than or equal to

$$\min_k[\min\{F(X_k), F(Y_k)\}].$$

Since

$$\min_k[\min\{F(X_k), F(Y_k)\}]$$

$$= \min[F(X_1), F(X_2), \ldots, F(X_n!); F(Y_1), F(Y_2), \ldots, F(Y_{n!})]$$

$$= \min[\min_k F(X_k), \min_k F(Y_k)]$$

$$= \min[S(X), S(Y)],$$

then

$$S[\lambda X + (1 - \lambda)Y]$$

$$\geq \min[S(X), S(Y)]$$

must be true, which proves that the social welfare function $S(X)$ based on the maximin strategy is indeed quasi-concave. It can be easily demonstrated that $S(X)$ is a nondecreasing and symmetric function of individual incomes. Thus, by Theorem 4, we have proved the following result.

THEOREM 7:   *The following statements are equivalent—*

(a) $\mu_x L_x(p) \geq \mu_y L_y(p)$

(b) $S(X) \geq S(Y)$,

where S(X) is the maximin social welfare function defined in Eq. (6.1).

Again substituting $\mu_x = \mu_y$ and $L_x(p) = p$ in (a), the following theorem, which was earlier proved by Sen (1973), follows immediately from the above result.

THEOREM 8:   *A maximin strategy for social welfare is to distribute income equally.*

Note that Theorem 8 is more general than the one proved by McManus et al. (1972). Their proof depends essentially on the assumption that the social welfare function $W(u_1, u_2, \ldots, u_n)$ is additive separable. Theorem

7 and 8 only require social welfare to be quasi-concave functions of individual utilities.

VII. AN INTERNATIONAL COMPARISON OF WELFARE USING CROSS-SECTION DATA

This section provides an international comparison of welfare using the ranking criterion developed in this paper. The calculations are based on income distribution data for 72 countries obtained from a compilation of Jain (1975), to whom the reader is referred for the definition of *income* and *income-receiving unit*.

It must be pointed out that there are several problems associated with the comparability of income distribution data from different countries. These problems have been discussed elsewhere (see, for instance, Kuznets, 1955; Adelman and Morris, 1971; Titmuss, 1962; Kravis, 1960). Unavoidably, then, conclusions emerging from this section have severe limitations.

In order to apply the new ranking criterion, it is necessary to have the estimates of GDP (gross domestic product) per capita for each country in the units of a single currency, e.g., U.S. dollars. The GDP per capita is available for almost all countries in terms of their domestic currencies. The conversion of these GDPs to U.S. dollars at the official exchange rate can be misleading because these rates do not necessarily reflect the purchasing power of different countries. Kravis et al. (1978) have recently computed the real GDP per capita in terms of U.S. dollars (adjusting for differences in the purchasing power of countries) for more than a hundred countries. These real GDP per-capita estimates were used in the present study after they were indexed with base 100 for the United States.

Given the decile shares and the GDP per-capita index, we computed the values of the function $L(\mu, p)$ for $p = .1, .2, .3, .4, .5, .6, .7, .8, .9,$ 1.0. In any pairwise comparison, the two countries can be ranked on the basis of their welfare value if and only if the two curves $L(\mu\ p)$ (one for each country) do not cross. It is, therefore, of interest to know how often these curves actually cross.

With 72 countries, we could make $72_{C_2} = 2,556$ all possible pairwise comparisons. The proposed curves crossed in 511 cases, which means that in about 80% of all pairwise comparisons it was possible to say which of the two countries was welfare superior. We consider this percentage to be fairly high, thereby suggesting the usefulness of the proposed ranking criterion. The Lorenz curves, on the other hand, crossed in more than 30% of all such pairwise comparisons. Thus, it can be concluded that the

Table 1. Indexes of GDP per Capita 1970 and $L(\mu, p)$ for Different Values of p

No.	Country	Index of GDP per Capita 1970	$L(\mu, p)$ for p Equal to:									
			.1	.2	.3	.4	.5	.6	.7	.8	.9	1.0
1	Bangladesh	4.29	.15	.34	.57	.84	1.15	1.52	1.95	2.47	3.14	4.29
2	Malawi	4.58	.10	.26	.45	.69	.96	1.29	1.68	2.16	2.80	4.58
3	India	5.48	.11	.28	.50	.78	1.13	1.56	2.10	2.80	3.78	5.98
4	Tanzania	6.04	.05	.14	.28	.47	.73	1.08	1.56	2.22	3.22	6.04
5	Pakistan	9.93	.32	.79	1.35	2.01	2.76	3.61	4.61	5.78	7.24	9.93
6	Sri Lanka	10.10	.28	.70	1.19	1.80	2.50	3.34	4.34	5.56	7.16	10.10
7	Philippines	10.40	.13	.41	.76	1.24	1.83	2.58	3.54	4.78	6.54	10.40
8	Korea	13.70	.42	.97	1.63	2.42	3.38	4.51	5.89	7.60	9.86	13.70
9	Hondurus	14.80	.07	.24	.53	.95	1.54	2.35	3.49	5.14	7.75	14.80
10	Turkey	18.10	.18	.52	1.03	1.70	2.57	3.69	5.16	7.13	10.01	18.10
11	Malaysia	18.90	.23	.72	1.38	2.23	3.27	4.57	6.20	8.28	11.13	18.90
12	Brazil	22.80	.20	.55	1.05	1.76	2.71	3.99	5.70	8.09	11.72	22.80
13	Costa Rica	25.30	.53	1.37	2.40	3.69	5.26	7.18	9.56	12.54	16.65	25.30
14	Mexico	28.30	.57	1.19	1.95	2.89	4.10	5.63	7.67	10.41	14.49	28.30
15	Chile	29.90	.57	1.43	2.54	3.89	5.33	7.53	10.12	13.22	17.55	29.90
16	Hong Kong	31.70	.67	1.77	3.20	4.94	7.01	9.48	12.46	16.17	21.02	31.70
17	Japan	58.20	1.98	5.12	8.79	12.98	17.81	23.16	29.27	36.32	44.76	58.20
18	United Kingdom	63.50	1.46	4.19	7.62	11.75	16.70	22.54	29.53	37.91	48.32	63.50
19	New Zealand	64.30	2.19	5.34	9.07	13.44	18.45	24.24	30.86	38.77	48.48	64.30
20	Australia	75.90	1.82	5.39	9.87	15.18	21.40	28.54	36.74	46.37	58.06	75.90
21	Germany	77.80	1.71	4.59	8.25	12.76	18.20	24.66	32.60	42.32	55.16	77.80
22	Canada	89.00	.98	3.46	7.46	12.98	20.05	28.67	38.92	51.10	65.68	89.00
23	United States	100.00	1.40	4.80	9.40	15.30	22.40	31.00	41.40	54.20	70.90	100.00

Table 2. Pairs of Countries for Which the New Welfare
Criterion Failed to Rank the Two Countries

Bangladesh	– Malawi	Korea	– Hondurus
Bangladesh	– India	Korea	– Turkey
Bangladesh	– Tanzania	Korea	– Malaysia
Bangladesh	– Philippines	Korea	– Brazil
Bangladesh	– Hondurus	Malaysia	– Brazil
Malawi	– Tanzania	Costa Rica	– Mexico
Malawi	– Hondurus	Japan	– U.K.
India	– Tanzania	Japan	– Germany
India	– Hondurus	Japan	– Canada
Pakistan	– Sri Lanka	Japan	– U.S.
Pakistan	– Philippines	U.K.	– Canada
Pakistan	– Hondurus	U.K.	– U.S.
Pakistan	– Turkey	New Zealand	– Australia
Pakistan	– Malaysia	New Zealand	– Germany
Pakistan	– Brazil	New Zealand	– Canada
Sri Lanka	– Philippines	New Zealand	– U.S.
Sri Lanka	– Hondurus	Australia	– Germany
Sri Lanka	– Turkey	Australia	– Canada
Sri Lanka	– Malaysia	Australia	– U.S.
Philippines	– Brazil	Germany	– Canada
		Germany	– U.S.

new curves are likely to cross less often than the well-known Lorenz curves.

The fact that the income distribution data have been obtained from different studies renders intercountry comparisons difficult because of the differences in income units, population coverage, and the year of the survey. In order to remedy these difficulties, we selected only 23 countries, data for which were more or less comparable in terms of these three criteria (i.e., income units, population coverage, and the year of the survey).[9] Table 1 presents the index of GDP per capita and the value of $L(\mu, p)$ for $p = .1, .2, \ldots, .9, 1.0$ for each of these 23 countries.

The new welfare criterion failed to rank the two countries in 16.6% of all possible pairs of countries. These pairs of countries are listed in Table 2. For instance, in this list of 23 countries, the United States is the richest country in GDP per-capita terms but in terms of welfare it can be ranked neither higher nor lower than, say, Japan, New Zealand, Australia, or the United Kingdom.

The Lorenz curves intersected in 50 pairwise comparisons, which means that in more than 21% cases it was not possible to say which of the two countries had unambiguously higher inequality. Interestingly

Table 3. Pairs of Countries for Which the Lorenz Curve Intersected but which Could Still Be Ranked by the Welfare Criterion[a]

Malawi	– India	Malawi	– Germany
Bangladesh	– Pakistan	Bangladesh	– Canada
Malawi	– Philippines	Malawi	– Canada
Sri Lanka	– Korea	India	– Canada
Tanzania	– Brazil	Pakistan	– Canada
Hondurus	– Brazil	Sri Lanka	– Canada
India	– Mexico	Phillipines	– Canada
Tanzania	– Mexico	Korea	– Canada
Philippines	– Mexico	Malaysia	– Canada
Hondurus	– Mexico	Costa Rica	– Canada
Turkey	– Mexico	Mexico	– Canada
Malaysia	– Mexico	Chile	– Canada
Brazil	– Mexico	Hong Kong	– Canada
India	– Chile	Uruguary	– Canada
Philippines	– Chile	Malawi	– U.S.
Malaysia	– Chile	India	– U.S.
Mexico	– Chile	Costa Rica	– U.S.
Malawi	– Hong Kong	Mexico	– U.S.
Bangladesh	– U.K.	Chile	– U.S.
Pakistan	– U.K.	Hong Kong	– U.S.
U.K.	– New Zealand	Sri Lanka	– U.K.
Bangladesh	– Australia	Korea	– U.K.
Pakistan	– Australia	Malawi	– Costa Rica
Sri Lanka	– Australia		
Korea	– Australia		

[a] The second country in each pair is welfare superior to the first.

Table 4. Pairs of Countries for Which the Ranking by the Lorenz Curve was the Same as That by the Welfare Criterion[a]

Malawi	– Pakistan	Tanzania	– Malaysia
India	– Pakistan	Hondurus	– Malaysia
Tanzania	– Pakistan	Turkey	– Malaysia
Malawi	– Sri Lanka	India	– Costa Rica
India	– Sri Lanka	Tanzania	– Costa Rica
Tanzania	– Sri Lanka	Philippines	– Costa Rica
Tanzania	– Philippines	Hondurus	– Costa Rica
Malawi	– Korea	Turkey	– Costa Rica
India	– Korea	Malaysia	– Costa Rica
Tanzania	– Korea	Brazil	– Costa Rica
Philippines	– Korea	Tanzania	– Chile
Tanzania	– Turkey	Hondurus	– Chile
Hondurus	– Turkey	Turkey	– Chile

206

Table 4. (Continued)

Brazil	– Chile	Malaysia	– Japan
Bangladesh	– New Zealand	Brazil	– Japan
Malawi	– New Zealand	Costa Rica	– Japan
India	– New Zealand	Mexico	– Australia
Tanzania	– New Zealand	Chile	– Australia
Pakistan	– New Zealand	Hong Kong	– Australia
Sri Lanka	– New Zealand	U.K.	– Australia
Philippines	– New Zealand	India	– Germany
Korea	– New Zealand	Tanzania	– Germany
Hondurus	– New Zealand	Philippines	– Germany
Turkey	– New Zealand	Hondurus	– Germany
Malaysia	– New Zealand	Turkey	– Germany
Brazil	– New Zealand	Malaysia	– Germany
Costa Rica	– New Zealand	Brazil	– Germany
Mexico	– New Zealand	Costa Rica	– Germany
Chile	– New Zealand	Mexico	– Germany
Hong Kong	– New Zealand	Chile	– Germany
Uruguary	– New Zealand	Hong Kong	– Germany
Japan	– New Zealand	Uruguary	– Germany
Malawi	– Australia	Tanzania	– Canada
India	– Australia	Hondurus	– Canada
Tanzania	– Australia	Turkey	– Canada
Philippines	– Australia	Brazil	– Canada
Hondurus	– Australia	Tanzania	– U.S.
Turkey	– Australia	Philippines	– U.S.
Malaysia	– Australia	Hondurus	– U.S.
Brazil	– Australia	Turkey	– U.S.
Costa Rica	– Australia	Malaysia	– U.S.
India	– Hong Kong	Brazil	– U.S.
Tanzania	– Hong Kong	Mexico	– Japan
Hondurus	– Hong Kong	Chile	– Japan
Turkey	– Hong Kong	India	– U.K.
Malaysia	– Hong Kong	Korea	– U.K.
Brazil	– Hong Kong	Turkey	– U.K.
Costa Rica	– Hong Kong	Brazil	– U.K.
Mexico	– Hong Kong	Mexico	– U.K.
Chile	– Hong Kong	Hong Kong	– U.K.
Bangladesh	– Japan	Tanzania	– U.K.
Malawi	– Japan	Canada	– U.S.
India	– Japan	Hong Kong	– Japan
Tanzania	– Japan	Malawi	– U.K.
Pakistan	– Japan	Philippines	– U.K.
Sri Lanka	– Japan	Hondurus	– U.K.
Philippines	– Japan	Malaysia	– U.K.
Korea	– Japan	Costa Rica	– U.K.
Hondurus	– Japan	Chile	– U.K.
Turkey	– Japan		

[a] The second country is welfare superior as well as inequality superior to the first country in each pair.

207

Table 5.   Pairs of Countries for Which the Ranking by the
Lorenz Curve Was Opposite to That by the Welfare
Criterion

India	– Philippines	Korea	– Mexico
Bangladesh	– Sri Lanka	Pakistan	– Chile
Pakistan	– Korea	Sri Lanka	– Hong Kong
Tanzania	– Hondurus	Korea	– Hong Kong
Bangladesh	– Turkey	Bangladesh	– Chile
Malawi	– Turkey	Malawi	– Chile
India	– Turkey	Sri Lanka	– Chile
Philippines	– Turkey	Korea	– Chile
Bangladesh	– Malaysia	Costa Rica	– Chile
Malawi	– Malaysia	Bangladesh	– Hong Kong
India	– Malaysia	Pakistan	– Hong Kong
Philippines	– Malaysia	Japan	– Australia
Bangladesh	– Brazil	Bangladesh	– Germany
Malawi	– Brazil	Pakistan	– Germany
India	– Brazil	Sri Lanka	– Germany
Philippines	– Brazil	Korea	– Germany
Turkey	– Brazil	U.K.	– Germany
Pakistan	– Costa Rica	Bangladesh	– U.S.
Sri Lanka	– Costa Rica	Pakistan	– U.S.
Korea	– Costa Rica	Sri Lanka	– U.S.
Bangladesh	– Mexico	Korea	– U.S.
Malawi	– Mexico	Bangladesh	– Korea
Pakistan	– Mexico	Bangladesh	– Costa Rica
Sri Lanka	– Mexico		

enough, we could still rank 48 such pairs of countries according to their
welfare value. These countries are listed in Table 3. The second country
in each pair is welfare superior to the first. There were only two pairs of
countries where it was not possible to rank the two countries either by
the Lorenz curve or by the new welfare criterion. These two pairs of
countries are new Zealand–Australia and Germany–Canada.

Table 4 lists 119 pairs of countries for which the ranking by the Lorenz
curve was the same as that by the proposed welfare criterion. The second
country in each pair is welfare superior as well as inequality superior to
the first. There were 47 pairs of countries for which the Lorenz ranking
was opposite to the welfare ranking. These pairs of countries are given
in Table 5. In each pair, the first country is inequality superior to the
second whereas the second country would have the effect of lowering the
welfare, but this effect was offset by the higher mean income in the second
country.

Table 6. Indexes of GDP per Capita and L(μ, p) for the United Kingdom, the United States, Finland, Netherlands, Sweden, and Norway for the Years 1952, 1953, 1957, 1962, 1967, and 1970

Year	Index of GDP per Capita	L(μ, p) for p Equal to:									
		.1	.2	.3	.4	.5	.6	.7	.8	.9	1.0
UNITED STATES:											
1952	87	.835	2.297	7.064	12.598	19.497	27.683	37.323	48.363	62.196	87.00
1957	91	.883	3.303	7.453	13.368	20.875	29.848	40.295	52.589	68.032	91.00
1962	98	.999	3.538	7.722	13.690	21.384	30.694	41.719	56.546	73.392	98.00
1967	117	1.240	4.399	9.547	16.789	26.032	37.206	50.497	66.780	86.943	117.00
1970	122	1.318	4.587	9.894	17.324	26.877	38.515	52.643	69.638	91.890	122.00
UNITED KINGDOM:											
1953	81	1.482	3.985	7.565	12.263	18.160	25.280	33.631	43.691	55.914	81.00
1957	88	1.470	4.180	8.158	13.490	20.249	28.362	37.840	48.805	61.943	88.00
1962	98	1.676	4.332	8.624	14.416	21.805	30.831	41.552	54.331	70.354	98.00
1967	109	1.864	5.581	10.791	17.473	26.062	36.406	48.461	62.740	80.289	109.00
SWEDEN:											
1952	69	1.207	3.360	6.520	10.833	16.360	23.067	30.939	40.041	50.908	69.00
1957	80	1.312	3.664	7.064	11.80	18.04	25.768	34.968	45.808	59.032	80.00
1962	96	1.411	4.195	8.131	13.584	20.928	30.00	40.483	53.002	68.928	96.00
1967	115	1.817	5.462	10.603	17.549	26.530	37.559	50.634	65.964	84.663	115.00

Table 6. (Continued)

Year	Index of GDP per Capita	L(μ, p) for p Equal to:									
		.1	.2	.3	.4	.5	.6	.7	.8	.9	1.0
NORWAY:											
1952	74	.866	3.071	6.482	11.085	16.961	24.168	32.767	42.876	55.078	74.00
1957	84	1.142	3.847	7.845	13.154	19.841	27.905	37.355	48.342	61.706	84.00
1962	96	1.382	4.704	9.6288	16.0896	24.125	33.696	44.755	57.494	72.912	96.00
1967	119	1.702	5.890	12.126	20.278	30.381	42.447	56.620	73.030	93.498	119.00
NETHERLANDS:											
1952	69	.793	2.173	5.292	9.384	14.414	20.376	27.317	35.473	45.844	69.00
1957	87	1.331	4.237	9.109	15.312	22.028	29.824	38.732	49.120	62.301	87.00
1962	98	1.362	4.429	8.938	14.984	22.520	31.370	41.513	53.283	67.532	98.00
1967	119	1.440	5.081	10.555	18.290	27.656	37.985	50.170	64.914	83.385	119.00
FINLAND:											
1952	67	.730	2.68	5.762	9.802	14.787	20.891	28.287	37.306	49.104	67.00
1957	78	.709	2.605	5.756	10.171	15.865	22.916	31.473	42.120	55.700	78.00
1962	98	.715	2.675	6.096	11.152	17.934	26.587	37.387	50.813	68.541	98.00
1967	114	.661	2.565	6.110	11.662	19.426	29.492	42.134	58.015	78.740	114.00

Table 7.   Summary of Conclusions

Country		1952–1957[a]	1957–1962	1962–1967	1967–1970[b]
United States	Inequality	decreased	inconclusive	inconclusive	inclusive
	Welfare	increased	increased	increased	increased
United Kingdom	Inequality	inconclusive	inconclusive	decreased	N.A.
	Welfare	inconclusive	increased	increased	N.A.
Finland	Inequality	increased	increased	decreased	N.A.
	Welfare	inconclusive	increased	inconclusive	N.A.
Netherlands	Inequality	decreased	increased	inconclusive	N.A.
	Welfare	increased	inconclusive	increased	N.A.
Sweden	Inequality	inconclusive	increased	decreased	N.A.
	Welfare	increased	increased	increased	N.A.
Norway	Inequality	inconclusive	decreased	inconclusive	N.A.
	Welfare	increased	increased	increased	N.A.

[a] For the United Kingdom, the period considered is from 1953 to 1957.
[b] N.A. = not available.

VIII.   WELFARE COMPARISONS USING THE TIME SERIES DATA

In this section, the welfare comparisons are made over time. The discussion is limited to six developed countries (Sweden, Finland, Norway, Netherlands, the United States, and the United Kingdom).[10]

Table 6 presents the index of GDP per capita along with the value of $L(\mu, p)$ for $p = .1, .2, \ldots , .9, 1.0$, for the six countries covering the period from 1952 to 1970. The conclusions emerging from Table 6 are summarized in Table 7.

NOTES

1.   See Kakwani (1980, p. 31).

2.   Since the Lorenz curve is convex to the p axis, its second derivative will always be positive. For further details on this point, see Kakwani and Podder (1973, 1976) and Kakwani (1980).

3.   The symmetry of the social welfare function requires that, if two individuals interchange their incomes, the social welfare function remains unchanged. Quasi-concavity requires that the minimum of the two social welfare levels from any two distributions X and Y, respectively, should be less than or equal to the social welfare of the weighted average of the two distributions.

4.   Rothschild and Stiglitz (1973) proved a particular case of Theorem 4 when the two distributions have the same mean income. In their proof, however, they did not consider the possibility that $x_2 + s_1$ could be greater than x_3. Their proof of the theorem is, therefore, incomplete.

5.   Rothschild and Stiglitz (1973) have indicated an alternative proof of this theorem by defining an inefficient regressive transfer in which a poor man gives up d while a richer man receives less than d.

6.   Sen (1973a) has argued that the additive separable assumption is rather restrictive in the context of Friedman's (1947) criticism of Lerner's approach.

7.   See Sen (1973a, p. 85).

8.   Note that under Rawls (1971) "maximin" criterion, the level of welfare of the worst-off individual is maximized with no uncertainty about who has which welfare function.

9.   The income unit for these data was households; the survey covered the entire national population; and the year of the survey varied between 1967 and 1973.

10.   The income distribution data for these countries were obtained from the following: *for Finland*, Central Statistical Office, Statistical Year-book of Finland, Helsinki; *for Netherlands*, Netherlands Central Bureau of Statistics, Statistical Year-book of Netherlands, The Hague; *for Norway*, Norges Offisielle Statistikk, XII, 245, Historical Statistics, 1968, Oslo, 1969, Idem., XII, 274, Statistical Year-book of Norway; *for Sweden*, Statistical Abstract of Sweden, Statistiska Centralbyran, Stockholm; *for United Kingdom*, Central Statistical Office, National Income and Expenditure, London; *for United States*, U.S. Bureau of the Census, Current Population Reports, Consumer Income, Series P-60, Washington, D.C. The GDP per-capita index at constant prices (1963 = 100) for all these countries was obtained from the United Nations: Year-book of National Accounts Statistics 1969 and 1979, Vol. II, International Tables.

REFERENCES

Adelman, L. and C. Morris (1971) An Anatomy of Patterns of Income Distribution in Developing Nations, Part III of the Final Report, Grant AID/Csd-2236 (Northwestern University, Evanston, 12).

Atkinson, A. B. (1970) On the Measurement of Inequality, *Journal of Economic Theory*, 2, 244–63.

Bergson, A. (1938) A Reformulation of Certain Aspects of Welfare Economics, *Quarterly Journal of Economics*, Vol. 52, 310–34.

Breit, W. and W. P. Culbertson, Jr. (1970) Distributional Equality and Aggregate Utility: Comment, *American Economic Review* June, 60, 435–41.

Dasgupta, P., A. K. Sen, and D. Starrett (1973) Notes on the Measurement of Inequality, *Journal of Economic Theory* 6, 180–87.

Friedman, M. (1947) Lerner on the Economics of Control, *Journal of Political Economy* Vol. 55, reprinted in *Essays in Positive Economics*, University of Chicago Press, 1964.

Hardy, G. H., J. E. Littlewood and G. Polya (1929) Some Simple Inequalities Satisfied by Convex Functions, *Messenger of Maths* 26, 145–53.

Jain, S. (1975) *Size Distribution of Income: A Compilation of Data*, (The World Bank, Washington D.C.).

Kakwani, N. C. (1980) *Income Inequality and Poverty: Methods of Estimation and Policy Applications*, New York: Oxford University Press.

Kakwani, N. C. and N. Podder (1973) On the Estimation of Lorenz Curves from Grouped Observations, *International Economic Review* 14, 278–91.

Kakwani, N. C. and N. Podder (1976) Efficient Estimation of the Lorenz Curve and Associated Inequality Measures from Grouped Observations, *Econometrica* 44, 137–148.

Kuznets, S. (1955) Economic Growth and Income Inequality, *American Economic Review* 45.

Kravis, I. B. (1960) International Differences in the Distribution of Income, *Review of Economics and Statistics* Vol. 42, 408–416.

Kravis, I. B., A. W. Heston and Robert Summers (1978) Real G.D.P. Percapita for More than One Hundred Countries, *The Economic Journal* June, 215–241.

Lerner, A. P. (1944) *The Economics of Control*, New York.

McManus, M, Gary M. Walton and Richard B. Coffman (1972) Distributional Equality and Aggregate Utility: Further Comments, *The American Economic Review*, Vol. LXII, June, 489–496.

Rawls, J. (1971), *A Theory of Justice*, Cambridge, MA: Harvard University Press.

Rothschild, M. and J. E. Stiglitz (1973) Some Further Results on the Measurement of Inequality, *Journal of Economic Theory* 6, 188–204.

Samuelson, P. A. (1947) *Foundation of Economic Analysis*, Cambridge, MA: Harvard University Press.

Samuelson, P. A. (1964) A.P. Lerner at Sixty, *Review of Economic Studies*, (June) 31, 169–78.

Sen, A. K. (1969) Planners' Preferences: Optimality, Distribution and Social Welfare. In J. Margolis and H. Guitton (eds.), *Public Economics*, London, New York.

Sen, A. K. (1973) *On Economic Inequality*, Clarendon Press.

Sen, A. K. (1973a) On Ignorance and Equal Distribution'', *The American Economic Review* (December) Vol. LXIII, 1022–1024.

Titmass, R. M. (1962) *Income Distribution and Social Change*, (Allan and Unwin London).

ON ECONOMIC POVERTY:
A SURVEY OF AGGREGATE MEASURES

James E. Foster

I. INTRODUCTION

Amartya Sen's work on economic poverty has brought about a serious reconsideration of how poverty is measured. The time-tested method of counting the number of poor is now dismissed for failing to indicate the intensity of poverty; the more recent vintage of statistics based on the mean or aggregate income of the poor is criticized for failing to reflect the distribution of income among the poor. These observations have led to the development of several new summary statistics or measures of poverty, almost all of which are based firmly in the framework suggested by Sen. But what exactly is Sen's approach to poverty measurement, and how is it justified? How does the Sen measure compare to subsequent measures presented within his framework? Where does the traditional problem of setting a poverty line figure into this literature? In this paper

Advances in Econometrics, vol. 3, pages 215–251
Copyright © 1984 by JAI Press Inc.
All rights of reproduction in any form reserved.
ISBN: 0-89232-443-0

we shall examine critically the recent work on poverty measurement with the goal of providing clear answers to these basic questions.

We begin, of course, with Sen's approach to poverty measurement, examining first his three motivating axioms: the focus axiom, the monotonicity axiom, and the weak transfer axiom. Next the Sen measure is defined and we trace the steps leading from the general principles to the specific form Sen adopts. We shall pay particularly close attention to those aspects of the argument that reappear in the subsequent literature: Sen's conception of relative deprivation, the relation between poverty and inequality measurement, and the use for which the poverty measure is sought.

In Section III, we investigate the numerous poverty measures proposed by subsequent authors and evaluate their respective justifications. These contributions fall roughly into three groups: The first includes the more or less direct extensions of the Sen measure, obtained for instance by adding a constant to, or raising to a power, the weighting system used by Sen. The second group contains measures constructed using inequality measures or methodology drawn from the literature on inequality. The third group contains measures whose development was motivated by a practical concern—the analysis of poverty by population subgroup. The various measures are evaluated in terms of Sen's three axioms and contrasted with the Sen measure.

In the final section we summarize the major conclusions to be drawn from this literature. A particularly disturbing aspect is that all of the recent work depends rather crucially upon the setting of an appropriate poverty line, a step that is freely acknowledged in the traditional literature as being quite arbitrary. A first attempt at avoiding this problem has been made by Foster and Shorrocks (1983). We shall briefly describe their approach and give an outline of their main results linking poverty, inequality, and social welfare measurement.

II.   THE SEN APPROACH TO POVERTY
MEASUREMENT

Sen (1976) has noted that poverty measurement may be broken down into two steps: first, an *identification* step to determine who the poor are; and, second, an *aggregation* step which brings together the data on the poor into an overall measure of poverty. The fact that Sen considers the second step to be equally as important as the first is where he departs from the previous literature, and indeed this ranks as one of his major contributions to the area.[1]

Sen begins with a collection N of individuals $i = 1, 2, \ldots, n$, each receiving a respective quantity y_i of income. Implicitly, all problems with defining income (e.g., heterogeneous families, variations in regional cost of living) are presumed to be solved, and a common poverty line π for all individuals is assumed to be given.[2] The poor are identified as all persons whose incomes do not exceed the poverty line.[3] Where $y = (y_1, \ldots, y_n)$ is the income distribution and π is the poverty line, we denote the set of the poor by $T(y; \pi) = \{i \in N \mid y_i \leq \pi\}$, or simply T where there is no ambiguity. The number of persons in T is denoted by $q(y; \pi)$, or simply q.

The aggregation step entails combining this basic data to obtain a number which indicates the overall level of poverty. A *measure of poverty* is a real-valued function P which, given a poverty line π, assigns to each income distribution y a value $P(y; \pi)$ indicating its associated level of poverty. When the poverty line and all incomes are nonnegative, this may be denoted by $P \colon \mathbb{R}_+^{n+1} \to \mathbb{R}$. For Sen, the aggregation step is tantamount to choosing an appropriate poverty measure.

A.   The Sen Axioms

Now there are clearly many conceivable functions that do not correspond to anyone's notion of poverty, and so the first question to be answered is: What properties should a measure of poverty satisfy? Sen proposes a basic framework of three axioms:[4] first, a "focus axiom" which requires the measure to depend on the incomes of the poor and *not* on the incomes of the nonpoor; second, a "monotonicity axiom" which requires poverty to increase whenever, given other things, the income of a poor individual falls; and, third, a "weak transfer axiom" which requires poverty to increase whenever, given other things, a poor person gives a small sum of income to a richer person who remains poor after the transfer. We shall now present the rigorous definitions of these axioms and discuss their implications.

In the following, let x and y be two income distributions (among N) such that $T(x; \pi) = T(y; \pi) = T$. We say that x *is obtained from y by a change in nonpoor incomes* if $x_i = y_i$ for all $i \in T$, and $x_i \neq y_i$ for some $i \notin T$.

FOCUS AXIOM: *If x is obtained from y by a change in nonpoor incomes, then $P(x; \pi) = P(y; \pi)$.*

The focus axiom specifies that *once the poverty line is set* one should disregard information relating to the incomes of the nonpoor in determining an overall level of poverty.[5] This is not to say that such information cannot be of use in measuring other aspects which might be related to poverty. For instance, Beckerman (1979) expresses the aggregate poverty gap (i.e., the total amount of income necessary to leave all the poor at the poverty line) as a percentage of aggregate income to indicate the difficulty of ensuring that all incomes reach the poverty line. Anand (1977) obtains an alternative measure by expressing the aggregate poverty gap as a ratio of the aggregate income of the nonpoor. However, as Anand cautions, these measures should not be interpreted as measures of poverty but rather as "indicators of the ease of its alleviation." In a direct way, the focus axiom prevents such a misinterpretation.

We say that x *is obtained from* y *by a loss of income among the poor* if $x_i < y_i$ for some $i \in T$, and $x_i = y_i$ for every other $i \in N$.

MONOTONICITY AXIOM: *If* x *is obtained from* y *by a loss of income among the poor, then* $P(x; \pi) > P(y; \pi)$.

Perhaps the most important implication of the monotonicity axiom is that it rules out measures based upon a simple counting of the poor, in particular the head-count ratio (or the proportion of the population that is poor). While a loss of income among the poor will never decrease poverty as measured by the head-count ratio, neither will poverty be seen to increase. The head-count ratio is perfectly neutral with respect to such changes, and so it *just* fails to satisfy the monotonicity axiom.

In addition to ensuring that a poverty measure is sensitive to a loss of income among the poor, the monotonicity axiom indicates the direction of the change in poverty: it must increase. A direct implication is that, for a given population and a given set of poor, poverty will be the least when all poor persons have the largest income consistent with their being poor, i.e., the poverty line income.

Finally, x *is obtained from* y *by a regressive transfer among the poor* if for some pair of individuals in T, say i and j, we have (a) $y_i \leq y_j$, (b) $x_j - y_j = y_i - x_i > 0$, and (c) $x_k = y_k$ for all $k \neq i, j$. Note that (a) says that person i is initially poorer, or no richer, than person j; (b) says that the income of person j is increased by exactly the amount that the income of person i is decreased; and (c) says all other incomes remain unchanged.[6]

WEAK TRANSFER AXIOM: *If* x *is obtained from* y *by a regressive transfer among the poor, then* $P(x; \pi) > P(y; \pi)$.

The implications of the weak transfer axiom are plain enough. First, it requires a measure of poverty to be sensitive to changes in the distribution of income among the poor, at least to the extent that a "regressive" transfer does not pass unnoticed. Of course, this is where the aggregate poverty gap and the related measures based upon the mean income of the poor fall flat. They ignore the distribution among the poor in much the same way as the aggregate or mean income ignores the distribution of income among the population as a whole. Secondly, the weak transfer axiom specifies the direction that poverty must change as a result of such a transfer: it must increase. Simply put, any increase in inequality among the poor, due to one or a series of regressive transfers, must be reflected in a higher level of poverty.

The justification for the weak transfer axiom, though, is a bit less direct than the arguments for the other two axioms. While it is clear that a decrease in a poor person's income, taken by itself, leads to a higher overall level of poverty, we might be less certain of its effect if at the same time the income of another poor person is increased. Since the inclusion of distributional considerations into the measurement of poverty is central to the Sen approach, and since this is carried forth by the weak transfer axiom, we shall pause to examine the arguments for the axiom in greater detail.

Basically there are two general lines of argument. The first, which is mentioned by Sen (1981, pp. 31–32) but is not central to this thesis, depends on comparisons of utility gains and losses in a world where the marginal utility of income is positive but diminishing. If the utility functions of the poor are identical (or differ by a constant function), then any regressive transfer among the poor will lower the utility of the "giver" by more than the increase in the utility of the "receiver." This "net loss in utility" between the two poor persons might then be interpreted as leading to an increase in poverty.

Sen's main case for the weak transfer axiom is made in terms of a notion of relative deprivation: when a regressive transfer takes place from a more deprived to a less deprived person, Sen concludes that "in a straightforward sense the overall relative deprivation is increased."[7] If, in the analysis of poverty, relative deprivation is to supplement considerations of absolute deprivation (presumably unaffected in the aggregate by the transfer[8]), then we may conclude that a regressive transfer increases poverty.

B.   Implications of the Axioms

What do the three axioms taken together imply about the form of P? First, it should be noted that they only place constraints on comparisons between income distributions having the same poverty line and the same set of the poor. In fact, the focus axiom is equivalent to the requirement that for given π and T we may express P as a function of incomes in T alone; the monotonicity axiom says that this function must be decreasing in poor incomes; and the weak transfer axiom ensures that it decreases when two poor incomes move closer together.

We can obtain a more intuitive interpretation of these axioms if we require an additional property that, typically, is implicitly assumed in any case.[9] Where x and y are two income distributions (among N), we say that x is *obtained from y by a permutation of incomes* if $x = My$ for some permutation matrix M of order n.[10] Under a permutation of incomes, individuals' positions in the income distribution are switched around.

SYMMETRY: *If x is obtained from y by a permuation of incomes, then $P(x; \pi) = P(y; \pi)$.*

Thus, a symmetric poverty measure is unaffected by a permutation of incomes.

An implication of this property is that poverty may be defined over *ordered* income distributions without loss of generality. For any income distribution y, let $\hat{y}$ denote the ordered distribution associated with y; that is, $\hat{y}$ is obtained from y by a permutation of incomes and $\hat{y}_1 \le \hat{y}_2 \le \cdots \le \hat{y}_n$. By symmetry, then, $P(y; \pi) = P(\hat{y}; \pi)$.

This observation leads to a simple interpretation of Sen's axioms. When symmetry is assumed, the focus, monotonicity, and weak transfer axioms are equivalent to requiring that on each set of income distributions with constant q, the poverty measure $P(y; \pi)$ must be a strictly decreasing, strictly Schur-convex function of the first q incomes of $\hat{y}$. Strict Schur-convexity has the intuitive interpretation that, whenever the Lorenz criterion chooses one vector as having more inequality than another vector with the same mean, the function "follows" the Lorenz criterion by giving a higher value to the first.[11] Taken together with monotonicity it implies that, whenever $q(x; \pi) = q(y; \pi)$ and the poor incomes in x are dominated by the poor incomes in y by the *absolute* Lorenz criterion[12]

$$\sum_{i=1}^{k} \hat{x}_i \le \sum_{i=1}^{k} \hat{y}_i \qquad \text{(for } k = 1, \ldots, q)$$

and

$$\sum_{i=1}^{k} \hat{x}_i < \sum_{i=1}^{k} \hat{y}_i \qquad \text{(for some } k = 1, \ldots, q),$$

then $P(x; \pi)$ must be greater than $P(y; \pi)$. In other words, the three axioms proposed by Sen are equivalent to requiring that P be a function of poor incomes that follows the absolute Lorenz criterion when it applies.

C.   The Traditional Measures

As mentioned above, the commonly used measures of poverty violate one or more of Sen's axioms. We shall now define the traditional poverty measures and investigate their properties.

The most common measures are based on counting the poor. The aggregate head count $q(y; \pi)$ and the head-count ratio $H(y; \pi) = q/n$, which in the present framework—where n is fixed—yield precisely the same ranking, satisfy the focus axiom and violate the monotonicity and weak transfer axioms.[13] On each set of income distributions where q is fixed, the head-count measures are simply constant functions; thus they are constant in nonpoor incomes but are not strictly decreasing or mindful of the Lorenz criterion over poor incomes.

The family of measures based on the aggregate poverty gap satisfy the monotonicity axiom but still violate the weak transfer axiom. Given a distribution y and poverty line π, let the poverty gap $g_i(y; \pi)$ of individual i in $T(y; \pi)$ be defined by $g_i(y; \pi) = \pi - y_i$. The aggregate poverty gap may then be expressed as $g(y; \pi) = \sum_{i \in T} g_i(y; \pi)$. While this measure is often normalized to obtain the average poverty gap g/q, Sen focuses on a slightly different normalization $I(y; \pi) = g/(qz)$, which he calls the income gap ratio.[14] The poverty orderings given by g may differ from those given by g/q and I when the number of poor changes, but all three give *identical* rankings whenever q remains fixed.

Expressing the income gap ratio as $I = 1 - \bar{y}_p/z$, where $\bar{y}_p = \sum_{i \in T} y_i/q$ is the mean income of the poor, we see that I is surely a constant function of nonpoor incomes and a decreasing function of poor incomes. Yet for any two income distributions with the same number of poor and the same mean income among the poor, I indicates a constant poverty level. For such comparisons I, like H, has nothing to say, and so it goes against the Lorenz criterion. In sum, then, I, g and g/q satisfy the focus and monotonicity axioms but violate the weak transfer axiom.

D. The Sen Measure

The fact that neither H nor I satisfies all three axioms is mentioned by Sen to be the underlying motivation for his search for a new measure of poverty.[15] In this section we shall present the Sen poverty measure and examine its properties.

At the heart of the Sen measure lies the notion of a "ranking" of the poor. Given y and π, we define a ranking of the poor to be a one-to-one function,[16] $r:T \to \{1, 2, \ldots, q\}$, which satisfies $r(i) > r(j)$ whenever $g_i(y; \pi) > g_j(y; \pi)$. Note that r depends on the income distribution and the poverty line, and so we shall denote $r(i)$ by $r_i(y; \pi)$ or simply r_i. In the special case where no two poor persons have the same income, $r_i(y; \pi)$ is just the number of persons in $T(y; \pi)$ whose incomes are greater than or equal to y_i (or whose poverty gaps are less than or equal to g_i). Hence, the poorest person has a rank of q, while the poor person nearest the poverty line has a rank of 1.

The Sen poverty measure is defined by[17]

$$S(y; \pi) = \frac{2}{(q + 1)n\pi} \sum_{i \in T} g_i r_i(y; \pi),\tag{1}$$

where $r_i(y; \pi)$ is a ranking of the poor associated with y and π. Aggregate poverty is a normalized weighted sum of individual poverty gaps, where the weights are given by a ranking among the poor.

We can immediately verify that S does indeed satisfy Sen's three axioms: Suppose that x is obtained from y by a change in nonpoor incomes. Then it is clear that T, q, and g_i are the same for x and y, and they have identical ranking(s) of the poor. Thus, $S(x; \pi) = S(y; \pi)$, and the focus axiom is satisfied.

Now suppose that x is obtained from y by a loss of income among the poor. If x and y have a ranking of the poor in common, then $S(x; \pi) > S(y; \pi)$ since $g_i(x; \pi) > g_i(y; \pi)$ for some i with all else fixed. If the decrease in income among the poor disturbs the ranking of the poor, we need only note that each rank $k = 1, 2, \ldots, q$ has an associated poverty gap that is at least as large in x as it is in y, and some rank has a poverty gap that is strictly larger. Thus, once again, $S(x; \pi) > S(y; \pi)$, and the monotonicity axiom is verified.

Finally, let x be obtained from y by a regressive transfer among the poor. We may easily verify that if x and y have a ranking of the poor in common, then $S(x; \pi) > S(y; \pi)$. In this case, the poverty gap of a higher-ranked person is increased by the same amount that a lower-ranked person's poverty gap is decreased, leaving a net increase in S as a result of the regressive transfer.[18] However, when changes in ranking are caused by the regressive transfer, the argument becomes a bit messy. Instead, we shall take a more or less indirect route to the same goal. As shown by Sen (1976, pp. 224–225),

$$S(y; \pi) = H\left[I + (1 - I)G_p\left(\frac{q}{q + 1}\right)\right],\tag{2}$$

where G_p is the Gini measure of inequality taken over the vector of poor incomes.[19] As is well known, the Gini coefficient registers an increase whenever a regressive transfer occurs and, since q, H, and I are unaffected and $1 - I$ is positive, S must also be increased by a regressive transfer among the poor.

Thus, the Sen measure satisfies the three axioms set forth by Sen; but it is by no means the only conceivable measure that does.[20] Our next step is to examine the specific justifications given by Sen for this particular measure.

E.   Justifications and Interpretations

There are two main arguments offered by Sen to support his measure. The first comprises three steps that progressively limit a measure's form until only the Sen measure remains; the second depends on the relationship between the Sen measure and the Gini measure of inequality. We begin with the three-step procedure.

Sen proposes the following general form for poverty measures:

$$Q(y; \pi) = A(y; \pi) \sum_{i \in T} g_i v_i(y; \pi), \tag{3}$$

where it is required that $A(y; \pi) = A(x; \pi)$ whenever $q(y; \pi) = q(x; \pi)$.[21] A poverty measure is interpreted as a normalized weighted sum of individual poverty gaps, where the weights may depend on the entire income distribution. It is stressed that the restrictions placed on the form of poverty measure by (3) are almost nonexistent, since the weights v_i are general functions of y and π.[22] The real restriction comes in the second step where the form of v_i is fixed.

In the next step Sen chooses a weighting scheme based on a person's relative rank.

RANKED RELATIVE DEPRIVATION: *Poverty is measured in (3) with the weight v_i on person i's poverty gap equaling i's rank among the poor*

$$v_i(y; \pi) = r_i(y; \pi). \tag{4}$$

The justification for this weighting scheme is twofold. First, the similarity to the Borda rank-order voting scheme is noted, as well as Borda's argument for "choosing equal distances in the absence of a convincing case for any alternative assumption" (Sen, 1981, p. 36). Secondly, Sen interprets the weight on person i's poverty gap to be a proxy for i's sense of relative deprivation, which he argues might be represented by "i's relative position *vis-à-vis* others in the same reference group" (Sen, 1981, p. 187). Taking the set of the poor as a poor person's reference group, then, might lead to $v_i(y; \pi)$ being simply $r_i(y; \pi)$.

What are the implications of this weighting system? First, we should note that "rank-order weighting" means absolutely nothing outside the context of the general form (3). In the presence of (3), though, it is equivalent to assuming that

$$Q(y; \pi) = B(y; \pi)S(y; \pi), \tag{5}$$

where B is a normalization factor satisfying $B(x; \pi) = B(y; \pi)$ whenever $q(x; \pi) = q(y; \pi)$. This means that over each set of distributions having a fixed number of poor Q is simply a constant multiple of S.

The third step of Sen's procedure fixes the normalization factor. To do this, Sen chooses a somewhat indirect approach. He argues that, in the special case where every poor person has the same income, the traditional measures H and I might together form an adequate picture of poverty. Hence, we might reasonably require the poverty measure to depend on H and I alone in this case. One particularly simple requirement of this kind is given in the following condition.

NORMALIZED ABSOLUTE DEPRIVATION: *If y satisfies* $y_i = \bar{y}_p$, *for all i* $\in$ $T(y; \pi)$, then

$$Q(y; \pi) = H(y; \pi)I(y; \pi). \qquad (6)$$

Thus, the measure should take the value of the product of the head-count ratio and the income gap ratio when all the poor have the same income.

It follows immediately from this condition that B in (5) is a constant function which takes the value 1. Indeed, where y and π are given, let y' be the distribution which assigns $\pi/2$ to each $i \in T(y; \pi)$ and y_i to every $i \notin T(y; \pi)$. Then $B(y; \pi) = B(y'; \pi)$, and since the Gini coefficient among the poor vanishes for y', we obtain $S(y'; \pi) = Q(y'; \pi)$ from (2) and (6). This in turn implies $B(y; \pi) = 1.$[23] In sum, then, the conditions of "normalized absolute deprivation" and "ranked relative deprivation," in the context of the general form (3), yield precisely the Sen measure.

A second line of argument for the Sen measure arises from the relationship between S and the Gini measure of inequality. From (2) it is clear that the Gini coefficient is the measure of inequality underlying S in the sense that the ordering given by S over distributions having the same number of poor and the same mean income of the poor is exactly the ordering given by the Gini measure. Furthermore, the two measures are linked in another way: when S is applied to the entire distribution of incomes, in the sense that n replaces q, $\bar{y}$ (the mean income of y) replaces π, etc. (see Sen, 1976, p. 225), one obtains a multiple of the Gini coefficient.

F.   A Careful Reexamination

How effective are the arguments on behalf of the Sen measure? To be sure the three-step procedure offers an interesting interpretation of S in terms of relative deprivation—a notion that has achieved a central status in discussions of poverty.[24] In addition, the relationship between S and the Gini measure is quite appealing. The Gini coefficient is perhaps the most commonly used measure of inequality, and for those familiar with this inequality measure the Sen measure is a natural choice indeed. Finally, it should not be forgotten that S satisfies the three axioms of Sen, as they were the prime motivation for his search for a new measure. Thus, the various arguments lend considerable support to the Sen measure.

Yet one should not conclude that S is in any sense the *best* measure of poverty. Sen specifically acknowledges the presence of arbitrariness in his arguments (1976, p. 227), which he would consider unavoidable in light of the basic plurality and ambiguity that surround the concept of poverty itself (1981, p. 189). As a result, there have been many alternative measures proposed in the literature, each apparently justified by Sen's own arguments or a slight variation. To understand how this later work fits in, it would be useful to note precisely where the justifications for S admit alternative interpretations. This we shall now do beginning with (1) the three-step procedure, continuing with (2) the relation with the Gini measure, and ending with (3) considerations beyond the basic Sen axioms.

1. The Three-Step Procedure

a. The General Form. It is quite true that the general form (3) for poverty measures, taken by itself, is not very restrictive. Yet, as an integral part of Sen's condition of "ranked relative deprivation," it leads to very strong conclusions indeed. While the weights themselves receive a great deal of attention, no justification is given for the underlying context in which these weights are being considered.[25] Thus, there is room for any number of alternative general forms, which would clearly lead to a variety of alternative measures (e.g., see Takayama, 1979, p. 753).

b. The Weights. The condition of "ranked relative deprivation" is motivated by a notion of relative deprivation using the rank of an individual as a proxy for the relative deprivation he may suffer. Why is this notion particularly appropriate? It would seem that Sen's concept of relative deprivation is related to Runciman's (1966, p. 12) "frequency of relative deprivation" as exemplified by the paradigm of promotions in the military: a soldier's feeling of relative deprivation (if he is not promoted) depends on the *number* of others in his group who in fact are promoted. Similarly, a poor person's feeling of relative deprivation might depend on the *number* of others in his group who have more income.[26]

While this relationship is suggestive, it should be noted that there are many alternative concepts of relative deprivation which could be incorporated into the weight v_i (e.g., see Kakwani, 1977; Foster et al., 1981). Furthermore, even if a notion of relative deprivation based on "number of persons better off" is adopted, there is a certain amount of arbitrariness in restricting a poor person's field of vision to the set of the poor (see Sen, 1981, pp. 16 and 192), or in representing relative deprivation simply by the rank $r_i(y; \pi)$ rather than some increasing function of the rank (see Sen, 1981, p. 187).

This entire discussion of weights and relative deprivation, of course, is only relevant to the way relative deprivation enters at the aggregation step. Considerations of relative deprivation may also enter at the identification step, which is an issue discussed at length in a recent paper by Sen (1983). He suggests that a person might not only *feel* deprived, but in fact *is* deprived in an absolute sense, by having relatively less income than others. If person i's income remains constant while the incomes of his peers go up, then his income requirements for fulfilling exactly the same needs (e.g., participating in social activities, maintaining self-respect) may actually increase as well. This, in turn, leads to a heightened sense of deprivation—not due to a Runciman-like comparison of relative positions, but due to the fact that person i is simply less able to fulfill his needs. It would be interesting to see what implications (if any) this new approach might have for the weighting scheme.

c.   The Normalization.   The requirement that a poverty measure must depend only on H and I in the special case where all the poor have the same income, in fact, puts almost no restriction on the form of the measure.[27] However, specifying that a poverty measure must be precisely the product of H and I seems rather restrictive and arbitrary.[28] For example, the requirement that $P = HI^2$ when the poor have identical incomes would lead to *nonexistence*, even though it is equally justifiable, and equally arbitrary.

2.   Inequality and Poverty

The relationship between the Sen and Gini measures clearly does not uniquely choose the Sen measure as *the* poverty measure related to the Gini measure. Any number of poverty measures may, in fact, be associated with the Gini coefficient in either of the two ways considered by Sen (see Thon, 1979, or Takayama, 1979). Furthermore, if there is a single conclusion to be drawn from the literature on the measurement of inequality, it is that there is no *best* measure. The Gini coefficient is surely acceptable, but it cannot be regarded as unambiguously superior to, say, the coefficient of variation or the Atkinson family of measures. By simply varying the measure of inequality implicit in a poverty measure one might very well obtain perfectly acceptable poverty measures (e.g., see Blackorby and Donaldson, 1980; Clark et al., 1981).

3.   Additional Considerations

The Sen axioms may be regarded as necessary requirements for a distribution-sensitive poverty measure. However, just because a given measure satisfies these requirements, this by itself does not imply that the measure is suitable in any given application. In particular, if we were interested in assessing how subgroups in a given population "contribute" to total poverty, there might be some justification for requiring that the measure exhibit a simple decomposition (Anand, 1977, p. 12), or at least that it maintain some degree of consistency between subgroup and total poverty (Foster et al., 1981). If it can be shown that the given measure does not satisfy certain properties of this type, then the measure may not be particularly well suited for this purpose.

III.   ALTERNATIVE MEASURES

In the last section we presented Sen's general approach to poverty measurement, his specific measure, and its justification. The present section will consider variations of this approach and alternative measures that have been proposed in the subsequent literature. Our focus will be on how the various measures are justified and how the justifications depart from those of Sen.

A.   Weights and Normalizations

The first group consists of poverty measures that can be obtained by varying the weights and normalization factor used in Sen's three-step procedure. The two variants presented by Anand (1977) are distribution-sensitive measures of the "ease of poverty alleviation," which satisfy only the monotonicity and weak transfer axioms. Kakwani (1980a) and Thon (1979) are concerned with the way the Sen measure treats certain transfers of income among the poor, and they propose alternative measures that satify the Sen axioms and reflect their respective concerns. We begin with the paper of Anand.

In addition to presenting one of the earliest empirical applications of the Sen measure, Anand (1977) provides a particularly insightful critique of this measure. He notes the "rather special" nature of rank-order weighting and describes a method of incorporating different measures of inequality into poverty measures in the same way S incorporates the Gini measure.[29] He then applies S to Malaysian data and compares the value of S to the value of HI to indicate "the magnitude of the correction due to inequality among the poor." Further, he notes that S is not "decomposable" by population subgroups, and instead uses H to obtain a "profile of poverty in Malaysia."

Anand introduces two simple variants of the Sen measure. Where $a = n\pi$ is the amount of income necessary to place all persons at the poverty line, and $b = \sum_{i \in N} y_i$ is the aggregate income in y, Anand's first measure is

$$P(y; \pi) = \frac{a}{b} S(y; \pi). \tag{7}$$

Where $b' = \sum_{i \notin T} y_i$ is the aggregate income of the nonpoor, Anand's second measure is

$$P'(y; \pi) = \frac{a}{b'} S(y; \pi). \tag{8}$$

Anand points out that, when all the poor have the same income level, P reduces to the aggregate poverty gap as a proportion of total income (g/b) while P' reduces to the aggregate poverty gap as a proportion of total nonpoor income (g/b'), similar to the way that S reduces to $HI = g/a$ (the aggregate poverty gap as a proportion of $n\pi$). However, Anand is very careful to note that P and P', unlike S, are indicators of the ease with which poverty may be alleviated, rather than measures of poverty. This aspect of the measures is reflected in the fact that, while both satisfy the monotonicity and weak transfer axioms, they violate the focus axiom: any time a nonpoor income increases (with all other incomes fixed), the factors b and b' increase and the measures fall.[30]

Sen (1981, pp. 189–190) also interprets Anand's first measure as a measure of the "relative burden of poverty of a nation," and proceeds to derive the measure in a way similar to the three-step procedure given above. He proposes an "alternative normalized absolute deprivation" condition, which requires a measure to equal g/b when all poor incomes are the same. Recalling expression (5), though, we see that this requirement is inconsistent with the "ranked relative deprivation" condition, since the normalization factor can only change when q (or π) changes. To derive Anand's measure in this way, it would seem that the normalization factor should be defined to depend on both the number and the mean income of the poor.

Kakwani (1980a) obtains a simple variation of the Sen measure by raising each weight $r_i(y; \pi)$ to a power $k \geq 0$ and renormalizing. The resulting parameteric family is given by

$$P_k(y; \pi) = \frac{q}{n\pi\phi_k(q)} \sum_{i \in T} g_i r_i^k, \tag{9}$$

where $\phi_k(q) = \sum_{i=1}^{q} i^k$. When $k = 0$, the measure is simply HI; when $k = 1$, it becomes the Sen measure. Further, for $k > 0$ the measures satisfy the three Sen axioms. To see why the weak transfer axiom holds, let x be obtained from y by a regressive transfer among the poor. In fact, suppose person i transfers an amount $d > 0$ of income to person j, and for simplicity let the ranking of the poor be undisturbed by the transfer. Then it is easily seen that P_k changes by an amount

$$P_k(x) - P_k(y) = Ad(r_i^k - r_j^k), \qquad (10)$$

where $A = q/(n\pi\phi_k(q))$. Since $r_i^k > r_j^k$ for $k > 0$, we see that the measure increases as a result of a regressive transfer.

A curious thing happens when $k = 1$: the magnitude of the change is proportional to the number of persons with a rank between the transfer participants but is surely independent of their absolute ranks. For example, if $\pi = 15$ and the distribution among the poor associated with y is represented by (2, 9, 10), then the poverty level obtained when (1, 10, 10) becomes the distribution among the poor is just the same as when (2, 8, 11) represents the poor incomes. Kakwani finds this characteristic of the Sen measure undesirable.

He proposes a ranking-based "transfer sensitivity" property: Let x, x', and y be three distributions having a ranking r and a set T of the poor in common. Where $i, j, i', j', \in T$, suppose that x is obtained from y by a regressive transfer from i to j entailing a quantity $d > 0$ of income, and suppose that x' is obtained from y by a regressive transfer from i' to j', also involving an amount d. If $r_i > r_{i'}$ and $r_j - r_i = r_{j'} - r_{i'}$, then it must follow that $P(x; \pi) > P(x'; \pi)$. In other words, a transfer of a fixed amount of income between two poor persons a fixed number of ranks apart must have a larger effect on poverty the higher the income ranking of the pair.

This property is the motivation for Kakwani's class of measures, and it is easily seen from (8) and the properties of convex functions that it holds for $k > 1$.[31] Kakwani further justifies his class using a three-step procedure similar to Sen's,[32] and notes that P_k may be converted into a class of inequality measures that contains the Gini measure. Not unexpectedly, many of the arguments supporting the Sen measure also apply to this class of measures, at least for $k > 0$.

Kakwani also mentions a second form of income-based "transfer sensitivity" property discussed in the inequality literature by Atkinson (1970) and Sen (1973). Suppose that x, x', and y again share T and r and that x and x' are obtained from y by transfers involving a fixed amount d of income. If $x_i < x_{i'}$ and $x_j - x_i = x_{j'} - x_{i'}$, then it must follow that $P(x; \pi) > P(x'; \pi)$. In other words, a transfer of a fixed amount of income between two poor persons whose incomes differ by a fixed amount must have a larger effect the lower the incomes of the pair.

Kakwani then goes on to claim that one can always find a k large enough so that P_k satisfies this requirement. In fact, where n is given and fixed, this is quite true. For, to see whether x leads to a higher level of poverty than x' for P_k, we need only evaluate whether (8) is higher for x than x', or equivalently whether $(r_i^k - r_j^k) > (r_{i'}^k - r_{j'}^k)$. Note that the expression on the right achieves its highest possible value when $r_{i'} = n - 1$ and $r_{j'} = 1$, while the expression on the left is smallest when $r_i = n$ and $r_j = n - 1$. Since we can always find a $k > 1$ for which $(n^k - (n - 1)^k) > ((n - 1)^k - 1)$, it follows that x has more poverty than x'.

It should be noted, though, that the appropriate k depends very much on the population size n. In fact, we can easily see that for any given k there is a population size n for which P_k *violates* the income-based transfer sensitivity property. This should be borne in mind when one is considering this class of measures.[33]

The main concern of Thon's (1979) paper is the "transfer axiom" as introduced by Sen (1976, p. 219): "Given other things, a pure transfer of income from a person below the poverty line to anyone who is richer must increase the poverty measure." Under this axiom, an increase in poverty is expected to occur even if the transfer *lowers* the number of the poor. In contrast, the weak transfer axiom only applies if the number of poor is unchanged.

Sen (1977, p. 77) has pointed out that S does not satisfy the transfer axiom. Thon considers this to be a shortcoming of S and, to indicate its seriousness, gives an example in which a transfer from the poorest poor to a poor person having an income just below the poverty line in fact lowers the level of poverty as reckoned by S. He notes that this is a general phenomenon: S will inevitably register a drop in poverty when a poor person crosses the poverty line due to a "small" regressive transfer. Thon then asks whether this must be the case for *all* renormalizations (5) of S. He finds that any renormalization of S satisfying a "strong monotonicity" property (which requires poverty to decrease whenever an income strictly below the poverty line increases) must, in fact, violate the transfer axiom.[34]

Thon obtains an alternative variation of S by adding a fixed number $n - q$ to each weight $r_i(y; \pi)$ and renormalizing. The resulting measure is

$$P(y; \pi) = \frac{2}{n(n + 1)\pi} \sum_{i \in T} g_i(r_i + n - q). \tag{11}$$

By arguments similar to those for S, this measure satisfies all three of Sen's axioms. In fact, as Thon (1979; p. 438) notes

$$P(y; \pi) = \frac{q + 1}{n + 1} S(y; \pi) + \frac{2(n - q)}{n + 1} H \cdot I, \tag{12}$$

which immediately implies that a regressive transfer among the poor increases P. This also shows that P orders distributions having the same number of poor and same mean income among the poor in just the same way as the Sen measure and the Gini measure among the poor. Furthermore, the measure may be justified by a three-step procedure similar to Sen's, where the weights are interpreted as the ranks of the poor among *all* persons [i.e., the poorest person has a rank of n, while the poor person nearest the poverty line has a rank of $(n - q + 1)$].[35] Thus, Thon's variant is also justified by many of the arguments in favor of S.

In addition, though, the Thon measure satisfies the transfer axiom. To see this, we need only examine the effects of a transfer from a poor person to a person who is at the poverty line. It is clear that the increase in the recipient's income, by itself, has no effect on the measure; not directly, since the poverty gap of the recipient is initially zero; and not indirectly, since the factors $2(r_i + n - q)/(n(n + 1)\pi)$ are unchanged for all persons with positive povery gaps. The transfer, then, is equivalent to a loss in income among the poor, which implies that the Thon measure must register an increase in poverty.

For the Sen measure the story is slightly different. The increase in a poor person's poverty gap resulting from a loss of income among the poor is accompanied by a decrease in the factor $2r_i/(n(q + 1)\pi)$ for each i having a positive poverty gap. And since this decrease is independent of the size of the transfer, it follows that the overall effect may be to lower S. In fact, for some distributions, S will never increase when such a disequalizing transfer changes the number of the poor. For instance, suppose that the distribution of income among the poor is given by (5, 5, 10, 15, 26) where the poverty line is 30. Then *any* transfer from a poor person to a richer poor person that lowers the number of the poor will lead to a lower value for S. Since the Thon measure satisfies the transfer axiom, it will yield just the opposite results in this case.

The main motivation for the Thon measure is the transfer axiom. But how compelling is this axiom? Thon regards the transfer axiom as a self-evident requirement for poverty measures, so basic that it calls into question the traditional concern with the number of the poor.[36] Sen (1981, 1982) views the axiom as a perfectly suitable requirement for inequality measures, but he finds it less compelling as an axiom for poverty measures since in certain cases a decrease in the number of the poor might conceivable outweigh the poverty-augmenting effects of the transfer. Kundu and Smith (1983) present a general result which shows that if a measure is sufficiently responsive to the number of poor (and nonpoor) it cannot satisfy the transfer axiom. Since this could very well affect our assessment of the transfer axiom, we shall examine their theorem a bit more closely.

Kundu and Smith propose two "population monotonicity" properties: (a) when a nonpoor person is added to the population, the poverty value should decrease; and (b) when a poor person is added to the population, the poverty measure should not decrease. Their main theorem is that any poverty measure satisfying (a) and (b) *must violate* the transfer axiom.[37] Sen (1981, p. 193) sees this result as arising from a conflict in the way the properties regard the poverty line: The population monotonicity properties treat the poverty line "as the great divider," while the transfer axiom "takes no note whatever of the poverty line."[38] The result might then be taken as a criticism of the transfer axiom, although not of the weak transfer axiom since the weaker axiom *does* take into account the poverty line and, in fact, *does not* conflict with the population monotonicity properties.

Yet there may be another interpretation which focuses on the population monotonicity properties rather than the transfer axiom. Kundu and Smith illustrate their result by presenting a table of measures and the properties they satisfy. As follows from their theorem, all measures in their table violate one or more the the three properties. Looking more closely, though, one is struck by the fact that H is the only measure in their table to satisfy both (a) and (b), and g is the only other measure to satisfy (b). While the aggregate poverty gap is useful in capturing certain aspects of poverty, it is clear that it is after something quite different from, say, the Sen, Kakwani, or Thon measure. All of these measures approach poverty from a "per-capita" point of view, which is reflected in the fact that they satisfy (a). On the other hand, g would appear to approach poverty from the "absolute" point of view represented by property (b). It is interesting to note that in Kundu and Smith's table every measure that satisfies (a) and violates (b) can be converted into a measure that violates (a) and satisfies (b) by a simple renormalization. Moreover, this is true if we reverse the positions of (a) and (b).

While this proposition may be far from general, it does remind one of Sen's (1981, p. 190) advice that the choice of a poverty measure depends on the question the user wants to answer. If one wishes to measure how destitute the poor are, how unequally their incomes are distributed, and the proportion of the total population they represent, then one should adopt a "per-capita" measure and not expect the measure to be particularly sensitive to the absolute number of the poor. On the other hand, if one is interested in how destitute the poor are, how unequally their incomes are distributed, and their absolute number, then one should choose an "absolute" measure and not be too concerned if the measure does not decrease when a nonpoor person is added to the population.

Further, it can be seen that while (a) and (b) appear to be concerned with different aspects of poverty measurement, the transfer axiom is quite consistent with *either* of the two approaches. However, the transfer axiom has just enough to say about the change in population size of the poor vis-à-vis the nonpoor to precipitate the underlying conflict between (a) and (b). Seen in this light, the Kundu and Smith result is not so much a criticism of the transfer axiom as a warning not to try to measure too many aspects of poverty at the same time.

B. Inequality Measures and Poverty Measures

In the last section we noted how Sen's three-step procedure might be varied to obtain different inequality measures. The present section discusses an alternative route taken by Blackorby and Donaldson (1980), Hamada and Takayama (1977), Takayama (1979), and Clark et al. (1981): Poverty measures may be derived from inequality measures. As we shall see, though, some care must be taken to ensure that the resulting poverty measures satisfy monotonicity.

Blackorby and Donaldson (1980) present two ways of deriving poverty measures from measures of inequality. The first yields what they call "relative" measures of poverty which, like S, are unchanged when both the poverty line and all incomes are multiplied by a positive constant. The second yields "absolute" measures which are unaffected when the same positive constant is added to the poverty line and all incomes. We shall begin with the relative measures.

Sen (1976, p. 225) has noted that, if y and π are such that $q(y; \pi)$ is very large, then $S(y; \pi)$ is "close" to the following measure:

$$S'(y; \pi) = H(I - (1 - I)G_p),\qquad(13)$$

where, as before, G_p is the Gini measure of inequality as applied to the vector of poor incomes.[39] The measure S' is also called the Sen measure in the literature. Note that since H, I, and G_p are unaffected by a proportionate change in the poverty line and all incomes, S' is clearly a relative measure of poverty.

Blackorby and Donaldson suggest that to obtain alternative poverty measures one can simply apply alternative relative measures of inequality in (13). The class of relative poverty measures they obtain is thus given by

$$P_r(y; \pi) = H(I + (1 - I)R_p),\qquad(14)$$

where R_p is a relative inequality measure that is strictly Schur-convex and homogeneous of degree zero in the incomes of the poor.

To motivate their measures, Blackorby and Donaldson give a nice interpretation of P_r. Using the identity $I = (\pi - \bar{y}_p)/\pi$, they note that P_r may be written

$$P_r(y; \pi) = H\left[\frac{\pi - \bar{y}_p(1 - R_p)}{\pi}\right].\qquad(15)$$

The quantity $\bar{y}_p(1 - R_p)$ is of significance in recent work relating inequality measures to social welfare, or social evaluation, functions.[40] First,
when taken as a function of poor incomes, it is one representation of a
welfare function "associated" with R_p. Note that so long as $\bar{y}_p$ is fixed,
$\bar{y}_p(1 - R_p)$ increases whenever inequality as measured by R_p decreases
(and vice versa). Secondly, $\bar{y}_p(1 - R_p)$ may be specifically interpreted
as a "representative income" which, when equally distributed among the
poor, leads to the same level of welfare among the poor as the original
distribution. Thus, P_r, and in particular S', may be seen as a product of
the head-count ratio and an income gap ratio using the representative
income rather than the mean income of the poor.[41]

Using a similar motivation, Blackorby and Donaldson propose a class
of absolute poverty measures

$$P_a(y; \pi) = q(y; \pi)[\pi - \bar{y}_p + A_p], \tag{16}$$

where A_p is an absolute measure of inequality that is strictly Schur-convex
and regards an addition of the same absolute quantity to all incomes as
leaving inequality unchanged.[42] While P_r reduces to the measure HI when
all poor incomes are identical, P_a reduces to the aggregate poverty gap.
It shares with g the property that it is unchanged when the same absolute
quantity is added to all incomes and the poverty line.

The Blackorby and Donaldson approach to poverty measurement is
quite useful in that it allows various inequality measures to be incorporated explicitly into measures of poverty: their class of relative poverty
measures directly generalizes S', while their absolute measures extend
the aggregate poverty gap to distribution-sensitive measures of poverty.
However, we should take the following points into account when evaluating this approach.

First, it might be argued that the classes given by Blackorby and Donaldson are in a sense too small: while P_r and P_a allow for many alternative
notions of inequality, they do so in fairly restrictive ways. There are any
number of ways that R_p and A_p might be converted into poverty measures.
For example, we could choose $P'_r = H(I^2 + (1 - I)^2 R_p^2)$ and $P'_a = q(\pi$
$- \bar{y}_p^2 + A_p^2)$ with equal justification, and yet this would lead to quite
different classes of relative and absolute poverty measures. Thus, many
potentially useful measures of poverty are ruled out by the Blackorby
and Donaldson framework.[43]

Secondly, it could be argued that these classes of measures are in a
sense too large since they contain many measures that do not satisfy the
Sen axioms. While P_r and P_a will always satisfy the focus and weak
transfer axioms, there is no assurance that they will satisfy monotonicity.
This problem is easiest to see for inequality measures that do not take
values between 0 and 1. For instance, the coefficient of variation achieves

a highest value of $\sqrt{q - 1}$ when applied to distributions having q persons. Over distributions having an inequality level of, say, 2 by the coefficient of variation, P_r may be expressed as $H(\pi + \bar{y}_p)/\pi$. It is clear, then, that if all poor incomes are cut in half, the poverty measure will actually *decrease*.

Even if R_p takes nonnegative values less than 1, though, this does *not* ensure that P_r satisfies monotonicity. For instance, suppose that we adopt the *square root* of the Gini coefficient as the relative measure of inequality in P_r. Then $G_p^{1/2}$, like G_p, takes nonnegative values strictly less than 1, and yet when $\pi = 4$, $y = (1, 1, 5, 5)$, and $x = (1, 3, 5, 5)$, we obtain $P_r(x; \pi) = P_r(y; \pi) = 3/8$. Other examples show that P_r may decrease when a poor income falls.[44] In sum, then, we must be careful in choosing an appropriate inequality measure if the resulting poverty measure is to satisfy Sen's axioms.

Under what conditions will the poverty measures P_r and P_a satisfy the monotonicity axiom? We can see from (15) and (16) that this will only happen if R_p and R_a are "dominated" by the mean income of the poor in a specific way. In particular, P_r will satisfy monotonicity if and only if $\bar{y}_p(1 - R_p)$ is strictly increasing in each poor income; and, similarly, P_a satisfies monotonicity if and only if $\bar{y}_p - A_p$ is strictly increasing in each poor income. Thus, in order to obtain poverty measures that satisfy Sen's axioms using the Blackorby and Donaldson approach, one must ensure that the underlying "representative income" or "social welfare" function is *strictly increasing* in all poor incomes.[45]

Takayama (1979) and Hamada and Takayama (1977) have proposed an alternative way of obtaining poverty measures from inequality measures. Their approach is based upon the notion of a "censored distribution" $y^*(\pi)$ associated with a given distribution y and poverty line π, found by replacing all nonpoor incomes with π in the original distribution y. More rigorously, $y^*(\pi)$ is defined by $y_i^*(\pi) = y_i$ for $i \in T(y; \pi)$, and $y_i^*(\pi) = \pi$ for $i \notin T(y; \pi)$. Applying an inequality measure R to the censored distribution then yields a poverty measure associated with R, that is,

$$P_R(y; \pi) = R(y^*(\pi)). \tag{17}$$

It is clear that if R is a measure of inequality that is strictly Schur-convex—it follows the Lorenz criterion for distributions having the same mean—and homogeneous of degree zero in incomes, then P_R is a relative poverty measure (i.e., invariant to proportionate changes in π and all y_i) that satisfies the focus and weak transfer axioms.

Yet P_R cannot possibly satisfy the monotonicity axiom of Sen, since it takes a value of 0 for all distributions wherein all persons have the same income level.[46] Clearly it may not pay much attention to the average income of the poor. Further, P_R may actually register a decrease in poverty when all nonpoor persons experience a drop in income which leaves them below the poverty line. Hence P_R is not particularly attuned to the number of the poor.

Takayama (1979) focuses on the particular measure P_G obtained when the Gini coefficient G is used. His justifications for P_G are suggestive of those given in support of S. First, he obtains his measure using a three-step procedure: an alternative general form in terms of censored distributions is proposed, weights are specified, and the normalization fixed.[47] Secondly, the relationship between P_G and G is invoked in support of G. Thirdly, Takayama (p. 748) mentions that his measure has "the appropriate properties," although later he notes that P_G violates monotonicity.

The first two parts of this justification would seem to be no stronger and no weaker than the comparable arguments for S. Yet Takayama claims that his measure is superior to S in many respects. In particular: (i) the "truncated" vector of poor incomes used by Sen does not give "sufficient information on poverty," whereas the censored distribution does; (ii) S is "less geared to relativities than it need be," whereas P_G gives a more "full-blooded representation of the notion of relative deprivation" than S; and (iii) P_G is a more natural translation of the Gini coefficient. While one should judge for oneself the validity of these claims, it should be noted that (i) the truncated vector and the fixed number n give exactly the same information as the censored distribution; (ii) no notion of relative deprivation is ever explicitly given by Takayama; and (iii) what is meant by a "more natural translation" is not made very clear, and in any case it is hardly a basis upon which to choose a *poverty* measure.[48]

In the final analysis, though, it is the third part of the justification that presents the greatest difficulty for this approach. Given the properties of P_G, and in particular its violation of monotonicity, one might conclude that P_G is a bit too concerned with "relativities" and not enough with how many or how poor the poor really are. The next paper to be considered, though, provides one way of avoiding this difficulty.

Clark et al. (1981) investigate two additional methods of constructing poverty measures from inequality measures. The first uses measures of inequality taken over *poverty gaps* rather than incomes. The second modifies the approach of Hamada and Takayama (1977) and Takayama (1979), yielding a poverty measure that satisfies the monotonicity axiom.

The main insight of the first part of the paper by Clark and colleagues is that the measure S' [see Eq. (13)] may be expressed as

$$S'(y; \pi) = HI(1 + G_g), \tag{18}$$

where G_g is the Gini coefficient as applied to the distribution of poverty gaps.[49] The term G_g is then interpreted as reflecting "relative deprivation in aggregate" (p. 519). Given the form (18), it is clear how one might obtain alternative poverty measures: simply apply different inequality measures to the vector of poverty gaps and substitute for G_g in (18).

Clark et al. focus on a specific form of inequality measure in constructing their first measure of poverty. Since this form is never explicitly discussed in their paper, we shall take a moment to do so here. The Atkinson family of inequality measures (over the entire distribution) is defined by

$$A^{\alpha}(y) = 1 - \frac{\left(\frac{1}{n}\sum_{i \in N} y_i^{\alpha}\right)^{1/\alpha}}{\bar{y}}, \tag{19}$$

where $\alpha \le 1.$[50] For all values of α below 1, it is clear that A^{α} is a strictly Schur-convex function of all incomes. Note, though, that if (19) is used with a parametric value greater than 1, the resulting function will be strictly Schur-*concave*; it registers an *increase* in inequality whenever the Lorenz criterion indicates a *decrease* in inequality for distributions with a common mean. On the other hand, the negative of this function would work quite well as an inequality measure. We now define

$$B^{\alpha}(y) = \frac{\left(\frac{1}{n}\sum_{i \in N} y_i^{\alpha}\right)^{1/\alpha}}{\bar{y}} - 1 \tag{20}$$

for $\alpha > 1$. This is apparently the class of inequality measures used by Clark et al.[51]

Applying B^{α} to the vector of poverty gaps yields

$$B_g^{\alpha} = \frac{\left(\frac{1}{q}\sum_{i \in T} g_i^{\alpha}\right)^{1/\alpha}}{\bar{g}} - 1, \tag{21}$$

where $\bar{g} = \sum_{i \in T} g_i/q$ is the mean poverty gap. The first poverty measure proposed by Clark et al. is

$$C^{\alpha}(y; \pi) = HI(1 + B_g^{\alpha}). \tag{22}$$

It is easy to verify that C^{α} satisfies all the Sen axioms. In fact the focus axiom follows directly from the definition; and since a regressive transfer among the poor leads to a higher value for B_g^{α}, it follows that C^{α} satisfies the weak transfer axiom.[52]

To verify the monotonicity axiom, note that C^{α} may be expressed as

$$C^{\alpha}(y; \pi) = H \frac{\left(\frac{1}{q}\sum_{i \in T} g_i^{\alpha}\right)^{1/\alpha}}{\pi} \tag{23}$$

by substituting (21) into (22) and using the identity $I = \bar{g}/\pi$. Clearly, then, any decrease in income among the poor leads to a higher value for C^α.

A natural question to ask at this stage is: Why not instead use the Blackorby and Donaldson method to convert B_p^α into a poverty measure? One reason is that the resulting poverty measure need not satisfy monotonicity. For example, when $\alpha = 2$ the representative income associated with B_p^α is

$$2\bar{y}_p - \left(\frac{1}{q}\sum_{i \in T} y_i^2\right)^{1/2},$$

which is *not* strictly increasing in the poor incomes. Thus, the approach of Blackorby and Donaldson may not yield a poverty measure satisfying Sen's axioms (when B^α is the inequality measure), whereas the approach of Clark et al. does. On the other hand, it should be noted that, if Clark and associates' method is applied to the Atkinson measure A^α, the resulting poverty measure need not satisfy monotonicity.[53] Since the representative income associated with A_p^α is strictly increasing (for $\alpha < 1$), the Blackorby and Donaldson method would succeed here.

The second measure proposed by Clark et al. might be seen as a variant of the Hamada and Takayama approach. Recall that Blackorby and Donaldson (1980) have used a modified income gap notion in their measure, substituting the "representative income" of the poor for the mean income of the poor. Clark et al. propose a measure that is a different modification of the income gap ratio, using an alternative "representative income" based on the censored distribution of Takayama.

For simplicity of notation, let y^* denote the censored distribution associated with y and π, and denote the mean of y^* by $\bar{y}^* = \sum_{i \in N} y_i^*/n$. The second measure proposed by Clark et al. is

$$D^\alpha(y; \pi) = \frac{\pi - \bar{y}^*(1 - A^\alpha(y^*))}{\pi} \tag{24}$$

for $\alpha < 1$, where $A^\alpha(y^*)$ is the Atkinson measure of inequality as applied to the censored income distribution. Note that $\bar{y}^*(1 - A^\alpha(y^*))$ can be interpreted as the representative income associated with the censored distribution using the Atkinson measure. Thus the second measure is a modified income gap ratio with the representative income of the censored income distribution replacing the mean poor income.

How does this approach relate to the one taken by Hamada and Takayama (1977)? There, the Atkinson measure would be applied directly to the censored distribution to obtain $A^\alpha(y^*)$ as a poverty measure, or equivalently

$$A^\alpha(y^*) = \frac{\bar{y}^* - \bar{y}^*(1 - A^\alpha(y^*))}{\bar{y}^*}. \tag{25}$$

Clark et al., then, differ from Hamada and Takayama in that the former authors consider the proportional shortfalls from the poverty line rather than the mean censored income.

Of course, the main advantage of this approach is that the resulting measure D^α satisfies all of Sen's axioms. The focus axiom follows from the definition of y^*; and since a regressive transfer among the poor leads to a censored distribution having more inequality by the Lorenz criterion, it follows that A^α (hence D^α) increases. Thus D^α satisfies the weak transfer axiom. Once again, the monotonicity axiom requires a bit of algebra. By the definition of A^α we see that

$$y^*(1 - A^\alpha(y^*)) = \left(\frac{1}{n} \sum_{i \in N} (y_i^*)^\alpha \right)^{1/\alpha} ;$$

and since any decrease in income among the poor will lower this expression, D^α will increase as a result.[54]

C. Additional Considerations

Foster et al. (1981) have presented a parametric family of poverty measures[55]

$$P_\alpha(y; \pi) = \frac{1}{n} \sum_{i \in T} \left(\frac{g_i}{\pi} \right)^{\alpha - 1} , \qquad (26)$$

where $\alpha \geq 1$. When α takes on the value 1, the head-count ratio H is obtained. When $\alpha = 2$, the measure P_α becomes HI, the per-capita aggregate poverty gap expressed in poverty units, which has been used by Anand (1977, p. 11), Thon (1979, p. 439), and others.

Foster and colleagues pay considerable attention to the poverty measure obtained when $\alpha = 3$ and show how it may be justified along the lines of Sen (1976).

First, they interpret P_3 in terms of the general form (3) for poverty measures: it is a normalized weighted sum of individual poverty gaps, where the weights are simply the gaps themselves. Referring to Runciman (1966, p. 10), they note that, when the poverty line is taken as the "reference point" of the poor, the poverty gap g_i corresponds very closely to what is called the "magnitude of relative deprivation."[56] Thus, the weighting scheme employed by Foster et al. (1981) is also related to an aspect of relative deprivation, albeit a rather different one than Sen's.

Secondly, they note that P_3 is closely related to a well-known measure of inequality in the same ways that S is related to the Gini coefficient. In fact, they show that

$$P_3(y; \pi) = H[I^2 + (1 - I)^2 C_p^2], \qquad (27)$$

where $C_p^2 = \sum_{i \in T} (\bar{y}_p - y_i)^2/(q\bar{y}_p^2)$ is the squared coefficient of variation among the poor.[57] This implies that over distributions having the same number of poor and the same mean income among the poor, P_3 and C_p^2 give precisely the same ranking. In addition, P_3 "becomes" the squared coefficient of variation measure of inequality when π is replaced by $\bar{y}$ (the mean of y), q is replaced by n, etc., as suggested in Sen (1976, p. 225).

Thirdly, P_3 satisfies the Sen axioms. The focus and monotonicity axioms follow immediately from the definition, while the weak transfer axiom follows simply from (27) by the strict Schur-convexity of C_p^2 in the poor incomes. Note, though, that the identity (27) also implies that P_3 exhibits a "transfer neutrality" property based on income differences: a regressive transfer of a given amount of income between two poor persons whose incomes are a certain distance apart will always have the same effect on poverty irrespective of the absolute incomes of persons involved.

Just as Kakwani (1980a, p. 438) uses the "ranking-based" transfer sensitivity property to motivate his extension of the Sen measure, Foster et al. invoke the "income-based" transfer sensitivity property: the effect of a given-sized regressive transfer between poor persons whose incomes are a fixed distance apart should be greater when the absolute incomes of the persons involved are lower. They then show that P_α satisfies monotonicity when $\alpha > 1$; it satisfies the weak transfer axiom *and* the transfer axiom for $\alpha > 2$; and it satisfies the income-based transfer sensitivity property for $\alpha > 3$.

The primary motivation given by Foster et al. for their parametric family of measures is that each may be "decomposed" in a simple and useful manner. Suppose that a given population of size n is divided into subgroups $j = 1, 2, \ldots, m$ having population sizes n_j. Where $y^{(j)}$ is the distribution of income for subgroup $j = 1, 2, \ldots, m$ and $y = (y^{(1)}; y^{(2)}; \cdots ; y^{(m)})$ is the distribution for the entire population,[58]

$$P_\alpha(y; \pi) = \sum_{i=1}^{m} \frac{n_j}{n} P_\alpha(y^{(j)}; \pi). \qquad (28)$$

Thus, P_α is "additively decomposable" with population-share weights.

The decomposition (28) is quite useful in the analysis of poverty by population subgroup. Orshansky (1965, reprinted 1969) and Anand (1977) have used the head-count ratio to construct "profiles of poverty" in which the total population of a given region is divided into subgroups according to a given characteristic (e.g., occupation, race, or geographic location). One objective of this type of analysis is to identify subgroups that are particularly susceptible to poverty, as measured by the head-count ratio $H(y^{(j)}; \pi)$. Another quite separate objective is to determine how much each subgroup "contributes" to total poverty, which is obtained by weighting the poverty measure by the population share of the subgroup and expressing this as a percentage of total poverty, that is, $100(n_j/n)H(y^{(j)}; \pi)/H(y; \pi)$.[59]

Since H is a member of the class P_α, it exhibits the decomposition (28); but where exactly does this property help? It should be noted that *any* measure, decomposable or not, could be used to attain the first objective. If we are merely interested in comparing the subgroup poverty levels with one another, then decomposability is quite inessential. On the other hand, if the analysis involves comparisons between subgroup and *total* poverty levels (as in the second objective), then the decomposition (28) can be very useful indeed. To see this, let us apply a *non*decomposable measure to determine subgroup contributions, and see where the problems arise. Suppose that an income distribution y is divided into two subgroups having distributions $y^{(1)} = (3, 3, 10, 11, 15)$ and $y^{(2)} = (7, 8, 8, 11, 11)$, where the poverty line is $\pi = 10$. If the Sen measure is used to construct a poverty profile, we find that $S(y^{(1)}; \pi) = .35$, $S(y^{(2)}; \pi) = .15$, and $S(y; \pi) = 2/7$, while the respective contribution of subgroups 1 and 2 are $61\frac{1}{4}\%$ and $26\frac{1}{4}\%$. This illustrates one possible problem: for an arbitrary measure the sum of contributions may exceed or fall short of 100%.[60]

There is a second problem that seems even more fundamental. Suppose that the subgroup distributions become $x^{(1)} = (1, 6, 9, 11, 15)$ and $x^{(2)} = (7, 7, 9, 11, 11)$, so that poverty as measured by the Sen measure *increases* in both subgroups to $S(x^{(1)}; \pi) = .16$ and $S(x^{(2)}; \pi) = .36$. What happens to total poverty? In fact, as measured by the Sen measure total poverty falls.[61] Foster et al. (1981) propose a requirement that rules out this type of inconsistency between subgroups and total poverty, as follows.

SUBGROUP MONOTONICITY: *Let x and y be distributions of income (among N) broken down into m subgroups $j = 1, \ldots, m$. If $x^{(j)} = y^{(j)}$ for all subgroups $j \neq k$, and $P(x^{(k)}; \pi) > P(y^{(k)}; \pi)$ for subgroup k, then $P(x; \pi) > P(y; \pi)$.*

Thus an increase in a given subgroup's poverty ceteris paribus leads to an increase in total poverty.

How does P_α fare with respect to these two types of consistency requirements? First, dividing both sides of (28) by total poverty $P_\alpha(y; \pi)$, we find that subgroup contributions always sum to 100%. Secondly, subtracting $P_\alpha(x; \pi)$ from $P_\alpha(y; \pi)$, where x and y are as given in "subgroup monotonicity," we obtain $(n_k/n)(P_\alpha(x^{(k)}; \pi) - P_\alpha(y^{(k)}; \pi))$ from (28), which implies that total poverty increases whenever poverty in subgroup k increases. Since P_α satisfies both consistency properties, it may be considered particularly useful in analyzing poverty by population subgroup.

It should be noted, though, that these measures are not the only measures that might be used in this context. While P_α ($\alpha \geq 1$) or some renormalization[62] are the only measures in the existing literature that satisfy subgroup monotonicity, many other measures satisfying this property could easily be found. The same holds for the decomposition property (27). In addition, for applications that do not involve analyzing subgroup poverty, there is no particular reason for choosing P_α above other measures satisfying the same properties.

IV. SUMMARY AND CONCLUSIONS

This survey has examined the Sen approach to poverty measurement, the Sen measure, and the subsequent measures that have appeared in the literature. The focus has been the strengths and weaknesses of the respective justifications of these measures. In particular, we have observed that each of the arguments advanced on behalf of the Sen measure may also support alternative measures of poverty. The same is true for every poverty measure that we have examined. Hence, one conclusion of this survey is that the choice of a *single* poverty measure involves a certain degree of arbitrariness.

Where can we go from here? It would seem that the three-step procedure and the inequality-linked approach are not likely candidates for addressing this problem. While the three-step procedure leads to interesting interpretations of poverty measures, it is difficult to see how the specification of particular weights and normalization factors within an unjustified functional form can provide a strong basis for choice of a poverty measure.[63] Identical general arguments can lead to a multitude of possible measures via slight variations in the specific weights and normalization adopted, and the general form (3) may be changed to obtain even more. Similarly, it is clear that the approach linking poverty and inequality measures offers a useful way of looking at poverty measures but is unlikely to form an appropriate basis for choosing poverty measures since the specific link between poverty and inequality measures is bound to be arbitrary, and in any case the question of which inequality measure to use is quite a difficult problem in itself.

The third approach, basing the choice of poverty measures on properties beyond the Sen axioms, would appear to have the greatest chance of "reducing" arbitrariness. In general, though, we should not expect this approach to choose a single best measure, but rather to reduce the set of possibilities to a *class* of equally satisfactory measures. If no other general properties are specified, then any choice of a *single* measure from this set is apt to be arbitrary.[64] Similarly, if a given measure determines that one distribution has more poverty than another (at the given poverty line) and another measure drawn from the same class gives the opposite result, we might be forced to conclude that our ranking over these distributions is ambiguous. On the other hand, if a given distribution has less poverty than another for *all* poverty measures in the relevant class, we might be willing to rank the two without fear of contradiction. This leads quite naturally to considerations of *partial orderings* of poverty defined relative to the class of measures and the given poverty line.[65]

We have already considered the partial ordering implied by the class of poverty measures satisfying the three Sen axioms: one distribution is seen to have less poverty than another if its absolute Lorenz curve among the poor lies nowhere below, and somewhere above, the absolute Lorenz curve among the poor of the second distribution, given that q and n are the same for both distributions. Adding properties for poverty measures to satisfy can only *decrease* the set of acceptable measures and *strengthen* the resulting partial ordering. What, for instance, would be the implication of requiring measures to satisfy the transfer axiom in addition to the Sen axioms? Or alternatively, how might the partial ordering be affected if we adopt a property which captures the notion that poverty increases whenever the number of the poor increases, ceteris paribus.[66] Further work along these lines would surely be useful.

It should be noted that none of the above work addresses the problem of setting the poverty line and instead presupposes that π is already given. How reasonable is this assumption? The question of how to set an appropriate poverty line has been under discussion ever since the notion was developed by Booth (1889) and improved by Rowntree (1901). There are now many general approaches to fixing a poverty line, each of which admits a broad range of possible interpretations when it comes to practical applications.[67] It would not be unreasonable to claim that any choice of a *single* poverty line is bound to be arbitrary. If this is accepted, then any comparison of two distributions made by a poverty measure (or indeed a poverty partial ordering) at a particular poverty line is open to question, since by choosing a different poverty line the ranking may very well be reversed. Once again we are faced with the possibility of ambiguous poverty rankings.

Foster and Shorrocks (1983) present a first approach to avoiding this problem. Rather than accepting the complete ordering generated by a poverty measure at a specific poverty line, they consider the partial ordering generated by allowing the poverty line to vary.[68] In precise terms, given a poverty measure P and two distributions x and y (over N), we say that x has unambiguously less poverty than y, written $x\mathbf{P}y$, if $P(x; \pi) \le P(y; \pi)$ for all positive π, with strict inequality for some π.

Foster and Shorrocks study in detail the partial ordering $\mathbf{P}_\alpha$ generated by members of the class of poverty measures presented by Foster et al.

(1981). When the head count $P_1 = H$ is used, the partial ordering $\mathbf{P}_1$ generated is seen to be equivalent to coordinate-wise domination of ordered vectors; that is, $x\mathbf{P}_1 y$ if and only if $\hat{x}_i \geq \hat{y}_i$ for every $i = 1, 2, \ldots, n$, and $\hat{x}_i > \hat{y}_i$ for some i. This, in turn, is equivalent to requiring that for all symmetric and increasing social welfare functions W we have $W(x) > W(y)$. Hence, the "unambiguous" poverty ranking generated by P_1 is exactly the same as the "unanimous" welfare ranking generated by the class of symmetric and increasing welfare functions.

Next, the partial-ordering associated with the poverty gap $P_2 = HI$ is studied, and it is found that $x\mathbf{P}_2 y$ is equivalent to requiring that the aggregate income held by the poorest k persons is no lower in x than in y, and for some k it is higher. Hence $\mathbf{P}_2$ is precisely the partial ordering generated by the absolute Lorenz criterion (see Shorrocks, 1983b). It is then shown that $\mathbf{P}_2$ is equivalent to requiring welfare to increase under all symmetric, increasing, and equality-preferring[69] social welfare functions. In particular, if the two distributions in question have the same mean, then domination by the usual Lorenz criterion is equivalent to having unambiguously less poverty under the normalized aggregate poverty gap measure $P_2 = HI$.

Finally, the poverty measure P_3 of Foster et al. (1981) is shown to yield a particular ordering $\mathbf{P}_3$ that is equivalent to domination under all symmetric, increasing, and equality-preferring social welfare functions satisfying an additional (income-based) transfer sensitivity property. Suitable modifications of these results are given for the cases where distributions have different population sizes and where the possible poverty line must fall below a certain level. Thus, Foster and Shorrocks (1983) demonstrate that there is a strong relationship between certain poverty measures and certain classes of social welfare functions.

ACKNOWLEDGMENTS

The support of the Purdue Research Foundation and the Krannert School is gratefully acknowledged. I am greatly indebted to Amartya Sen for suggesting this project and helping me follow it through. Thanks also go to C. Blackorby, A. Shorrocks, and D. Ulph for helpful conversations, to S. Holland and M. Frierman for research assistance, and to J. and W. Lane, M. Tappas, and the editors for their patience. Of course, the opinions expressed here are my own, as are the inevitable errors and omissions.

NOTES

1. An important if overlooked exception is Watts (1968), who expresses many of Sen's concerns and even proposes a distribution-sensitive measure of poverty. Sen (1973b, pp.

78–81) discusses some of the issues raised in his 1976 paper and presents a poverty measure similar to his later measure S'. The identification-aggregation dichotomy is also used by Sen (1975, p. 9) in the measurement of employment.

2. That incomes are comparable to the extent that a common poverty line may be drawn is no small assumption [see Sen (1981, p. 28)], but it is apparently made by Sen to study the aggregation question without muddling the issue with admittedly serious comparability problems.

3. On this point, Sen differs from the usual practice of identifying those *below* the poverty line as poor. While, in general, we would expect this change in definition to have little effect, Atkinson (1977, fn. 6) and Beckerman (1979, pp. 264 and 278) note an instance where it *does* make a large difference.

4. Actually, the focus axiom was only implicitly present in Sen's 1976 paper but is explicitly used in later work. See Sen (1981, p. 186), Hamada and Takayama (1977, Axiom I), and also Sen (1973b, p. 80). On the difference between the transfer axiom in the earlier work and the weak transfer axiom used later, see Sen (1977, p. 77; 1981, p. 192) and Thon (1979, p. 11). Note that these are not the "axioms" used by Sen to derive his particular measure.

5. Of course, the focus axiom does *not* rule out the use of all incomes in fixing the poverty line.

6. In the presence of the focus and monotonicity axioms, this definition is equivalent to the one in Sen (1981, p. 186). Notice that it allows i and j to have the same initial income, whereas Sen's (1977, p. 77) verbal definition does not.

7. See Sen (1981, pp. 31–32). Of course, to evaluate the plausibility of this argument, one would have to know a bit more about the notion of relative deprivation that Sen is implicitly using.

8. While absolute deprivation as measured in income space might not be affected by a regressive transfer, there may be a case for saying that absolute deprivation in "capability" space is increased. See Sen (1982, pp. 367–369; 1983).

9. Some notion of symmetry is implicit in the use of the weak transfer axiom. In Sen (1976), Anand (1977), and nearly every other paper, symmetry is implicitly assumed by defining poverty measures over ordered income distributions. All measures discussed below satisfy symmetry.

10. That is, M is an $n \times n$ matrix of "0's" and "1's" having exactly one "1" in each row and column.

11. See Marshall and Olkin (1979) or Dasgupta et al. (1973). Schur-convexity is often shortened to "S-convexity."

12. In words, x dominates y by the absolute Lorenz criterion if the poorest k persons in x have no less income than the poorest k persons in y, and for some k they hold strictly more income. See Shorrocks (1983b), who uses the term "generalized" Lorenz. Note that the criterion holds for distributions having different means; it would be interesting to extend this partial ordering to distributions having different numbers of poor persons.

13. Early examples of the use of an aggregate poverty count are given in Eden (1797, Vol. III, p. cccv), while the use of a head-count ratio dates back at least to Perez y de Molina (1859, p. 121), Booth (1889, p. 36), and Rowntree (1901, p. 298).

14. The aggregate poverty gap would appear to have been used first by Orshansky (1965, p. 85; 1966, pp. 28–29), who also introduced the statistic $1 - I$ as the "percentage of estimated need" being met. For a recent application of g and g/q, see Beckerman (1979).

15. Sen (1976, p. 220). Note that the basic motivation must be a desire to find a *distribution-sensitive* measure, since I and g satisfy the remaining two axioms.

16. That is, $r(i) = r(j)$ implies $i = j$; or different poor persons must have different ranks.

17. Note that while the ranking of the poor may not be unique, any two rankings must give the same poverty value. Hence S is a well-defined function. There are two other meas-

ures that have also been called the Sen measure: measure S' defined in (13) below, and S'' = HS' presented in Sen (1973b, p. 80).

18.　In fact, the net change in S will be proportional to the number of persons between giver and receiver as reckoned by the common ranking. See expression (10) and the accompanying discussion.

19.　Where y and π are given, and $\hat{y}$ is y's ordered vector,

$$G_p = 1 + \frac{1}{q} - 2 \sum_{i=1}^{q} \frac{\hat{y}_i(q + 1 - i)}{q^2 \bar{y}_p}.$$

20.　In fact, to construct a measure satisfying the axioms, we first fix q and π and choose an arbitrary, strictly increasing, strictly Schur-convex function of q variables, say $f_{\pi,q}(\cdot)$. Now do so for *all* q and π, and define $P(y; \pi) = f_{\pi,q}(y)$, where $q = q(y; \pi)$. Then, P satisfies all three axioms.

21.　Sen (1976, p. 220) originally presented the form (3) with no restriction on A, but later (1977, p. 77) required A to be a function of π, q, and n. As Sen's approach takes N to be fixed, n is redundant; and since q is itself a function of y and π, the approach taken here seems a bit more explicit.

22.　In fact, if we rule out distributions wherein all poor individuals are at the poverty line, then (3) places no logical restrictions on the poverty measure at all. An arbitrary measure $Q(y; \pi)$ is obtained by letting $v_i = Q(y; \pi)/g_i$, where i is the poorest person in y, and fixing $v_i = 0$ for all other persons. This hardly does justice to the interpretation of (3), though.

23.　This argument shows that the "normalized absolute deprivation" property is much stronger than needed. For example, it may be replaced by the weaker requirement that, when all poor have half the poverty line income, the measure is half the head-count ratio.

24.　For a dissenting view, see Miller (1968).

25.　It could very well be argued that unless the context for the weights is fixed and justified any discussion of the weights must be meaningless. The discussion of weights by Clark et al. (1981, pp. 516–517) is particularly susceptible to this criticism.

26.　For further results linking this notion of relative deprivation to the Gini coefficient, see Yitzhaki (1979, 1980) and Hey and Lambert (1980).

27.　In fact, any symmetric measure that satisfies the focus axiom and is homogeneous of degree zero in the poverty line and all incomes must satisfy this requirement: when all poor have the same income the poverty measure can only depend on q and $\bar{y}_p/\pi$; and since $q = nH$ and $\bar{y}_p/\pi = 1 - I$, the measure can be expressed as a function of H and I.

28.　One might expect a priori that few measures possess this particular property. Recall, though, by note 24, above, that it can be weakened substantially.

29.　To be precise, Anand uses the "other" Sen measure S' [defined in (13), in Section III.B].

30.　See Sen (1973b; reprinted 1974, p. 79) for alternative measures of the "ease of poverty alleviation".

31.　Kakwani's original verification involves taking derivatives with respect to a discrete variable i, which would seem a bit problematic. Note further that his discussion on p. 440 relating Sen's axioms to the weights $v_i(y; \pi)$ is incorrect. For example, suppose that v_i is defined to be 1 when $y_i = \pi$, and $1/g_i$ otherwise. Does this measure satisfy monotonicity?

32.　Since Kakwani takes the normalization factor A as a function of π alone, a slight change is needed to make his procedure valid.

33.　Clark et al. (1981, p. 518) claim that the choice of k depends on the particular distribution under consideration. This is clearly not the case if n is fixed and given.

34.　Since all positive renormalizations of S must satisfy the "weaker" monotonicity axiom, it is clear that the trouble occurs once again where the number of poor changes.

35.　It is clear from (12) that a change in the third step to, say, $P = HI[1 + (n - q)/(n + 1)]$ is necessary. Note that this measure also satisfies the "strong monotonicity" property.

36. Thon (1979, p. 438) also argues that whether a person has π or slightly more income "does not matter to him" and that "a poverty index should be consistent with that fact." Yet this would appear to be an argument for continuity rather than the transfer axiom. See also Kundu and Smith (1981) on this point.

37. Note that Kundu and Smith adopt a broader definition of a poverty measure which covers all population sizes and define the poor to be all persons having incomes *strictly* less than π. In addition, they only require properties (a) and (b) to hold when there are both poor and nonpoor persons present.

38. Sen (1981, pp. 192–193). One should note, however, that the transfer axiom requires the "giver" to be poor, whereas the analogous condition for inequality measures (see Sen, 1973a, p. 27) does not.

39. The significance of this "closeness" is not entirely clear. While the disparity between the values given by S and S' may become small as q becomes large, these two measures still represent distinct poverty orderings.

40. See Blackorby and Donaldson (1978) and the references contained therein.

41. Note that Anand (1977, p. 9) gives an identical interpretation of S' and suggests the general approach of P_r.

42. See Kolm (1976) for a discussion of absolute and relative measures of inequality.

43. It should be noted, though, that Blackorby and Donaldson never claim that their classes are in any sense exhaustive.

44. For instance, compare $P(y; \pi)$ with $P(x'; \pi)$, where $x' = (1, 2, 5, 5)$.

45. This point is not mentioned by Blackorby and Donaldson (1980). It should be noted that Blackorby and Donaldson are mistaken when they claim (1980, p. 1054) that the inequality measure "corresponding to" a Schur-concave social welfare function will always take values between 0 and 1. The welfare function "associated with" the coefficient of variation (see Blackorby and Donaldson, 1978, p. 70) is one counterexample.

46. On the other hand, Kakwani (1981) shows that, for Takayama's (1979) measure, if the monotonicity axiom is violated for some x obtained from y by a loss of income among the poor, then $q(y; \pi) > n/2$.

47. There is no special justification given by Takayama on behalf of his general form. His weights are—as with Thon (1979)—the ranks of individuals among the whole population; but given the difference in the respective general forms, the two rank-order conditions are strictly noncomparable. It is not clear that Takayama is aware of this point (see 1979, p. 759).

48. Takayama's (1979) paper would appear to have more than its share of careless slips. For instance, where is "axiom M" ever used? Why must the richest poor person have an income of π? In what sense is Sen's measure "essentially ordinal"?

49. This follows immediately from the fact that $I \cdot G_g = (1 - I)G_p$.

50. Note that where $\alpha = 0$ the measure is defined to be $1 - (\prod_{i \in N} y^{1/n})/\bar{y}$. Of course, the measure obtained when $\alpha = 1$ is not very interesting.

51. See Cowell (1980) or Shorrocks (1983a) for a discussion of this class of inequality measures.

52. Chakravarty (1981, p. 70) and Thon (1982) note that C^α may not satisfy the transfer axiom.

53. For example, let $\alpha = \frac{1}{2}$ and compare the distributions $x = (1, \frac{199}{100}, 4, 4)$ and $y = (1, \frac{799}{400}, 4, 4)$, where $\pi = 2$. The measure $HI(1 + A_g^\alpha)$ will register a higher level of poverty for y than x, and yet x is obtained from y by a loss of income among the poor.

54. In fact, it can be shown to satisfy the transfer axiom as well. See Thon (1982). Note that while this approach yields a monotonic poverty measure when A^α is used, this is not necessarily the case for *any* given inequality measure. The coefficient of variation provides a simple counterexample. However, the poverty measure *will* satisfy monotonicity if $\bar{y}^*(1 - R(y^*))$ is strictly increasing in each poor income.

55.   In their original paper the parameter α is lower by 1; that is, P_0 in their paper is P_1 here, and so on. We have taken the liberty of renumbering the measures so that the results in Foster and Shorrocks (1983) are more natural.

56.   That a sizeable proportion of the poor regard the poverty line as a reference point is well-documented for the United Kingdom. See Townsend (1979, p. 894).

57.   Note that the squared coefficient of variation is simply the variance (where each observation has equal probability) divided by the square of the mean. Kundu (1981, p. 94) independently derived P_3 and noted its relationship with C_p.

58.   In this context P_α is being regarded as a function over distributions of any population size n.

59.   See columns (4) and (2), respectively, of the table in Anand (1977, pp. 13–15).

60.   The notion of a subgroup's "contribution" to total poverty is not above criticism, nor is the particular way in which it is measured here. Why not use $100P(y^{(j)}; \pi)/\sum_{k=1}^{m} P(y^{(k)}; \pi)$, which would ensure that the sum of the contributions would be 100% for any arbitrary measure?

61.   The precise amount it falls is 1/175. See also the related example for the Gini coefficient given in Cowell (1980), and his "General Decomposition" property.

62.   See Clark et al. (1981) or Chakravarty (1981).

63.   A further complication is that the three-step procedure leads to a *numerically significant* measure of poverty; that is, it leads to the unique functional form S. This rather extreme result seems hard to justify if the measure is only to be used for ordinal comparisons. It should be noted that the "ordinal" in the title of Sen's paper refers to the welfare information used to construct his measure, and not the *measurability* properties of the measure itself. This point is apparently missed by Takayama (1979).

64.   The issue is whether a measure is supported by a given property or whether it is supported *uniquely*. Note that *none* of the measures discussed in this survey is supported uniquely by its motivating properties; for example, many measures besides Thon's satisfy the transfer axiom, and many measures besides the class proposed by Foster et al. (1981) satisfy their decomposability property.

65.   See the discussion of Sen (1973a, pp. 47–48) on the similar issue in inequality measurement.

66.   What exactly should be held fixed is a difficult question.

67.   Surveys of the literature on setting the poverty line can be found in Ornati (1966), Atkinson (1975), Fiegehen (1977), and Townsend (1979). Atkinson (p. 187) stresses that even the so-called absolute approach based on subsistence diets (e.g., that of Rowntree, 1901) is not free from arbitrariness.

68.   A number of studies use two or more poverty lines (e.g., see the "poverty band" of Ornati (1966, pp. 10–11)).

69.   A welfare function is equality preferring if it regards a regressive transfer of income (from poor to rich) as welfare reducing.

REFERENCES

Ahluwalia, M. S. (1978) Rural Poverty and Agricultural Performance in India, *Journal of Development Studies* 14, 298–322.

Anand, S. (1977) Aspects of Poverty in Malaysia, *Review of Income and Wealth* 23, 1–16.

Anand, S. (1983) *Inequality and Poverty in Malaysia,* New York: Oxford University Press.

Atkinson, A. B. (1970) On the Measurement of Inequality, *Journal of Economic Theory* 2, 244–263.

Atkinson, A. B. (1975) *The Economics of Inequality,* Oxford: Clarendon Press.

Atkinson, A. B. (1977) Poverty and Social Security Research: An Agenda, in *Social Security Research,* Papers presented at a DHSS Seminar on 7–9 April 1976, HMSO, London: (Paper 1).

Beckerman, W. (1979) The Impact of Income Maintenance Payments on Poverty in Britain, 1975, *Economic Journal* 89, 261–279.

Blackorby, C. and D. Donaldson. (1978) Measures of Relative Equality and Their Meaning in Terms of Social Welfare, *Journal of Economic Theory* 18, 59–80.

Blackorby, C. and D. Donaldson. (1980) Ethical Indices for the Measurement of Poverty, *Econometrica* 48, 1053–1060.

Booth, C. (1889) *Life and Labour of the People,* Vol. 1, London: Williams & Norgate.

Bourguignon, F. (1979) Decomposable Income Inequality Measures, *Econometrica* 47, 901–920.

Chakravarty, S. R. (1981) On Measurement of Income Inequality and Poverty, Ph.D. Dissertation, Indian Statistical Institute.

Clark, S., R. Hemming and D. Ulph (1981) On Indices for the Measurement of Poverty, *Economic Journal,* 91, 515–526.

Cowell, F. A. (1980) The Structure of American Income Inequality, mimeographed, London School of Economics, (forthcoming, *Review of Income and Wealth*).

Dasgupta, P., A. Sen and D. Starrett (1973) Notes on the Measurement of Inequality, *Journal of Economic Theory* 6, 180–187

Dutta, B. (1978) On the Measurement of Poverty in Rural India, *Indian Economic Review* 13, 23–32.

Eden, F. M. (1797) *The State of the Poor,* London.

Fiegehen, G. C., P. S. Lansley and A. D. Smith (1977) *Poverty and Progress in Britain, 1953–73,* Cambridge England: Cambridge University Press.

Fields, G. S. and J. C. H. Fei (1978) On Inequality Comparisons, *Econometrica* 46, 303–316.

Fields, G. (1980) *Poverty, Inequality and Development,* Cambridge England: Cambridge University Press.

Foster, J. E. (1982) Essays on Inequality and Equilibrium, Ph.D. Dissertation, Cornell University.

Foster, J. E. (1983) An Axiomatic Characterization of the Theil Measure of Income Inequality, *Journal of Economic Theory* 31, 105–121.

Foster, J. E. and A. F. Shorrocks (1983) Welfare Dominance and Poverty Orderings, mimeographed, London School of Economics.

Foster, J. E., J. Greer and E. Thorbecke (1981) *A Class of Decomposable Poverty Measures,* Working Paper No. 243, Department of Economics, Cornell University, (forthcoming, *Econometrica*).

Hamada, K. and N. Takayama (1977) Censored Income Distributions and the Measurement of Poverty, *Bulletin of the International Statistical Institute* 47, 617–630.

Hey, J. D. and P. J. Lambert (1980) Relative Deprivation and the Gini Coefficient: Comment, *Quarterly Journal of Economics,* 95, 568–573.

Kakwani, N. C. (1977) Measurement of Poverty and the Negative Income Tax, *Australian Economic Papers* 16, 237–248.

Kakwani, N. C. (1980a) On a Class of Poverty Measures, *Econometrica* 48, 437–446.

Kakwani, N. C. (1980b) *Income Inequality and Poverty,* New York: Oxford University Press.

Kakwani, N. (1981) Note on a New Measure of Poverty, *Econometrica* 49, 525–526.

Kolm, S. C. (1976) Unequal Inequalities, *Journal of Economic Theory* 12, 416–442, and 13, 82–111.

Kundu, A. (1981) Measurement of Poverty—Some Conceptual Issues, *Anvesak* 11, 80–96.

Kundu, A. and T. E. Smith (1983) An Impossibility Theorem on Poverty Indices, *International Economic Review* 24, 423–434.

Marshall, A. W. and I. Olkin (1979) *Theory of Majorization and Its Applications*, New York: Academic Press.

Metcalf D. (1981) Review of *Poverty in the United Kingdom* (by P. Townsend), *British Journal of Industrial Relations*, 19, 112–116.

Miller, W. (1968) The Elimination of the Lower Class as National Policy. In D. P. Moynihan (ed.), *On Understanding Poverty* New York: Basic Books, 260–315.

Ornati, O. (1966) *Poverty Amid Affluence*, New York: The Twentieth Century Fund.

Orshansky, M. (1969) Counting the Poor: Another Look at the Poverty Profile, *Social Security Bulletin*, 28 (1965), 3–29. Reprinted in *Poverty in America: A Book of Readings* (L. A. Ferman, J. L. Kornbluh, and A. Haber, eds.), Ann Arbor: The University of Michigan Press, 67–106.

Orshansky, M. (1966) Recounting the Poor: A Five-Year Review, *Social Security Bulletin* 29, 20–37.

Osmani, S. R. (1982) *Economic Inequality and Group Welfare*, Oxford: Clarendon Press.

Perez y de Molina, M. (1859) *Del Pauperismo*, Jerez.

Randolph, S. M. (1982) Measures of Absolute Poverty, Cornell University Rural Development Committee Occasional Paper.

Rowntree, B. S. (1901) *Poverty: A Study of Town Life*, London: Macmillan and Co.

Runciman, W. G. (1966) *Relative Deprivation and Social Justice*, Berkeley, CA: University of California Press.

Sen, A. (1973a) *On Economic Inequality*, Oxford: Clarendon Press.

Sen, A. (1974) Poverty, Inequality and Unemployment: Some Conceptual Issues in Measurement, *Economic and Political Weekly* (Bombay), 8 (1973b). Reprinted in *Poverty and Incomes Distribution in India* (T. N. Srinivasan and P. K. Bardhan, eds.), Calcutta: Statistical Publishing Society, 67–82.

Sen, A. (1975) *Employment, Technology and Development*, Oxford: Clarendon Press.

Sen, A. (1976) Poverty: An Ordinal Approach to Measurement, *Econometrica* 44, 219–231.

Sen, A. (1977) Social Choice Theory: A Re-examination, *Econometrica* 45, 53–89.

Sen, A. (1979) Issues in the Measurement of Poverty, *Scandinavian Journal of Economics* 81, 285–307.

Sen, A. (1981) *Poverty and Famines: An Essay on Entitlement and Deprivation*, Oxford: Clarendon Press.

Sen, A. (1982) *Choice, Welfare and Measurement*, Cambridge, MA: The MIT Press.

Sen, A. K. (1983) Poor, Relatively Speaking, Economic and Social Research Institute (forthcoming, *Oxford Economic Papers*).

Shorrocks, A. F. (1980) The Class of Additively Decomposable Inequality Measures, *Econometrica* 48, 613–625.

Shorrocks, A. F. (1983a) Inequality Decomposition by Population Subgroups, mimeographed, London School of Economics, (forthcoming, *Econometrica*).

Shorrocks, A. F. (1983b) Ranking Income Distributions, *Economica* 50, pp. 3–17.

Takayama, N. (1979) Poverty, Income Inequality, and Their Measures: Professor Sen's Axiomatic Approach Reconsidered, *Econometrica* 47, 747–759.

Thon, D. (1979) On Measuring Poverty, *Review of Income and Wealth* 25, 429–440.

Thon, D. (1981) Income Inequality and Poverty: Some Problems, *Review of Income and Wealth*, 27, 207–210.

Thon, D. (1982) A Note on a Troublesome Axiom for Poverty Indices, mimeographed, Norwegian School of Economics and Business Administration, (forthcoming, *Economic Journal*).

Townsend, P. (1979) *Poverty in the United Kingdom*, London: Penguin.

Van Ginneken, W. (1980) Some Methods of Poverty Analysis: An Application to Iranian Data, 1975–76, *World Development*, 8, 639–646.

Watts, H. (1968) An Economic Definition of Poverty. In D. P. Moynihan (ed.), *On Understanding Poverty* New York: Basic Books, 316–329.

Yitzhaki, S. (1979) Relative Deprivation and the Gini Coefficient, *Quarterly Journal of Economics* 93, 321–324.

Yitzhaki, S. (1980) Relative Deprivation and the Gini Coefficient: Reply, *Quarterly Journal of Economics* 95, 575–576.

ISSUES IN MEASURING POVERTY

Nanak Kakwani

ABSTRACT

The measurement of poverty involves two distinct problems. First is the specification of the poverty line, the threshold income below which one is considered to be poor, and which may reflect the socially accepted minimal standard of living. A probabilistic model of social choice is utilized to incorporate the value judgments about the poverty line of all members of the society. Once the poverty line is determined, the second problem is that of constructing an index which would measure the intensity of poverty suffered by those below the poverty line. This paper provides a critical evaluation of alternative indexes of poverty and proposes a new class of poverty indexes. A numerical method of computing the poverty indexes from grouped data is also given, along with an international comparison of poverty using data from 31 developing countries.

I. INTRODUCTION

Poverty has been in existence in the world for many centuries. But an awareness of its existence in Western societies has increased only recently.[1] Social attitudes toward poverty have changed, and the fact that

Advances in Econometrics, vol. 3, pages 253–282
Copyright © 1984 by JAI Press Inc.
All rights of reproduction in any form reserved.
ISBN: 0-89232-443-0

many of the Western economies have achieved a level of affluence where poverty can be eliminated without causing any significant hardship to the nonpoor sections of the community is increasingly recognized. It is also being increasingly realized that the developing countries will continue to need outside assistance to eliminate poverty or at least to reduce its intensity.[2] The prior problem, however, is to identify the poor and measure the intensity of their poverty so that methods can be devised to wage a war against it.

Consequently, the measurement of poverty involves two distinct problems. First is the identification of the poor. The poor are those who lack resources to obtain the "minimum necessities of life." The "poverty line" is the level of income which is just sufficient to buy these so-called minimum necessities of life. A person is poor if his or her income falls below that line.

The problem of specification of the poverty line is discussed in Sections II and III of this paper. It is argued that the poverty line should depend on the nutritional needs of a person or a family as well as society's values about the minimum standard of living. A probabilistic model of social choice proposed by Intriligator (1973) is utilized to incorporate the value judgments of all members of the society. Once the poverty line is determined, the second problem is that of constructing an index which would measure the intensity of poverty suffered by those below the poverty line.

Most of the literature on poverty concerns the number of individuals or families below the poverty line. The proportion of individuals (or families) below the poverty line, as such, does not reflect the intensity of poverty suffered by the poor. The problem is to determine how poor are the poor. They may have incomes that approximate the threshold level, or they may have incomes of almost zero. If the deviation of a poor person's income from the poverty line is proportional to the degree of misery suffered by that individual, the sum total of these deviations divided by the number of poor may be considered an adequate measure of poverty. This index, which has been used by the U.S. Social Security Administration, is called the *poverty gap*. It indicates the average shortfall of income from the poverty line of all the poor taken together. There are two main drawbacks with this index: (1) it is completely insensitive to to the number of poor; and (2) it does not take into account the inequality of income among poor.

Sections IV to VIII provide a discussion of alternative measures of poverty that avoid the drawbacks of previous measures. The only work which has so far appeared on this subject is that of Sen (1976, 1979) Kakwani (1977a, 1980a,b,c), Takayama (1979), and Drewnowski (1977).[3] The purpose of this paper is to provide an evaluation of alternative measures without giving detailed derivations. A new class of poverty measures is proposed, and the earlier measures by Sen (1976) and Kakwani (1980a) are shown to be particular members of this class. A numerical method of computing the measures from grouped data is discussed in Sections IX, and Section X provides an international comparison of poverty using data from 31 developing countries.

II. SPECIFICATION OF THE POVERTY LINE

One of the earlier studies on poverty was done by Rowntree (1901), who defined families as being in primary poverty if their total earnings are insufficient to obtain the "minimum necessities of merely physical efficiency." He estimated the minimum money costs for food which would satisfy the average nutritional needs of families of different sizes. To these costs he added the rent paid and certain minimum amounts for clothing, fuel, and sundries to arrive at a poverty line of a family of given size. This poverty line based on the concept of physical subsistence involves a number of serious problems.[4]

One of the main criticisms against this concept of poverty is that it does not take into account the current living standards of the society. This concept of poverty may be valid in many developing countries where malnutrition is still prevalent, but in developed countries poverty no longer means starvation or near starvation. The old standards of poverty are not relevant to contemporary society.[5] The new approach to the definition of poverty is based on the concept of "relative deprivation," which denotes the feelings of deprivation relative to others.[6] In view of this, it seems best to recognize explicitly that any poverty line will be influenced by current living standards and should only be defined in relation to the living standards of a particular society at a particular time.[7]

Sen (1979), recognizing these different aspects of poverty, defined two poverty lines: (1) the nutritional poverty line and (2) the cultural poverty line. The first corresponds to the level of income at which the consumption level of an individual or of a family is nutritionally adequate, and the second identifies the level of income adequate for meeting necessities defined in terms of the overall living standards of that society. It seems useful to define a single poverty line which takes into account both these aspects of poverty. One such poverty line is

$$z(\beta) = z_0 + \beta(m - z_0), \tag{2.1}$$

where z_0 is the nutritional poverty line income and m denotes either the median or the mean income of the society;[8] β lies in the range $0 \le \beta \le 1$, which implies that the poverty line can be neither lower than z_0 (which represents a standard of minimum subsistence) nor higher than the mean or median income of the society.[9] The value of β depends on the society's value judgment about the minimum standard of living which all its members must enjoy. The problem is that of obtaining social preferences about the alternative values of β from the individual preferences. This is discussed in the next section.

III.   A PROBABILISTIC APPROACH TO MEASURING POVERTY

Suppose in a given society there are n families who are arranged in ascending order of their incomes $x_1 \leq x_2 \leq \cdots \leq x_n$. These incomes are denoted by a vector $\mathbf{x} = (x_1, x_2, \ldots, x_n)$. If $z(\beta)$ is the poverty line, then the poverty index $\theta(\mathbf{x}, z(\beta))$ is defined as being a unique function of $x_1, x_2, \ldots, x_n$ and $z(\beta)$, satisfying certain axioms. Assume that β takes m alternative values $\beta_1, \beta_2, \ldots, \beta_m$ (all of which lie in the range $0 \leq \beta \leq 1$), which lead to m alternative poverty lines, as defined in (2.1). Each individual in the society has certain preferences among alternative poverty lines, which are summarized by individual probability vector

$$\mathbf{p}_i = (p_{i1}, p_{i2}, \ldots, p_{im});$$

$$p_{ij} \geq 0 \quad \text{(for all } i, j);$$

$$\sum_{j=1}^{m} p_{ij} = 1 \quad \text{(for all } i),$$

where p_{ij} is the probability that an individual i will choose the poverty line $z(\beta_j)$.[10] Let the social probability vector $\mathbf{p}$ derived from individual probability vectors $\mathbf{p}_1, \mathbf{p}_2, \ldots, \mathbf{p}_n$ be given by

$$\mathbf{p} = (p_1, p_2, \ldots, p_m); \quad p_j \geq 0 \quad \text{(for all } j); \quad \sum_{j=1}^{m} p_j = 1,$$

where p_j is the probability that the society will choose the poverty line $z(\beta_j)$.

The problem is then of obtaining the social probability vector $\mathbf{p}$ from the individual vectors $\mathbf{p}_i$. To tackle this problem, the following three axioms are proposed.[11]

AXIOM 3.1:   *Existence of Social Probabilities—Given any set of n nonnegative vectors $\mathbf{p}_i$ with unit sums, there exists a nonnegative vector $\mathbf{p}$, such that meaningful individual probabilities will yield meaningful social probabilities.*

AXIOM 3.2: *Unanimity Preserving for a Loser—If all individuals reject a poverty line with certainty then so does society, i.e., if $p_{ij} = 0$ for all i, then $p_j = 0$. Similarly if all individuals accept a poverty line with certainty so does society, i.e., if $p_{ij} = 1$ for all i, then $p_j = 1$.*

AXIOM 3.3: *Strict and Equal Sensitivity to Individual Probabilities— Social probabilities are strictly sensitive to individual probabilities in that an increase (decrease) in the probability that any one individual will choose a particular poverty line always increases (decreases) the probability that society will choose this poverty line.*

Given these axioms, Intriligator (1973) proved that there is a unique rule for determining social probabilities, the *average rule*, according to which the social probabilities are simple averages of individual probabilities,[12] i.e.,

$$p_j = \frac{1}{n} \sum_{i=1}^{n} p_{ij} \qquad \text{(for all } j = 1, 2, \ldots, m\text{)}.$$

There are m poverty indexes $\theta_j = \theta(\mathbf{x}, z(\beta_j))$, each of which is associated with a social probability p_j, which is derived from individual probabilities. A weighted average of all these poverty indexes, as given by

$$E(\theta) = \sum_{j=1}^{m} \theta_j p_j = \frac{1}{n} \sum_{j=1}^{m} \sum_{i=1}^{n} \theta_j p_{ij},$$

provides an aggregated index of poverty which incorporates the value judgments (expressed in terms of probabilities) of all the members of a society. The problem of deriving a suitable index of poverty from given income distribution $\mathbf{x}$ and a poverty line $z(\beta_j)$ is discussed in subsequent sections.

IV. A GENERAL CLASS OF POVERTY MEASURES

In this and later sections, the poverty line will be denoted by z instead of $z(\beta)$. Let q ($\leq n$) be the number of the poor who have income below the poverty line z. The ratio q/n has been widely used as a poverty measure and is called *the head-count* ratio.

The head-count ratio is a crude measure of poverty because of two main drawbacks. It is insensitive, first, to decreases in income of individuals below the poverty line and, second, to transfers of income among the poor as well as from the poor to the nonpoor. To counter these shortcomings, Sen (1976) proposed that a suitable measure of poverty must satisfy the following two axioms.

AXIOM 4.1 (*Monotonicity*):   *Other things remaining the same, a re-duction in income of a person below the poverty line must increase the poverty measure.*

AXIOM 4.2 (*Transfer*):   *Other things remaining the same, a pure trans-fer of income from a person below the poverty line to anyone who is richer must increase the poverty measure, unless the number of people below the poverty line is strictly reduced by the transfer.*[13]

The head-count ratio violates both axioms. The alternative poverty meas-ures will now be considered that satisfy these axioms.

If μ is the mean income of a society and ξ^* the mean income of indi-viduals below the poverty line, a poverty index proposed by Kakwani (1977a) is

$$K = \frac{q(z - \mu^*)}{n\mu}, \qquad (4.1)$$

where K is interpreted as the percentage of total income that must be transferred from the nonpoor to the poor so that the poverty is completely wiped out. This measure, therefore, reflects the relative burden of poverty on the nation compared with its aggregate income.[14] Further, if $z = \mu$, then it can be shown that K reduces to the relative mean deviation, which is a well-known measure of income inequality.[15]

Next, we divide the whole population into k mutually exclusive regions or groups. We denote μ_i as the mean income of the ith region and f_i as the proportion of population in the ith region; then K can be written as

$$K = \frac{1}{\mu} \sum_{i=1}^{k} \mu_i f_i K_i,$$

K_i being the poverty index in the ith region. This result may have inter-esting policy implications. It helps one to analyze the contribution of poverty within each socioeconomic group (or geographic region) to the aggregate poverty.[16]

Although the measure K [as defined in Eq. (4.1)] has an intuitively appealing interpretation in terms of income transfer from the nonpoor to the poor, it suffers from the drawback that it is sensitive to decrease (or increase) in income of the poor as well as the nonpoor. Other things remaining the same, a decrease (increase) in income of a poor or nonpoor person will increase (decrease) the poverty measure. If every person below the poverty line gets zero income, in which case μ^* will be equal to zero, then

$$K = \frac{qz}{(n - q)\bar{\mu}^*},$$

where $\bar{\mu}^*$ is the mean income of the nonpoor.

This equation implies that the poverty measure decreases monotonically as the income of the nonpoor increases, even if the income of the poor remains zero. It means that the poverty can be reduced by any amount only by increasing the affluence of the nonpoor. This is clearly an undesirable feature of this poverty measure. The poverty measure, as Sen (1979) points out, should reflect exclusively the interests of the poor and not permit a trade-off with the fortunes of the rich. One such measure is by Sen (1976):

$$S = \frac{q(z - \mu^*)}{nz},$$

which differs from K only by a multiplicative constant. This measure remains unaffected by the increase in the mean income of the nonpoor provided the poverty line is fixed.[17]

The poverty measure S is the product of two ratios, namely, the headcount ratio q/n, which measures the percentage of families below the poverty line, and the income gap ratio $(z - \mu^*)/z$, which indicates the proportion of the mean income shortfall of the poor families from the poverty line. These ratios reflect two different aspects of poverty, both of which are important. It can, therefore, be argued that the product of these ratios can be used as a measure of poverty, but this product is completely insensitive to income transfers among the poor. Thus, the measure S violates the transfer axiom 4.2.

The measure S will provide adequate information about the intensity of poverty if all the poor families are assumed to have exactly the same income, which is less than the poverty level. In actual practice, the income among the poor is unequally distributed and, therefore, S cannot be an adequate measure of intensity of poverty. More inequality of income among the poor with mean income remaining unchanged should imply greater hardship to the extremely poor in a society; therefore, the value of the poverty should be higher in this case.

In order to take into account the inequality of income among the poor, we need to consider the social welfare function of the poor only,[18] which we assume can be written as

$$W = W(\mu^*, G^*), \tag{4.2}$$

G^* being a measure of inequality of income among the poor. We have selected G^* to be the Gini index, which is the most widely used measure of inequality. Further, we impose the following restrictions on the social welfare function:

$$\frac{\partial W}{\partial \mu^*} > 0 \quad \text{and} \quad \frac{\partial W}{\partial G^*} < 0, \qquad (4.3)$$

which seem intuitively reasonable. Let ξ be the level of income which is received by every poor person, which would result in the same level of social welfare of the poor as their current distribution; then

$$W(\xi, 0) = W(\mu^*, G^*), \qquad (4.4)$$

which gives

$$\xi = \xi(\mu^*, G^*), \qquad (4.5)$$

ξ being the equally distributed equivalent level of income among the poor.[19]

Let us assume that the welfare function of the poor is homothetic in incomes; then we must have

$$\xi(k\mu^*, G^*) = k\,\xi(\mu^*, G^*), \qquad (4.6)$$

where k is any scalar.[20] A simple functional form satisfying (4.6) is

$$\xi(\mu^*, G^*) = \mu^* \, g(G^*), \qquad (4.7)$$

where $g(G^*)$ in view of restrictions (4.3) and (4.4) must satisfy the following conditions:

$$g(G^*) = 1 \qquad \text{if } G^* = 0; \qquad (4.8)$$

$$g(G^*) < 1 \qquad \text{for } G^* > 0; \qquad (4.9)$$

$$g'(G^*) < 0, \qquad (4.10)$$

$g'(G^*)$ being the first derivative of $g(G^*)$ with respect to G^*.

We can interpret $\xi = \xi(\mu^*, G^*)$ as the effective income of the poor after taking into account the inequality of income among them. Conditions (4.8) and (4.9), above, imply that the effective income will always be less than the actual mean income because of income inequality. Obviously, the income gap ratio now defined as $(z - \xi)/z$ will also be higher in the presence of income inequality among the poor than in its absence. Defining the poverty measure as a product of the head-count ratio and the income gap ratio $(z - \xi)/z$, we arrive at a class of poverty measures

$$Pg = \frac{q}{nz} [z - \mu^* g(G^*)], \qquad (4.11)$$

which in view of Eqs. (4.8) and (4.9) satisfy the following conditions:

$$\frac{\partial Pg}{\partial \mu^*} < 0;$$

$$\frac{\partial \mathbf{P}g}{\partial G^*} > 0;$$

$$Pg = \frac{q(z - \mu^*)}{nz} \quad \text{if } G^* = 0;$$

$$Pg = \frac{q}{n} \quad \text{if } \mu^* = 0 \text{ (i.e., all the poor get zero income)};$$

$$Pg = 0 \quad \text{if } \mu^* = z \text{ and } G^* = 0$$

(i.e., when all the poor get incomes exactly equal to z).

Since the Gini index increases if any transfer of income takes place from an individual to anyone who is richer,[21] any poverty index satisfying the above conditions will necessarily satisfy both Axioms 4.1 and 4.2.

A simple functional form of $g(G^*)$ in which Pg increases with G^* at a constant rate and at the same time satisfying conditions (4.8)–(4.10) is

$$g(G^*) = (1 - G^*),$$

which on substituting in (4.11) leads to Sen's (1976) poverty measure:

$$S^* = \frac{q\,[z - \mu^*(1 - G^*)]}{zn}. \tag{4.12}$$

The elasticity of the measure S^* with respect to G^* is

$$\eta_s = \frac{G^*}{S^*}\frac{\partial S^*}{\partial G^*} = \frac{\mu^* G^*}{(z - \mu^*) + \mu^* G^*},$$

which is clearly less than unity. Thus, if income among the poor is redistributed so that the Gini index reduces by 1%, the poverty index reduces by less than 1%. This elasticity provides the information regarding the effect on the poverty index of income inequality among the poor.

An alternative index proposed by Kakwani (1980) is obtained by substituting

$$g(G^*) = \frac{1}{(1 + G^*)}$$

into (4.11), which, if denoted by K^*, gives

$$K^* = \frac{q}{nz}\left[z - \frac{\mu^*}{(1 + G^*)}\right]. \tag{4.13}$$

The elasticity of K^* with respect to G^* will be

$$\eta_k = \frac{\mu^* G^*}{(1 + G^*)(z - \mu^* + zG^*)} .$$

Comparing the elasticities of η_s and η_k, note that $\eta_k < \eta_s$, which shows that the poverty index S^* is more sensitive to the change in inequality of income among the poor than the alternative index K^*. If the society attaches relatively greater importance to the inequality of income among the poor, the measure S^* will be preferred to the measure K^*.

   A class of measures depending on a single parameter λ in the range $0 < \lambda < 1$ is obtained by substituting

$$g(G^*) = \frac{(1 - \lambda\, G^*)}{1 + (1 - \lambda)\, G^*} \tag{4.14}$$

into (4.11), where $g(G^*)$ in (4.14) satisfies the restrictions (4.8) to (4.10). This class of measures, if denoted by θ_λ, gives

$$\theta_\lambda = WS^* + (1 - W)K^*, \tag{4.15}$$

where

$$W = \frac{\lambda}{\lambda + (1 - \lambda)(1 + G^*)} .$$

Note that, if $\lambda = 1$, W becomes unity and therefore θ_λ leads to Sen's measure S^*. When $\lambda = 0$, W is zero, and then θ_λ gives Kakwani's measure K^*. Since $S^* > K^*$ for all nonzero G^*, Eq. (4.15) will provide the following upper and lower bounds on θ_λ:

$$S^* > \theta_\lambda > K^*$$

for all λ in the range $0 < \lambda < 1$.

   This class of poverty measures, which includes both Sen's and Kakwani's measures as particular members, has been derived using a homothetic welfare function of the poor. One can further generalize this analysis to include nonhomothetic welfare functions, but the measures so obtained will not be the relative measures of poverty, i.e., will not remain unchanged when all incomes and the poverty line itself are multiplied by a positive scalar.[22]

V. SEN'S AXIOMATIC APPROACH TO MEASURING POVERTY

Sen's approach to measuring poverty is based on ordinal welfare comparisons. He defines a general measure of poverty as

$$\theta = A(z, q, n) \sum_{i=1}^{q} g_i v_i(z, x), \tag{5.1}$$

where $g_i = z - x_i$ is the income shortfall of the *i*th poor, and $v_i(z, \mathbf{x})$ is the weight attached to his income shortfall given the income distribution $\mathbf{x}$. It should be understood that $v_i(z, x)$ has been defined as a function of the whole income distribution vector $\mathbf{x}$ and not of x_i alone, which implies a more general welfare function than the one that is additive separable.[23] One could also define the poverty measure as the sum total of disutilities arising from being poor. This definition would correspond to the utilitarian welfare function, and in that case v_i must depend only on the income x_i of the *i*th person and not also on the incomes of others. Sen (1979) dismissed this approach because it misses the idea of relative deprivation, which is rather central to the notion of poverty. Instead, he determines the weights v_i on the basis of ranking of poor individuals, which in some ways captures the relative deprivation aspect of poverty.[24]

A brief discussion of Sen's (1976) axioms will now be provided.

AXIOM 5.1 (*Relative Equity*):   *For any pair of individuals i and j, if $W_i(\mathbf{x}) < W_j(\mathbf{x})$ then $v_i(z, \mathbf{x}) > v_j(z, x)$, where $W_i(\mathbf{x})$ and $W_j(\mathbf{x})$ are the welfare levels of i and j under a given income configuration $\mathbf{x}$.*

This axiom implies that if a person *i* is considered to be worse off than person *j* in a given income configuration $\mathbf{x}$, the income shortfall g_i of the *i*th person should have higher weight than the income shortfall g_j of the *j*th person. Note that $W_i(\mathbf{x})$ is assumed to be ordinally measurable, which only indicates who is worse off than whom by saying nothing about the welfare differences.

AXIOM 5.2 (*Monotonic Welfare*):   *For any i and j, if $x_i < x_j$, then $W_i(\mathbf{x}) < W_j(\mathbf{x})$.*

This axiom gives the relationship between income and welfare, implying that a person *i* with lower income is always considered to be worse off than person *j* with higher income. The axiom rules out the other factors that might affect the individual welfare; for instance, a richer person with poor health may feel worse off than a poorer person with sound health. Axioms 5.1 and 5.2 together imply that the larger the income shortfall, the greater should be the weight attached to it; that is, $v_i(z, \mathbf{x})$ should decrease as *i* increases.

AXIOM 5.3 (*Rank-Order*):   *The weight $v_i(z, x)$ on the income shortfall of person i equals the rank order of i in the interpersonal welfare ordering of the poor.*

This is the most demanding axiom. Sen (1976) justifies it by viewing deprivation as an essentially relative concept. The lower a person is on the welfare scale, the greater is his sense of deprivation with respect to others in the same category. Therefore, the poverty measure must make the weight $v_i(z, \mathbf{x})$ decrease with rank value $r(i)$ of the ith person; the poorest person has the largest rank value q, while the least poor has the rank value of 1. The axiom is equivalent to saying that $v_i(z, \mathbf{x})$ on the income shortfall g_i is proportional to the number of poor persons with income level at least as high as that of person i.

An alternative justification of Sen's rank-order axiom rests on the weighting procedure used in the Borda rule of voting. If there are, say, only four alternatives A, B, C, and D arranged in order of preference, then this rule implies that the intensity of preference of A over B is the same as that of B over C and C over D. This equidistance weighting rule motivated Sen (1974) to propose a primitive axiom O which leads to his Axiom 5.3. If the situation of being the ith person in the distribution $\mathbf{x}$ is denoted by $(\mathbf{x}, i)$, then axiom O states that "if everyone prefers $(\mathbf{x}, i)$ to $(\mathbf{x}, j)$ with no intermediately ranked alternative and $(x, \mathbf{m})$ to (x, l) also with no intermediately ranked alternative, then the excess of weight on j's income over that of i should be no more and no less than the excess of weight on l's income over that of m."

AXIOM 5.4 (Normalized Poverty Value): *If all the poor have the same income, then*

$$\theta = \frac{q(z - \mu^*)}{nz}.$$

This axiom does not need explanation because it was argued in the previous section that the measure S provides adequate information about the intensity of poverty if all the poor have exactly the same income.

The following theorem, which is due to Sen (1976), emerges from the above axioms.

THEOREM 1:   *For large numbers of the poor, the only poverty index satisfying Axioms 5.1, 5.2, 5.3, and 5.4 is S^* [as defined in Eq. (4.12)].*

VI.   AN ALTERNATIVE SET OF AXIOMS

It was pointed out in the previous section that Sen's rank-order axiom (5.3) is most demanding. This axiom makes the weight $v_i(z, \mathbf{x})$ on the income shortfall of person i depend only on the number of people among the poor who are better off than i, thus ignoring completely their actual income. Kakwani (1980a) proposed an axiom alternative to Sen's which makes the i's sense of deprivation depend on the actual income enjoyed by those who are richer than *i* but still belonging to the category of poor. His axiom is formally stated as follows.

AXIOM 6.1: *The weight $v_i(z, \mathbf{x})$ on the income shortfall of person i is proportional to the income of all other persons above him/her but below the poverty line z.*

The following theorem, which is due to Kakwani (1980a), can now be stated:

THEOREM 2: *For large numbers of the poor, the only poverty index satisfying Axioms 5.1, 5.2, 5.4, and 6.1 is K^*, where K^* is defined in Eq. (4.13).*

The poverty measure S^* differs from K^* in its characterization of the relative deprivation among the poor: whereas S^* concentrates on persons, K^* focuses on income.[25] Sen (1979) believes that the sense of relative deprivation is more readily captured by knowing how many people are richer than in knowing what their aggregate income happens to be. He therefore prefers S^* over K^*. There may be some who might believe that the aggregated income of the richer rather than their number is more important in capturing the deprivation aspect of poverty. Ideally, the sense of deprivation should take note of both factors: the actual incomes enjoyed by those who are richer and the number of such persons who enjoy these incomes. To achieve this objective, the following new axiom is introduced.

AXIOM 6.2: *The weight $v_i(z, \mathbf{x})$ on the income shortfall of the ith person is given by*

$$v_i(z, \mathbf{x}) = [\lambda a_i(z, \mathbf{x}) + (1 - \lambda)b_i(z, x)]$$

where $a_i(z, \mathbf{x})$ is the proportion of poor persons with income level at least as high as that of person i and $b_i(z, \mathbf{x})$, is the proportion of their actual income; λ being the constants such that $0 \leq \lambda \leq 1$.

Here $\lambda = 1$ makes the sense of relative deprivation depend only on the number of the poor who are better off than the person in question, whereas $\lambda = 0$ implies that the sense of relative deprivation depends only on the actual income enjoyed by these people. Thus, Sen takes the value of λ to be 1 and Kakwani assumes λ to be 0. It will be more desirable to assume the value of λ to lie between 0 and 1. The particular choice of λ should depend on one's values regarding the sense of relative deprivation.

The following theorem provides a class of poverty measures satisfying Axioms 6.2.

THEOREM 3:   *For the large number of the poor, the only poverty index satisfying Axioms 5.1, 5.2, 5.4, and 6.2 is* θ_λ, *where* θ_λ *is defined in Eq. (4.15).*

VII.   A GENERALIZATION OF SEN'S MEASURE

This section presents a generalization of Sen's measure which was proposed by Kakwani (1980b). The generalization is motivated by the failure of Sen's measure to satisfy some sensitivity axioms, discussed below.

AXIOM 7.1   (*Transfer-Sensitivity I*):   *For any positive integer* ρ *and any pair of poor individuals i and j, if j > i, then* $(\Delta\theta)i, i + \rho > (\Delta\theta)j, j + \rho$, *where* $(\Delta\theta)i, i + \rho$ *is the increase in poverty measure due to a transfer of income from the ith poor to the* $(i + \rho)$*th poor.*

This axiom implies that the sensitivity of the poverty measure depends on the position of the transferer in the ordering of poor people when the number of positions between the transfer and the recipient is fixed. The poorer the transferer, the greater should be the increase in the poverty measure. Sen's measure gives equal weight to transfers of income at different positions of the ranking, i.e., the impact of a small transfer from the ith person to say the $(i + 1)$th person is the same for all values of i. This neutral position, Kakwani argues, may not be a desirable thing if the poverty measure is based on the concept of relative deprivation.

AXIOM 7.2   (*Transfer-Sensitivity II*):   *If a transfer of income takes place from the ith poor with income* x_i *to a poor with income* $(x_i + h)$, *then for a given h > 0, the magnitude of increase in poverty measure decreases as i increases.*

This axiom gives more weight to transfers of income at the lower end of the distribution than at higher ends. Under this axiom, it is the income difference, not the number of income positions, which is fixed between the transferee and the transfer recipient. If a society is particularly averse to inequality among the poor, the poverty measure must give maximum weight to a transfer from the poorest and the weight should decrease with the level of income. Sen's measure implies precisely the opposite weighting system; i.e., it gives least weight to the poorest and the weight increases with the level of income. Kakwani argues that such a weighting system is incongruent with existing social values. Therefore, he has derived a class of poverty measures which includes all the three possible weighting systems: increasing, decreasing, and constant (or neutral). The choice of a particular member should then depend on the preference for alternative weighting systems. His generalization is based on an alternative rank-order axiom given below.

AXIOM 7.3 (*Generalized Rank-Order*): *For any poor individual i,* $v_i(z, \mathbf{x}) = [q + 1 - i]^k$.

This axiom implies that the weight $v_i(z, \mathbf{x})$ on the income shortfall g_i is equal to the kth power of the number of people among the poor with at least as high an income level as that of person i. Note that, if $k = 1$, this axiom is identical to Sen's rank-order axiom (Axiom 5.3).

It was pointed out earlier that Sen's axiom is based on the equidistant weighting rule proposed by Borda in voting theory. His axiom gives

$$v_i(z, \mathbf{x}) - v_{i+\rho}(z, \mathbf{x}) = A(z)\rho,$$

which implies that the excess of weight on the ith person's income shortfall over that of the $(i + \rho)$th person's income shortfall depends only on the number of positions between the ith and the $(i + \rho)$th person. This makes the poverty measure θ equally sensitive to a transfer of income at all income positions. In order to derive a class of poverty measures that allows the transfer of sensitivity to be increasing or constant or decreasing with the level of income, Borda's procedure of equidistanced weights needs to be generalized. One such generalization of the Borda procedure is

$$v_i(z, \mathbf{x}) - v_{i+\rho}(z, \mathbf{x}) = \psi_i(\rho, k),$$

where k is a parameter and the function $\psi_i(\rho, k)$ either increases or decreases or remains constant with i depending on the value of k. The value of k may be chosen according to the society's preference for the sensitivity of the measure to an income transfer at different income positions. One of the simplest function forms of $\psi_i(\rho, k)$ leads to Axiom 7.4.[26,27]

THEOREM 7.4: *The only class of poverty measures satisfying Axioms 5.1, 5.2, 5.4, and 7.3. is given by*

$$\theta(k) = \frac{q}{nz \, \phi_q(k)} \sum_{i=1}^{q} (z - x_i)(q + 1 - i)^k, \tag{7.1}$$

where $\phi_q(k) = \sum_{i=1}^{q} i^k$.

Consider now the special cases. Substituting $k = 1$ and using the fact that $\phi_q(1) = q(q + 1)/2$, poverty measure $\theta(k)$ reduces to Sen's measures

S^*. If $k = 0$, $\theta(k)$ reduces to

$$\frac{q}{n} \frac{(z - \mu^*)}{z},$$

which is a suitable measure of poverty in the specific case wherein all poor people have exactly the same income.

Next, we consider the possible values of k for which the transfer-sensitivity axioms are satisfied. Kakwani (1980b) has demonstrated that the poverty measure $\theta(k)$ satisfies Axiom 7.1 only for $k > 1$ and, therefore, Sen's measure S^* for which $k = 1$ violates this axiom. Further Kakwani (1980b) has demonstrated that the measure $\theta(k)$ will satisfy the transfer-sensitivity axiom 7.2 for a value of k sufficiently larger than unity, which means that this axiom is also violated by Sen's measure. Thus, this class of poverty measures allows one to choose any of the three possible weighting systems one considers appropriate.

Sen (1976) defined the measure of inequality for the whole population corresponding to the poverty index S^* as the value obtained in place of S^* by replacing z (the poverty level) by μ (the mean income of the community) and replacing q (the number of poor) by n (the total number of people in the community).

Therefore, substituting $q = n$ and $z = \mu$ in Eq. (7.1) gives a new class of inequality measures $\eta(k)$ corresponding to the poverty measure $\theta(k)$:

$$\eta(k) = \frac{1}{\mu \phi_n(k)} \sum_{i=1}^{n} (\mu - x_i)(n + 1 - i)^k, \qquad (7.2)$$

which for $k = 1$ leads to the Gini index. Thus $\eta(k)$ is a general class of inequality measures of which the Gini index is a particular member.

VIII.   TWO MORE MEASURES OF POVERTY

Takayama (1979) proposed a measure of poverty which is based on the "censored" income distribution. This censored income distribution is obtained from the actual income distribution by replacing all incomes above the poverty line by the poverty line income. The Gini index of the censored income distribution leads to his measure of poverty.

Algebraically, the measure is written as

$$T = \frac{1}{mn^2} [(z - \mu^*)q(n - q) + G^* q^2 \mu^*], \qquad (8.1)$$

where m is the mean income of the censored income distribution and is given by

$$mn = q\mu^* + (n - q)z. \qquad (8.2)$$

If every poor person gets exactly the same income, the measure becomes

$$T = \frac{(z - \mu^*)q(n - q)}{mn^2}, \tag{8.3}$$

which shows that this measure does not satisfy the normalization axiom 5.4. Note that all the measures discussed in the previous sections (with the exception of Kakwani's measure K) are based on Sen's normalization rule, which clearly has an intuitively appealing interpretation, whereas this new normalization rule appears to be arbitrary, with no interpretation. This may be regarded as a serious drawback of Takayama's measure.

A still more serious objection to Takayama's measure lies in its robust violation of the monotonicity axiom 4.1. The author himself points out that the measure has the disturbing property that a reduction in the income of someone below the poverty line can reduce (rather than increase) the degree of poverty. This drawback, although it appears to be disturbing, is of no serious consequence for most practical work. Kakwani (1980c) has demonstrated that the monotonicity axiom will be violated by this measure only in an unusual situation when the poverty line strictly exceeds the median income of the distribution, i.e., when the poor comprise more than 50% of the society's population. Further, it can be easily demonstrated that, like Sen's measure, this measure also violates the transfer-sensitivity axioms 7.1 and 7.2.

The elasticity of T with respect to G^* is

$$\eta_T = \frac{q\mu^*G^*}{(z - \mu^*)(n - q) + G^*\mu^*q}, \tag{8.4}$$

and, comparing it with η_s, note that $\eta_s > \eta_T$ for $q < n/2$, which means that Sen's measure is more sensitive to the changes in equality of income among the poor than Takayama's measure provided the number of poor is less than the 50% of the population. This means that if the society attaches relatively greater importance to the inequality of income among the poor, Sen's measure will, in general, be preferred to Takayama's measure.

Another objection to Takayama's measure is that it can show a decrease in poverty when the proportion of poor increases. This is clearly an undesirable feature of his measure, but fortunately such a situation will occur only if the distribution of the poor is perfectly equal and income of the poor is near the poverty line z (or $q/n > \frac{1}{2}$). Takayama defends his measure by pointing out that in this special case, which should be considered as an unrealistic and therefore negligible one, it could be argued that the perfectly equal distribution of the poor who form almost the entire population ought to be weighed more heavily than the narrow poverty gap in measuring poverty.

Takayama's measure is based on axioms which are essentially the same as those of Sen. Therefore, the ranking of income distributions according to this measure should not differ significantly from that of Sen's measure because both measures are based on essentially the same value judgments. The significant differences in ranking observed in the next section are, therefore, attributed to the different normalization rules adopted by the two measures. Takayama's measure has an interesting interpretation in terms of censored distribution, but one can argue that he arrived at this interpreation by utilizing an arbitrary normalization rule.

Drewnowski (1977) proposed a measure of poverty which in Figure 1 is given by the distance *PE*, where the point *P* corresponds to the poverty line income *z* and line *OE* is drawn so as to make the area of the triangle *ODE* equal to the area under the Lorenz curve up to the point *P*. The

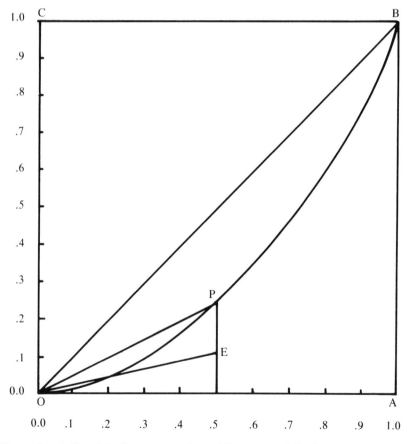

Figure 1 A Graphic Representation of Drewnowski's Poverty Measure.

Gini index G^* is then given by area *OEP* divided by area *ODP*. It can now be shown that Drewnowski's poverty index is given by

$$D = \frac{q\mu^* G^*}{n\mu},$$

which becomes zero when $G^* = 0$. This implies that if all the poor have exactly the same income, however small, this measure will indicate no poverty, which is a serious objection against this measure. If all the poor have zero income, the poverty should be maximum, but this measure again shows no poverty. The objection makes this measure unattractive for any practical use.

IX. AN INTERNATIONAL COMPARISON OF POVERTY

This section provides an international comparison of poverty using the measures discussed in the previous sections. The calculations are based on the income distribution data for 31 developing countries compiled by Jain (1975), to whom the reader is referred for the definitions of income and income-receiving units.

There are several difficulties associated with the use of income distribution data from different countries. These data are generally subject to large errors, and the magnitude of the errors is not likely to be the same for all countries. The definitions of income and income units as well as the year of the survey may also differ from one country to another. These and some other deficiencies have been discussed at length elsewhere (see, for instance, Kuznets, 1955; Adelman and Morris, 1971; Kravis, 1960). Therefore, the conclusions that emerge from the computations in this paper must be qualified.

For the purpose of comparing the poverty in different countries, it is necessary to have the estimates of GDP (gross domestic product) per capita for each country in the units of a single currency, e.g., the U.S. dollar. The GDP per capita is available for almost all countries in terms of their domestic currencies. The conversion of these GDPs to U.S. dollars at official exchange rates can be misleading because these rates do not necessarily reflect the purchasing power of different countries. Kravis et al. (1978) have computed the real GDP per capita in terms of U.S. dollars (adjusting for differences in the purchasing power of currencies) for more than a hundred countries. Their estimates of GDP derived by extrapolations are subject to large margins of error but are still superior to the GDP estimates based on official exchange rates. These real GDP per-capita estimates were indexed with base 100 for the United States. The values of this index are presented in column 1 of Table 1.

Table 1. Index of GDP per Capita and Other Measures of Poverty When the Poverty Line is 4.0% of the U.S. per-Capita Real GDP

Country	Index of GDP per Capita	Percent of Poor	Poverty Measures θ_λ values of λ				
			.00	.25	.50	.75	1.00
Bangladesh	4.29	59.4	.275	.278	.281	.283	.285
		(4)	(4)	(4)	(4)	(4)	(4)
Chad	4.58	60.1	.261	.264	.267	.69	.271
		(3)	(10)	(10)	(10)	(10)	(10)
Melawi	4.58	67.0	.350	.355	.359	.362	.365
		(1)	(2)	(2)	(2)	(2)	(2)
Burma	4.81	52.2	.275	.278	.281	.283	.284
		(7)	(5)	(5)	(5)	(5)	(5)
Indonesia	5.12	65.4	.272	.275	.278	.260	.282
		(2)	(6)	(8)	(8)	(7)	(7)
India	5.98	50.4	.272	.277	.280	.282	.283
		(8)	(7)	(6)	(6)	(6)	(6)
Tanzania	6.04	58.0	.393	.403	.408	.412	.414
		(5)	(1)	(1)	(1)	(1)	(1)
Uganda	7.90	29.2	.115	.117	.118	.118	.119
		(17)	(17)	(17)	(17)	(17)	(17)
Sudan	8.10	34.9	.162	.164	.166	.166	.167
		(11)	(13)	(13)	(13)	(13)	(13)
Kenya	8.30	54.8	.271	.276	.278	.279	.280
		(6)	(8)	(7)	(7)	(8)	(8)
Botswana	8.66	42.6	.298	.309	.314	.316	.318
		(10)	(3)	(3)	(3)	(3)	(3)
Sri Lanka	10.10	15.6	.041	.042	.042	.042	.042
		(25)	(27)	(27)	(27)	(27)	(27)
Thailand	10.10	33.7	.088	.089	.089	.089	.089
		(13)	(19)	(19)	(19)	(20)	(20)
Philippines	10.40	29.6	.147	.150	.151	.152	.152
		(16)	(15)	(15)	(15)	(15)	(15)
Egypt	11.90	20.2	.087	.089	.089	.090	.090
		(21)	(20)	(20)	(20)	(19)	(19)
Ecuador	14.10	42.8	.268	.273	.275	.276	.276
		(9)	(9)	(9)	(9)	(9)	(9)
Rhodesia	14.70	33.5	.127	.128	.129	.129	.129
		(14)	(16)	(16)	(16)	(16)	(16)
Tunisia	14.70	24.6	.062	.062	.062	.062	.062
		(19)	(24)	(25)	(26)	(26)	(26)
Honduras	14.80	34.8	.225	.231	.232	.233	.234
		(12)	(11)	(11)	(11)	(11)	(11)

Table 1. *(Continued)*

Country	Index of GDP per Capita	Percent of Poor	Poverty Measures θ_λ values of λ				
			.00	.25	.50	.75	1.00
El Salvador	15.10	18.2	.084	.086	.086	.086	.086
			(24)	(21)	(21)	(21)	(22)
Peru	16.80	28.2	.176	.182	.183	.184	.185
			(18)	(12)	(12)	(12)	(12)
Colombia	17.40	19.9	.062	.063	.063	.063	.063
			(22)	(25)	(24)	(24)	(25)	(25)
Ivory Coast	17.40	20.4	.038	.038	.038	.038	.038
			(20)	(29)	(29)	(29)	(29)	(29)
Dominican Rep.	18.10	11.5	.031	.032	.032	.032	.032
			(28)	(30)	(30)	(30)	(30)	(30)
Turkey	18.10	19.9	.090	.092	.093	.093	.093
			(23)	(18)	(18)	(18)	(18)
Guyana	18.30	9.3	.064	.069	.070	.071	.071
			(29)	(22)	(22)	(22)	(22)
Iraq	18.70	31.7	.157	.158	.158	.159	.159
			(15)	(14)	(14)	(14)	(14)
Malaysia	18.90	13.5	.063	.065'	.065	.066	.066
			(26)	(23)	(23)	(23)	(23)
Iran	19.40	8.7	.058	.062	.063	.064	.064
			(30)	(26)	(26)	(25)	(24)	(24)
Fiji	20.30	5.3	.007	.007	.007	.007	.007
			(31)	(31)	(31)	(31)	(31)
Brazil	22.80	11.9	.041	.041	.042	.042	.042
			(27)	(28)	(28)	(28)	(28)

The poverty line in this illustration is defined as the income level of the 50th percentile in India in 1970. Using the "dollar of Kravis et al. (1978)," which is adjusted for purchasing power, the poverty line corresponds to $216 (approximately equal to 4% of the U.S. per-capita real GDP in 1970). This definition is based on the belief that 50% of the population of India have income levels that are insufficient to provide adequate nutrition. For the purpose of international comparison of poverty, the same nutritional standards are used in all the developing countries.[28]

The data on income distribution of these 31 countries were available only in grouped form giving (1) the number of persons with incomes in each range and (2) totals (for each range) of their incomes. From these basic data, we derived data on p's and $L(p)$'s for each income range, where p is the cumulative proportion of persons and $L(p)$ is the cumulative proportion of their incomes. Here $L(p)$, which is called the Lorenz curve, is interpreted as the percentage of income received by the bottom p percent of such persons.[29] The Gini index is defined as 1 minus twice the area under the Lorenz curve.

In order to compute the poverty measures, the following equation of the Lorenz curve proposed by Kakwani (1980b) was estimated by ordinary least squares analysis after applying logarithmic transformation:

$$L(p) = p - Ap^\alpha (1 - p)^\beta, \qquad (9.1)$$

where A, α, and β are parameters each greater than zero. Note that $L(p) = 0$ for $p = 0$ and $L(p) = 1$ for $p = 1$. The sufficient conditions for $L(p)$ to be convex to the p axis are $0 < \alpha < 1$ and $0 < \beta < 1$. The first derivative of the Lorenz curve is always equal to x/μ, which for Eq. (9.1) gives

$$Ap^\alpha(1 - p)^\beta \left[\frac{\alpha}{p} - \frac{\beta}{1 - p} \right] = \frac{\mu - x}{\mu}.$$

This equation provides values of p for a given value of x. Let p^* be the value of p when $x = z$; then p^* is the proportion of the poor in the population and $L(p^*)$ is the income share of the poor. The mean income of the poor μ^* is then equal to $L(p^*)\mu/p^*$. The Gini index of the poor only was then computed by numerical integration:

$$G^* = 1 - \frac{2\mu}{p^{*2} \mu^*} \int_0^{p^*} L(p) \, dp,$$

where $L(p)$ is defined as in (9.1).

The class of poverty measures in (7.1) was computed by numerical integration:

$$\theta(k) = \frac{p^* z}{\mu} - \frac{k(k + 1)}{p^{*k}} \int_0^{p^*} L(p)(p^* - p)^{k-1} \, dp,$$

which for $k = 1$ leads to Sen's measure S^*.

The class of inequality measures (7.2) can similarly be written as

$$\eta(k) = 1 - k(k + 1) \int_0^1 L(p)(1 - p)^{k-1} \, dp,$$

which can also be evaluated numerically using (9.1).

Tables 1 and 2 present the computed values of the alternative poverty measures, and Table 3 gives the inequality measures for different values of k. The figures in the parentheses are the rankings of countries according to different poverty measures (or inequality measures).

The developing countries selected for this illustration were those which had a value of GDP index less than 25. Among the 31 countries selected,

Table 2. k-Class Poverty Measures and Takayama Poverty Index When the Poverty Line is 4.0% of the U.S. per-Capita Real GDP

Country	Values of k					Takayama's Index
	0.0	0.5	1.0	1.5	2.0	
Bangladesh	.219	.266	.285	.302	.315	.164
	(7)	(5)	(4)	(5)	(5)	(9)
Chad	.204	.251	.271	.290	.305	.152
	(10)	(10)	(10)	(9)	(8)	(10)
Melawi	.282	.339	.365	.388	.405	.207
	(2)	(2)	(2)	(2)	(2)	(3)
Burma	.228	.269	.284	.296	.304	.179
	(5)	(4)	(5)	(7)	(9)	(6)
Indonesia	.209	.260	.282	.305	.323	.152
	(9)	(9)	(7)	(4)	(4)	(11)
India	.219	.265	.283	.300	.313	.181
	(8)	(6)	(6)	(6)	(6)	(5)
Tanzania	.329	.387	.414	.435	.450	.280
	(1)	(1)	(1)	(1)	(1)	(1)
Uganda	.089	.112	.119	.128	.135	.078
	(17)	(17)	(17)	(17)	(17)	(17)
Sudan	.130	.158	.167	.176	.183	.112
	(14)	(13)	(13)	(13)	(13)	(14)
Kenya	.221	.264	.280	.295	.306	.170
	(6)	(8)	(8)	(8)	(7)	(8)
Botswana	.248	.295	.318	.335	.348	.229
	(3)	(3)	(3)	(3)	(3)	(2)
Sri Lanka	.031	.042	.042	.045	.048	.029
	(29)	(28)	(27)	(27)	(27)	(29)
Thailand	.074	.091	.089	.092	.092	.059
	(18)	(18)	(20)	(21)	(21)	(21)
Philippines	.117	.143	.152	.162	.169	.105
	(15)	(15)	(15)	(14)	(14)	(15)
Egypt	.068	.086	.090	.096	.101	.063
	(20)	(20)	(19)	(19)	(19)	(19)
Ecuador	.231	.265	.276	.283	.286	.197
	(4)	(7)	(9)	(10)	(10)	(4)
Rhodesia	.102	.125	.129	.136	.141	.086
	(16)	(16)	(16)	(16)	(16)	(16)
Tunisia	.057	.067	.062	.060	.057	.047
	(22)	(22)	(26)	(26)	(26)	(23)
Honduras	.191	.223	.234	.241	.246	.172
	(11)	(11)	(11)	(11)	(11)	(7)

Table 2. k(Continued)

Country	Values of k					Takayama's Index
	0.0	0.5	1.0	1.5	2.0	
El Salvador	.066	.083	.087	.092	.096	.062
	(21)	(21)	(21)	(20)	(20)	(20)
Peru	.146	.174	.185	.193	.200	.136
	(12)	(12)	(12)	(12)	(12)	(12)
Colombia	.051	.064	.063	.066	.068	.046
	(23)	(23)	(25)	(25)	(25)	(24)
Ivory Coast	.036	.044	.038	.036	.035	.030
	(27)	(27)	(29)	(29)	(30)	(27)
Dominican Rep.	.024	.033	.032	.034	.036	.023
	(30)	(30)	(30)	(30)	(29)	(30)
Turkey	.071	.089	.093	.099	.103	.066
	(19)	(19)	(18)	(18)	(18)	(18)
Guyana	.050	.064	.071	.079	.085	.049
	(24)	(24)	(22)	(22)	(22)	(22)
Iraq	.139	.158	.159	.159	.157	.117
	(13)	(14)	(14)	(15)	(15)	(13)
Malaysia	.048	.062	.066	.071	.075	.046
	(25)	(25)	(23)	(23)	(24)	(25)
Iran	.044	.058	.064	.071	.078	.044
	(26)	(26)	(24)	(24)	(23)	(26)
Fiji	.006	.010	.007	.008	.008	.006
	(31)	(31)	(31)	(31)	(31)	(31)
Brazil	.032	.042	.042	.044	.046	.030
	(28)	(29)	(28)	(28)	(28)	(28)

Bangladesh was the poorest according to the GDP index, but it ranked fourth on the basis of head-count ratio (which is given in column 2 of Table 1). There are substantial differences among countries with respect to the level of poverty. These differences are displayed by all the measures of poverty.

The sensitivity of poverty measures θ_λ with respect to λ in Table 1 is shown by the fact that the measures increase monotonically with λ for all the countries. It should be noted that $\lambda = 1$ leads to Sen's measures S^* and $\lambda = 0$ gives Kakwani's measures K^*. Therefore, Sen's measures display higher poverty value than Kakwani's measures, although the differences between them are not very great.

The ranking of the countries according to measures θ_λ may change with

Table 3. k-Class Inequality Measures

Country	Values of k for η(k)			
	.5	1.0	1.5	2.0
Bangladesh	.248	.342	.407	.451
	(31)	(31)	(31)	(31)
Chad	.280	.361	.427	.467
	(28)	(30)	(30)	(30)
Melawi	.365	.466	.528	.570
	(19)	(20)	(21)	(23)
Burma	.264	.380	.460	.513
	(30)	(28)	(28)	(28)
Indonesia	.374	.449	.497	.529
	(16)	(22)	(26)	(26)
India	.355	.477	.554	.604
	(21)	(19)	(19)	(20)
Tanzania	.456	.597	.680	.732
	(6)	(6)	(6)	(6)
Uganda	.293	.400	.472	.521
	(27)	(27)	(27)	(27)
Sudan	.323	.446	.526	.580
	(23)	(23)	(22)	(21)
Kenya	.521	.623	.678	.710
	(3)	(4)	(7)	(8)
Botswana	.422	.574	.668	.729
	(10)	(8)	(8)	(7)
Sri Lanka	.275	.377	.446	.493
	(29)	(29)	(29)	(29)
Thailand	.399	.509	.572	.610
	(12)	(14)	(16)	(19)
Philippines	.364	.494	.576	.630
	(20)	(17)	(15)	(15)
Egypt	.309	.434	.518	.575
	(24)	(24)	(23)	(22)
Korea	—	—	—	—
Ecuador	.544	.684	.760	.804
	(1)	(1)	(1)	(1)
Rhodesia	.543	.651	.708	.742
	(2)	(2)	(3)	(4)
Tunisia	.366	.502	.586	.640
	(18)	(15)	(14)	(14)

Table 3.   (*Continued*)

Country	Values of k for η(k)			
	.5	1.0	1.5	2.0
Honduras	.468	.620	.708	.763
	(5)	(5)	(4)	(3)
El Salvador	.332	.465	.553	.613
	(22)	(21)	(20)	(18)
Peru	.446	.594	.683	.739
	(7)	(7)	(5)	(5)
Colombia	.426	.555	.631	.679
	(9)	(10)	(10)	(10)
Ivory Coast	.402	.534	.614	.663
	(11)	(11)	(11)	(11)
Dominican Rep.	.369	.492	.570	.620
	(17)	(18)	(18)	(17)
Turkey	.435	.567	.645	.695
	(8)	(9)	(9)	(9)
Guyana	.298	.419	.504	.564
	(26)	(26)	(24)	(24)
Iraq	.483	.630	.714	.764
	(4)	(3)	(2)	(2)
Malaysia	.390	.517	.597	.649
	(14)	(13)	(13)	(13)
Iran	.383	.499	.572	.621
	(15)	(16)	(17)	(15)
Zambia	—	—	—	—
Fiji	.302	.422	.503	.559
	(25)	(25)	(25)	(25)
Brazil	.392	.524	.606	.660
	(13)	(12)	(12)	(12)

λ, but the changes are not substantial. Therefore, it may be concluded the different assumptions about the relative deprivation do not lead to significantly different conclusions about the relative poverty in different countries.

Table 2 presents the numerical results on k-class poverty measures, where k is a measure of the degree of inequality aversion—or the relative sensitivity to transfers at different income levels. As k rises, the more weight is attached to transfers at the lower end of the distribution than at the middle and the top. The classes of measures $\theta(k)$ increase monotonically with k for all countries, showing that the measures are sensitive to the degree of inequality aversion. The numerical results clearly show that the differences of poverty among the countries become more prominent for larger values of k, although the ranking of countries does not change very significantly for different values of k.

The numerical results in Table 3 show that the inequality measure $\eta(k)$ increases monotonically with k. It is interesting to note that the larger values of k do not necessarily increase the differences of inequality among the countries, as in the case of poverty. The ranking of countries according to inequality may change with k, but the changes are not very prominent. There appears to be no positive correlation between inequality of income and poverty on the basis of cross-country comparisons. A very poor country can have a small inequality of income.

NOTES

1. Harrington (1962) was perhaps the first to emphasize the poverty issue in the United States. For other outstanding contributions on the subject of poverty in advanced countries since 1962, see Atkinson (1969), Ferman et al. (1965), Fishman (1966), Townsend (1965), Tobin (1965), and Budd (1967). There is also a considerable amount of excellent work done on poverty in India for which Bardhan and Srinivasan (1974) is the best reference. An international comparison of poverty is provided by Kakwani (1980a).

2. For a number of years, the World Bank has been particularly interested in financing projects in the developing countries leading to a reduction in poverty.

3. For empirical work using the refined poverty measures see Bhatty (1974), Seastrand and Diwan (1975), Alamgir (1976), Kakwani (1977a, 1980a,b), Anand (1977) and Ahluwalia (1977).

4. These problems have been discussed at length by Townsend (1954, 1962). For a brief but illuminating discussion, see Sen (1979).

5. See Wedderburn (1974, p. 1).

6. The term *relative deprivation* was coined by Stouffer (1949) and subsequently developed by Merton (1957) and Runciman (1966). This term is used here in a narrower sense meaning a level of income sufficiently low to be regarded as creating hardship in terms of society's current living standards.

7. See Atkinson (1974, p. 48).

8. Note that the basic unit of measurement of poverty should be the nuclear family instead of individuals because of the income-sharing phenomenon which is common between married couples and dependent children. Naturally, the income required to maintain any given level of living will be different for the families of different sizes and composition. In order to measure the effect of family composition, attempts have been made to construct consumer unit scales which must be used to arrive at the poverty lines for families of different composition. This problem has been discussed at length by Kakwani (1977b, 1980a). Here it is assumed that the incomes of families have been adjusted (by the consumer unit scale) to take into account the effect of family composition.

9. Fuschs (1969) argues that the poverty standard should be linked to the median income. Drewnowski (1977) suggests that the poverty line should be equal to the mean income of the society. Under this definition, the poor are those who gain when income becomes more evenly distributed and the nonpoor are those who lose.

10.   Note that this procedure of assigning probabilities to the alternative poverty line takes into account the intensity of preferences of individuals (i.e., it introduces an element of cardinality). If an individual feels very strongly for a poverty line, then he will choose the most preferred line with probability unity and the probabilities assigned to the remaining poverty lines will then be zero.

11.   These are basically Intriligator's axioms, slightly modified for the poverty line.

12.   In addition to the three axioms, 3.1, 3.2, and 3.3, the average rule satisfies a number of other important conditions discussed by Intriligator (1973). Note that this collective choice rule violates one of Arrow's (1963) conditions, namely, the condition of "independence of irrelevant alternatives." This is because each pairwise comparison is affected by the probabilities assigned to the remaining poverty lines.

13.   Note that this is the modified version of Sen's (1976) earlier transfer axiom. "Given other things, a pure transfer of income from a person below the poverty line to anyone who is richer must increase the poverty measure," which did not rule out the possibility of the richer person crossing the poverty line owing to a transfer. This modification was motivated because Sen's poverty measure could violate his earlier axiom. For further discussion, see Sen (1979).

14.   See Sen (1979, p. 33).

15.   Sen's (1976) poverty measure, to be discussed in Section V, corresponds to the Gini index, which is another widely known measure of inequality.

16.   For an empirical application of this result on Malaysian data, see Kakwani (1977b).

17.   It seems reasonable to assume that the poverty line changes with the general level of living only in the long run. Even if the poverty line changes with the mean income of the society according to Eq. (2.1), the above condition is still satisfied provided $0 < \beta < 1$.

18.   This is because we want to derive a poverty measure which is unaffected by the incomes of the nonpoor.

19.   This concept of the equally distributed equivalent level of income was introduced by Atkinson (1970).

20.   Homotheticity of the welfare function implies that if all incomes are multiplied by a scalar, then ξ is also multiplied by the same scalar. Since G^* remains unchanged if all incomes are multiplied by a scalar, (4.6) must be true.

21.   See Atkinson (1970), Sen (1973), and Kakwani (1980a).

22.   A relative poverty index is one which is homogeneous of degree zero in the incomes of the poor and the poverty line (see Blackorby and Donaldson, 1978).

23.   Clark et al. (1981), following a welfare-based approach, have proposed two new indices of poverty by employing the group welfare function which is additive separable in individual welfares. But this is a strong assumption. Sen (1973), in particular, has discussed the restrictions implied by additive separability, namely, that the relative social valuation of the incomes of two individuals is independent of the levels of any other income. In view of these shortcomings, discussion of poverty indices in this paper is restricted to the ones which imply a non-additive-separable group welfare function.

24.   The rank-order weighting has been widely used in voting theory; see for instance, Borda (1781), Black (1958), Fine and Fine (1974), Fishburn (1975), Hansson (1975), and Gardenfors (1973).

25.   See Sen (1979).

26.   See Kakwani (1980b).

27.   It seems reasonable to choose the simplest functional form in the absence of a convincing case for any alternative forms.

28.   This may not be realistic because the nutritional requirements of people depend on physical features, climatic conditions, and work habits.

29.   For a more formal definition of the Lorenz curve, see Kakwani and Podder (1973, 1976) and Kakwani (1977a, 1980a).

REFERENCES

Adelman, I. and C. Morris (1971) *An Anatomy of Patterns of Income Distribution in Developing Nations, Part III of the Final Report* (Grant AID/Csd—2236), Northwestern University.

Ahluwalia, M. S. (1977) Rural Poverty and Agricultural Growth in India, mimeographed, Development Research Center, IBRD, (June).

Alamgir, M. (1976) Poverty, Inequality and Development Strategy in the Third World, mimeographed, Bangladesh Institute of Development Studies, (February).

Anand, S. (1977) Aspects of Poverty in Malaysia, *Review of Income and Wealth* 23.

Arrow, K. (1963) *Social Choice and Individual Values*, 2nd edition, New Haven: Yale University Press.

Atkinson, A. B. (1969) *Poverty in Britain and the Reform of Social Security*, Cambridge, MA: Cambridge University Press.

Atkinson, A. B. (1970) On the Measurement of Inequality, *Journal of Economic Theory* 2, 244–63.

Atkinson, A. B. (1974) Poverty and Income Inequality in Britain. In Dorothy Wedderburn (ed.), *Poverty, Inequality and Class Structure*, Cambridge, MA: Cambridge University Press.

Bardhan, P. K. and T. N. Srinivasan (1974), *Poverty and Income Distribution in India*, Calcutta, Statistical Publishing Society.

Bhatty, I. Z. (1974) Inequality and Poverty in Rural India. In Bardhan and Srinivasan (1974), above.

Black, D. (1958) *The Theory of Committees and Elections*, Cambridge, MA: Cambridge University Press.

Blackorby, C. and D. Donaldson (1978) Ethical Indices for the Measurement of Poverty, Discussion Paper 78-04, University of British Columbia.

Borda, J. C. (1781) Mémoire sur les Elections au Scrutin. In *Mémoires de l'Académie Royale des Sciences*, Paris.

Budd, E. (1967) *Inequality and Poverty*, W. W. Norton and Company, Inc.

Clark, Stephen, Richard Hemming and David Ulph (1981) On Indices for the Measurement of Poverty, *The Economic Journal* 91, 515–526.

Drewnowski, D. (1977) Poverty: Its Meaning and Measurement, *Development and Challenge* 8.

Ferman, L., J. Kornbluh, and A. Haber (1956), *Poverty in America*, Ann Arbor, MI: Michigan University Press.

Fine, B. and K. Fine (1974) Social Choice and Individual Ranking, *Review of Economic Studies* 41, 303–22, 549–75.

Fishburn, P. C. (1975) *The Theory of Social Choice*, Princeton, N.J.: Princeton University Press.

Fishman, L. (1966) *Poverty Amid Affluence*, New Haven, CT: Yale University Press.

Fuschs, V. (1969) Comment. In L. Sottow (ed.), *Six Papers on the Size Distribution of Income and Wealth*, New York.

Gardenfors, P. (1973) Positional Voting Functions, *Theory and Decision*, 4, pp. 1–24.

Hansson, B. (1975) The Independence Condition in the Theory of Social Choice, *Theory and Decision*, 4, pp. 25–50.

Harrington, Michael (1962) *The Other America*, The Macmillan Company.

Intriligator, M. (1973) A Probabilistic Model of Social Choice, *Review of Economic Studies* Vol. 40 553–60.

Jain, S. (1975) *Size Distribution of Income: A Compilation of Data*, World Bank.

Kakwani, N. C. (1977a) Applications of Lorenz Curves in Economic Analysis, *Econometrica*, (April) Vol. 45, 719–727.

Kakwani, N. C. (1977b) Measurement of Poverty and Negative Income Tax, *Australian Economic Papers*, (December) Vol. 16, 237–248.

Kakwani, N. C. (1977c) On the Estimation of Consumer Unit Scale, *Review of Economics and Statistics* (November) Vol. 59, 507–510.

Kakwani, N. C. (1980a) *Income Inequality and Poverty: Methods of Estimation and Policy Applications*, Oxford University Press, New York.

Kakwani, N. C. (1980b) On a Class of Poverty Measures, *Econometrica* (March) Vol. 48.

Kakwani, N. C. (1980c) Note on a New Measure of Poverty, forthcoming *Econometrica*.

Kakwani, N. C. and N. Podder (1973) On the Estimation of Lorenz Curves from Grouped Observations, *International Economic Review* 14.

Kakwani, N. C. and N. Podder (1976) Efficient Estimation of the Lorenz Curve and Associated Inequality Measures from Grouped Observations, *Econometrica* 44, (1) 137–48.

Kravis, I. B. (1960) International Differences in the Distribution of Income, *Review of Economics and Statistics* Vol. 42, 408–16.

Kravis, I. B., A. Heston and R. Summers (1978) Real GDP Per Capita for More Than One Hundred Countries, *The Economic Journal* 88, (June) 215–42.

Kuznets, S. (1955) Economic Growth and Income Inequality, *American Economic Review* 45.

Merton, R. K. (1957) *Social Theory and Social Structure*, Illinois.

Rowntree, S. (1901) *Poverty: A Study of Town Life*, London: Macmillan.

Runciman, W. G. (1966), *Relative Deprivation and Social Justice*, Routledge and Kegan Paul, London.

Seastrand, F. and R. Diwan (1975) Measurement and Comparison of Poverty and Inequality in the United States, presented at the Third World Econometric Congress, Toronto.

Sen, A. K. (1973) *On Economic Inequality*, Oxford: Clarendon Press.

Sen, A. K. (1974) Informational Bases of Alternative Welfare Approaches: Aggregation and Income Distribution, *Journal of Public Economics* 4.

Sen, A. K. (1976) Poverty: An Ordinal Approach to Measurement, *Econometrica* 44, (2) (March) 219–31.

Sen, A. K. (1979) Issues in the Measurement of Poverty, *Scandanavian Journal of Economics*.

Stouffer, S. A. (1949) *The American Soldier*, Princeton, N.J.

Takayama, N. (1979) Poverty, Income Inequality and their Measures: Professor Sen's Axiomatic Approach Reconsidered, *Econometrica* 47, (3) (May), 747–60.

Tobin, J. (1965) Improving the Economic Status of the Negro, *Daedalus* 94, 878–98.

Townsend, P. (1954) Measuring Poverty, *British Journal of Sociology* V.

Townsend, P. (1962) Meaning of Poverty, *British Journal of Sociology* XIII.

Townsend, P. (1965) The Scale and Meaning of Poverty in Contemporary Western Society, *Dependency and Poverty* Colloquium Series Paper, Waltham, MA: Brandeis University.

Townsend, P. (1974) Poverty as Relative Deprivation: Resources and Style of Living. In D. Wedderburn (1974).

Wedderburn, D. (ed.), (1974) *Poverty, Inequality and Class Structure*, Cambridge, MA: Cambridge University Press.

Research Annuals in
ECONOMICS

Advances in Applied Micro-Economics
Series Editor: V. Kerry Smith,
University of North Carolina

Advances in Econometrics
Series Editors: R. L. Basmann,
Texas A & M University
and George F. Rhodes, Jr.,
Colorado State University

Advances in the Economics of Energy and Resources
Series Editor: John R. Moroney,
Tulane University

Advances in Health Economics and Health Services Research
(Volume 1 published as Research in Health Economics)
Series Editor: Richard M. Scheffler, *George Washington University.* Associate Series Editor: Louis F. Rossiter, *National Center for Health Services Research*

Applications of Management Science
Series Editor: Randall L. Schultz, *University of Texas at Dallas*

Research in Corporate Social Performance and Policy
Series Editor: Lee E. Preston,
University of Maryland

Research in Domestic and International Agribusiness Management
Series Editor: Ray A. Goldberg,
Harvard University

Research in Economic Anthropology
Series Editor: George Dalton, *Northwestern University*

Research in Economic History
Series Editor: Paul Uselding,
University of Illinois

Research in Experimental Economics
Series Editor: Vernon L. Smith,
University of Arizona

Research in Finance
Series Editor: Haim Levy,
The Hebrew University

Research in Human Capital and Development
Series Editor: Ismail Sirageldin,
The Johns Hopkins University

Research in International Business and Finance
Series Editor: Robert G. Hawkins,
New York University

Research in Labor Economics
Series Editor: Ronald G. Ehrenberg, *Cornell University*

Research in Law and Economics
Series Editor: Richard O. Zerbe, Jr.,
University of Washington

Research in Marketing
Series Editor: Jagdish N. Sheth, *University of Illinois*

Research in Organizational Behavior
Series Editors: Barry M. Staw, *University of California at Berkeley*
and L. L. Cummings, *University of Wisconsin—Madison*

Research in Philosophy and Technology
Series Editor: Paul T. Durbin,
University of Delaware

Research in Political Economy
Series Editor: Paul Zarembka, *State University of New York—Buffalo*

Research in Population Economics
Series Editor: Julian L. Simon,
University of Illinois

Research in Public Policy Analysis and Management
Series Editor: John P. Crecine,
Carnegie-Mellon University

Research in Real Estate
Series Editor: C. F. Sirmans,
University of Georgia

Research in Urban Economics
Series Editor: J. Vernon Henderson, *Brown University*

Please inquire for detailed brochure on each series.

Ⓐ JAI PRESS INC.